Image Processing
and Analysis
A Primer

Primers in Electronics and Computer Science

Print ISSN: 2516-6239
Online ISSN: 2516-6247

(*formerly known as ICP Primers in Electronics and Computer Science* — ISSN: 2054-4537)

Series Editor: Mark S. Nixon *(University of Southampton, UK)*

This series fills a gap in the market for concise student-friendly guides to the essentials of electronics and computer science. Each book will address a core elements of first year BEng and MEng courses and will stand out amongst the existing lengthy, dense and expensive US textbooks. The texts will cover the main elements of each topic, with clear illustrations and up-to-date references for further reading.

Published

Vol. 3   *Image Processing and Analysis: A Primer*
          by Georgy Gimel'farb and Patrice Delmas

Vol. 2   *Programming: A Primer – Coding for Beginners*
          by Tom Bell

Vol. 1   *Digital Electronics: A Primer – Introductory Logic Circuit Design*
          by Mark S. Nixon

Primers in Electronics and Computer Science ○─── Vol. 3

Image Processing and Analysis
A Primer

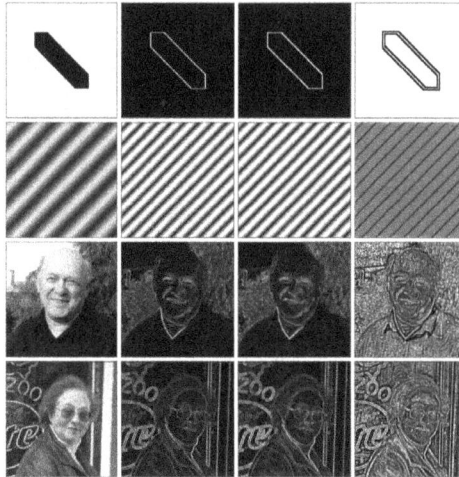

Georgy Gimel'farb
Patrice Delmas
The University of Auckland, New Zealand

World Scientific

NEW JERSEY · LONDON · SINGAPORE · BEIJING · SHANGHAI · HONG KONG · TAIPEI · CHENNAI · TOKYO

Published by

World Scientific Publishing Europe Ltd.

57 Shelton Street, Covent Garden, London WC2H 9HE

Head office: 5 Toh Tuck Link, Singapore 596224

USA office: 27 Warren Street, Suite 401-402, Hackensack, NJ 07601

Library of Congress Cataloging-in-Publication Data

Names: Gimel'farb, Georgy, author. | Delmas, Patrice, author.
Title: Image processing and analysis : a primer / by
    Georgy Gimel'farb (The University of Auckland, New Zealand),
    Patrice Delmas (The University of Auckland, New Zealand).
Description: New Jersey : World Scientific, 2018. | Series: Primers in electronics and
    computer science ; volume 3 | Includes bibliographical references and index.
Identifiers: LCCN 2018026885 | ISBN 9781786345813 (hc : alk. paper)
Subjects: LCSH: Image processing--Digital techniques. | Computer vision.
Classification: LCC TA1630 .G555 2018 | DDC 621.36/7--dc23
LC record available at https://lccn.loc.gov/2018026885

British Library Cataloguing-in-Publication Data

A catalogue record for this book is available from the British Library.

For any available supplementary material, please visit
https://www.worldscientific.com/worldscibooks/10.1142/Q0173#t=suppl

Desk Editors: Anthony Alexander/Jennifer Brough/Shi Ying Koe

Typeset by Stallion Press
Email: enquiries@stallionpress.com

Preface

What is this textbook for?

Vision, our main source of information about a surrounding natural scene, exploits inherent abilities of the human brain to collect, combine, and interpret a constant flow of images perceived by eyes. The image, formed in an instant by retinal eye sensors, encodes electromagnetic radiation emitted or reflected by a rather small part of the observed scene in a narrow spectral band, referred to as *visible light*. The brain converts a flow of these loosely dependent small patches observed by our eyes into an apparently continuous, stable, and detailed (often perceived as complete) image of the scene. This image is constantly updated (at the rate of about 25 frames per second) in line with movements of the eyes and changes in the observer's position, while the brain forms a comprehensive inner scene model of the environment to guide the observer's behaviour.

How this has been achieved, has been the topic of intense research for many decades. Unfortunately, this fast and highly effective process of visual perception, is performed almost completely at a subconscious level. As such, it still eludes satisfactory explanation and understanding, although many of its aspects have been already explored in-depth in various research domains, from biology, psychology and brain science to engineering and computer vision.

Our goals

This textbook intends to help a reader in their first steps into a magic and challenging world of mimicking human vision with computational tools and techniques. Compared to a wealth of today's image processing and computer vision tutorials, textbooks, research publications, and user guides dealing with images (see Appendix A), this textbook focuses on notions and ideas behind a few basic image processing operations, which are widely used in today's computer vision, computer graphics, and image processing. It is intended to be an entry level guide to any reader dealing with images on the basis of computers. Despite applications and research tasks of this kind have too fuzzy boundaries and share many common mathematical models and computational techniques, a simplified taxonomy by input and output data roughly separates them into three main areas: **image processing** that transforms input natural or synthetic images into new images; **computer vision** that analyses natural images to formally describe, or model an observed scene, and **computer graphics** that generates synthetic images of a scene from its formal description.

Professor Azriel Rosenfeld [19.02.1931–22.02.2004], a pioneer of computational image processing, who authored the very first book in this field [Rosenfeld (1969)][1], coined the term *pixel* for an individual visual cell, or the smallest element of a digital image. This term gave rise to several subsequent image-related notions, such as, e.g., a *voxel* (a volume cell), an *edgel* (an edge element), and a texel (an elementary area of an image texture).

Although the primer considers mostly greyscale images with scalar signals, in a few cases it touches also on colour images with three-element vectorial signals. The greyscale, or panchromatic images are captured in a wide interval of electromagnetic wavelengths. A continuous sensed interval is usually called a *band*. The colour images are captured in three smaller bands relating to primary red (R), blue (B), and green (G) colours as perceived by the human eyes. More intricate *multi-band*, or *multi-spectral* images sensed in three to 12–15 separate narrow bands, and *hyper-spectral* images with dozens to hundreds of such intervals per pixel are outside of the scope of this primer. Accordingly, the notions *spectrum* and *spectral* will relate here to only spatial oscillations that any greyscale image consists of and can be decomposed into.

How to interpret image signals, such as scalar intensities or colour vectors, depends on the problem at hand. Conventional optical images represent points of a depicted scene with colours or grey shades. To be processed and analysed, the optical signals are coded numerically with typically integer grey levels or intensities of primary colours. These integer codes may

---

[1]Today's **image processing** was born in the 1950s–1960s as **picture processing**.

also be used to represent labels of regions occupied by different objects in an optical image in order to build and visualise a so-called *region map*. An alternative parametric, or *feature map* encodes a certain scalar feature of optical signals and/or region labels, associated with each image location.

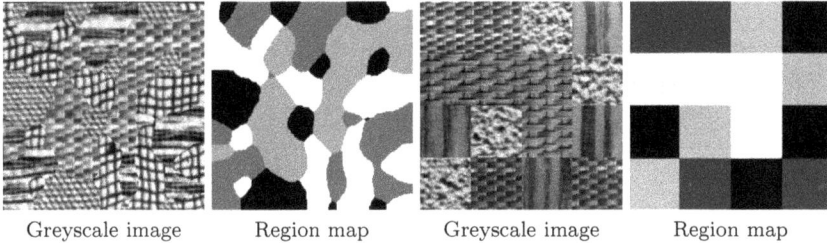

| Greyscale image | Region map | Greyscale image | Region map |

Extracting information about a scene or its components (individual objects) in computer vision also might be considered a complex image-to-image transformation. For instance, medical image analysis for computer-aided diagnostics often calls for segmenting input images into region maps, while computational stereo vision builds a distance map, encoding observer-to-surface distances from two or more optical images showing different overlapping views of the same scene.

Scope

While this primer may refer to the above or other complicate and challenging problems, it is confined to a collection of simpler, albeit critical image-to-image transformations, which *normalise, filter,* and *segment* an input image. These transformations are used frequently to enhance and adjust visual appearance of a depicted scene in order to suppress or eliminate some types of incoherent signal deviations (noise), as well as find quantitative features to separate objects-of-interest from background and quantitatively (e.g., area, orientation, shape, intensity) describe these objects. Due to being in common use, these transformations are implemented in a majority of available graphical editors and similar software tools, and typically form part of the solution to many image-based applied problems. In these cases both the input and output image are of the same or similar size; every output signal depends only on a single input signal or a rather small subset of input signals (e.g., neighbours in the image plane), and this dependency is easily formalised in terms of analytical or numerical computations. Every output signal is computed from the input signals, located in a rather small region (called a *window*), its shape and computation defining the whole normaliser (filter). Three arbitrary examples of transforming a left-most input facial image are shown below:

| Original image | Enhanced | Filtered | Enhanced/deformed |

The window shape determines relative positions of the input signals with respect to the output signal. If the latter is a weighted linear combination of the inputs, the filter is called linear, otherwise it is non-linear. To form the entire output, the window moves around the input image in line with positions of the output signals to be computed. Typically, both the filter shape and computations are fixed (pre-defined), although in some cases they might depend on the input data.

Milestones

In practice one might encounter a multitude of different types of static or dynamic two- and three-dimensional (2D/3D) images with greyscale, colour (three-band), multi-band (multi-spectral), or hyper-spectral pixel/voxel-wise signals. Although the primer will focus mostly on static 2D greyscale images and their region or feature maps, a large part of the models and techniques presented can be also applied, after natural modifications and extensions, to other types of images.

Image filtering is readily understood and becomes especially simple when the "window" is reduced to select a single input signal. It is a natural point to start our journey into a vast land of image processing and analysis, as such transformations are widely used in practice to enhance or even segment images. In so doing, an introduction to digital images and their simple descriptors in Chapter 1 comprises the first milestone along this way. This chapter will detail main image-related notions, such as pixels/voxels and dynamic ranges, as well as introduce simple descriptors, such as, e.g., normed *histograms* of pixel/voxel-wise signals or their pairwise co-occurrences. The signal histogram shows how frequent each signal value is, in a given image, i.e., provides marginal empirical probabilities of these values. Although it is anticipated that the reader knows basics of applied statistics, minimal required knowledge (including window-wide statistical characteristics of signals to form maps of regions or pixel/voxel-wise features) will be presented in this primer.

Chapter 2 will focus on adjusting visual appearance (in terms of integral brightness and contrast) to normalise an image and make it invariant to a few unessential signal deviations. Manually controlled or automated adjustments of the image contrast and brightness might enhance a depicted scene, improve its visual perception, and/or help in its subsequent computational analysis.

Chapter 3 will present one of the most popular processing tools, namely, a moving-window filtering to suppress some types of image noise and estimate local, or window-wide statistical signal features. The chapter details linear mean and Gaussian filters, as well as non-linear median and more general rank filters. The filtering takes account of dependencies between adjacent signal values to decrease noise-caused signal deviations or forms maps of local features (functions of signals) describing such dependencies.

Chapter 4 will present two simple techniques for image segmentation: building a binary region map by pixel-wise classification, or thresholding signal values after analysing their histogram, and growing continuous regions in an arbitrary binary map.

Chapter 5 will describe basic morphological moving-window filtering to modify shapes of objects in a binary region map or change appearance of a greyscale image. The greyscale morphology extends the non-linear rank filtering.

Chapter 6 will describe a more advanced segmentation of a greyscale image or a feature map by evolving a deformable boundary, defined explicitly (active contours), implicitly (level sets) or statistically (active shape models), to outline a (set of) goal object(s).

Chapter 7 will consider edges, corners, and more specific points of interest (POI) in an image to be used, e.g., for co-aligning the images or finding certain objects. Both the deformable boundaries and the POIs help in segmenting and analysing intricate goal objects.

Chapter 8 details basic geometric transformations of a digital image, namely, affine transformations and polynomial (mostly, quadratic and cubic) warps.

More complicated spectral representations of images presume a deeper mathematical background of the reader, than other chapters, and thus are postponed to Chapter 9. It will detail forward and backward image–

spectrum transformations, filtering in the Fourier spectral domain, and closely related wavelet decompositions, which facilitate image compression and analysis.

Chapters 1–5 and 8 comprise an introductory single-semester under-graduate course on image processing and analysis. A more advanced two-semester course could include all the topics.

Basic notation

We will denote $\mathbb{S}$ as continuous or discrete set of image sites (points) $\mathbf{s}$ (individually denoted as $\mathbf{s}$) in a 2D plane supporting an image or map, and $\mathbb{Q}$ as continuous interval or a finite set of numerical signals assigned to, or supported in the sites $\mathbf{s} \in \mathbb{S}$. For a 3D image the set $\mathbb{S}$ contains sites in a 3D volume. Planar or spatial positions (locations) of individual sites are specified, respectively, in an orthogonal Cartesian coordinate system with width (x), height (y), and depth (z) axes.

A planar, $\mathbf{s} = (x, y)$, or spatial, $\mathbf{s} = (x, y, z)$, site is considered, if necessary, a vector-column or, what is the same, a transposed vector-row of the coordinates:

$$\mathbf{s} = \begin{bmatrix} x \\ y \\ z \end{bmatrix} \equiv [x, y, z]^\mathsf{T} \text{ and } \mathbf{s} = \begin{bmatrix} x \\ y \end{bmatrix} \equiv [x, y]^\mathsf{T}$$

where the superscript T indicates the vector-matrix transposition.

For brevity, our consideration is restricted mostly to 2D images and maps. Although their support, $\mathbb{S}$, may be, generally, of an arbitrary geo-metric shape, a majority of continuous images are supported in a rectangle of size $M \times N$ with usually integer lengths of sides: $M \geq 1$ and $N \geq 1$. The related discrete support $\mathbb{S}$ is a 2D arithmetic lattice (grid) of sites, $\mathbf{s}$, with integer coordinates:

$$\mathbb{S} = \{(m, n) : m = 0, 1, \ldots, M - 1; \ n = 0, 1, \ldots, N - 1\}$$

Depending on physical meaning or interpretation of the signals, a collection $\mathbf{g} = (g(\mathbf{s}) : \mathbf{s} \in \mathbb{S}; \ g(\mathbf{s}) \in \mathbb{Q})$ could be a greyscale image of a natural or artificial scene, or a region map with signals encoding region labels, or a map of numerically encoded site-wise features to be analysed or/and visualised.

About the Authors

Georgy Gimel'farb, PhD, is a Professor in the Department of Computer Science at the University of Auckland, Auckland, New Zealand. His interests include image processing and analysis, texture modelling, 3D vision, and statistical pattern recognition. He has authored more than 420 publications, including the monograph *Image Textures and Gibbs Random Fields* (Kluwer, 1999) and the textbook *Stochastic Modeling for Medical Image Analysis* (CRC Press, 2016).

    Patrice Delmas, PhD, is an Associate Professor in the Department of Computer Science at the University of Auckland, Auckland, New Zealand. His interests include image processing and analysis, and 3D computer vision. He has authored more than 170 publications in theoretical and experimental computer vision, as well as in image processing for soil sciences, marine sciences, and hydraulic engineering. He was partially supported by the European Union's Horizon 2020 research and innovation programme PROTINUS under grant agreement N°645717, while working on this book.

Contents

Chapter 1

Continuous and Digital Images

To begin our journey through a vast land of image processing and analysis, it is natural to define main objects of interest: images of realistic or artificial objects and maps of regions or features exemplified in Fig. 1.1.

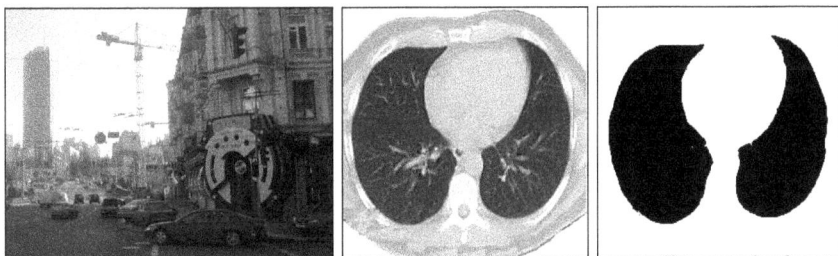

Fig. 1.1 Realistic urban scene and a computed tomographic chest slice with its region map (black/white encoding of lung/background labels).

What will you find here? This chapter presents basic notions associated with continuous images and maps, as well as with their discrete (digital) analogues. Section 1.1 will detail spatial resolution of digitisation (sampling), the smallest discrete elements (points), called *pixels* in 2D or *voxels* in 3D digital images, and point-wise scalar or vectorial signals, in particular, grey values and colours in the images or region labels and numerical feature values in the maps.

Sections 1.2 and 1.3 describe a few features, or quantitative descriptors of global (image-wide) or local (point- and window-wide) signal behaviour. The descriptors include global brightness and contrast, as well as global or local statistical properties, called simply *statistics*, of signal co-occurrences in pixel or voxel k-tuples. The size, k, and spatial shapes of these signal patterns are mostly prescribed, but generally might depend on the signals. The first-order statistics follow from a global or local grey level histogram (GLH) and its cumulative histogram (CH). The second-order statistics follow from grey level difference or co-occurrence histograms (GLDH or GLCH, respectively) characterising prescribed or adaptively chosen signal pairs. This primer will consider only most common first- and second-order statistics, as well as briefly outlining popular higher-order ones, called local binary and ternary patterns (LBPs and LTPs).

Human vision is of great importance in perceiving, describing, and understanding the surrounding world. Our eyes receive electromagnetic waves reflected from or emitted by an observed (and thus called *optical*) spatial surface. The *visible light* has wavelengths from 0.4 to 0.7 μm (micrometers, or microns), sensed as colours from violet to red, respectively. Special optical sensors help to visualise certain ranges of ultraviolet (UV: $0.01 - 0.4 \ \mu m$) and infrared light (IR: 0.7–$1,000 \ \mu m$). By various estimates, up to 35–50% of the human brain participate, in one way or another, in processing and analysing optical data acquired by multiple light receptors (cones and rods) in retinas of both eyes.

The eyes are constantly scanning their fields of view using rapid instinctive and slower deliberate movements, guided by observation goals. Sequences of retinal neural signals encoding the data acquired are compressed firstly in the retinas and then secondly by other vision-related parts of the brain in order to be combined at each time instant into a stable continuous image of the currently observed three-dimensional (3D) scene. The image perceived may be considered similar in many aspects to a central projection of the observed optical surfaces onto a 2D plane.

Older photo and cinematographic cameras with light-sensitive films produced continuous images with a continuous range of optical signals (grey shades or colours) encoding the perceived light. A majority of other imaging tools, including modern digital photo cameras and even the human eye retina (due to its limited spatial, intensity, and colour resolution), capture a finite set of isolated 2D image elements and mostly distinguish among a finite number of element-wise shades or colours.

Special imaging devices can visualise inner structures of realistic 3D objects, such as, e.g., human bodies, industrial parts, or soil samples to mention only a few, with the aid of penetrating magnetic fields or electromagnetic rays with wavelengths below 0.01 μm (X-rays). The latter are used in conventional X-ray radioscopy and computed tomography (CT), whereas the combination of strong static and pulsing magnetic fields enable magnetic resonance imaging (MRI). Radioscopic 2D images encode integral attenuations of multiple X-rays passing through an object, and 3D CT images or MRI encode point-wise X-ray attenuations or hydrogen (primarily, water) densities, respectively, at different spatial locations within the object.

1.1 Images and maps

Optical geometry of both a human eye and most common imaging devices, such as photo cameras, are closely modelled with a *pinhole camera model* (see, e.g., Fig. 1.2). It projects each 3D point **S** of an observed surface to a 2D point **s** on the image plane and assigns to this point an optical signal (intensity or colour) encoding properties of the light reflected or emitted in direction of the projecting ray. All projecting rays go through the same 3D point **O**, called the *optical centre*. The ray, orthogonal to the projection plane, and the distance from the optical centre to the projection, or image plane is called the *principal*, or *optical axis* of the camera, and the *focal distance*, respectively.

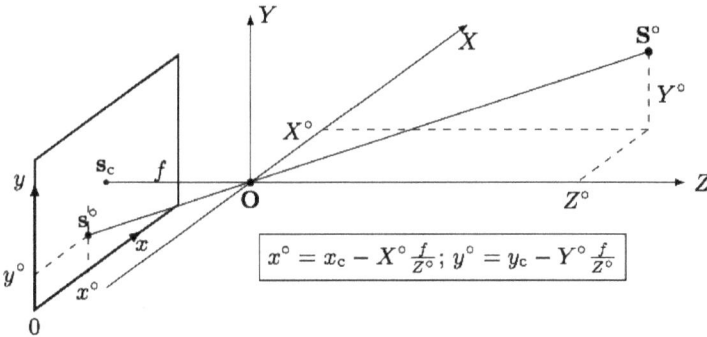

Fig. 1.2   Projecting a spatial point $\mathbf{S}^\circ = (X^\circ, Y^\circ, Z^\circ)$ onto a planar point $\mathbf{s}^\circ = (x^\circ, y^\circ)$ by a pinhole camera with the focal distance f and the principal point $\mathbf{s}_c$ (the counter-clockwise planar coordinate system).

The origin attached to the pinhole camera Cartesian coordinate system is in the optical, or projection centre, $\mathbf{O} = (0,0,0)$. The axis Z of depths (distances) of 3D points to the XY-plane coincides with the optical axis. The X- and Y-axes are parallel to the respective Cartesian x- and y-axes on the image plane. The optical axis crosses the plane in the *image centre*, or *principal point*, $\mathbf{s}_c = (x_c, y_c)$. The planar coordinate origin, $(0,0)$, is often in the bottom left corner, rather than the centre, $\mathbf{s}_c$.

Definition 1.1 (Continuous 2D and 3D images). *A continuous 2D or 3D image is supported in a continuous planar rectangle or a spatial parallelepiped, respectively, and takes point-wise values from a continuous or finite set of bounded non-negative numerical values (often, integers), encoding grey shades or colours (triplets of grey shades).*

Integer encoded grey shades are frequently called grey levels. When a 2D greyscale or colour image is formed with a pinhole-like camera, each point-wise signal represents the sensed light intensity or colour. The grey values in a 3D image, or within its 2D slices, encode other point-wise scalar properties, e.g., X-ray attenuations in a CT image or hydrogen densities in an MR image of a human body (Fig. 1.3).

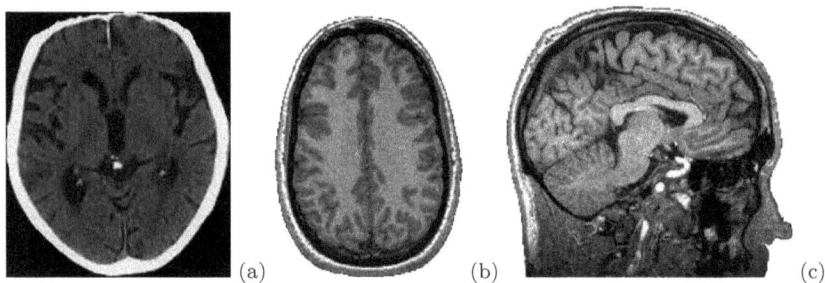

(a)   (b)   (c)

Fig. 1.3   2D slices of 3D CT (a) and MRI (b, c) brain images.

Formally, a continuous image can be considered a visual representation of values of an intricate non-negative function $g : \mathbb{S} \to \mathbb{Q}$ mapping points of a 2D plane or 3D volume $\mathbb{S}$ onto a continuous or finite set $\mathbb{Q}$ of signals. The function is specified implicitly, by its values, $g(\mathbf{s}) \in \mathbb{Q}$, measured at or assigned to every point $\mathbf{s} \in \mathbb{S}$. A continuous range $\mathbb{Q} = [0, q_{\max}]$ of the light intensities; $q_{\max} > 0$, spans from zero (typically, the darkest grey shade) to a certain numerical code, $q_{\max}$, of the brightest shade. A colour is encoded by either an integer index, pointing to an entry of a colour table, or a triplet of continuous or discrete intensities, one per red (R), green (G), and blue (B) primary colour.

Conversely, a continuous function of two or three variables can be illustrated with an image if these variables are interpreted as Cartesian coordinates and values of the functions can be encoded by grey values between

0 and q_{max} or colours. This is the basis of *scientific visualisation* – a computer graphics branch that facilitates visual assessment and analysis of non-intuitive numerical data records.

Such interpretation should account for limited angular and optical (intensity or colour) resolution of human vision. Daylight angular resolution of a "normal" eye is about 1 arc minute (0.003 radians), or about 3 mm at distance of 10 m. Because optical signals at smaller than resolved distances are perceived as a single point, spatial continuity of an image means that a supporting plane or volume has no resolved gaps. Thus, a discrete image is perceived continuous if no individual point can be resolved visually along any path across the supporting plane (see, e.g., Fig. 1.4).

Fig. 1.4 Perceiving a pencil of lines: a subjective spatial resolution boundary.

For integer encoding, a continuous dynamic range of sensed light intensities or other measurements to be visualised is quantised uniformly or sometimes non-uniformly into $Q = 2^b$ distinct grey levels where the exponent b, also known as the *bit-depth*, determines the chosen number of bits (binary digits) in the grey levels.

Definition 1.2 (Dynamic range of optical signals). *The dynamic range is specified by the ratio between the maximal and minimal sensed signals. The ratio is measured in bits, also referred as* stops *(the ratio's logarithm by base 2), or* decibels *(the decibel is the ratio's logarithm by base 10): 1 dB = 0.301 stops.*

Table 1.1 details correspondences between the signal ratios and relevant dynamic ranges in stops.

Table 1.1   Dynamic range in stops (bits).

Range	2 : 1	8 : 1	32 : 1	128 : 1	256 : 1	1024 : 1
Stops	1	3	5	7	8	10

Range	16384 : 1	65536 : 1	10^5 : 1	1.05×10^6 : 1	1.68×10^7 : 1	1.07×10^9 : 1
Stops	14	16	16.6	20	24	30

Dynamic range of human eyes, perceiving static scenes, is about 10–14 stops, but increases up to 20–25 stops or more for dynamic scenes. It is larger for daylight (*photopic*) vision perceiving colours, than for low-light night (*scotopic*) vision with no colours. Human eyes can distinguish between 12–16 grey shades and up to about 1–2 million colours. The most popular bit-depths of imaging devices are listed in Table 1.2. The common ones are 8-bit greyscale and 24-bit colour images encoding more grey shades and colours, respectively, than could be resolved visually; see Fig. 1.5 with almost invisible borders between uniformly changing 32 ($b = 5$) or more successive grey levels and 64 ($b = 6$) or more colours from blue to red.

Table 1.2   Typical bit-depths for greyscale and colour images.

b	Q	Class of images
1	2	Binary, or "black-white" images
2...5	4...32	Quantised greyscale images
8	256	Common greyscale images
10...16	1024...65536	High dynamic range (HDR) images
24	3×256	Common colour RGB images
30	3×1024	HDR colour RGB images

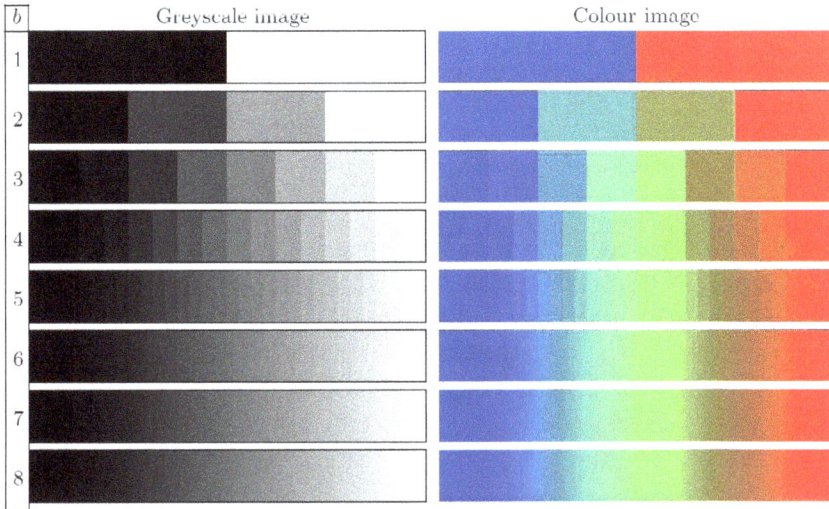

Fig. 1.5   Successive blocks of 2 to 256 uniformly scattered grey levels or colours.

Definition 1.3 (Discrete, or digital images). *A digital image is supported in a set of sites obtained by sampling a supporting plane or volume of a continuous image. The sampling associates each individual site with a certain continuous planar or spatial area. Each site-wise sampled signal is quantised, the quantisation encoding a continuous set of signals with a finite set of integers.*

The "basic" 2D or 3D area of sampling is called the *pixel* or *voxel*, respectively. Each pixel or voxel is characterised by its location, $\mathbf{s}$, with typically integer Cartesian coordinates $((x, y)$ or $(x, y, z))$ and supports an integer grey level, q, or other quantised signal. Sometimes, the entire location–signal pair, $(\mathbf{s}, q)$, is considered the pixel or voxel.

Most common digital images are supported in finite 2D or 3D lattices with integer coordinates. To geometrically transform a digital image, its continuous version is to be restored, transformed, and *resampled*, i.e., once again its transformed continuous support is sampled and the sampled signals are quantised (Chapter 8 will detail this process).

Definition 1.4 (Feature maps). *A feature map assigns to each pixel or voxel supporting an input image a scalar or vectorial numerical property, called a* feature*, which depends on one or more relevant input signals.*

To be visualised, the feature values are grey- or colour-coded. If the feature is a label that indicates non-intersecting regions or objects, its map is called a *region*, or *segmentation map*.

1.1.1 *Resolution, 2D lattice, and pixels*

Pixels in a most common digital image relate to same-size rectangular or square areas organised into a rectangular planar grid, or lattice with integer coordinates, $\mathbb{S} = \{(x,y) : x = 0,1,\ldots,M-1; \ y = 0,1,\ldots,N-1\}$, exemplified in Fig. 1.6. The coordinate origin is usually at the left bottom corner with the x- and y-axes pointing rightward and upward, respectively, but it may be sometimes at the top left corner with the y-axis pointing downwards.

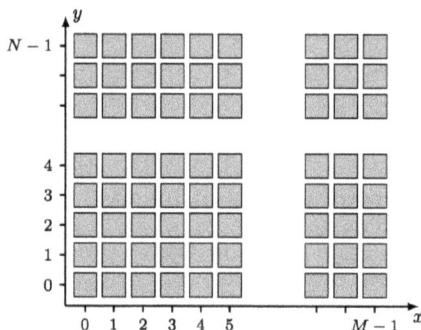

Fig. 1.6 $M \times N$ rectangular lattice of square pixels supporting a digital image.

The pixel or voxel size is not necessarily the same along each coordinate axis depending on spatial resolution of sampling. Uniformly spaced sampling simplifies restoration of original continuous images, as well as helps to accelerate certain image processing operations, such as, e.g., moving-window filtering in Chapter 3 and fast Fourier or wavelet transforms in Chapter 9.

Given a sampling origin, $\mathbf{s}^\circ = (x^\circ_{\text{cont}}, y^\circ_{\text{cont}})$ and width-height resolution, $\boldsymbol{\varepsilon} = (\varepsilon_{\text{x}}, \varepsilon_{\text{y}})$ on a continuous plane, the original position, $\mathbf{s}_{\text{cont}} = (x_{\text{cont}:m}, y_{\text{cont}:n})$, of a pixel, $\mathbf{s} = (m,n)$, with integer lattice coordinates is

$$x_{\text{cont}:m} = x^\circ_{\text{cont}} + \varepsilon_{\text{x}} m; \ y_{\text{cont}:n} = y^\circ_{\text{cont}} + \varepsilon_{\text{y}} n$$

Assuming an origin, q°_{c} and resolution, ε_{q} of uniform quantisation, the original grey value in a continuous 2D image is restored approximately as: $q_{\mathrm{cont}} = q_{\mathrm{cont}}^{\circ} + \varepsilon_{\mathrm{q}} q$. Signals for all other spatial points $\mathbf{s}$ of the continuous image are obtained by interpolation (see Chapter 8 for more details).

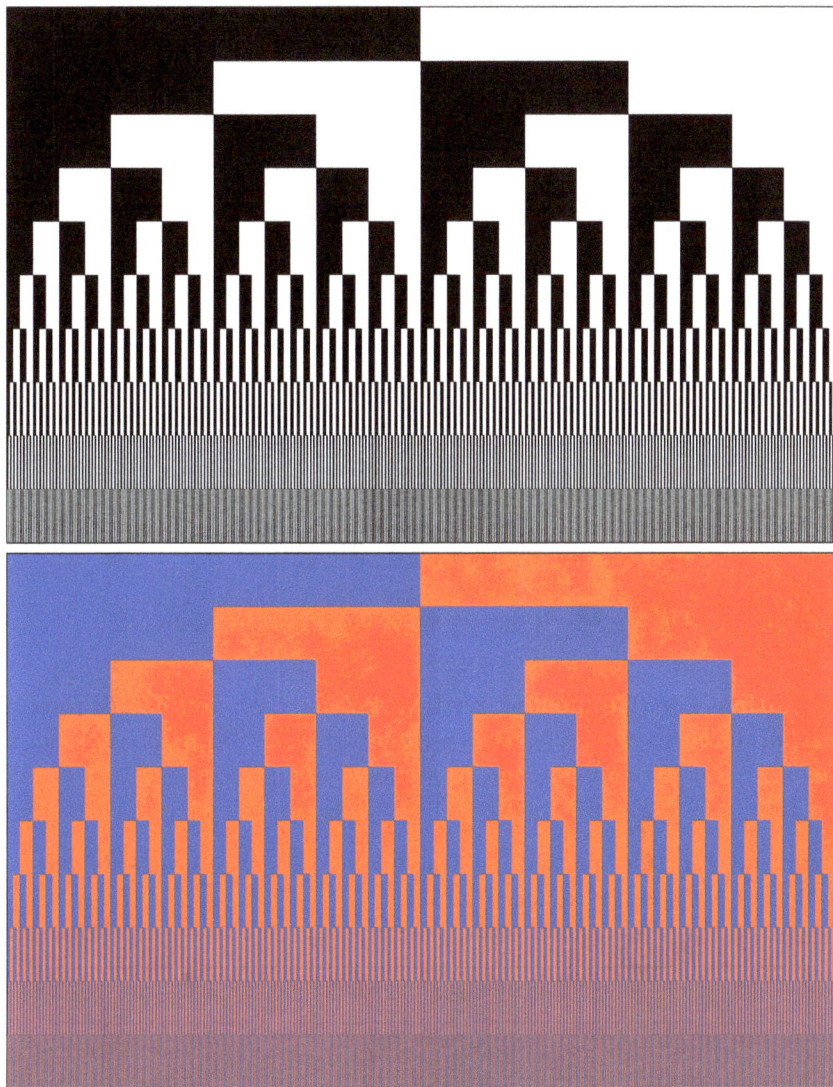

Fig. 1.7 Alternate black ($q = 5$) / white ($q = 250$) or red ($\mathbf{q} = [255, 0, 0]$) / blue ($\mathbf{q} = [0, 0, 255]$) blocks of gradually halving width: from 512 (top) to 1 (bottom).

Figure 1.7 illustrates the limited spatial resolution of human eyes in more detail. Both the images contain 640×1024 pixels with black/white or red/blue blocks of widths from 512 pixels to 1 pixel. Unless the reader has an extraordinary fine vision, the bottom stripes with smaller block widths might be perceived uniformly grey or magenta because of averaging adjacent optical signals due to limited spatial resolution of human eyes.

1.1.2   *Pixel neighbourhood and lattice connectivity*

Each square or rectangular pixel $\mathbf{s} = (x, y)$ in a supporting lattice, $\mathbb{S} = \{(x,y) : x = 0, 1, \ldots, M-1; y = 0, 1, \ldots, N-1\}$, has two basic types of the nearest neighbourhood, shown in Fig. 1.8:

4-neighbourhood: $\mathbb{N}_\mathbf{s} = \{(x, y \pm 1), (x \pm 1, y)\}$ and
8-neighbourhood: $\mathbb{N}_\mathbf{s} = \{(x \pm 1, y \pm 1), (x, y \pm 1), (x \pm 1, y)\}$.

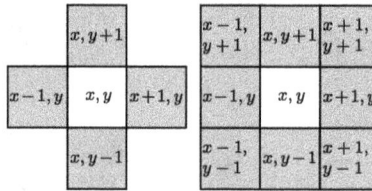

Fig. 1.8   4- and 8-neighbourhoods of a pixel $\mathbf{s} = (x, y)$.

Definition 1.5 (Connected path). *A 4- or 8-connected path from a pixel $\mathbf{s}_1$ to another pixel $\mathbf{s}_n$ is a sequence of pixels $\{\mathbf{s}_1, \mathbf{s}_2, \ldots, \mathbf{s}_n\}$, such that $\mathbf{s}_{i+1}$ is a 4- or 8-neighbour, respectively, of $\mathbf{s}_i$, i.e., $\mathbf{s}_{i+1} \in \mathbb{N}_{\mathbf{s}_i}$, for all $i = 1, \ldots, n-1$.*

Example 1.1 (Connected path). *Figure 1.9 demonstrates 4- and 8-connected paths in a rectangular lattice.*

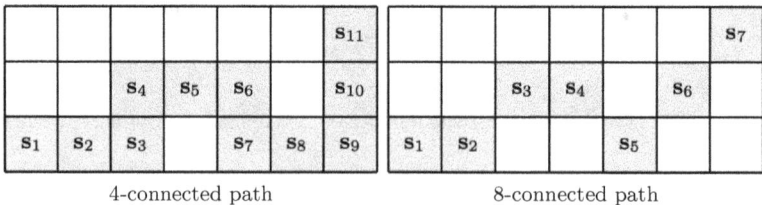

Fig. 1.9   4- and 8-connectivity in a lattice.

Definition 1.6 (Connected region). *A set of pixels is a 4- or 8-connected region if there exists at least one 4-connected or 8-connected path, respectively, between any pair of pixels from that set.*

Both the 4- and 8-connectedness may not preserve connectivity of regions in a continuous image before the sampling. In particular, a 4-connected single-pixel-wide horizontal or vertical line breaks into a sequence of disconnected strokes after being rotated by an angle, which differs from $90°$, $180°$, $270°$, or $360°$.

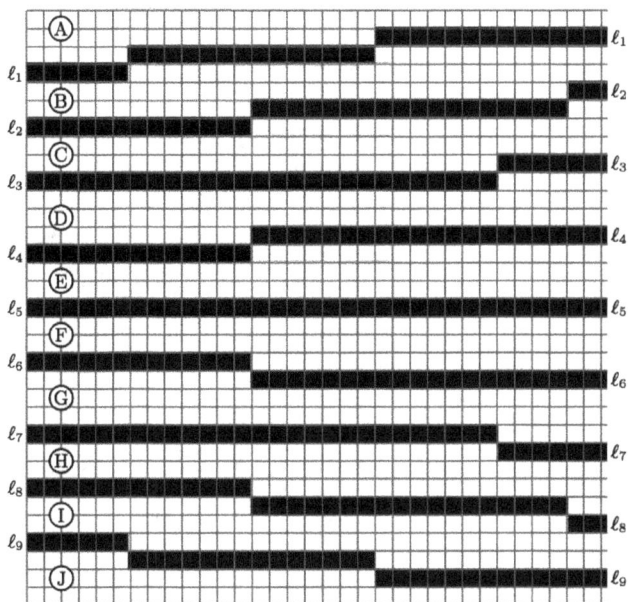

Fig. 1.10   Nine black lines, ℓ_1–ℓ_9, separating white areas A–J.

Example 1.2 (4- vs. 8-connectedness). *Figure 1.10 shows that the 8-connectedness preserves a slant line as a single continuous object, but simultaneously merges two regions, which are separate when the line was vertical or horizontal. Out of the nine pairs (A,B), (B,C), ..., (I,J) of white regions in Fig. 1.10, separated by a pencil of thin lines ℓ_1, ℓ_2, ..., ℓ_9 in the continuous image, only the pair (E,F) remains disjoint in the lattice.*

The 4-connectedness keeps all these pairs disjoint, but each slant continuous line, ℓ_1–ℓ_4 and ℓ_6–ℓ_9, is now a sequence of disjoint horizontal strokes: three for ℓ_1, ℓ_2, ℓ_8, and ℓ_9 or two for ℓ_3, ℓ_4, ℓ_6, and ℓ_7.

To avoid impractically complex definitions of connectedness, objects of interest are often supposed 8-connected, but on a 4-connected background. Then if a pixel-wide vertical line is considered an object, it continues to separate two background regions after any rotation.

1.1.3   *Greyscale, colour, and multiband signals*

A number of bits in an integer scalar pixel/voxel-wise signal is called *bit-depth*. Typical bit-depth is 1 for a binary image and 8 for a common monochrome, or greyscale image. The binary images (1-bit signals) have only two codes (0 and 1), visualised, typically, as black and white. The 8-bit signals allow for 256 codes represented with grey shades or selected colours. To capture subtle differences between objects, today's special imaging devices often have larger bit-depths, e.g., 10-, 12-, 14-, or 16-bit monochrome signals ($Q = 1024, 4096, 16384$, or 65536, respectively).

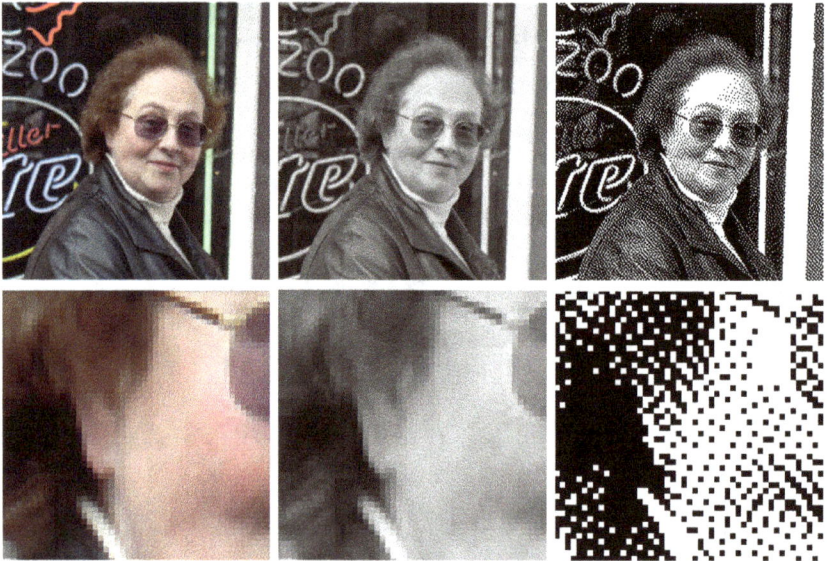

Fig. 1.11   Colour, greyscale, and pseudo-greyscale binary images of the same scene and their 8-times-enlarged pieces.

Example 1.3 (Colour, greyscale, and binary signals). *Figure 1.11 shows a 24-bit colour and 8-bit greyscale image of the same scene, together with a binary (1-bit) image encoding grey shades by spatial densities of* *purely black and white pixels scattered over small, e.g., 4×4, blocks. The lat-ter are perceived as grey points due to limited spatial resolution of human vi-sion. Their scaled up pieces clarify the black-white encoding of grey shades.*

Relatively small colour palettes can be encoded with just a single integer colour index per pixel or voxel. A "true-colour" RGB image of bit-depth $3 \times b$ (or b for each primary colour) has vectorial signals, $\mathbf{g}(x, y) = [g_r(x, y), g_g(x, y), g_b(x, y)] : (x, y) \in \mathbb{S}$, from a set of Q^3 distinct colours in the RGB colour space ($Q = 2^b$). Three 8-bit colour components produce in total $2^{24} = 16,777,216$ colours. So-called *multi-band* and *multi-spectral* images, sensed simultaneously in more than three bands of electromagnetic waves, are also encoded by vectorial pixel-wise signals. These vectors are sometimes called *signatures* of signals.

From now on, this primer will mostly consider greyscale 2D images and their feature or region maps, although a majority of the concepts and techniques presented can be easily applied or extended to colour and multi-band images.

1.1.4 *Regions and features*

Image analysis usually exploits various feature and region (segmentation) maps of the same observed scene to associate an object of interest with sensed scalar or vectorial signals. Each pixel-wise feature is a computable property (in a metric or interval scale) of image signals in a certain neigh-bourhood of, or a window around the respective pixel. Most commonly, the features are selected among local window-wise statistics (a few of them will be detailed in Section 1.3).

Each site of a region map presents a numerical or symbolic label, and sites with the same label are attributed to an individual class, called often a region, segment, or individual object on the optical image.

1.2 Global signal statistics

The simplest first-order descriptors are based on a grey level histogram (GLH), $\mathbf{H}(\mathbf{g})$, or its normed version, an empirical probability distribution function (p.d.f.) of grey levels, $\mathbf{P}(\mathbf{g})$ in a given image, $\mathbf{g}$.

Let $S = |\mathbb{S}|$ be *cardinality* (size) of a lattice, i.e., the total number of its sites (pixels). Because the number, Q^k, of different k-tuples of Q-level signals is growing exponentially, the k-order histograms remain computationally feasible for characterising signal variations over the lattice only if $Q^k < S$, i.e., $k < \log S / \log Q$. As a result, the descriptors are mostly limited to the second-order statistics based on certain grey level co-occurrence histograms (GLCHs) or grey level difference histograms (GLDHs).

To make the histogram-based descriptors invariant to global brightness and contrast deviations, the input images might be normalised as it will be detailed in Chapter 2. Alternatively, the statistics themselves might be combined into contrast-brightness-invariant descriptors.

1.2.1   *Grey-level histogram (GLH)*

Definition 1.7. *The GLH* $\mathbf{H}(\mathbf{g}) = (H(q|\mathbf{g}) : q \in \mathbb{Q})$ *of an image* $\mathbf{g}$ *is a collection of (unnormed) frequencies,* $H(q|\mathbf{g})$ *of signals* $q \in \mathbb{Q}$ *in* $\mathbf{g}$*, i.e., of numbers of sites supporting each signal* $q \in \mathbb{Q}$ *in the lattice* $\mathbb{S}$*:*

$$H(q|\mathbf{g}) = \sum_{\mathbf{s} \in \mathbb{S}} \delta\big(q - g(\mathbf{s})\big); \quad \sum_{q \in \mathbb{Q}} H(q|\mathbf{g}) = S$$

where $\delta(\dots)$ *is the Kronecker's delta-function.*

Algorithm 1 details the GLH computation for a given digital image. For an 8-bit or 16-bit image, $\mathbb{Q} = \{0, 1, \dots, 255\}$ or $\{0.1. \dots, 65535\}$, respectively. In a common true-colour image with three 8-bit RGB channels, each site supports one of $2^{24} = 1,677,216$ distinct colours.

Algorithm 1 Computing the GLH.

Input: a greyscale image $\mathbf{g} = (g(\mathbf{s}) : \mathbf{s} \in \mathbb{S})$.
Output: the GLH $\mathbf{H} = (H(q) : q \in \mathbb{Q} = \{0, 1, \dots, Q-1\})$
Initialisation: **for** $q = 0$ **step** $q \leftarrow q + 1$ **until** $q = Q - 1$ **do**
    $H(q) = 0$
end for
GLH: **for** $\mathbf{s} \in \mathbb{S}$ **do**
    $H\big(g(\mathbf{s})\big) \leftarrow H\big(g(\mathbf{s})\big) + 1$
end for

The GLH, $\mathbf{H}$, provides a basis for various generic first-order statistics to characterise an original (and possibly unknown) image, including, in particular, its minimum, $q_{\min}$, maximum, $q_{\max}$, and average, or mean μ, grey values; its standard deviation, σ, of grey values; its most frequent grey value, q_{mode}, indicated by the global GLH mode, or position of its maximal component, and so forth:

$$q_{\min} = \min_{q \in \mathbb{Q}}\{q : H(q) > 0\} \qquad q_{\max} = \max_{q \in \mathbb{Q}}\{q : H(q) > 0\}$$
$$\mu = \frac{1}{S}\sum_{q \in \mathbb{Q}} q \cdot H(q) \qquad \sigma^2 = \frac{1}{S-1}\sum_{q \in \mathbb{Q}}(q - \mu)^2 \cdot H(q) \qquad (1.1)$$
$$q_{\text{mode}} = \max_{q \in \mathbb{Q}} H(q) \qquad S = \sum_{q \in \mathbb{Q}} H(q)$$

Table 1.3 summarises these statistics for the images in Fig. 1.12.

Table 1.3   Integral characteristics of images in Fig. 1.12.

Image	Size MN	$q_{\min}$	$q_{\max}$	q_{mean}	S.t.d.	q_{mode}	$H(q_{\text{mode}})$
Left	43,621	11	255	134.1	79.4	255	8,479
Middle	64,108	3	255	112.4	43.1	96	1,210
Right	69,156	2	255	65.5	44.0	49	1,162

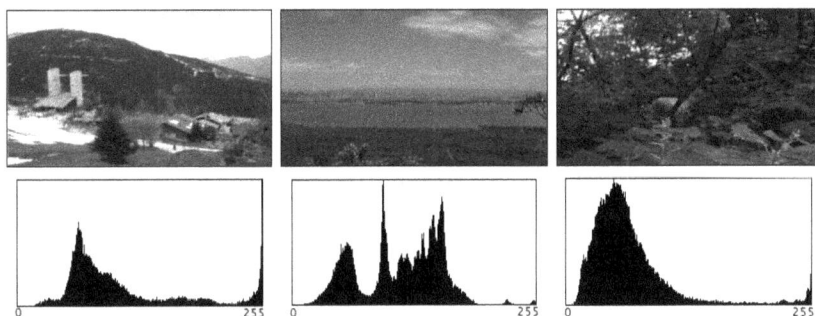

Fig. 1.12   Digital greyscale images and their GLHs.

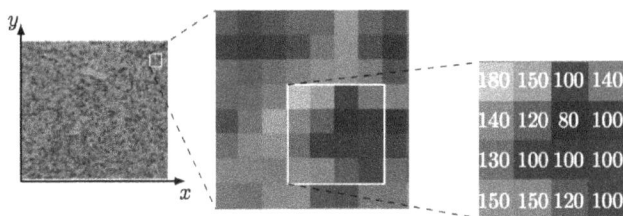

Fig. 1.13 4×4 image patch in Example 1.4 (numbers – the pixel-wise grey levels).

Example 1.4 (Collecting a GLH with Algorithm 1). *Scanning a particular 4×4 patch (magnified in Fig. 1.13) updates the GLH* **H** *collected* *so far as:*

$H(80) \leftarrow H(80) + 1;$ $H(100) \leftarrow H(100) + 6;$ $H(120) \leftarrow H(120) + 2;$
$H(130) \leftarrow H(130) + 1;$ $H(140) \leftarrow H(140) + 2;$ $H(150) \leftarrow H(150) + 3;$
$H(180) \leftarrow H(180) + 1$

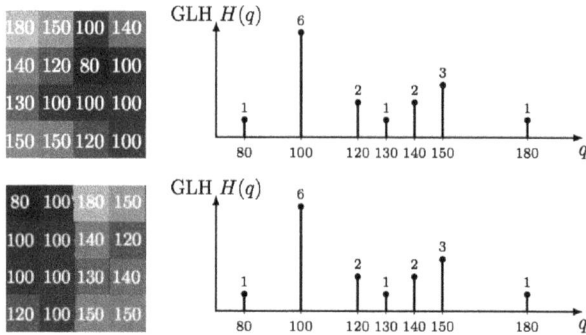

Fig. 1.14   The same GLHs after permuting sites of the 4×4 patch.

Example 1.5 (Invariance to pixel permutations). *A GLH and its normed version, an empirical probability distribution of grey levels, detailed in Section 1.2.2, remain the same after the lattice sites are arbitrarily permuted, as shown in Fig. 1.14. Also, the normed GLH is almost invariant to scaling the image size up and (to some extent) down.*

Therefore, both the original and normed GLHs are rather weak image descriptors. However, they are useful for a global image assessment. In particular, a GLH, which is overly shifted to one end of the signal interval $[0, \ldots, Q-1]$, indicates that the image is excessively bright or dark, as will be detailed in Section 1.2.4.

1.2.2 *Empirical vs. theoretical probabilities*

Definition 1.8 (Empirical p.d.f.). *The empirical p.d.f.,* $\mathbf{P(g)} = (P(q|\mathbf{g}) : q \in \mathbb{Q})$, *of grey values in an image* $\mathbf{g}$ *is a collection of the normed frequencies (relative counts), or empirical marginal probabilities of signals,* $q \in \mathbb{Q}$, *over* $\mathbb{S}$:

$$P(q|\mathbf{g}) = \frac{1}{S} H(q|\mathbf{g}); \quad \sum_{q \in \mathbb{Q}} P(q|\mathbf{g}) = 1$$

For a lattice with M rows and N columns, $S \equiv |\mathbb{S}| = M \times N$ pixels.

An empirical p.d.f. is a *statistical estimate* of the unknown theoretical p.d.f. The estimate can be confidently accurate if the image size, i.e., the number S of signals to build the GLH, exceeds a certain threshold. The latter depends on a chosen confidence level and a tolerable maximal absolute difference, $\varepsilon_{\mathrm{pr}}$, between the empirical probability and its true value.

For a common in practice confidence level of 95%, the threshold is approximately equal to $\varepsilon_{\mathrm{pr}}^{-2}$, so that the required image size is $S \geq \varepsilon_{\mathrm{pr}}^{-2}$. If $\varepsilon_{\mathrm{pr}} = \frac{1}{Q}$, the minimum size is Q^2. A less restrictive statistical "rule of thumb", calling for 7 to 10 image signals per histogram bin to closely estimate the true p.d., decreases the required image size to $S \geq (7 - 10)Q$.

Example 1.6 (Image sizes to estimate a true p.d. of grey levels).
The minimum size of a training square patch of an 8-bit ($Q = 256$) or 4-bit ($Q = 16$) image to estimate the p.d. of grey levels is 256×256 or 16×16, respectively. The less tight "rule of thumb" decreases the minimal patch size to $S \approx 9Q$, i.e., to the patch $3\sqrt{Q} \times 3\sqrt{Q}$, i.e., 48×48 or 12×12, respectively, for the same sets of grey levels.

Therefore, both the GLHs and their statistics of Eq. 1.1, as well as their derived CHs and percentiles in Section 1.2.3, can serve as not only global, but also local image descriptors.

1.2.3 *Cumulative histogram (CH) and percentiles*

Definition 1.9. *A CH $\mathbf{C}$ counts the total number of pixel intensities in all the GLH's bins up to the current bin q:*

$$\mathbf{C} = \left[C(q) = \sum_{\gamma=0}^{q} H(\gamma) : q = 0, \ldots, Q - 1 \right]$$

Given a GLH, the CH is built with Algorithm 2.

Algorithm 2 Computing the CH.

Input: an GLH $\mathbf{H} = (H(q) : q = 0, \ldots, Q - 1)$.
Output: the CH $\mathbf{C} = (C(q) : q = 0, 1, \ldots, Q - 1)$
$C(0) = H(0)$
for $q = 1$ **step** $q \leftarrow q + 1$ **until** $q = Q - 1$ **do**
$\quad C(q) = C(q - 1) + H(q)$
end for

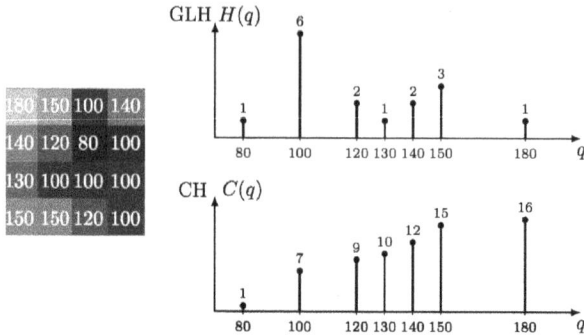

Fig. 1.15   Building a CH for a 4 × 4 patch.

Example 1.7 (Building a CH). *Let a 10×10 image with 3-bit signals, $q \in \mathbb{Q} = \{0, 1, \ldots, 7\}$, have the GLH $\mathbf{H} = [40, 0, 18, 6, 10, 3, 7, 16]$. Then its CH, $\mathbf{C} = [40, 40, 58, 64, 74, 77, 84, 100]$, is formed by Algorithm 2 as follows:*

$C[0] = H[0] = 40;$ $\qquad$ $C[1] = C[0] + H[1] = 40 + 0 = 40;$
$C[2] = C[1] + H[2] = 40 + 18 = 58;$ $\quad$ $C[3] = C[2] + H[3] = 58 + 6 = 64;$
$C[4] = C[3] + H[4] = 64 + 10 = 74;$ $\quad$ $C[5] = C[5] + H[5] = 74 + 3 = 77;$
$C[6] = C[5] + H[6] = 77 + 7 = 84;$ $\quad$ $C[7] = C[6] + H[7] = 84 + 16 = 100$

One more example for a 4×4 patch is presented in Fig. 1.15. Figure 1.16 shows the cumulative histogram for a greyscale 8-bit image. The CH is useful for some pixel-wise intensity corrections, e.g., *histogram equalisation*, and helps in computing rank statistics, e.g., percentiles, of grey levels.

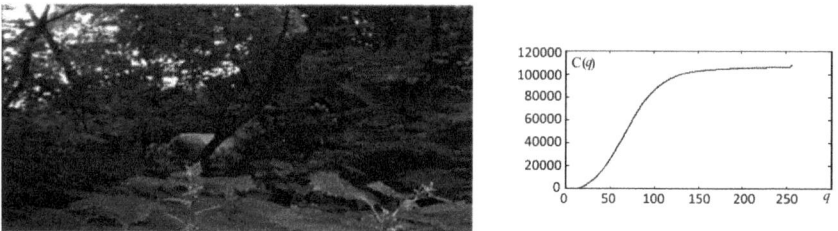

Fig. 1.16   Greyscale image and its CH.

Definition 1.10 (Percentiles). *Given a GLH $\mathbf{H}$, the α-percentile q_α is the minimum grey level with the cumulative probability $\alpha\%$, i.e., the value, such that $\alpha\%$ of the lattice sites have grey values below than or equal to q_α:*

$$q_\alpha = \min\left\{q : q \in \mathbb{Q}; \ C(q) \geq \frac{\alpha}{100}C(Q-1)\right\}$$

Most common percentile statistics are the minimum (q_0), the first quartile (q_{25}), the median (q_{50}), the third quartile (q_{75}), and the maximum (q_{100}) signal value.

1.2.4 *Global brightness and contrast*

Visual or automatic selection of areas of interest, such as, e.g., lungs and their background in a CT chest image of Fig. 1.17, is impossible without significant differences in their visual appearances. Informally, an entire greyscale image or its part are often characterised by overall, or global brightness and contrast.

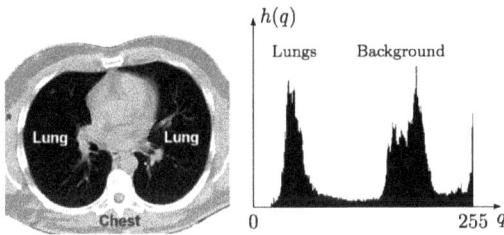

Fig. 1.17   2D CT chest slice and its GLH.

The GLH, collected for the image or its region, is helpful for assessing these properties, which relate to the mean (average) signal value, standard deviation, and grouping (clustering) of signals around prominent peaks of the GLH. In particular, two prominent clusters in Fig. 1.17 around the mean suggest two characteristic (dark and bright) regions, and a majority of grey levels for an overly dark or bright image are strongly biased to the respective side of the GLH (Fig. 1.18).

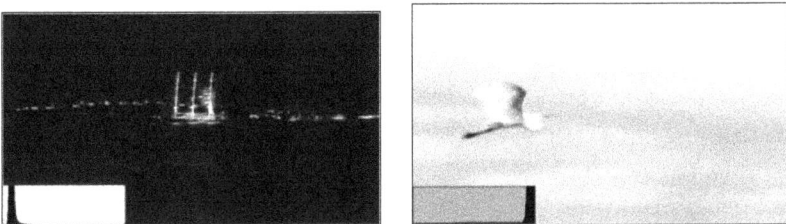

Fig. 1.18   Too dark and too bright images with the overlaid GLHs.

Global brightness is measured by the mean signal μ in Eq. (1.1).

Global contrast, in spite of its widespread use, has no universal definition. The frequently used *Michelson contrast* measures relative difference between the maximal, q_{max} and minimum, q_{min}, image signals:

$$c = \frac{q_{max} - q_{min}}{q_{max} + q_{min}} \equiv 1 - \frac{2q_{min}}{q_{max} + q_{min}}$$

A blank frame with $q_{min} = q_{max}$ obviously has zero contrast, otherwise the larger the signal span, $q_{max} - q_{min}$, the closer the contrast to the unit value. However, with such a definition the perceived and measured contrast may contradict each other. Provided that $q_{min} = 0$, the unit contrast is for any $q_{max} > 0$. In other words, the same minimal signal difference, $q_{max} - q_{min} = 1$, yields the unit contrast, $c = 1$, for $q_{min} = 0$ irrespectively of q_{max}, i.e., for any maximal signal from 1 to $Q - 1$, whereas the expected low contrast $c = \frac{1}{2Q-1}$ appears only at the opposite side of the minimal signal range, for $q_{min} = Q - 2$.

The *Weber contrast* presumes an object/background image, like in Fig. 1.17, and measures a relative difference between two signals, q_{ob} and q_{bg}, which are typical for an object and its background, respectively:

$$c = \frac{|q_{ob} - q_{bg}|}{q_{ob} + q_{bg}} \equiv 1 - 2\frac{\min\{q_{ob}, q_{bg}\}}{q_{ob} + q_{bg}}$$

The relative maximal signal difference in an image with respect to the full dynamic signal range, e.g., $Q - 1$ for $\mathbb{Q} = \{0, 1, \ldots, Q-1\}$, gives a more intuitive definition of the overall contrast:

$$c = \frac{q_{max} - q_{min}}{Q - 1}$$

In this case, the contrast is still in the range $[0, 1]$; and any image spanning across the whole dynamic range has a unit contrast. An alternative measure that is more robust to outliers is *root mean square (RMS) contrast* which measures the relative empirical standard deviation of signals in Eq. (1.1):

$$c = \frac{\sigma}{Q - 1}$$

1.2.5   *Grey-level co-occurrence histograms (GLCH)*

Definition 1.11 (GLCH). *Given a coordinate offset, $\boldsymbol{\nu} = (\xi, \eta)$, the GLCH $\mathbf{H}_{\boldsymbol{\nu}}(\mathbf{g}) = (H_{\boldsymbol{\nu}}(q, q') : q, q' \in \mathbb{Q})$ of an image $\mathbf{g}$ is a collection of (unnormed) frequencies of co-occurring signals $q \in \mathbb{Q}$ and $q' \in \mathbb{Q}$ in pairs of sites, $\mathbf{s}$ and $\mathbf{s}' = \mathbf{s} + \boldsymbol{\nu}$, respectively, i.e., of numbers of sites pairs supporting each signal pair, $(q, q'); q, q' \in \mathbb{Q}$, in the lattice $\mathbb{S}$:*

$$H_{\boldsymbol{\nu}}(q, q') = \sum_{\mathbf{s}, \mathbf{s}+\boldsymbol{\nu} \in \mathbb{S}} \delta(q - g(\mathbf{s}))\delta(q' - g(\mathbf{s} + \boldsymbol{\nu})); \quad \sum_{q \in \mathbb{Q}} \sum_{q' \in \mathbb{Q}} H_{\boldsymbol{\nu}}(q, q') = S_{\boldsymbol{\nu}}$$

where $\delta(\dots)$ is the Kronecker's delta-function and S_{ν} is the cardinality of the subset $\mathbb{S}_{\nu} \subset \mathbb{S}$ of all sites $\mathbf{s}$, such that $\mathbf{s} + \nu \in \mathbb{S}$.

For an 8-bit image, $Q = |\mathbb{Q}| = 256$, and each individual GLCH is a 256×256 matrix (thus, the GLCH is called also the GLCM where M stands for "matrix").

The GLCH, $\mathbf{H}_{\nu}$, provides various second-order descriptors of an original image, which are usually specified in terms of the normed GLCH, or a $Q \times Q$ matrix $\mathbf{P}_{\nu}$ of empirical marginal probabilities of the pairwise signal co-occurrences:

$$\mathbf{P}_{\nu} = \left[P_{\nu}(q, q') = \frac{1}{S_{\nu}} H_{\nu}(q, q') \right]_{q, q' \in \mathbb{Q}} ; \quad \sum_{q \in \mathbb{Q}} \sum_{q' \in \mathbb{Q}} P_{\nu}(q, q') = 1$$

Popular global descriptors of this type are means and ranges of generic GLCH-based statistics computed for the four nearest-neighbour offsets $\nu \in \{(-1, 0), (-1, 1), (0, 1), (1, 1)\}$. The latter statistics include the angular second moment, $f_{\text{asm}:\nu}$, textural contrast, $f_{\text{tec}:\nu}$, inverse difference moment, $f_{\text{idm}:\nu}$, entropy, $f_{\text{ent}:\nu}$ and a few others:

$$f_{\text{asm}:\nu} = \sum_{q \in \mathbb{Q}} \sum_{q' \in \mathbb{Q}} P_{\nu}^2(q, q');$$

$$f_{\text{tec}:\nu} = \sum_{\kappa \in \mathbb{Q}} \kappa^2 \left(\sum_{q, q+\kappa \in \mathbb{Q}} P_{\nu}(q, q + \kappa) + \sum_{q, q-\kappa \in \mathbb{Q}} P_{\nu}(q, q - \kappa) \right);$$

$$f_{\text{idm}:\nu} = \sum_{q \in \mathbb{Q}} \sum_{q' \in \mathbb{Q}} \frac{1}{1+(q-q')^2} P_{\nu}(q, q'); \tag{1.2}$$

$$f_{\text{ent}:\nu} = - \sum_{q \in \mathbb{Q}} \sum_{q' \in \mathbb{Q}} P_{\nu}(q, q') \log \left(P_{\nu}(q, q') \right)$$

In accord with Section 1.2.2, a large square $Q^2 \times Q^2$ patch, e.g., 256×256 for $Q = 16$, will be required to accurately estimate the $Q \times Q$ matrix of true co-occurrence probabilities with confidence of 95% and admissible errors of $\frac{1}{Q^2}$. Moreover, even the loose "rule of thumb" asks for no less than $S = 9Q^2$ signals, i.e., at least a $3Q \times 3Q$ square patch (48×48 for $Q = 16$).

Therefore, it is difficult to use the GLCH-based statistics for describing local signal variations, unless the cardinality, Q, of an original signal set is sufficiently small. The lesser cardinality could be obtained by quantising the original signals with fixed or data-driven thresholds, or considering only contrast-offset invariant properties of signal pairs, (q_1, q_2), such as, e.g., their binary ($q_1 \leq q_2$ and $q_1 > q_2$) or ternary ($q_1 < q_2$; $q_1 = q_2$, and $q_1 > q_2$) ordinal relations.

The normed GLHs and the GLH-based statistics of Eq. (1.1) are more feasible local descriptors that need at least $3\sqrt{Q} \times 3\sqrt{Q}$ patches to be accurately estimated, e.g., 12×12 for $Q = 16$ or 4×4 for $Q = 2$. The normed second-order GLDHs, i.e., marginal empirical distributions of absolute or signed signal differences, have just the same (Q) or twice larger $(2Q)$ numbers, respectively, of the histogram bins.

Thus, the means and ranges of the GLDH-based statistics, which are similar to the GLH- or selected GLCH-based ones and are computed for several coordinate offsets, can be used as feasible local descriptors, too. Also, some linear and non-linear scalar K-variate functions; $K \gg 1$, with relatively small sets of their distinct values are frequently used to describe large signal K-tuples (see, e.g., Section 1.3.2).

1.3 Mapping local features

Spatial variations of image signals provide information about depicted scenes and objects. In some cases, it is sufficient to account only for individual pixel/voxel-wise signals, but a majority of practical problems deal with k-tuples of signals with $k \gg 1$, rather than individual signals. Associating each lattice site with a feature depending on image signals (intensities or colours) in this and neighbouring sites produces a *dense feature map*. A lesser number of the lattice sites are associated each with a relevant feature in a *sparse feature map*. Regions attributed to different objects and their background in the lattice are supposed to have detectable differences of characteristic signal features.

1.3.1 *Pixel-wise signal statistics*

Statistical properties of scalar signals in a moving window $\mathbb{W}_{\mathbf{s}}$ of fixed size and shape are the simplest features describing the window centre, $\mathbf{s}$. The moving, or local mean value, $\mu(\mathbf{s})$, standard deviation, $\sigma(\mathbf{s})$, and range, $r(\mathbf{s})$, or difference between the maximum and minimum signals in a square $J \times J$ window $\mathbb{W}_{\mathbf{s}}$; $J = 3, 5, \ldots$, are among the common statistics:

$$\mu_{\mathbf{s}} = \frac{1}{J^2} \sum_{\mathbf{t} \in \mathbb{W}_{\mathbf{s}}} g(\mathbf{t}); \quad \sigma_{\mathbf{s}} = \sqrt{\frac{1}{J^2 - 1} \sum_{\mathbf{t} \in \mathbb{W}_{\mathbf{s}}} (g(\mathbf{t}) - \mu_{\mathbf{s}})^2}$$

and

$$r_{\mathbf{s}} = \max_{\mathbf{t} \in \mathbb{W}_{\mathbf{s}}} \{g(\mathbf{t})\} - \min_{\mathbf{t} \in \mathbb{W}_{\mathbf{s}}} \{g(\mathbf{t})\}$$

Example 1.8 (First-order statistics). *As shown in Fig. 1.19, both the local standard deviation and range of signals in a small 3×3 window centred at each pixel are similar in emphasising boundaries between almost homogeneous (uniform or slowly varying) regions. Additional boundaries are revealed by combining these statistics, e.g., by computing ratios between the signal ranges in the windows of different sizes.*

More informative features are based on the higher-order statistics, e.g., statistics of signal pairs or even k-tuples, $k > 2$, related to each pixel $\mathbf{s}$. The size and, possibly, shape of the window, $\mathbb{W}_\mathbf{s}$, might also be adapted to the signals supported.

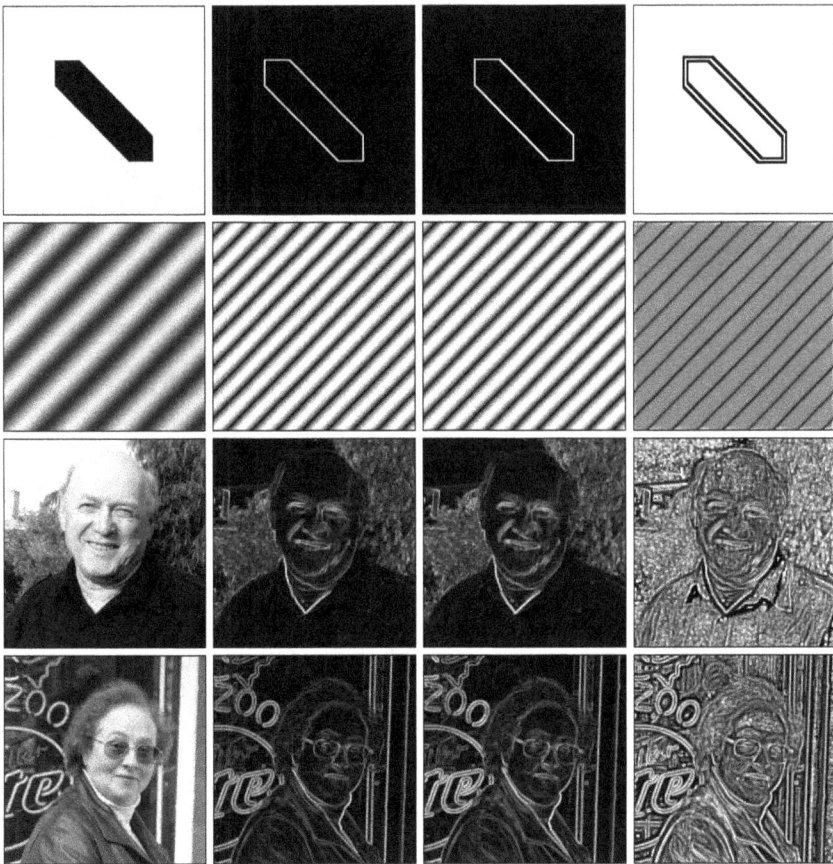

Fig. 1.19   Test images and grey coded dense maps (from left to right) of st.d. and ranges in 3×3 windows, and ratios of ranges in 3×3 and 9×9 windows.

1.3.2 *Local binary patterns (LBP)*

Contrast–offset invariant properties of signal variations in the nearest 8-neighbourhood of a pixel $\mathbf{s} = (x, y)$ are often described with a binary 8-digit code of pairwise relationships between the pixel-wise signal $q = g(x, y)$ and its 8 nearest neighbours, $q_i = g(x + \xi_i, y + \eta_i)$:

$$\lambda_{\mathbf{s}} = \sum_{i=0}^{7} 2^i \mathrm{U}_\varepsilon(q - q_i);$$

i	0	1	2	3	4	5	6	7
ξ_i	-1	-1	-1	0	1	1	1	0
η_i	-1	0	1	1	1	0	-1	-1

(1.3)

where offsets (ξ_i, η_i) specify the nearest 8-neighbours of the origin, $\xi = 0, \eta = 0$, in the counter-clockwise order and $\mathrm{U}_\varepsilon(\Delta)$ denotes a *boxcar function* of signal difference, Δ, with the interval $[-\varepsilon, \varepsilon]$ of unit values:

$$\mathrm{U}_\varepsilon(\Delta) = \begin{cases} 1 \text{ if } |\Delta| \leq \varepsilon \\ 0 \text{ otherwise} \end{cases} \tag{1.4}$$

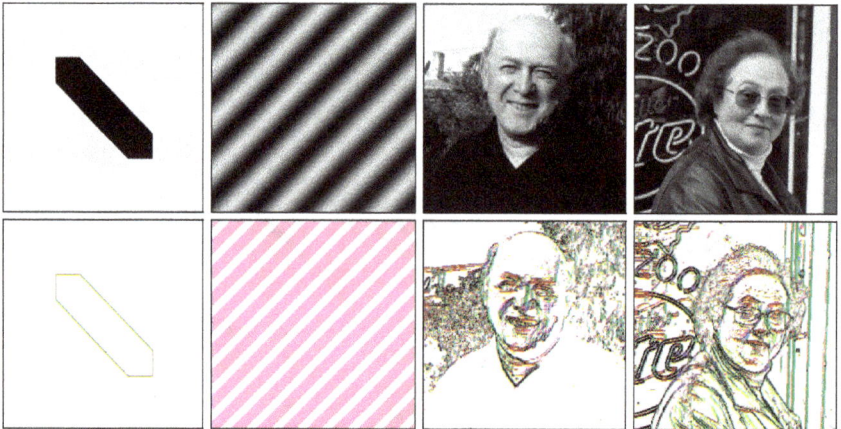

Fig. 1.20   Colour-coded LBP maps of test images (the nearest 8-neighbours; $\varepsilon = 10$).

Each LBP encodes simultaneous relations of approximate equality or inequality between the central signal and the nearest eight signals to within a given tolerance, ε. Obviously, some of the LBPs can be associated with local "edges" on their 3×3 supports (see Fig. 1.20).

Example 1.9 (LBP). *Let a 3×3 patch of an 8-bit greyscale image:*

$$\begin{array}{|c|c|c|} \hline 220 & 50 & 175 \\ \hline 100 & 115 & 25 \\ \hline 75 & 125 & 200 \\ \hline \end{array} \longleftarrow i = \begin{array}{ccc} 2 & 3 & 4 \\ 1 & & 5 \\ 0 & 7 & 6 \end{array} \tag{1.5}$$

have the rightward x and upward y-coordinate axes. The counter-clockwise order of Eq. (1.3) for the nearest 8-neighbours of the central pixel, $\mathbf{s}$, is shown in Eq. (1.5). Given the tolerance, $\varepsilon = 15$, for the boxcar function, $U_\varepsilon(\Delta)$, of Eq. (1.4), the LBP of Eq. (1.3) is computed as follows:

$$\begin{aligned}
\lambda_{\mathbf{s}} = {}& 2^0 U_{15}(115 - 75) + 2^1 U_{15}(115 - 100) + 2^2 U_{15}(115 - 220) + \\
& 2^3 U_{15}(115 - 50) + 2^4 U_{15}(115 - 175) + 2^5 U_{15}(115 - 25) + \\
& 2^6 U_{15}(115 - 200) + 2^7 U_{15}(115 - 125) \\
= {}& 1 \cdot 0 + 2 \cdot 1 + 4 \cdot 0 + 8 \cdot 0 + 16 \cdot 0 + 32 \cdot 0 + 64 \cdot 0 + 128 \cdot 1 = 130
\end{aligned}$$

In more general cases, the number of neighbours may vary (up to 10–12 for keeping computational feasibility). Coordinate offsets of the neighbours with respect to the origin may be arbitrary fixed or data-dependent. Also, other contrast invariant pairwise signal relations may be taken into account, e.g., "$\geq$" and "$<$", rather than $=$ and $\neq$ in the LBPs, or $<$, $=$, and $>$ ("less than", "equal to", and "greater than" to within the tolerance ε) in the so-called *local ternary patterns* (LTP). With an adaptive tolerance ε, being a fraction of the dynamic range of an image, the LBP or LTP histogram is sometimes used as an integral contrast-offset-invariant image descriptor. A rotation-invariant LBP property, called a *local uniformity grade* (LUG), is the sum of individual binary codes:

$$\lambda_{\text{lug:s}} = \sum_{i=0}^{7} U_\varepsilon(q - q_i)$$

The resulting nine grades, $0, 1, \ldots, 8$, characterise uniformity of the corresponding 3×3 block of pixels: from 0 (totally non-uniform) to 8 (uniform).

One more high-order local descriptor, called an *univalue segment assimilating nucleus* (USAN), will be met in Chapter 7 (Section 7.1.3).

1.4 Questions and exercises

(1) How a continuous image is formed with a pinhole camera?
(2) Given a pinhole camera of Fig. 1.2 with the optical centre, $\mathbf{O} = (0, 0, 0)$, at the origin of the 3D coordinate system, the focal distance, $f = 2$, and the principal point, $\mathbf{s}_c = (30, 20)$, find the projection, $\mathbf{s}$, of the spatial point, $\mathbf{S} = (2000, 3000, 500)$, to the image plane.
(3) Using a pencil of lines like in Fig. 1.4, determine your own spatial resolution boundary.
(4) Why an object-of-interest and its background are usually considered 8- and 4-connected, respectively, in a digital image?

(5) How many entries, $H(q)$, called usually bins, have GLHs, **H**, of digital images with the bit-depth, $b = 3$?

(6) Let a 10×10 digital image with bit-depth of 2 have the GLH

$$\mathbf{H} = \begin{array}{|cccc|c} 0 & 1 & 2 & 3 & q \\ \hline 36 & 16 & 32 & 16 & H(q) \end{array}$$

   (a) Find the mean, μ, and st.d., σ, of signals in the image **g** in accord with Eq. (1.1).

   (b) Find the CH for the image **g**.

(7) Let an 8-bit image ($Q = 256$) contain an uniform object on an uniform background, such that all object and background pixels have the same grey levels of 125 and 25, respectively. Find and compare the Michelson, Weber, and overall contrast (see Section 1.2.4) of this image.

(8) Given a 4×4 GLCH matrix for the nearest 4-neighbourhoods, $\boldsymbol{\nu}$, of an image with bit-depth of 2, compute the angular second moment, $f_{\text{asm}:\boldsymbol{\nu}}$ in Eq. (1.2):

$$\mathbf{H}_{\boldsymbol{\nu}} = \begin{bmatrix} 76 & 12 & 16 & 4 \\ 12 & 28 & 24 & 0 \\ 16 & 24 & 56 & 32 \\ 4 & 0 & 32 & 28 \end{bmatrix} \longrightarrow \mathbf{P}_{\boldsymbol{\nu}} = \frac{\mathbf{H}_{\boldsymbol{\nu}}}{364} = \begin{bmatrix} 0.209 & 0.033 & 0.044 & 0.011 \\ 0.033 & 0.077 & 0.066 & 0.000 \\ 0.044 & 0.066 & 0.153 & 0.088 \\ 0.011 & 0.000 & 0.088 & 0.077 \end{bmatrix}$$

(9) Using the same assumptions as in Example 1.9, compute the LBPs and LUGs for the following two 3×3 blocks of pixels:

160	157	165
142	150	136
163	138	155

and

200	75	140
100	120	150
90	140	165

Chapter 2

Transforming Appearance

Let us begin with the simplest operations that adjust the overall brightness and contrast of a depicted scene. Both the input and output images have the same set, $\mathbb{Q} = \{0, 1, \ldots, Q - 1\}$, of integer signals. For simplicity, the examples presented in this chapter will feature 8-bit grey levels ($Q = 256$). However, it should be noted that the presented operations are applicable to any dynamic signal range, $[0, Q - 1]$.

After processing, every distinct input signal is replaced at all its locations with a generally different output signal from the same dynamic signal range, which depends *only* on the corresponding input signal.

These image-to-image transformations may be classified as *perceptual* and *global*. The former term indicates their role in aiding visual perception, while the latter sets them apart from *local* operations that depend on other signal locations in the supporting plane, volume, or 2D/3D lattice.

Due to simplicity, global perceptual transformations are commonly found in image processing systems. Due to spatial uniformity, every transformation can be fully characterised by its impact on GLHs. An example is depicted in Fig. 2.1, where the input and output GLHs have a similar shape, but different spans along signal axes.

Definition 2.1. *Each global perceptual transformation, T, is an one-way mapping, $T : \mathbb{Q} \to \mathbb{Q}$, of a set of signals, $\mathbb{Q}$, onto itself. The mapping links the input, q, and output, s, signals via some scalar function of a single scalar argument: $s = T(q)$.*

For our integer set $\mathbb{Q}$, any such function, T, is conveniently represented with a look-up table (LUT), $\mathbb{T} = \{(q, T(q)) : q \in \mathbb{Q}\}$, relating every integer key, q, to its value, $T(q)$.

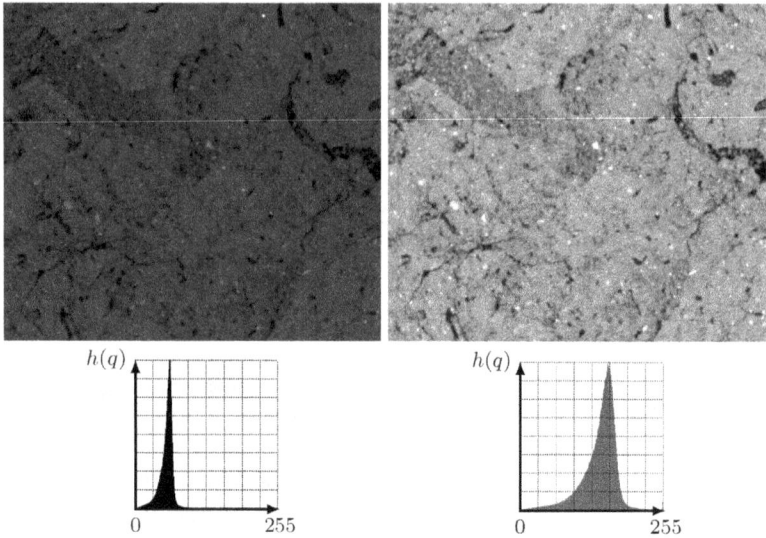

Fig. 2.1   Original (left) and enhanced (right) 2D slice of a 3D soil sample, acquired with an X-ray CT scanner, with their GLHs.

Example 2.1 (LUT). *The LUT for the transformation,* $T(q) = 0.5q + 50$; $q \in \{0, 1, \ldots, 255\}$, *is:*

q	0	1	2	...	139	140	141	...	254	255
$T(q)$	50	50	51	...	119	120	120	...	177	177

What will you find here? This chapter will describe first an arbitrary global linear transformation (Section 2.1) changing brightness and contrast of an input image in accord with two manually chosen or data-driven control parameters. Then Section 2.2 will detail the automated min-max and α-β-percentile selection of these parameters for linear *normalisation* of an input image. The normalisation makes the output image invariant to unessential brightness and contrast variations of input images of the same scene. More complicated nonlinear normalisation by equalising the output histogram (Section 2.3) provides the invariance to an arbitrary monotone transformation, T_{mon}, of the input signals. The latter transformation preserves ordering of the original and transformed signals: if $q < q^\circ$, then $T_{\mathrm{mon}}(q) \leq T_{\mathrm{mon}}(q^\circ)$ for all signal pairs (q, q°). Linear brightness and contrast variations are a particular case of the more general monotone transformation.

2.1   Global linear transformation

This transformation produces outputs that are scaled and biased. Typically these outputs are also rounded and trimmed to remain in the set $\mathbb{Q}$:

$$s = T_{a,b}(q) = \begin{cases} 0 \text{ if } aq + b \leq 0 \\ 255 \text{ if } aq + b \geq 255 \\ \lfloor aq + b \rceil \text{ otherwise} \end{cases} \tag{2.1}$$

Here, a; $a \neq 0$, is a non-zero *gain*, or scaling factor; b is a *bias*, or offset, and $\lfloor t \rceil$ denotes rounding an argument t to the nearest integer.

When the signal set $\mathbb{Q}$ is continuous and unbounded, both the gain and bias could be arbitrary, as well as the output signal, s, is just the linear combination, $aq + b$. However, our integer and bounded signals, like $\mathbb{Q} = \{0, 1, \ldots, 255\}$, call for rounding the floating-point values $aq + b$ and trimming to the range $[0, 255]$. Both the operations introduce non-linearities that might make the transformation non-invertible. Only if the gain and bias are integer, their linear combinations, $aq + b$, are also integer and may need only trimming.

2.1.1   *Linear mapping*

Generally, any one-to-one scalar mapping, $T : \mathbb{Q} \to \mathbb{Q}$, can be graphically represented with a collection of points $(q, s = T(q))$ in the (q, s)-plane. Applying the gain, a, and the bias, b, in Eq. (2.1) in order to adjust the signals is called *linear mapping* because the points $(q, s = aq + b)$ form a line in the continuous and unbounded (q, s)-plane.

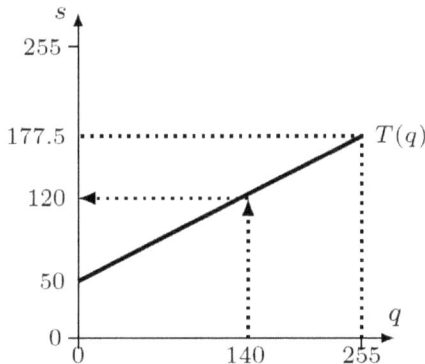

Fig. 2.2   Linear mapping of continuous signals: $s = 0.5q + 50$; $0 \leq q \leq 255$.

Example 2.2 (Linear mapping). *Figure 2.2 illustrates linear mapping in the case of the bounded continuous signal interval,* $\mathbb{Q} = \{q : 0 \le q \le 255\}$.

Accordingly, any global perceptual transformation, such that points representing it in the (q, s)-plane are sitting, at least, approximately, along a straight line, is called *linear*, all the others being *non-linear*.

2.1.2   *Inverse linear mapping*

Most often, the rounding and trimming in Eq. (2.1) make the transformation non-invertible. Thus, in practice, both the gain and bias should be selected carefully to avoid severe corruptions of the output image.

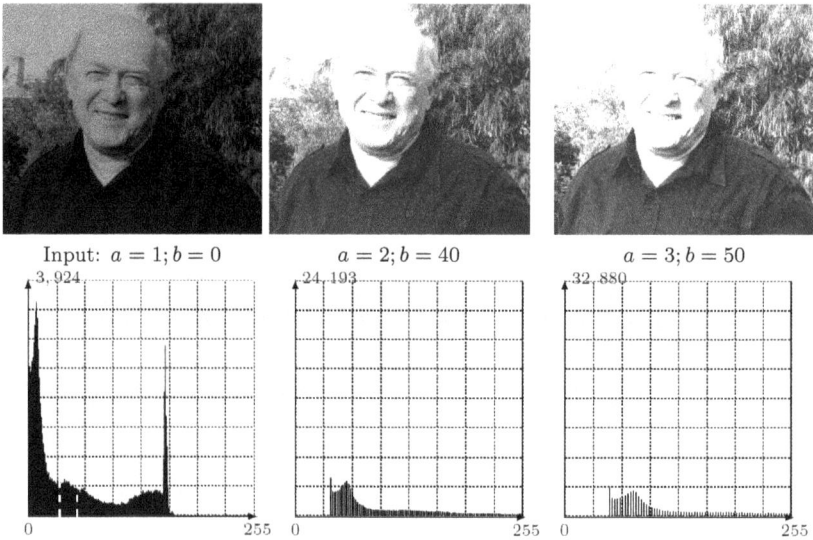

Fig. 2.3   Linearly transformed facial image and its GLHs.

Example 2.3 (Linear mapping: image corruption). *Figure 2.3 shows how an input image might be corrupted by the linear mapping. Here, all the input signals above 108 for $a = 2.0$ and $b = 40$ (in total, 24,193, out of 104,200 pixels) or above 68 for $a = 3.0$ and $b = 50$ (32,880 pixels) are replaced with the upper bound of 255. The resulting high peaks of the output histograms for $s = 255$ in these cases indicate that up to 23% and 32% of the image, respectively, had been irreparably corrupted.*

Generally, the inverse linear transformation, $q = T_{a_\circ, b_\circ}(s)$ with $a_\circ = a^{-1}$ and $b_\circ = -ba^{-1}$, cannot restore an input image after two or more original signals, $q_1, q_2, \ldots$, have been replaced, like in Fig. 2.3, with the same signal s. This "non-invertibility" is caused by rounding and trimming signals in the forward transformation of Eq. (2.1) for most of the control pairs (a, b).

Thus, to manually adjust an input image, both the gain and bias are mostly selected interactively, by inspecting each output image visually. Alternatively, as shown in Section 2.2, these parameters can be adapted to each particular input image in order to enhance, if possible, its appearance.

2.1.3 *Bias and gain adjustment*

Varying the gain, a, and bias, b, of the global linear perceptual transformation changes both the image brightness, B, and contrast, A. Suppose that rounding and trimming of Eq. (2.1) only weakly affect the linear combinations, $aq + b$. Then the output brightness and contrast depend, at least approximately, on the gain, bias, and input brightness, $B_{\text{output}} \approx aB_{\text{input}} + b$, and on the gain and input contrast, $A_{\text{output}} \approx aA_{\text{input}}$, respectively.

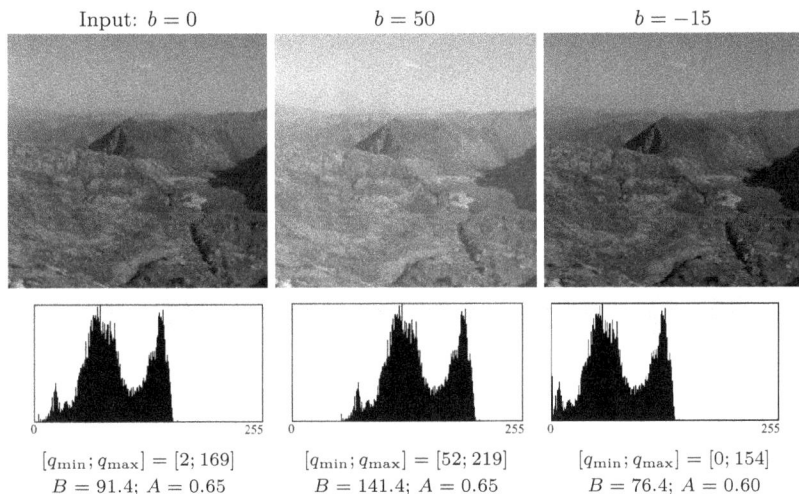

Input: $b = 0$	$b = 50$	$b = -15$
$[q_{\min}; q_{\max}] = [2; 169]$	$[q_{\min}; q_{\max}] = [52; 219]$	$[q_{\min}; q_{\max}] = [0; 154]$
$B = 91.4;\ A = 0.65$	$B = 141.4;\ A = 0.65$	$B = 76.4;\ A = 0.60$

Fig. 2.4 Bias adjustment: images and histograms.

Adding only a constant positive or negative bias to signals increases or decreases, respectively, the brightness, but affects no contrast if trimming is low or absent, whereas applying only a constant gain affects both the

Input: $a = 1$ $a = 1.5$ $a = 0.5$

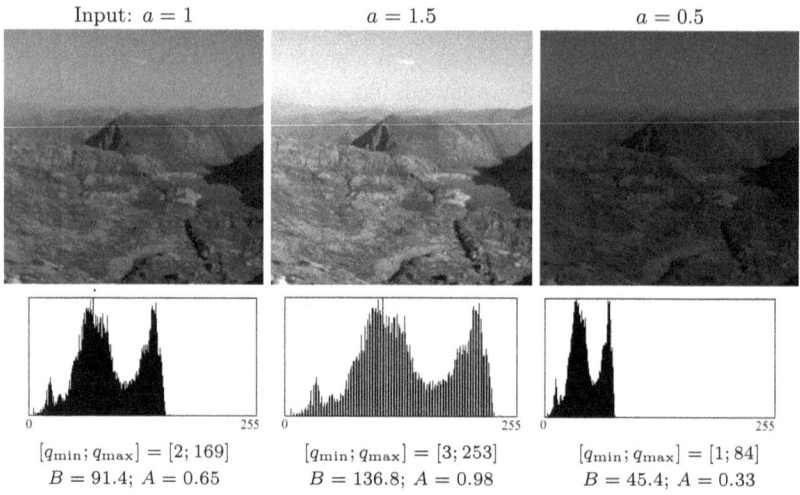

$[q_{min}; q_{max}] = [2; 169]$ $[q_{min}; q_{max}] = [3; 253]$ $[q_{min}; q_{max}] = [1; 84]$
$B = 91.4; A = 0.65$ $B = 136.8; A = 0.98$ $B = 45.4; A = 0.33$

Fig. 2.5   Gain adjustment: images and histograms.

Input: $a = 1; b = 0$ $a = 1.5; b = -15$ $a = 0.5; b = 50$

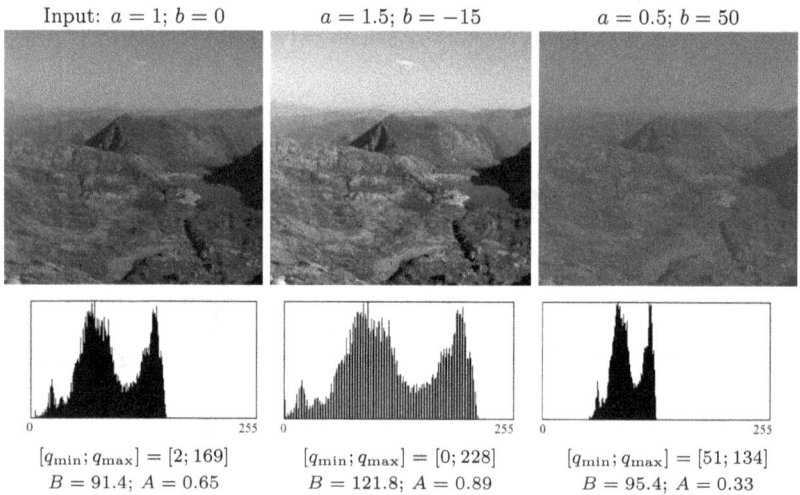

$[q_{min}; q_{max}] = [2; 169]$ $[q_{min}; q_{max}] = [0; 228]$ $[q_{min}; q_{max}] = [51; 134]$
$B = 91.4; A = 0.65$ $B = 121.8; A = 0.89$ $B = 95.4; A = 0.33$

Fig. 2.6   Linear mapping: images and histograms.

brightness and contrast (Figs. 2.4 and 2.5). The latter grows or decreases if the gain is above or below the unit value. Figure 2.6 illustrates impacts of simultaneous bias and gain adjustments on the brightness and contrast.

2.1.4 *Negation*

This transformation of Eq. (2.1) with the gain $a = -1$ and bias $b = 255$ is graphically illustrated in Fig. 2.7).

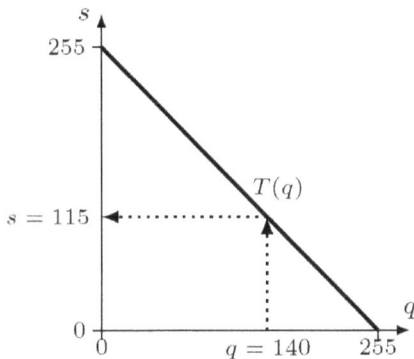

Fig. 2.7 Greyscale negation $T(q) = 255 - q$.

The negation outputs a complementary image with the reversed histogram (Fig. 2.8).

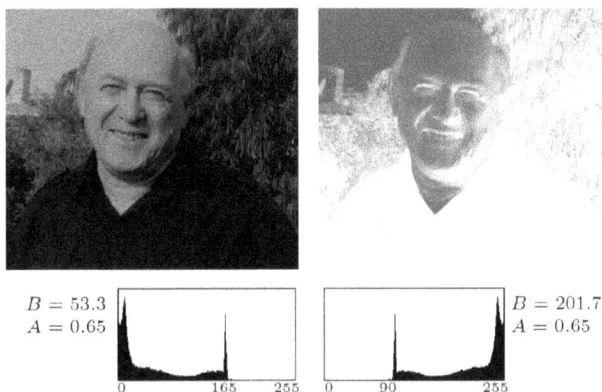

Fig. 2.8 Original and negated images with histograms.

Every input signal q is replaced by its complement $s = 255 - q$, making the output similar to a photographic negative. Obviously, summing the overlaid initial and negated images forms a blank frame.

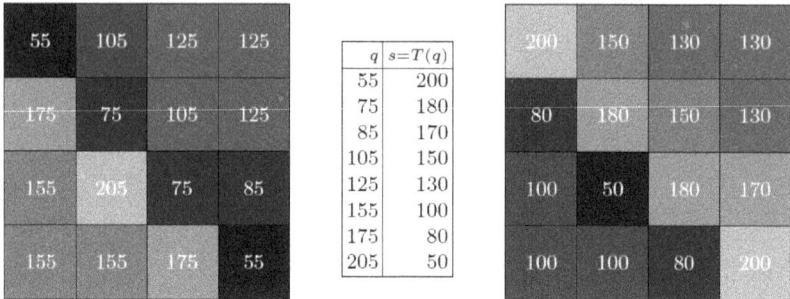

Fig. 2.9   Greyscale negation.

Example 2.4 (Negation). *Figure 2.9 details this transformation for a small 4×4 image patch with integer signals.*

2.2   Linear normalisation

Special contrast and brightness adjustment, called *normalisation*, increases dynamic range of low-contrast dark or bright images, having been acquired, e.g., under poor illumination or with an improper imaging device. The normalisation facilitates visual perception of an observed scene by "stretching" (extending) the input GLH to its full dynamic range of $[0, 255]$. The normalised output image becomes invariant to changes in global brightness and contrast of the input image.

Let q_{bb} and q_{ub} denote the bottom and upper borders, respectively, of a central part of the input histogram to be extended. Generally, these borders need not necessarily be equal to the respective minimum and maximum input signals:

$$0 \leq q_{min} \leq q_{bb} < q_{ub} \leq q_{max} \leq 255$$

An input range $[q_{bb}, q_{up}]$ is linearly mapped to the output range, $[0, 255]$, with the gain and bias in Eq. (2.1):

$$a_n = \frac{255}{q_{ub} - q_{bb}}; \quad b_n = -a_n q_{bb}$$

that solve an obvious system of linear equations for the borders:

$$a_n q_{bb} + b_n = 0; \quad a_n q_{ub} + b_n = 255.$$

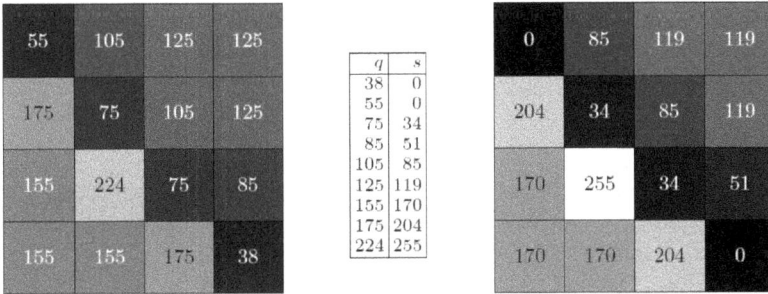

Fig. 2.10   Histogram stretching by linear mapping.

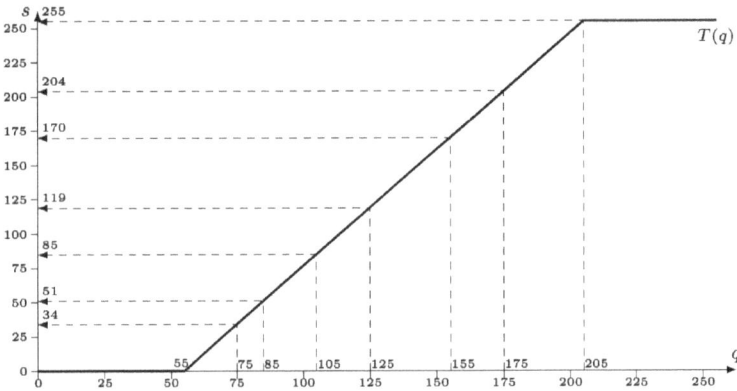

Fig. 2.11   Linear mapping: $q_{bb} = 55$ and $q_{ub} = 205$.

Example 2.5 (Histogram stretching). *Figures 2.10 and 2.11 demonstrate the linear mapping to stretch the GLH between the borders $q_{bb} = 55$ and $q_{ub} = 205$ to the dynamic range of $[0, 255]$. Here, $a_n = 1.7$ and $b_n = -93.5$.*

2.2.1   *Min-max normalisation*

Example 2.6 (Min-max normalisation). *Mapping the entire signal range between $q_{bb} = q_{min} = 38$ and $q_{ub} = q_{max} = 205$ of the GLH in Example 2.5 to the range of $[0, 255]$ leads to the following normalising gain and bias:*

$$a_n = \frac{255}{q_{max} - q_{min}} = 1.58; \quad \text{and} \quad b_n = -a_n q_{min} = -69.7$$

This min-max normalisation is illustrated in Fig. 2.12.

However, such a selection might be severely affected by outliers, i.e., a few outstanding signals forming tiny left and/or right "tails" of the input GLH.

Input image	Normalised image

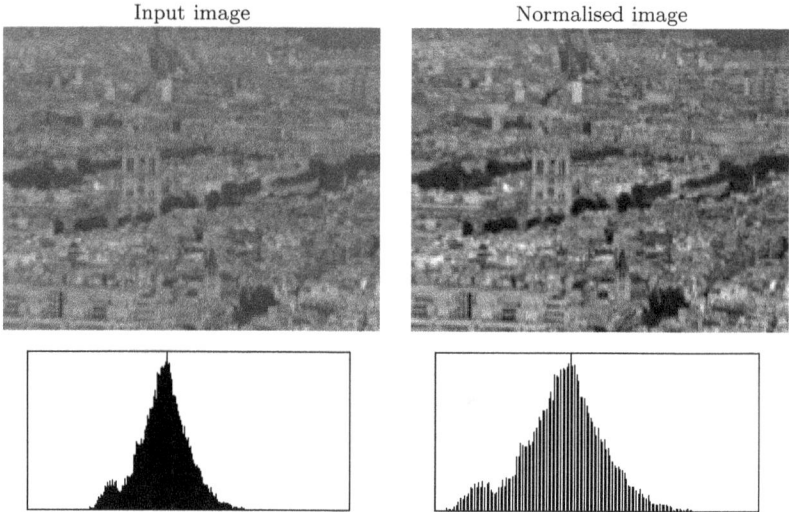

Fig. 2.12   Min-max normalisation.

2.2.2 $\alpha - \beta$-*percentile normalisation*

A more robust image normalisation that mostly leads to better visual appearance is based on a conjecture that too bright and/or dark outliers are rare and convey no useful information about an observed scene. Then only the main GLH body embracing a prescribed percentage of the image area (often, about $90 - 95\%$) is associated, with objects of interest and should be stretched.

The percentile-based normalisation excludes unessential left and right tails of the input GLH by making the bottom, q_{bb}, and upper, q_{ub}, borders equal to the α- and β-percentiles (q_α, and q_β, respectively) of the cumulative histogram; $0 \le \alpha < \beta \le 100$. The chosen borders keep at least $(\beta - \alpha)\%$ of the entire image area. Algorithm 3 details the $\alpha - \beta$-percentile mapping.

Example 2.7 ($5-95$-**percentile normalisation**). *Figure 2.13 illustrates the $5 - 95$-percentile normalisation using the borders $q_{bb} = q_{5\%} = 68$ and $q_{ub} = q_{95\%} = 141$, so that $a_n = 3.49$ and $b_n = -237.5$.*

Algorithm 3 $\alpha - \beta$-percentile normalisation.

---

(1) Collect the input histogram $\mathbf{H} = (H(q) : q \in \mathbb{Q})$.

(2) Compute the cumulative histogram $\mathbf{C} = (C(q) : q \in \mathbb{Q})$.

(3) Find the α- and β-percentiles:

    (a) The smallest value, q_α, such that $C(q_\alpha) \geq \frac{\alpha}{100} C(255)$.

    (b) The largest value, q_β, such that $C(q_\beta) \leq \frac{\beta}{100} C(255)$.

(4) Perform linear mapping $s = T_{a_n, b_n}(q)$ of Eq. (2.1) with

$$a_n = \frac{255}{q_\beta - q_\alpha} \text{ and } b_n = -a_n q_\alpha = -\frac{255 q_\alpha}{q_\beta - q_\alpha}$$

Input image   Normalised image

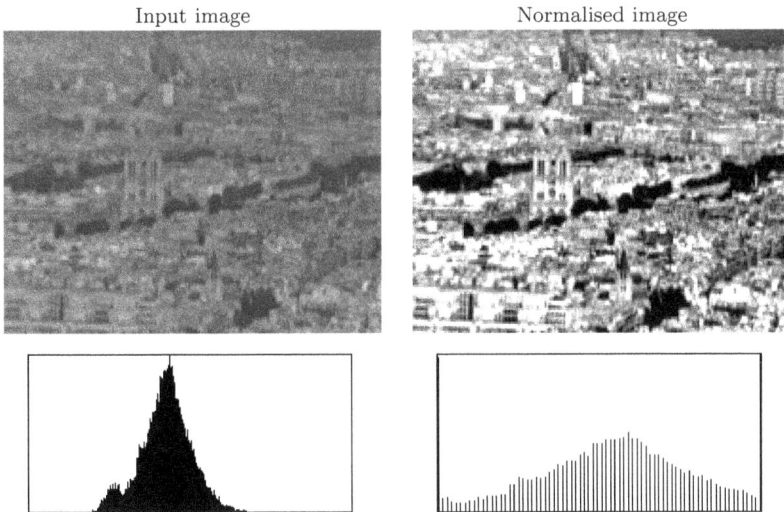

Fig. 2.13 $5-95$-percentile normalisation (note the large peaks for $q = 0$ and $q = 255$ in the output histogram due to trimming the input histogram).

2.3 Histogram equalisation

Linear normalisation in Section 2.2 replaces all input images, which differ only by brightness and contrast, with the same normalised image. The resulting invariance to global perceptual transformations helps in analysing objects if their brightness and contrast are unessential.

    The perceptual transformations are a particular case of more general and mostly non-linear *monotone transformations* that keep the same ordering of the initial and transformed grey levels. To replace all input images, which can be converted one into another by monotone transformation, the histogram equalisation linearises the cumulative histogram of the normalised image, i.e., distributes its signals more evenly in the entire range of $[0, 255]$, than the input histogram.

Example 2.8 (Equalisation). *The output histogram in Fig. 2.14 is more even than the input histogram of a low-contrast image. Despite the dynamic range, $[69, 255]$, of the input histogram is rather wide (73% of the entire $[0, 255]$ range), its main body is much more narrow, e.g., the 5-95-percentile range, $[113, 195]$, occupies less than 32% of the entire range.*

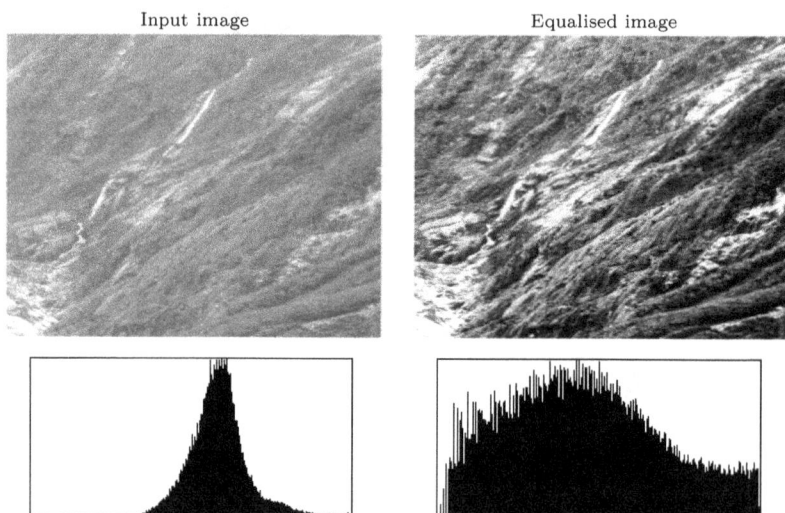

Fig. 2.14 Input and equalised images with histograms.

Algorithm 4 Histogram equalisation to normalise an input image.

(1) Collect the input GLH $\mathbf{H} = (H(q) : q \in \mathbb{Q})$.

(2) Compute the CH $\mathbf{C} = (C(q) : q \in \mathbb{Q})$.

(3) Convert the CH $\mathbf{C}$ into the equalising LUT,

$$\mathbb{T} = \left\{ \left(q, T_{\mathrm{eq}}(q) = \left\lfloor 255 \frac{C(q) - C(0)}{C(255) - C(0)} \right\rfloor \right) : q \in \mathbb{Q} \right\}$$

Algorithm 4 details the equalising transformation derived from the input histogram. Every input signal, q, is replaced with the signal, $T_{eq}(q)$, being approximately proportional to the area, occupied by all the signals from 1 to q in the input image. Thus, relative brightness and contrast of common visible objects might look unrealistic, especially, in equalised photos of natural environment. However, the equalisation is widely used for enhancing more special scientific or industrial images, such as medical, soil, or other x-ray, ultrasound, or magnetic resonance scans in non-visible (including thermal and microwave) bands of electromagnetic radiation; remotely sensed aerial and satellite images of the Earth's surface etc.

Just as linear normalisation, the equalisation increases, if possible, the dynamic range and therefore contrast of the input images. But also it may make uneven steps between the successive grey levels in the output histogram. As follows from Algorithm 4, any input unit step from q to $q + 1$ transforms into a step between $T_{eq}(q)$ and $T_{eq}(q + 1)$, i.e., into the step of

$$255\frac{C(q+1) - C(q)}{C(255) - C(0)} = 255\frac{H(q+1)}{S - H(0)}$$

before the rounding where $S = C(255)$ is the image size. As a result, every step $T_{eq}(q) \to T_{eq}(q+1)$ is roughly proportional to a rounded relative area, $\frac{H(q+1)}{S-H(0)}$, occupied by the signal $q + 1$ in the input image. Thus, if the relative area is less than 0.4% of the image size, both the signals q and $q+1$ might be replaced with the same output signal. The enlarged output steps help to reveal certain details that would have not been visually perceived because of the too small signal differences in the input image. At the same time, some minor, by the relative area occupied, low-contrast details might be lost. However, as a whole, the equalisation proved to be very useful for aiding visual perception, as well as, in some cases, automated image analyses.

Equalising the image in Fig. 2.15.

q	64	76	89	102	115	128	153	179	205
$H(q)$	1	6	2	8	5	6	4	2	2
$C(q)$	1	7	9	17	22	28	32	34	36
$s = T_{eq}(q)$	0	44	58	117	153	197	226	240	255
$H_{out}(s)$	1	6	2	8	5	6	4	2	2
$C_{out}(s)$	1	7	9	17	22	28	32	34	36

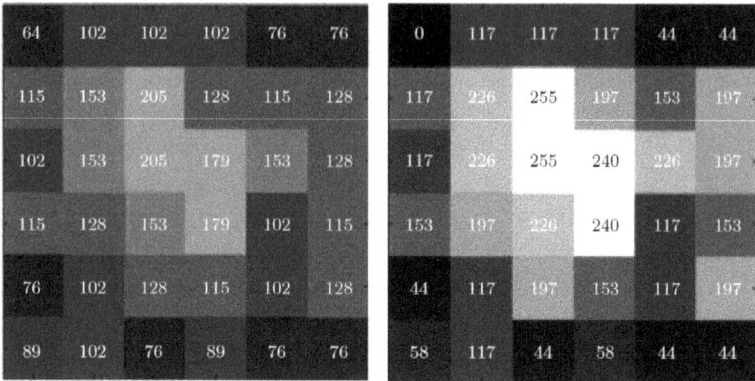

Fig. 2.15   Enlarged input (left) and equalised (right) 6 × 6 image.

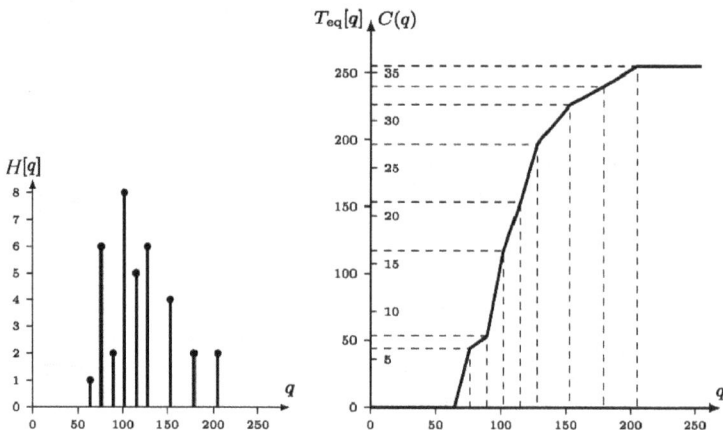

Fig. 2.16   Transformation $T_{eq}(q)$ for the input image in Fig. 2.15.

Example 2.9 (Image equalisation). *Figures 2.15 – 2.17 detail the equalisation of an enlarged 6×6 image with Algorithm 4, and Table 2.3 lists nonzero entries of the input histogram, together with the entries of the cumulative histogram and equalising transformation, illustrated also in Fig. 2.16. In this example,*

$$T_{eq}(q) = \left\lfloor 255 \frac{C(q) - C(64)}{C(205) - C(64)} \right\rfloor = \left\lfloor 255 \frac{C(q) - 1}{36 - 1} \right\rfloor = \lfloor 7.29(C(q) - 1) \rceil$$

The more evenly distributed output histogram, $\mathbf{h}_{out}$, *and the resulting linearised cumulative output histogram,* $\mathbf{C}_{out}$, *are shown in Fig. 2.17.*

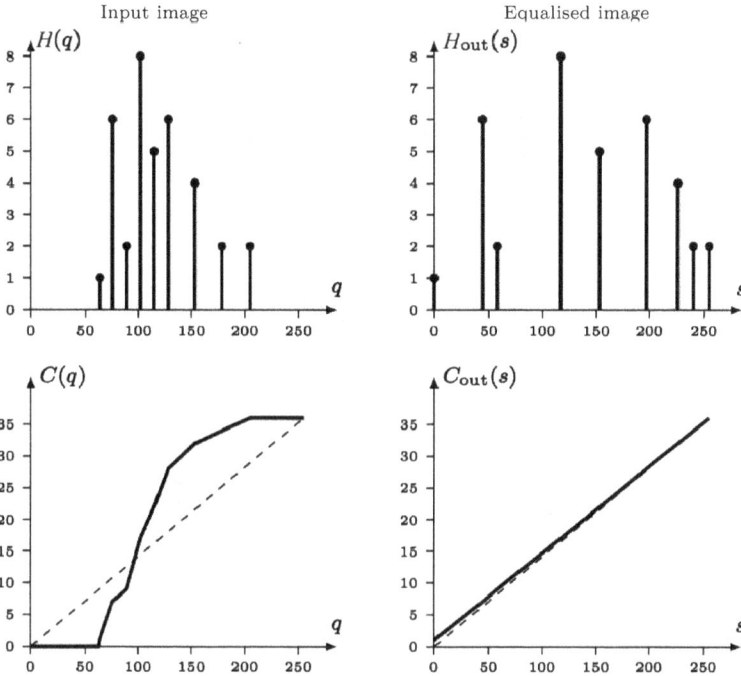

Fig. 2.17   Image histograms before and after equalisation.

In this particular case, every output signal is obtained from a single input signal, so that the normalisation is invertible. Generally, as was already mentioned, some input signals could be compressed into a single output signal, making the equalisation non-invertible. Still, in a majority of applications, non-linear equalisation outperforms linear normalisation by visual quality of the output images.

Example 2.10 (Normalisation vs. equalisation). *Figures 2.18 and 2.19 compare results of the linear min-max and (5-95)-percentile normalisation with the histogram equalisation of the same input images as in Figs. 2.12 – 2.14.*

As follows from Example 2.10, the linear normalisation tends to preserve the shape of the input histogram, i.e., relative contributions of the successive grey levels into appearance of the observed scene. But the linear normalisation may need to substantially trim the histogram tails to notably enhance the appearance. The non-linear equalisation tends to preserve the whole input histogram, but at the expense of changing its shape.

Input image   Min-max normalisation

5-95 percentile normalisation   Equalisation

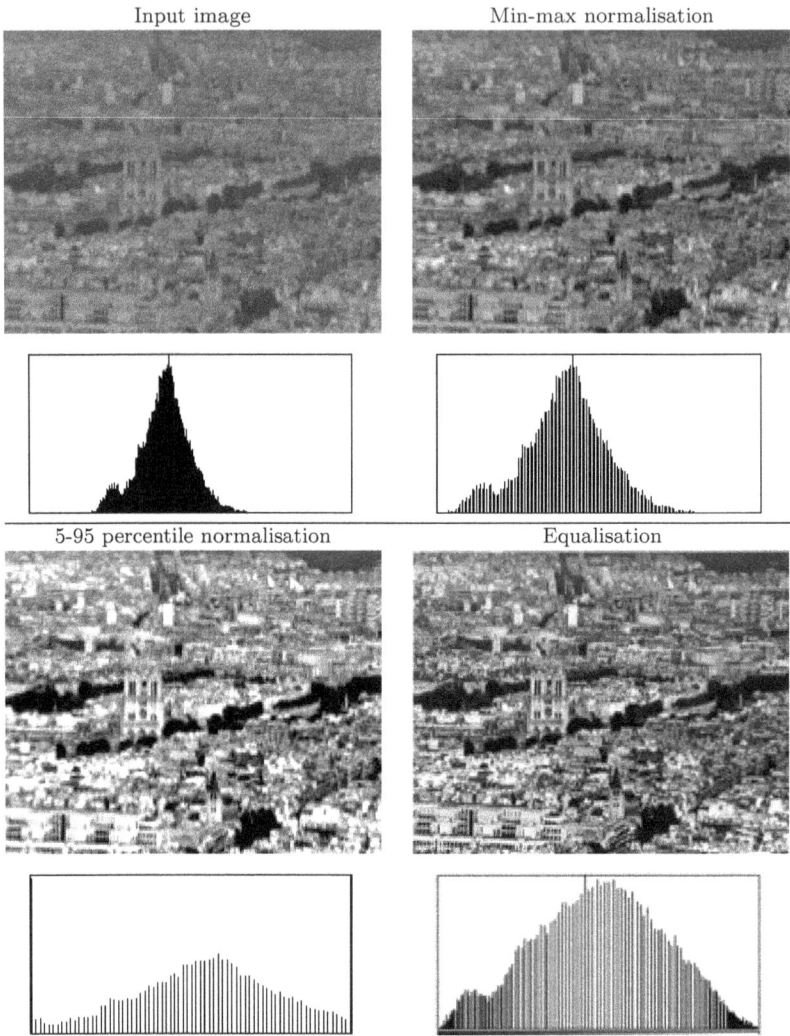

Fig. 2.18 Linear vs. non-linear normalisation (note the large peaks at the ends of the histogram after the 5-95-percentile normalisation due to trimming the input histogram).

Input image
$a_n = 1; b_n = 0$

Min-max normalisation
$a_n = 1.37; b_n = -96.6$

5-95-percentile normalisation
$a_n = 3.11; b_n = -351.4$

Equalisation

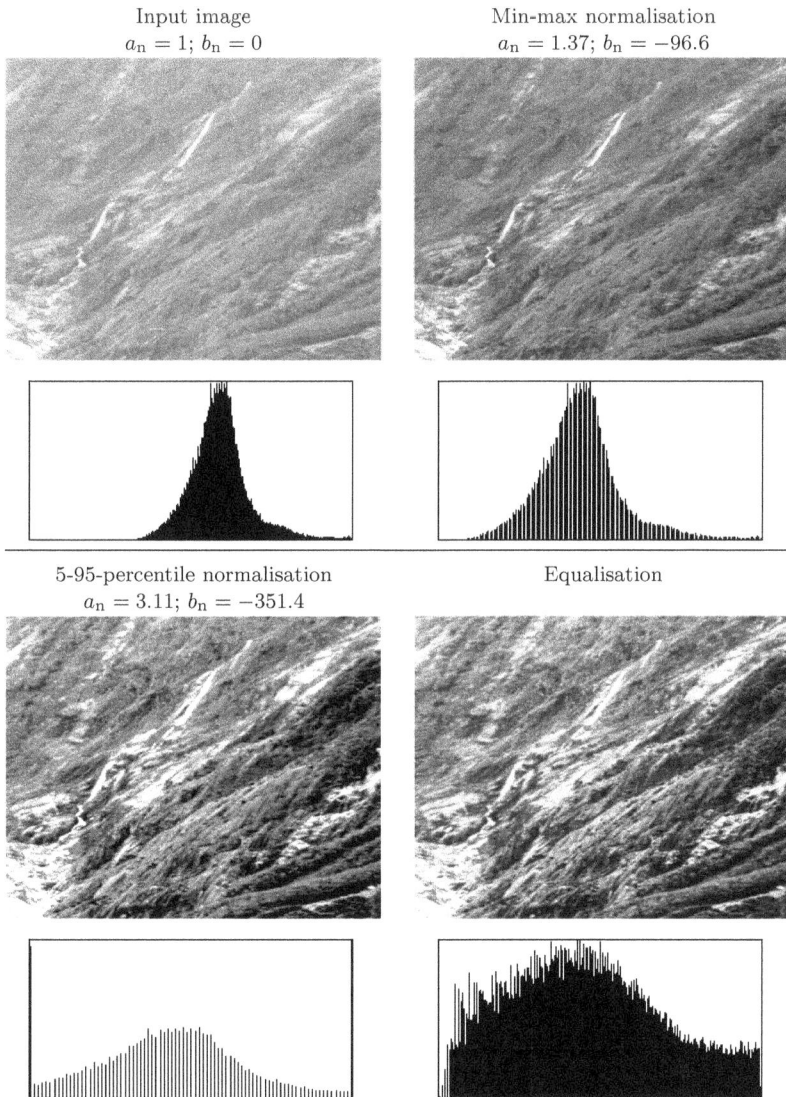

Fig. 2.19   Linear vs. non-linear normalisation (note the large peaks at the ends of the histogram after the 5-95-pecentile normalisation due to trimming the input histogram).

2.4   Questions and exercises

(1) Which and why are non-linearities involved in a global linear transformation?

(2) Rewrite the general linear transformation in Eq. (2.1) to deal with an arbitrary set of input signals, $\mathbb{Q} = \{0, 1, \ldots, Q - 1\}$.

(3) Let an input 10×10 digital image with the set $\mathbb{Q} = \{0, 1, \ldots, 9\}$ of $Q = 10$ integer signal values have the following GLH:

$$\mathbf{H} = \begin{array}{|ccccccccccc|} \hline 0 & 1 & 2 & 3 & 4 & 5 & 6 & 7 & 8 & 9 & q \\ \hline 0 & 1 & 2 & 12 & 40 & 30 & 12 & 2 & 1 & 0 & H(q) \\ \hline \end{array}$$

(a) Find the LUT for the min-max normalisation of this image.

(b) Find the LUT for the $5 - 95$-percentile normalisation of this image.

(c) Form the CH and find the LUT for the histogram equalisation of this image.

(d) Compare the Michelson and RMS contrast (see Section 1.2.4 of Chapter 1) for the input and three normalised images.

Chapter 3

Filtering to Denoise or Enhance

More complex image adjustments, e.g., to decrease irrelevant illumination-caused inhomogeneities or sharpen boundaries of depicted objects of interest, are performed with linear and nonlinear image filtering (Fig. 3.1).

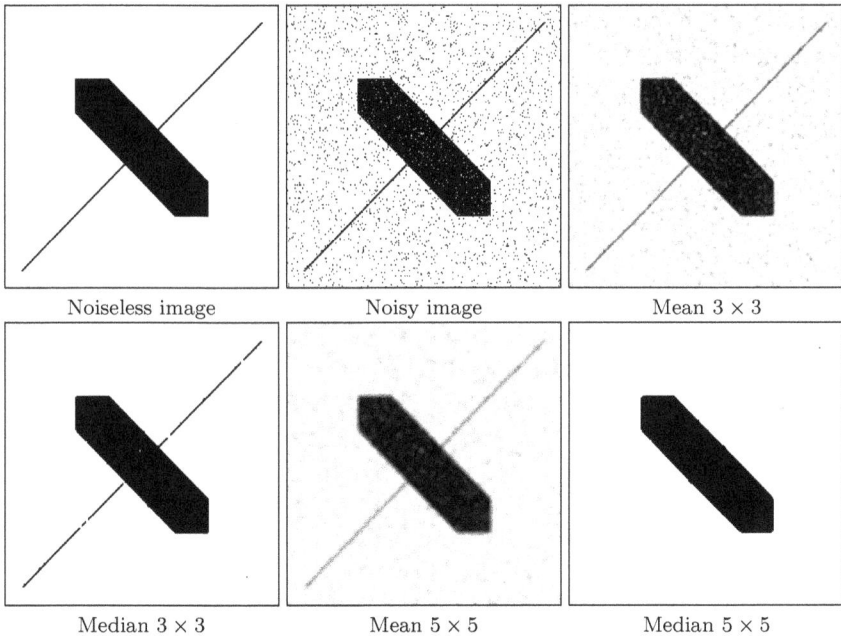

Noiseless image	Noisy image	Mean 3 × 3
Median 3 × 3	Mean 5 × 5	Median 5 × 5

Fig. 3.1 Suppressing additive "salt-and-pepper" noise (note that median filtering removes more noise, but simultaneously may destroy fine details).

Just as in Chapter 2, both the input, **g**, and output, $\widetilde{\mathbf{g}}$, digital images are on the same lattice, $\mathbb{S}$, and have the same set, $\mathbb{Q}$, of integer grey levels. However, unlike the global perceptual transformation, the filtering performs local transformations, where every output signal depends on more than one, but a rather small number of related input signals. Different filters can be applied sequentially for better image denoising or enhancement. The like transformations can be used also to build dense feature maps to represent and use local empirical signal statistics of an input image, such as, e.g., mean, median, or extremal values, standard deviations, mean-to-standard-deviation ratios etc.

Generally, the filtering may be adaptive, i.e. its algorithm may vary in accord with local properties of the input image.

What will you find here? This chapter will begin with a few typical math models of image noise or degradation (Section 3.1) to be reduced by filtering. It is followed by a general-case *moving window transform* (MWT) — being one of the most-widely used image processing tools. Section 3.2 will discuss the MWT in the signal domain, and a few popular linear and nonlinear filters for the MWT will be detailed in Sections 3.3 and 3.4, respectively. Figure 3.1 gives preliminary examples of using the MWTs with linear mean and nonlinear median square filters to denoise a black geometric object on a white background, which were corrupted with a so-called "salt-and-pepper" noise.

You will encounter image filtering also in Chapters 7 and 9. Chapter 7 will describe simple MWTs for detecting "edges", which might relate in part to actual boundaries, or "corners" and other points-of-interest (POIs) indicating intersections or sharp bends of the edges and other characteristic details of observed objects. Chapter 9 will detail common low-, band-, and high-pass filtering in the spectral, or Fourier frequency domain, as well as more intricate homomorphic and "cepstrum" filtering to suppress specific types of spatially variant image degradation.

3.1 Modelling image noise

What to call an "image noise" depends on a particular processing or analysis problem, namely, on dependences between sensed signals and desired information about visual appearances and shapes of depicted objects of interest. All irrelevant random and/or deterministic deviations of sensed image signals from "ideal" goal values are considered the noise that corrupts, or degrades the ideal (noiseless) images. In particular, imaging a real-world scene may be affected by uneven illumination, shadows, unstable gain and nonlinearities of light-to-signal conversion in a sensor, and other external and internal nuisance influences.

To place noise suppression (called *denoising*) on a sound theoretical basis, a collection of noisy images are described with a probabilistic model of lattice-supported signals. The model relates image probabilities to deviations of pixel/voxel-wise signals from their ideal values, which should be statistically estimated from the available noisy signals. Among a menagerie of global and local deterministic or random deviations, the primer will focus on a few most widespread models of statistically independent pixel/voxel-wise deviations. These models include a bi-valued "*salt-and-pepper*" noise; a more general *additive noise*, which can be also combined with arbitrary global contrast and bias, and a *multiplicative noise* that affects pixel/voxel-wise scaling factors to describe gradually changing local contrast and bias deviations, e.g., due to uneven illumination and shadows.

Let an observed surface be optically uniform, i.e., its ideal image signals are constant. To what extent its realistic image is affected by noise is roughly evaluated with a ratio between the mean and the standard deviation of the sensed signals, called a *signal-to-noise ratio* (SNR). Its nominator and denominator are statistical estimates of the constant ideal signal and its noise-caused deviations, respectively, so that the larger the SNR, the lesser the noise.

Salt-and-pepper noise exemplified in Fig. 3.1 replaces ideal image signals, $g_{id}(\mathbf{s})$, at arbitrary chosen lattice sites with the most distant extremal values in the set $\mathbb{Q} = \{0, 1, \ldots, Q-1\}$ of grey levels: $g(\mathbf{s}) = Q-1$ if $g_{id}(\mathbf{s}) \leq (Q-1)/2$ and $g(\mathbf{s}) = 0$ otherwise. Every lattice site, $\mathbf{s}$, is affected independently of the other sites with a probability α; $0 \leq \alpha < 1$, specifying the expected fraction of corrupted sites.

Additive noise biases the ideal image signals randomly at all the lattice sites: $g(\mathbf{s}) = g_{id}(\mathbf{s}) + \varepsilon(\mathbf{s})$; $\mathbf{s} \in \mathbb{S}$. Probability distributions of the individual deviations, $\varepsilon(\mathbf{s})$, are the same at all the sites, have zero mathematical expectation, and are centre-symmetric (i.e., the deviations of the same absolute value are equiprobable).

Most popular additive noise models employ uniform or Gaussian (normal) probability density functions of variations of sensed image signals around their ideal values. The Gaussian p.d.f. with standard deviation σ presumes continuous and infinite noisy and ideal signals, as well as their differences:

$$p(\varepsilon(\mathbf{s})) = \frac{1}{\sqrt{2\pi}\sigma} \exp\left(-\frac{\varepsilon^2(\mathbf{s})}{2\sigma^2}\right); \quad -\infty \le \varepsilon(\mathbf{s}) \le \infty$$

To form a discrete set $\mathbb{Q}$ of grey levels, the axis is bounded and quantised. Because both the noisy and ideal images take signals from the same set, $\mathbb{Q}$, p.d.f.s for individual differences, $\varepsilon(\mathbf{s})$, may actually depend on the ideal signals. However, if the continuous ideal differences span over three or more quantisation steps, the Gaussian densities can be sufficiently accurate approximations of actual probabilities of the discrete (e.g., integer) signal differences.

Global contrast and bias deviations depend on no location in the lattice and are combined with an additive noise: $g(\mathbf{s}) = a \cdot g_{\mathrm{id}}(\mathbf{s}) + b + \varepsilon(\mathbf{s})$. Here, the contrast factor, a, and the bias, b, may take arbitrary values, provided that the noisy grey levels remain in the set $\mathbb{Q}$.

Multiplicative noise scales the ideal image signals at all the lattice sites: $g(\mathbf{s}) = a_{\mathbf{s}} g_{\mathrm{id}}(\mathbf{s})$. To keep visual appearance of a depicted scene in noisy images, the neighbouring factors, $a_{\mathbf{s}}$, have to be strongly interrelated. One of the popular models assumes the factors vary slowly over the lattice.

3.2   Moving window transform (MWT)

To denoise or enhance an input image $\mathbf{g}$ by filtering, each output signal at location $\mathbf{s} \in \mathbb{S}$ is computed from K input signals; $|\mathbb{S}| \gg K > 1$, at locations specified by K relative offsets, $\mathbb{W} = \{\boldsymbol{\nu}_k : k = 1, \ldots, K\}$ from $\mathbf{s}$. The offsets $\mathbb{W}$ determine the filter's *shape*, often called a moving, or sliding *window*.

Definition 3.1 (MWT). *A moving window transform of an input image, $\mathbf{g}$ makes every output signal, $\widetilde{g}(\mathbf{s})$ a function (denoted below* MWT*) of K input signals from a relevant window of shape $\mathbb{W}$:*

$$\widetilde{g}(\mathbf{s}) = \mathsf{MWT}\big(g(\mathbf{s} + \boldsymbol{\nu}_1), \ldots, g(\mathbf{s} + \boldsymbol{\nu}_K)\big) \tag{3.1}$$

The output location, $\mathbf{s}$, coincides with the window origin, i.e., zero offset, $\boldsymbol{\nu} = \mathbf{0}$. The origin locates usually in the window, i.e., zero offset is in the shape $\mathbb{W}$. Sometimes the origin of the window coincides with a geometric centre of the shape. But generally the origin may be at any inner position of the window or even at an outer position. i.e., outside the shape. Most frequently, a 2D filter has a rectangular window with odd-length sides, $J_{\mathrm{x}} \times J_{\mathrm{y}}$, which is centred at every output location (x, y). The centre of the rectangle is the window origin.

In many cases the window shape, size, and function of input signals, which is denoted MWT in Eq. 3.1, remain the same for all the output locations. Typical windows are rectangular or rounded (like, e.g., in Fig. 7.11 of Chapter 7). However, generally, the shape may be arbitrary and not necessarily contiguous, as well as both the shape, size, and filtering function may vary over the lattice, e.g., to adapt the MWT to changing signal properties of the input image.

Linear filters, known also as *convolution* filters, form every output signal as a linear combination, $w_1 q_1 + w_2 q_2 + \ldots + w_K q_K$, of the K input signals, q_k, factored each with an own weight, w_k; $k = 1, \ldots, K$. **Nonlinear filters** implement more intricate scalar functions of the K input signals, such as, e.g., thresholded linear combinations or rank statistics, like the minimum, maximum, or median of the K signals, to mention just a few.

The most common linear mean, Gaussian, and Laplacian filters, as well as the nonlinear rank filters, together with a few others, will be detailed in Sections 3.3 and 3.4, respectively.

| Image | Zero padding | Toroidal lattice | Mirroring |

Fig. 3.2   Common extensions across image borders.

Border effects. If the offset locations partially leave the lattice, the filtering either omits such signals (e.g., by setting zero weights in linear filtering), or assumes an input image is extended beyond its borders to include these locations. For this imaginary extension, either an input image is zero-padded, or its lattice is made toroidal (or circular in the 1D case), or the image is mirrored at the lattice borders, as illustrated in Fig. 3.2. Given a 2D image $\mathbf{g}$ on a rectangular $M \times N$ lattice, $\mathbb{S} = \{(x, y) : x = 0, \ldots, X - 1; \; y = 0, \ldots, Y - 1\}$, any location (x°, y°) beyond the lattice borders, i.e., $x^\circ < 0$, or $y^\circ < 0$, or $x^\circ \geq X$, or $y^\circ \geq Y$, is assigned either zero or some image signal, q°:

$$q^\circ = \begin{cases} 0 & \text{Zero padding} \\ g\left(\xi^\circ, \eta^\circ\right) & \text{Toroidal lattice} \\ g\left(X - 1 - \xi^\circ, \, Y - 1 - \eta^\circ\right) & \text{Mirrored image} \end{cases} \qquad (3.2)$$

where $\xi^\circ = x^\circ \bmod X$ and $\eta^\circ = y^\circ \bmod Y$.

One more option is to process only "inner" lattice sites, such that the window centred on each such site does not leave the lattice.

3.3 Linear filtering

Linear filter, $\mathbf{w} = \{w(\boldsymbol{\nu}) : \boldsymbol{\nu} \in \mathbb{W}\}$, consists of scalar weights attributed to coordinate offsets, in the moving window, $\mathbb{W}$. This spatial configuration, often called *kernel*, is centred at each output location, $\mathbf{s} \in \mathbb{S}$, to fetch coinciding pairs of input signals and weights, $(g(\mathbf{s} + \boldsymbol{\nu}); w(\boldsymbol{\nu}))$, for summing:

$$\widetilde{g}(\mathbf{s}) = \sum_{\boldsymbol{\nu} \in \mathbb{W}} w(\boldsymbol{\nu}) g(\mathbf{s} + \boldsymbol{\nu}); \quad \mathbf{s} \in \mathbb{S} \qquad (3.3)$$

Any new offset, $\boldsymbol{\nu}$, can be added to or any existing offset can be excluded from a certain kernel $\mathbb{W}$ by assigning zero weight, $w(\boldsymbol{\nu}) = 0$.

The linear filtering of Eq. (3.3) is usually represented as *convolution*, often denoted $\mathbf{g} * \mathbf{w}$, of an input image, $\mathbf{g}$, with the kernel in Eq. (3.3), but mirrored w.r.t. its centre, $\boldsymbol{\nu} = 0$:

$$\widetilde{g}(\mathbf{s}) = \left(g * w\right)(\mathbf{s}) \equiv \sum_{\boldsymbol{\nu} \in \mathbb{W}} w(\boldsymbol{\nu}) g(\mathbf{s} - \boldsymbol{\nu}); \quad \mathbf{s} \in \mathbb{S} \qquad (3.4)$$

Both Eqs. (3.3) and (3.4) are equivalent. However, the convolution is more convenient for describing linear spectral filtering (Chapter 9), as well as replacing a sequence of linear MWTs that perform *cascaded filtering* with a single linear MWT. In line with basic properties of the convolution, the latter filter is obtained by convolving all the cascade filters:

$$\widetilde{g}(\mathbf{s}) = \underbrace{\left(\ldots\left((\mathbf{g} * \mathbf{w}_1) * \mathbf{w}_2\right) * \cdots \mathbf{w}_n\right)}_{\text{cascade of } n \text{ filters}} \equiv \mathbf{g} * \underbrace{\left(\ldots\left(\mathbf{w}_1 * \mathbf{w}_2\right) * \cdots \mathbf{w}_n\right)}_{\text{single filter } \mathbf{w}}$$

The 1D convolution is easily represented with a matrix-vector product, $\widetilde{\mathbf{g}} = W\mathbf{g}$ where components of the input, $\mathbf{g}$, and output, $\widetilde{\mathbf{g}}$, vectors are signals at successive integer locations of the same 1D lattice. Every row of the matrix W contains weights of the input components, taking part in computing the related output component.

Example 3.1 (1D convolution: mirrored signals). *Let an 1D sequence*

$$\mathbf{g} = (g(x);\ x = 0, ..., 9) \equiv \left\{ \begin{array}{c|ccccccccccc} x & 0 & 1 & 2 & 3 & 4 & 5 & 6 & 7 & 8 & 9 \\ \hline g(x) & 3 & 9 & 4 & 52 & 3 & 8 & 6 & 2 & 2 & 9 \end{array} \right.$$

be convolved with the averaging kernel, $\mathbf{w} = \{(-1; 1/3), (0; 1/3), (1; 1/3)\}$, *of size 3. In other words, the filter shape is specified by three offsets:* $\mathbb{W} = \{-1, 0, 1\}$, *each offset being associated with the same weight,* $w(\xi) = 1/3$.

Assuming the sequence is mirrored at the borders, so that the related weights are also mirrored and summed, this convolution filter performs the MWT, $\widetilde{\mathbf{g}} = M_{\mathbf{w}}\mathbf{g}$, *with the matrix of the kernels in all the output locations:*

$$M_{\mathbf{w}} = \frac{1}{3} \begin{bmatrix} 2 & 1 & 0 & 0 & 0 & 0 & 0 & 0 & 0 & 0 \\ 1 & 1 & 1 & 0 & 0 & 0 & 0 & 0 & 0 & 0 \\ 0 & 1 & 1 & 1 & 0 & 0 & 0 & 0 & 0 & 0 \\ 0 & 0 & 1 & 1 & 1 & 0 & 0 & 0 & 0 & 0 \\ 0 & 0 & 0 & 1 & 1 & 1 & 0 & 0 & 0 & 0 \\ 0 & 0 & 0 & 0 & 1 & 1 & 1 & 0 & 0 & 0 \\ 0 & 0 & 0 & 0 & 0 & 1 & 1 & 1 & 0 & 0 \\ 0 & 0 & 0 & 0 & 0 & 0 & 1 & 1 & 1 & 0 \\ 0 & 0 & 0 & 0 & 0 & 0 & 0 & 1 & 1 & 1 \\ 0 & 0 & 0 & 0 & 0 & 0 & 0 & 0 & 1 & 2 \end{bmatrix}$$

The successive steps of computing the means at nine window positions and rounding these real numbers to the closest integer are detailed below:

Input signals	Moving mean	Rounding $\widetilde{g}(x)$
$0 : (\mathbf{3}, 3, 9)$	$\Rightarrow (3 + 3 + 9)/3 = 5$	$\Rightarrow \widetilde{g}(0) = 5$
$1 : (3, 9, 4)$	$\Rightarrow (3 + 9 + 4)/3 = 5.33$	$\Rightarrow \widetilde{g}(1) = 5$
$2 : (9, 4, 52)$	$\Rightarrow (9 + 4 + 52)/3 = 21.67$	$\Rightarrow \widetilde{g}(2) = 22$
$3 : (4, 52, 3)$	$\Rightarrow (4 + 52 + 3)/3 = 19.67$	$\Rightarrow \widetilde{g}(3) = 20$
$4 : (52, 3, 8)$	$\Rightarrow (52 + 3 + 8)/3 = 21$	$\Rightarrow \widetilde{g}(4) = 21$
$5 : (3, 8, 6)$	$\Rightarrow (3 + 8 + 6)/3 = 5.67$	$\Rightarrow \widetilde{g}(5) = 6$
$6 : (8, 6, 2)$	$\Rightarrow (8 + 6 + 2)/3 = 5.33$	$\Rightarrow \widetilde{g}(6) = 5$
$7 : (6, 2, 2)$	$\Rightarrow (6 + 2 + 2)/3 = 3.33$	$\Rightarrow \widetilde{g}g(7) = 3$
$8 : (2, 2, 9)$	$\Rightarrow (2 + 2 + 9)/3 = 4.33$	$\Rightarrow \widetilde{g}(8) = 4$
$9 : (2, 9, \mathbf{9})$	$\Rightarrow (2 + 9 + 9)/3 = 6.67$	$\Rightarrow \widetilde{g}(9) = 7$

Therefore, the output sequence is

$$\widetilde{\mathbf{g}} = (\widetilde{g}(x);\ x = 0, ..., 9) \equiv \left\{ \begin{array}{c|cccccccccc} x & 0 & 1 & 2 & 3 & 4 & 5 & 6 & 7 & 8 & 9 \\ \hline \widetilde{g}(x) & 5 & 5 & 22 & 20 & 21 & 8 & 5 & 3 & 4 & 7 \end{array} \right.$$

To compute $\widetilde{g}(0)$ *and* $\widetilde{g}(9)$, *the signals* $g(0)$ *and* $g(9)$, *respectively, are mirrored with respect to the boundaries, i.e.,* $g(-1) = g(0)$ *and* $g(10) = g(9)$.

This mirroring is equivalent to adding the relevant two weights, i.e., using the weights $W[0,0] = W[9,9] = 2/3$ at these border positions.

Example 3.2 (1D convolution: circular lattice). *For the same averaging kernel and the same signal sequence, as in Example 3.1, the MWT matrix is slightly different:*

$$
M_{\mathbf{w}} = \frac{1}{3}
\begin{bmatrix}
1 & 1 & 0 & 0 & 0 & 0 & 0 & 0 & 0 & 1 \\
1 & 1 & 1 & 0 & 0 & 0 & 0 & 0 & 0 & 0 \\
0 & 1 & 1 & 1 & 0 & 0 & 0 & 0 & 0 & 0 \\
0 & 0 & 1 & 1 & 1 & 0 & 0 & 0 & 0 & 0 \\
0 & 0 & 0 & 1 & 1 & 1 & 0 & 0 & 0 & 0 \\
0 & 0 & 0 & 0 & 1 & 1 & 1 & 0 & 0 & 0 \\
0 & 0 & 0 & 0 & 0 & 1 & 1 & 1 & 0 & 0 \\
0 & 0 & 0 & 0 & 0 & 0 & 1 & 1 & 1 & 0 \\
0 & 0 & 0 & 0 & 0 & 0 & 0 & 1 & 1 & 1 \\
1 & 0 & 0 & 0 & 0 & 0 & 0 & 0 & 1 & 1 \\
\end{bmatrix}
$$

so that the filtered signals $\tilde{g}(0)$ and $\tilde{g}(9)$ become as follows:

Input signals	Moving mean	Rounding $\tilde{g}(x)$
$0 : (\mathbf{9}, 3, 9)$	$\Rightarrow (9 + 3 + 9)/3 = 7$	$\Rightarrow \tilde{g}(0) = 7$
$9 : (2, 9, \mathbf{3})$	$\Rightarrow (2 + 9 + 3)/3 = 4.67$	$\Rightarrow \tilde{g}(9) = 5$

and the output sequence is

$$
\tilde{\mathbf{g}} = (\tilde{g}(x);\ x = 0, ..., 9) \equiv
\left\{
\begin{array}{c|cccccccccc}
x & 0 & 1 & 2 & 3 & 4 & 5 & 6 & 7 & 8 & 9 \\
\hline
\tilde{g}(x) & 7 & 5 & 22 & 20 & 21 & 8 & 5 & 3 & 4 & 5
\end{array}
\right.
$$

Example 3.3 (1D convolution: zero padding). *For the same averaging kernel and the same signal sequence, as in Example 3.1, the MWT matrix is slightly different:*

$$
M_{\mathbf{w}} = \frac{1}{3}
\begin{bmatrix}
1 & 1 & 0 & 0 & 0 & 0 & 0 & 0 & 0 & 0 \\
1 & 1 & 1 & 0 & 0 & 0 & 0 & 0 & 0 & 0 \\
0 & 1 & 1 & 1 & 0 & 0 & 0 & 0 & 0 & 0 \\
0 & 0 & 1 & 1 & 1 & 0 & 0 & 0 & 0 & 0 \\
0 & 0 & 0 & 1 & 1 & 1 & 0 & 0 & 0 & 0 \\
0 & 0 & 0 & 0 & 1 & 1 & 1 & 0 & 0 & 0 \\
0 & 0 & 0 & 0 & 0 & 1 & 1 & 1 & 0 & 0 \\
0 & 0 & 0 & 0 & 0 & 0 & 1 & 1 & 1 & 0 \\
0 & 0 & 0 & 0 & 0 & 0 & 0 & 1 & 1 & 1 \\
0 & 0 & 0 & 0 & 0 & 0 & 0 & 0 & 1 & 1 \\
\end{bmatrix}
$$

so that the filtered signals $\widetilde{g}(0)$ and $\widetilde{g}(9)$ become as follows:

Input signals	Moving mean	Rounding $\widetilde{g}(x)$
$0 : (\mathbf{0}, 3, 9)$	$\Rightarrow (0+3+9)/3 = 4$	$\Rightarrow \widetilde{g}(0) = 4$
$9 : (2, 9, \mathbf{0})$	$\Rightarrow (2+9+0)/3 = 3.67$	$\Rightarrow \widetilde{g}(9) = 4$

and the output sequence is

$$\widetilde{\mathbf{g}} = (\widetilde{g}(x);\ x = 0, ..., 9) \equiv \left\{ \begin{array}{c|cccccccccc} x & 0 & 1 & 2 & 3 & 4 & 5 & 6 & 7 & 8 & 9 \\ \hline \widetilde{g}(x) & 4 & 5 & 22 & 20 & 21 & 8 & 5 & 3 & 4 & 4 \end{array} \right.$$

Weighted mean x-derivative y-derivative Laplacian #1 Laplacian #2

Fig. 3.3 3×3 kernels of 2D convolution filters (the origin, $(0,0)$, is shaded).

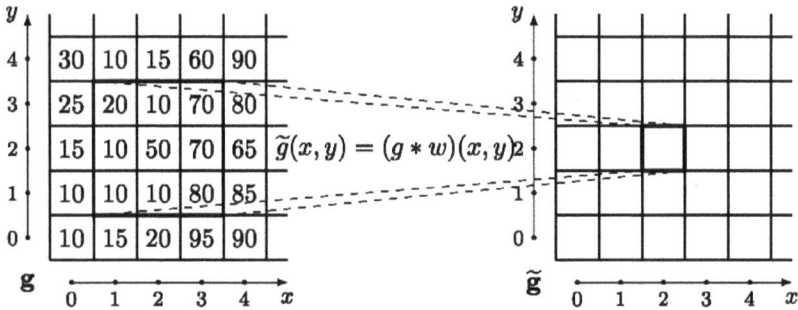

Fig. 3.4 2D convolution: $\widetilde{g}(x, y) = \sum\limits_{\xi=-1}^{1} \sum\limits_{\eta=-1}^{1} w(\xi, \eta)g(x - \xi, y - \eta)$

Example 3.4 (2D convolution). *Linear filtering by convolving in Eq. (3.4) a 2D image, $\mathbf{g} = (g(x,y) : x = 0, 1, \ldots, M-1; y = 0, 1, \ldots, N-1)$ with 3×3 kernels $\mathbf{w} = (w(\xi,\eta) : \xi = -1, 0, 1; \eta = -1, 0, 1)$ of Fig. 3.3 is illustrated in Eq. 3.5 for a 3×3 input area and a single output* *location in Fig. 3.4:*

Kernel	Convolution $\widetilde{g}(2,2)=\sum\limits_{\xi=-1}^{1}\sum\limits_{\eta=-1}^{1} w(\xi,\eta)g(2-\xi,2-\eta)$	
Wei. mean	$+\frac{10}{8}+\frac{10}{8}+\frac{20}{8}+\frac{10}{8}+0{\cdot}50+\frac{10}{8}+\frac{80}{8}+\frac{70}{8}+\frac{70}{8}$ $= 35$	
x-deriv.	$-\frac{10}{3}-\frac{10}{3}-\frac{20}{3}+0{\cdot}10+0{\cdot}50+0{\cdot}10+\frac{80}{3}+\frac{70}{3}+\frac{70}{3}$ $= 60$	(3.5)
y-deriv.	$-\frac{10}{3}+0{\cdot}10+\frac{20}{3}-\frac{10}{3}+0{\cdot}50+\frac{10}{3}-\frac{80}{3}+0{\cdot}70+\frac{70}{3}$ $= 0$	
Lapl. 1	$+0{\cdot}10-\frac{10}{4}+0{\cdot}20-\frac{10}{4}+1{\cdot}50-\frac{10}{4}+0{\cdot}80-\frac{70}{4}+0{\cdot}70$ $= 25$	
Lapl. 2	$-\frac{10}{8}-\frac{10}{8}-\frac{20}{8}-\frac{10}{8}+1{\cdot}50-\frac{10}{8}-\frac{80}{8}-\frac{70}{8}-\frac{70}{8}$ $= 15$	

The x-/y-derivative and Laplacian kernels are finite-difference approximations of partial first-order derivatives and a second-order Laplace operator:

$$\frac{\partial}{\partial x}g_{\mathrm{c}}(x,y);\ \ \frac{\partial}{\partial y}g_{\mathrm{c}}(x,y),\ \ and\ \ \frac{\partial^2 g_{\mathrm{c}}(x,y)}{\partial x^2}+\frac{\partial^2 g_{\mathrm{c}}(x,y)}{\partial y^2}$$

respectively, for a continuous image g_{c}, represented by a digital image, g. Laplacian filtering of two facial images is shown in Fig. 3.5.

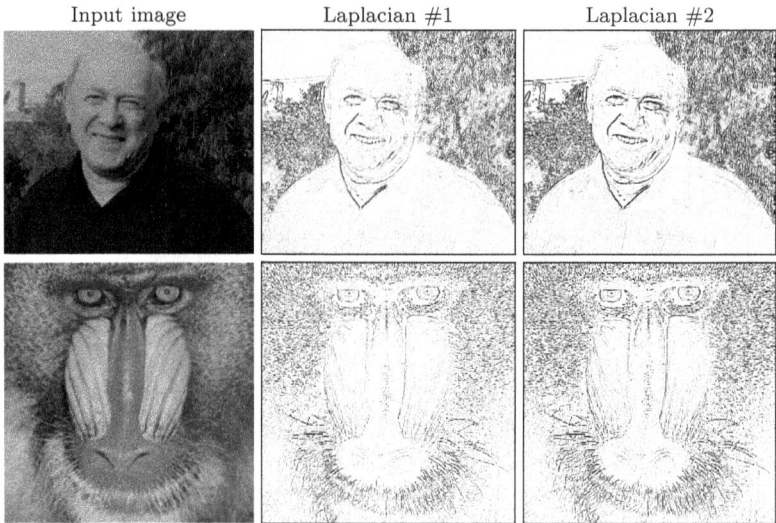

Fig. 3.5   Linear filtering with the 3×3 Laplacian kernels of Fig. 3.3 (the outputs are negated and enhanced for visualisation).

Separable linear filters. Linear filtering can be performed faster and implemented easier when the filter is separable, i.e., when its kernel is represented by a product of simpler kernels. A rectangular 2D filter is separable if its matrix of weights, W, is decomposed into a product of two vectors of weights, $\mathbf{w}_1$ and $\mathbf{w}_2$, for the 1D filters: $W = \mathbf{w}_1\mathbf{w}_2^{\mathsf{T}}$, e.g.,

$$\begin{bmatrix} \frac{1}{9} & \frac{1}{9} & \frac{1}{9} \\ \frac{1}{9} & \frac{1}{9} & \frac{1}{9} \\ \frac{1}{9} & \frac{1}{9} & \frac{1}{9} \end{bmatrix} = \begin{bmatrix} \frac{1}{3} \\ \frac{1}{3} \\ \frac{1}{3} \end{bmatrix} \begin{bmatrix} \frac{1}{3} & \frac{1}{3} & \frac{1}{3} \end{bmatrix}; \qquad \begin{bmatrix} -\frac{1}{4} & 0 & \frac{1}{4} \\ -\frac{1}{2} & 0 & \frac{1}{2} \\ -\frac{1}{4} & 0 & \frac{1}{4} \end{bmatrix} = \begin{bmatrix} \frac{1}{4} \\ \frac{1}{2} \\ \frac{1}{4} \end{bmatrix} \begin{bmatrix} -1 & 0 & 1 \end{bmatrix};$$

$$\begin{bmatrix} \frac{1}{16} & -\frac{1}{8} & \frac{1}{16} \\ -\frac{1}{8} & \frac{1}{4} & -\frac{1}{8} \\ \frac{1}{16} & -\frac{1}{8} & \frac{1}{16} \end{bmatrix} = \begin{bmatrix} -\frac{1}{4} \\ \frac{1}{2} \\ -\frac{1}{4} \end{bmatrix} \begin{bmatrix} -\frac{1}{4} & \frac{1}{2} & -\frac{1}{4} \end{bmatrix}; \qquad \begin{bmatrix} -\frac{1}{3} & \frac{1}{3} \\ -\frac{1}{3} & \frac{1}{3} \\ -\frac{1}{3} & \frac{1}{3} \end{bmatrix} = \begin{bmatrix} \frac{1}{3} \\ \frac{1}{3} \\ \frac{1}{3} \end{bmatrix} \begin{bmatrix} -1 & 1 \end{bmatrix}$$

3.3.1 Mean filter

The mean filtering, which is the simplest linear MWT, replaces each signal located at the window origin with the average signal for the entire window:

$$\widetilde{g}(\mathbf{s}) = \frac{1}{|\mathbb{W}|} \sum_{\boldsymbol{\nu} \in \mathbb{W}} g(\mathbf{s} + \boldsymbol{\nu})$$

In other words, each kernel location has the same positive weight: $w(\boldsymbol{\nu}) = 1/|\mathbb{W}|$. Filtering with a fixed-weight rectangular kernel is also called *box filtering*. The mean filtering reduces signal variations between the neighbouring image sites and thus results in a smoother or blurred image.

Potential problems of the mean filtering have been already shown in Examples 3.1 – 3.3: a single "outlier" (i.e., a very prominent signal value) significantly affects all the average signals in its neighbourhood, e.g., in all locations of the window origin, such that this outlier is within the window. Also, this MWT results in edge blurring: when the window crosses a step-like edge, the signals on each side of the step are interpolated across the window-dependent area, so that the output edges become less sharp.

Example 3.5 (3 × 3 **mean filter**). *Suppressing a large "salt-and-pepper" noise on a realistic 2D scene by using this filter:*

$$\widetilde{g}(x, y) = \frac{1}{9} \sum_{\xi=-1}^{1} \sum_{\eta=-1}^{1} g(x + \xi, y + \eta)$$

– is illustrated in Figs. 3.6 – 3.9.

Figures 3.7 – 3.9 detail the 3×3-averaging with subsequent rounding to the closest integer and three ways of accounting for border effects, for an artificial 6×6 image with a small signal set, $\mathbb{Q} = \{0, 1, \ldots, 4\}$.

Input noisy image   Filtered output image

Fig. 3.6 3×3 mean filtering to reduce "salt-and-pepper" noise.

0	1	4	0	1	3	1
0	②	2	4	2	2	3
0	1	0	1	0	1	0
	1	2	1	0	2	2
	2	5	3	1	2	5
g	1	1	4	2	3	0

1	1	1	1	1	1
①	2	2	2	1	1
1	2	1	1	1	1
1	2	1	1	1	1
1	2	2	2	2	2
1	2	2	2	1	1

$\widetilde{\mathbf{g}}$

Fig. 3.7   Mean filtering with the 3×3 window and zero padding.

The output signals at a single location: $\mathbf{s} = (0,4)$ for zero padding or mirroring and $(1,4)$ for keeping the input border signals, – are in these cases as follows:

Zero padding: $\widetilde{g}(0,4) = \frac{0}{9} + \frac{1}{9} + \frac{4}{9} + \frac{0}{9} + \frac{2}{9} + \frac{2}{9} + \frac{0}{9} + \frac{1}{9} + \frac{0}{9} = 1$

Image mirroring: $\widetilde{g}(0,4) = \frac{1}{9} + \frac{1}{9} + \frac{4}{9} + \frac{2}{9} + \frac{2}{9} + \frac{2}{9} + \frac{1}{9} + \frac{1}{9} + \frac{0}{9} = 2$

Keeping borders: $\widetilde{g}(1,4) = \frac{1}{9} + \frac{4}{9} + \frac{0}{9} + \frac{1}{9} + \frac{2}{9} + \frac{4}{9} + \frac{1}{9} + \frac{0}{9} + \frac{1}{9} = 2$

3.3.2   *Fast box filtering*

The box or mean filtering of a sequence, $\mathbf{g} = (g(x) : x = 0, 1, \ldots, X-1)$, of scalar signals on an 1D lattice can be considerably accelerated by using an auxiliary array, $\mathbf{a} = (a(x) : x = 0, 1, \ldots, X-1)$, of accumulators, one per lattice site. Each accumulator, $a(x)$, contains the sum of all signals from

1	1	4	0	1	3	1
2	②	2	4	2	2	3
1	1	0	1	0	1	0
	1	2	1	0	2	2
	2	5	3	1	2	5
	1	1	4	2	3	0

g

2	2	2	2	2	2
②	2	2	2	1	2
1	2	1	1	1	2
2	2	1	1	1	2
2	2	2	2	2	2
2	2	3	3	2	2

g̃

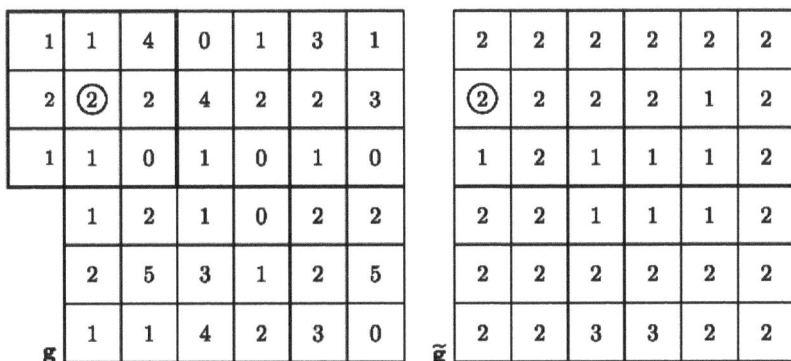

Fig. 3.8   Mean filtering with the 3 × 3 window and image mirroring at the borders.

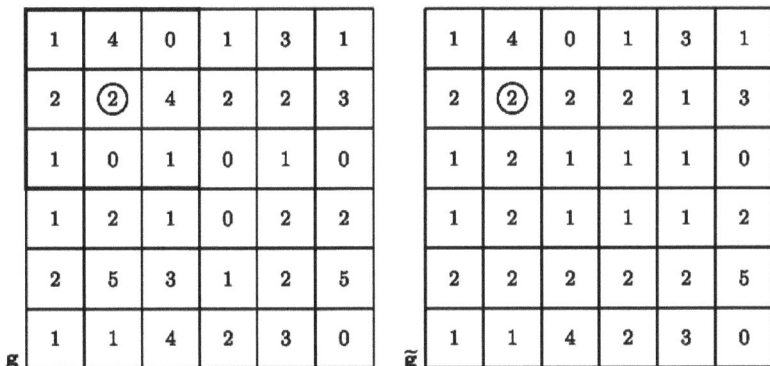

1	4	0	1	3	1
2	②	4	2	2	3
1	0	1	0	1	0
1	2	1	0	2	2
2	5	3	1	2	5
1	1	4	2	3	0

g

1	4	0	1	3	1
2	②	2	2	1	3
1	2	1	1	1	0
1	2	1	1	1	2
2	2	2	2	2	5
1	1	4	2	3	0

g̃

Fig. 3.9   Mean filtering with the 3 × 3 window and border signals unchanged.

$g(0)$ to $g(x)$, i.e.,

$$a(x) = \sum_{t=0}^{x} g(t); \quad x = 0, 1, \ldots, X - 1, \text{ or}$$
$$a(0) = g(0) \text{ and } a(x) = a(x - 1) + g(x); \quad x = 1, \ldots, X - 1$$

After forming the accumulator array, any partial sum of successive signals is obtained by a single subtraction:

$$\sum_{x=x_b}^{x_e} g(x) \equiv \sum_{x=0}^{x_e} g(x) - \sum_{x=0}^{x_b-1} g(x) = a(x_e) - a(x_b - 1)$$

Example 3.6 (Fast 1D mean filtering). *Let the same 1D sequence,* **g**, *of scalar signals, as in Example 3.1, be convolved with the averaging kernels* *of size 3, 5, and 7. For the assumed zero padding, as in Example 3.3, the accumulator array is as follows:*

x	0	1	2	3	4	5	6	7	8	9
$g(x)$	3	9	4	52	3	8	6	2	2	9
$a(x)$	3	12	16	68	71	79	85	87	89	98

where

$$a(0) = 3$$
$$a(1) = 3 + 9 = 12$$
$$a(2) = 3 + 9 + 4 = 16$$
$$a(3) = 3 + 9 + 4 + 52 = 68$$
$$a(4) = 3 + 9 + 4 + 52 + 3 = 71$$
$$\cdots \quad \cdots \cdots$$
$$a(9) = 3 + 9 + 4 + 52 + 3 + 8 + 6 + 2 + 2 + 9 = 98$$

with zero accumulated value for all $x < 0$ and the value of 98 for all $x > 9$. Each partial sum of the signals in the window is obtained by subtracting two corresponding accumulators:

$$\widetilde{g}(x) = \begin{cases} \frac{1}{3}\left(a(x+1) - a(x-1)\right) & \text{for the window size of 3} \\ \frac{1}{5}\left(a(x+2) - a(x-2)\right) & \text{for the window size of 5} \\ \frac{1}{7}\left(a(x+3) - a(x-3)\right) & \text{for the window size of 7} \end{cases}$$

so that $\widetilde{g}(0) = (12 - 0)/3 = 4$, $(16 - 0)/5 = 3.2$, or $(68 - 0)/7 = 9.7$ and $\widetilde{g}(5) = (85 - 71)/3 = 4.7$, $(87 - 68)/5 = 3.8$, or $(89 - 16)/7 = 10.4$ for the kernel size 3, 5, or 7, respectively.

For a 2D image $\mathbf{g} = (g(x, y) : x = 0, 1, \ldots, X - 1; y = 0, 1, \ldots, Y - 1)$ on a rectangular lattice of the size XY, the fast 2D mean filtering employs a 2D accumulator array,

$$\mathbf{a} = (a(x, y) : x = 0, 1, \ldots, X - 1; y = 0, 1, \ldots, Y - 1)$$

Each accumulator, $a(x, y)$, summing signals over the rectangular sublattice, is formed sequentially by three additions/subtractions:

$$a(x, y) = \sum_{\xi=0}^{x} \sum_{\eta=0}^{y} g(x, y)$$
$$\equiv g(x, y) + a(x - 1, y) + a(x, y - 1) - a(x - 1, y - 1) \tag{3.6}$$

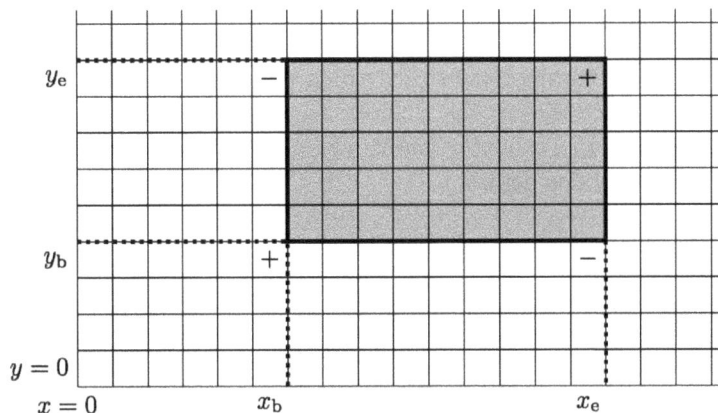

Fig. 3.10   Using accumulators for the fast 2D mean filtering.

Example 3.7 (Forming 2D accumulators). *Given a binary 4×8 image, the 4×8 array of accumulators is formed in accord with Eq. (3.6):*

$$
\mathbf{g} =
\begin{array}{|c|c|c|c|c|c|c|c|}
\hline
0 & 0 & 0 & 1 & 1 & 1 & 0 & 0 \\
\hline
1 & 0 & 1 & 0 & 0 & 1 & 0 & 0 \\
\hline
1 & 0 & 0 & 1 & 1 & 1 & 1 & 1 \\
\hline
1 & 1 & 1 & 1 & 0 & 1 & 1 & 1 \\
\hline
\end{array}
\quad \rightarrow \mathbf{a} =
\begin{array}{|c|c|c|c|c|c|c|c|}
\hline
3 & 4 & 6 & 9 & 11 & 15 & 17 & 19 \\
\hline
3 & 4 & 6 & 8 & 9 & 12 & 14 & 16 \\
\hline
2 & 3 & 4 & 6 & 7 & 9 & 11 & 13 \\
\hline
1 & 2 & 3 & 4 & 4 & 5 & 6 & 7 \\
\hline
\end{array}
$$

In particular,

$a(0,0) = g(0,0) = 1;$

$a(1,0) = g(1,0) + a(0,0) = 1 + 1 = 2;$

$a(0,1) = g(1,0) + a(0,0) = 1 + 1 = 2;$

$a(x,0) = g(x,0) + a(x-1,0) \text{ for } x = 2, \ldots, 7;$

$a(0,y) = g(0,y) + a(0,y-1) \text{ for } y = 2, 3;$

$a(1,1) = g(1,1) + a(1,0) + a(0,1) - a(0,0) = 0 + 2 + 2 - 1 = 3;$

$a(2,1) = g(2,1) + a(2,0) + a(1,1) - a(1,0) = 0 + 3 + 3 - 2 = 4;$

$\ldots$

$a(7,3) = g(7,3) + a(7,2) + a(6,3) - a(6,2) = 0 + 16 + 17 - 14 = 19$

Then the sum of signals in a rectangular window of any size, $J_x \times J_y$, is obtained with also only three additions/subtractions (Fig. 3.10):

$$
\tilde{g}(x,y) = \frac{1}{J_x J_y} \big(a(x_e, y_e) + a(x_b, y_b) - a(x_e, y_b) - a(x_b, y_e)\big) \qquad (3.7)
$$

where $x_b = x_e - J_x$ and $y_b = y_e - J_y$. Therefore, the fast box or mean filtering reduces $J_x J_y - 1$ additions for each window position to six additions/subtractions per position to form the accumulators and the sum of signals over the window.

3.3.3 *Gaussian filter*

Weighted mean filtering relates each signal weight to the distance from the supporting window site to the window origin. One of very popular filters of this kind uses approximate Gaussian weights to blur an input image and remove noise and fine detail.

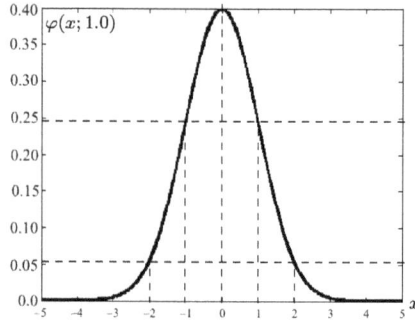

Fig. 3.11   Zero-mean Gaussian probability density function with the s.t.d. $\sigma = 1.0$.

The weights follow zero-mean Gaussian probability density function (called simply a *Gaussian*):

$$\varphi(x; \sigma) = \frac{1}{\sigma\sqrt{2\pi}} \exp\left(-\frac{x^2}{2\sigma^2}\right) \tag{3.8}$$

where σ is the standard deviation, commonly abbreviated "std", or "st.d.". For the 1D Gaussian with the unit standard deviation ($\sigma = 1.0$) in Fig. 3.11 68%; 95%, 99.7% of the x-values are within the range of $[-1, 1]$; $[-2, 2]$, and $[-3, 3]$, respectively. The 1D Gaussian $\varphi(x; \sigma)$ is transformed into $\varphi(x; 1.0)$ after scaling x/σ of its variable.

Discrete 1D Gaussian kernels $\mathbf{w}$ for filtering are built by sampling the normed Gaussian of Eq. (3.8). The norming factor, λ, for the sampled weights, $\lambda\varphi(x; \sigma)$, is not unique and should only make subsequent integer rounding sensible, i.e., the smallest weight before rounding should not be less than 1.

Cascaded Gaussian filtering, i.e., repeated filtering with a sequence of Gaussian filters, is equivalent to a single Gaussian filtering with a convolved kernel. The equivalence is easily shown because convolving two Gaussians with variances σ_1^2 and σ_2^2 produces the Gaussian with the variance. $\sigma_{cs}^2 = \sigma_1^2 + \sigma_2^2$ (in particular, $\sigma_{cs} = \sigma\sqrt{2}$ if $\sigma_1 = \sigma_2 = \sigma$):

$$\varphi(x; \sigma_1) * \varphi(x, \sigma_2) = \varphi\left(x, \sigma_{cs} = \sqrt{\sigma_1^2 + \sigma_2^2}\right) \tag{3.9}$$

Example 3.8 (1D Gaussian kernel of size 3). *Scaling of the Gaussian of Eq. (3.8) for $\sigma = 1.0$, followed by integer rounding and norming to keep the unit sum of the weights yields the following kernel of size 3:*

ξ	-1	0	1
$\varphi(\xi; 1.0)$	0.242	0.399	0.242
$\lambda = 5$	1.210	1.995	1.210
Rounding	1	2	1
Kernel $w(\xi)$	$\frac{1}{4}$	$\frac{1}{2}$	$\frac{1}{4}$

Example 3.9 (1D Gaussian kernel of size 5). *Scaling the Gaussian of Eq. (3.8) for $\sigma = 1.0$, followed by integer rounding and norming to keep the unit sum of the weights yields, in particular, the following two kernels of size 5:*

ξ	-2	-1	0	1	2
$\varphi(\xi; \sigma = 1.0)$	0.054	0.242	0.399	0.242	0.054
$\lambda = 10$	0.54	2.42	3.99	2.42	0.54
Rounding	1	2	4	2	1
Kernel $w(\xi)$	$\frac{1}{10}$	$\frac{2}{10}$	$\frac{4}{10}$	$\frac{2}{10}$	$\frac{1}{10}$
$\lambda = 20$	1.08	4.88	7.98	4.88	1.08
Rounding	1	5	8	5	1
Kernel $w(\xi)$	$\frac{1}{20}$	$\frac{5}{20}$	$\frac{8}{20}$	$\frac{5}{20}$	$\frac{1}{20}$

2D Gaussian filters using the 2D Gaussian:

$$\varphi(\xi, \eta; \sigma) = \varphi(\xi; \sigma)\varphi(\eta; \sigma) = \frac{1}{2\pi\sigma^2} \exp\left(-\frac{\xi^2 + \eta^2}{2\sigma^2}\right) \tag{3.10}$$

have in-built separability, i.e., the matrix of weights for a rectangular 2D kernel is a product of the vectors for 1D Gaussian kernels.

Example 3.10 (2D Gaussian kernels). *The following three separable 3×3 and 5×5 filters are formed from the 1D filters of Examples 3.8 and 3.9:*

$$\frac{1}{16}\begin{bmatrix} 1 & 2 & 1 \\ 2 & 4 & 2 \\ 1 & 2 & 1 \end{bmatrix} ; \quad \frac{1}{100}\begin{bmatrix} 1 & 2 & 4 & 2 & 1 \\ 2 & 4 & 8 & 4 & 2 \\ 4 & 8 & 16 & 8 & 4 \\ 2 & 4 & 8 & 4 & 2 \\ 1 & 2 & 4 & 2 & 1 \end{bmatrix} ; \quad \frac{1}{400}\begin{bmatrix} 1 & 5 & 8 & 5 & 1 \\ 5 & 25 & 40 & 25 & 5 \\ 8 & 40 & 64 & 40 & 8 \\ 5 & 25 & 40 & 25 & 5 \\ 1 & 5 & 8 & 5 & 1 \end{bmatrix}$$

The larger the standard deviation σ, the wider the Gaussian kernel and the larger the blurring. Just as the mean filtering, the non-uniform Gaussian filters perform low-pass filtering in the Fourier spectral domain. Both the mean and Gaussian filters of square shape are radially symmetric, i.e., have no directional bias; allow for fast computations due to their separability, but may reduce the signal range (i.e., decrease the overall image brightness). With a rectangular shape of these filters, the blurring prevails in the direction of the longer side.

3.4 Nonlinear filtering

Section 1.3 had already discussed dense feature maps, such that each individual feature of a lattice site is a local statistical descriptor of a configuration of image signals in a window centred on the site. Such a map is built by combining results of linear and nonlinear MWTs with fixed or adaptive window shapes and functions of signals depending on the signal descriptor under consideration.

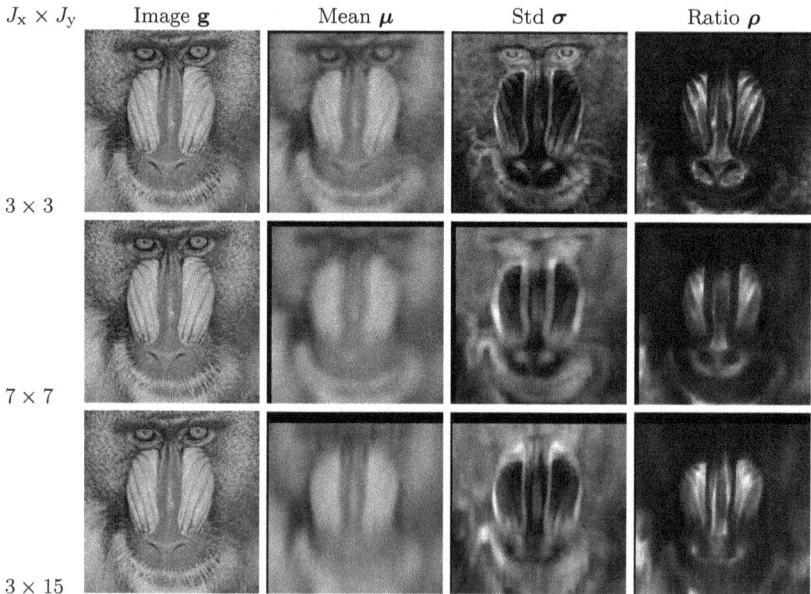

Fig. 3.12   Maps of local means, stds, and SNRs in rectangular $J_x \times J_y$ windows.

Let an image be a collection of contiguous non-intersecting regions covering the entire lattice and having constant grey levels, which differ for adjacent uniform regions and form step-wise edges between these regions. Such images are called sometimes "piecewise-constant". When the region map is absent, some local features can emphasise locations of the region borders. In particular, while the window origin, $\mathbf{0}$, visits each location $\mathbf{s}$ in the lattice $\mathbb{S}$, the window either resides within an individual region, or crosses one or more region borders. Thus, the window-wise feature at such a location depends either on only the signal and its possible noise-caused variations for the region, or also on the differences between the region-wise signals, respectively.

The simplest window-wise statistical characteristics, which are expected to emphasise in different ways locations of region borders in a piecewise-constant image corrupted with an unknown additive noise, include the local standard deviations, $\boldsymbol{\sigma} = (\sigma(\mathbf{s}) : \mathbf{s} \in \mathbb{S})$, of signals around their local mean values, $\boldsymbol{\mu} = (\mu(\mathbf{s}) : \mathbf{s} \in \mathbb{S})$, where

$$\sigma(\mathbf{s}) = \sqrt{\tfrac{1}{|\mathbb{W}|-1} \sum_{\boldsymbol{\nu} \in \mathbb{W}} \left(g(\mathbf{s} - \boldsymbol{\nu}) - \mu(\mathbf{s})\right)^2}$$
$$\mu(\mathbf{s}) = \tfrac{1}{|\mathbb{W}|} \sum_{\boldsymbol{\nu} \in \mathbb{W}} g(\mathbf{s} - \boldsymbol{\nu})$$

or the local mean-to-standard-deviation ratios

$$\boldsymbol{\rho} = \left(\rho(\mathbf{s}) = \frac{\mu(\mathbf{s})}{\max\{\sigma(\mathbf{s}), 1.0\}} : \mathbf{s} \in \mathbb{S} \right)$$

being local estimates of unknown regional signal-to-noise ratios (SNR).

Example 3.11. *Figure 3.12 demonstrates the grey-coded maps of the pixel-wise features $\boldsymbol{\mu}$, $\boldsymbol{\sigma}$, and $\boldsymbol{\rho}$ for the 3×3, 7×7, and 3×15 windows.*

Other applications of nonlinear filtering include image denoising (by median filters) and appearance transformations (by other rank filters).

3.4.1 *Median filter*

Median filtering is a frequent and efficient tool for removing "salt-and-pepper" noise in a piecewise-constant image, while preserving step-wise edges between the adjacent regions. It replaces each signal $g(\mathbf{s})$ with the median of signals in a window centred on that lattice site:

$$\widetilde{g}(\mathbf{s}) = \text{median}\{g(\mathbf{s} + \boldsymbol{\nu}) : \boldsymbol{\nu} \in \mathbb{W}\}$$

Let $q_0 = g(\mathbf{s} + \boldsymbol{\nu}_{[1]}) \leq q_1 = g(\mathbf{s} + \boldsymbol{\nu}_{[2]}) \leq \ldots \leq q_{n-1} = g(\mathbf{s} + \boldsymbol{\nu}_{[K]})$ be a sequence of all $K = |\mathbb{W}|$ signals from the window, which are sorted in ascending numerical order. The median is the signal at the middle position, $\widetilde{g}(\mathbf{s}) = q_{[(K+1)/2]}$ for the odd K and is the average of the two middle values, $\widetilde{g}(\mathbf{s}) = 0.5(q_{[K/2]} + q_{[K/2+1]})$, for the even K.

Example 3.12 (1D median filtering). *Figures 3.13 – 3.14 detail successive steps of the 1D median filtering of the same 1D input signal, **g** as in Example 3.1. The border signals are mirrored in order to fill in the window outside the lattice.*

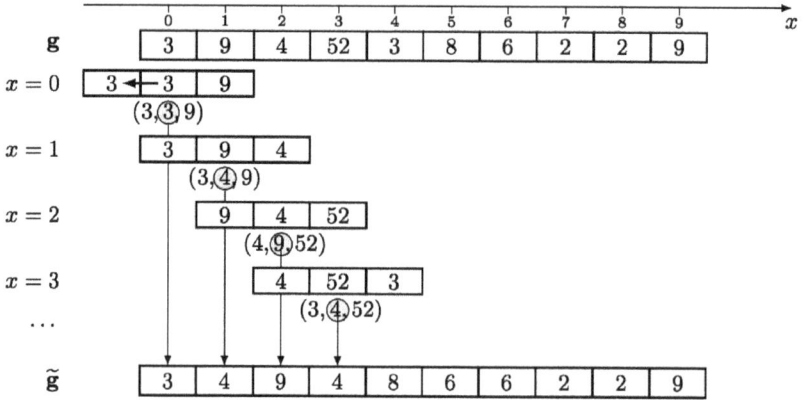

Fig. 3.13   1D median filtering with the contiguous window of size 3.

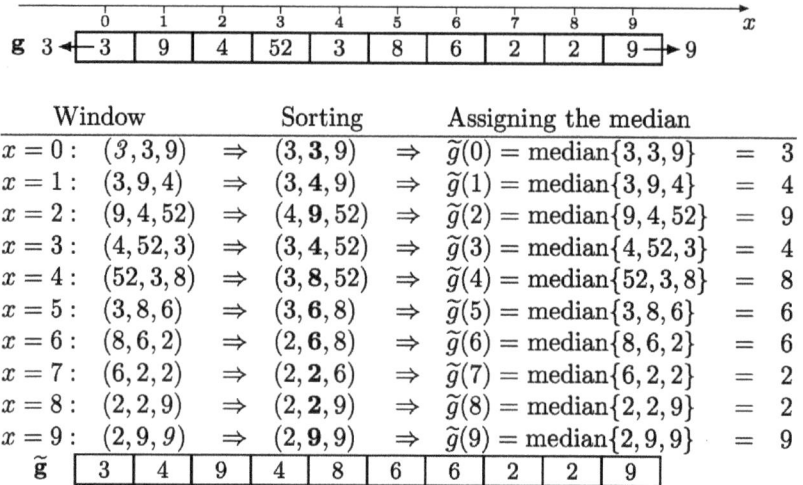

Window		Sorting		Assigning the median		
$x = 0$:	$(3,3,9)$	$\Rightarrow$	$(3,3,9)$	$\Rightarrow$	$\widetilde{g}(0) = \text{median}\{3,3,9\}$	$= 3$
$x = 1$:	$(3,9,4)$	$\Rightarrow$	$(3,4,9)$	$\Rightarrow$	$\widetilde{g}(1) = \text{median}\{3,9,4\}$	$= 4$
$x = 2$:	$(9,4,52)$	$\Rightarrow$	$(4,9,52)$	$\Rightarrow$	$\widetilde{g}(2) = \text{median}\{9,4,52\}$	$= 9$
$x = 3$:	$(4,52,3)$	$\Rightarrow$	$(3,4,52)$	$\Rightarrow$	$\widetilde{g}(3) = \text{median}\{4,52,3\}$	$= 4$
$x = 4$:	$(52,3,8)$	$\Rightarrow$	$(3,8,52)$	$\Rightarrow$	$\widetilde{g}(4) = \text{median}\{52,3,8\}$	$= 8$
$x = 5$:	$(3,8,6)$	$\Rightarrow$	$(3,6,8)$	$\Rightarrow$	$\widetilde{g}(5) = \text{median}\{3,8,6\}$	$= 6$
$x = 6$:	$(8,6,2)$	$\Rightarrow$	$(2,6,8)$	$\Rightarrow$	$\widetilde{g}(6) = \text{median}\{8,6,2\}$	$= 6$
$x = 7$:	$(6,2,2)$	$\Rightarrow$	$(2,2,6)$	$\Rightarrow$	$\widetilde{g}(7) = \text{median}\{6,2,2\}$	$= 2$
$x = 8$:	$(2,2,9)$	$\Rightarrow$	$(2,2,9)$	$\Rightarrow$	$\widetilde{g}(8) = \text{median}\{2,2,9\}$	$= 2$
$x = 9$:	$(2,9,9)$	$\Rightarrow$	$(2,9,9)$	$\Rightarrow$	$\widetilde{g}(9) = \text{median}\{2,9,9\}$	$= 9$

Fig. 3.14   1D median filtering with the contiguous window of size 3.

Depending on filtering goals, other ways of accounting for border effects might be preferred, e.g., to exclude processing at the boundaries with or without cropping the output border signals, or fetch signals from other places (image padding by twisting an image lattice into a torus), or shrink the window near the boundaries, so that every window is completely filled in. However, each strategy may notably affect the output border values.

Example 3.13 (3×3 **median filter**). *Figure 3.15 illustrates suppressing with this filter a "salt-and-pepper" noise on a realistic 2D scene:*

$$\widetilde{g}(x,y) = \text{median}\{g(x+\xi, y+\eta) : \xi = -1, 0, 1; \ \eta = -1, 0, 1\}$$

Figures 3.16 – 3.18 detail the 3×3 median filtering of the same artificial 6×6 image with a small signal set, $\mathbb{Q} = \{0, 1, \ldots, 4\}$, as in Example 3.5, for three ways of confronting the border effects.

Input noisy image   Filtered output image

Fig. 3.15 3×3 median filtering to reduce "salt-and-pepper" noise.

Median filtering effectively suppresses outliers (outstanding values), but destroys relations between adjacent signal values because the adjacency relations are not preserved. Mean filtering averages adjacent signals, i.e., blurs step-wise edges and decreases differences between the adjacent signals, but does not destroy the adjacency by itself.

Example 3.14 (Mean vs. median filtering). *Figures 3.19 and 3.20 compare results of applying the mean and median filters to the same images.*

Comparing to the mean filtering, Gaussian filtering produces less blurred edges, while it has more residual noise. Both the mean and Gaussian linear filters are inefficient for removing "salt-and-pepper" noise, because averaging does not suppress outliers (large deviations).

Sorted: (0, 0, 1, 1, ①, 2, 2, 4, 4)

0	0	0	0	0	0	0	0
0	1	4	0	1	3	1	0
0	2	②	4	2	2	3	0
0	1	0	1	0	1	0	0
0	1	2	1	0	2	2	0
0	2	5	3	1	2	5	0
0	1	1	4	2	3	0	0
0	0	0	0	0	0	0	0

g $\widetilde{g}$

0	2	1	1	1	0
0	①	1	1	1	1
0	1	1	1	2	1
0	1	1	1	1	1
1	2	2	2	2	2
0	1	1	1	1	0

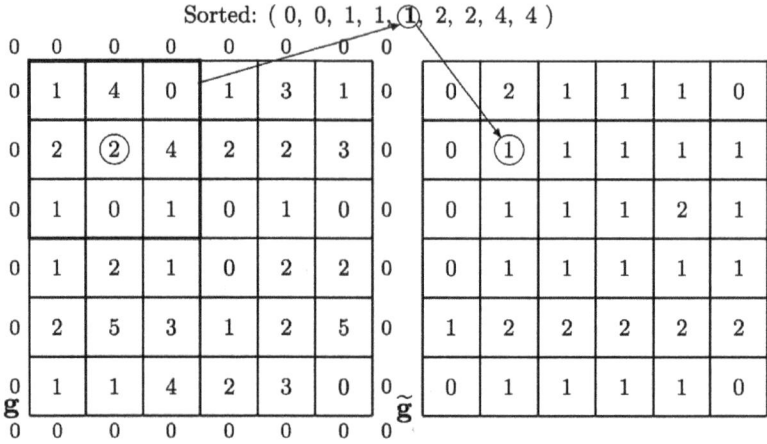

Fig. 3.16   Median filtering with the 3 × 3 window and zero padding.

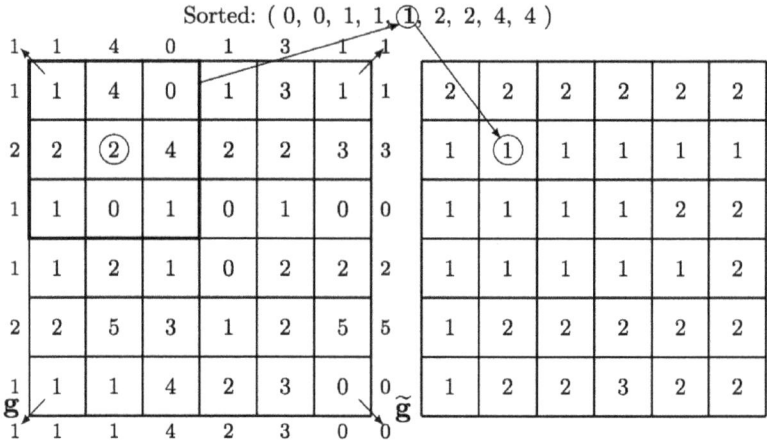

Sorted: (0, 0, 1, 1, ①, 2, 2, 4, 4)

1	1	4	0	1	3	1	1
1	1	4	0	1	3	1	1
2	2	②	4	2	2	3	3
1	1	0	1	0	1	0	0
1	1	2	1	0	2	2	2
2	2	5	3	1	2	5	5
1	1	1	4	2	3	0	0
1	1	1	4	2	3	0	0

g $\widetilde{g}$

2	2	2	2	2	2
1	①	1	1	1	1
1	1	1	1	2	2
1	1	1	1	1	2
1	2	2	2	2	2
1	2	2	3	2	2

Fig. 3.17   Median filtering with the 3 × 3 window and image mirroring at the borders.

Example 3.15 (Median vs. Gaussian filtering). *Figures 3.21 and 3.22 compare the median and Gaussian filtering in application to image denoising and smoothing.*

The median filtering is much more robust with respect to the outliers. But the Gaussian filtering is efficient for smoothing an image because of better approximation of spatial signal derivatives that are often used in edge detection (Fig. 3.23).

Sorted: (0, 0, 1, 1, ①, 2, 2, 4, 4)

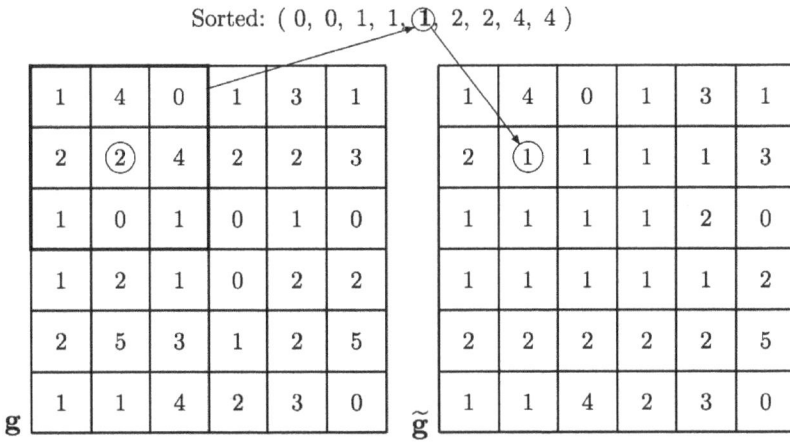

Fig. 3.18 Median filtering with the 3 × 3 window and border signals unchanged.

Input image   Median 3 × 3   Mean 3 × 3

Fig. 3.19 Median vs. mean filtering.

3.4.2 Rank filtering

The median MWT belongs to a family of rank MWTs, such that an output signal at each window position is selected by sorting and ranking input signals in the window, as well as to a similar family of percentile filters.

Input image

50	50	50	50	50	50
50	50	50	50	150	50
50	150	50	150	50	50
50	50	50	50	50	50
50	150	50	150	50	50
50	50	50	50	50	50

Median 3 × 3

50	50	50	50	50	50
50	50	50	50	50	50
50	50	50	50	50	50
50	50	50	50	50	50
50	50	50	50	50	50
50	50	50	50	50	50

Mean 3 × 3

50	50	50	50	50	50
50	61	72	72	72	50
50	61	72	72	72	50
50	72	94	72	72	50
50	61	72	61	61	50
50	50	50	50	50	50

50	50	50	150	50	50
50	50	50	150	50	50
50	150	150	150	50	50
50	50	50	150	50	50
50	50	50	150	50	50
50	50	50	150	50	50

50	50	50	150	50	50
50	50	150	50	50	50
50	50	150	50	50	50
50	50	150	50	50	50
50	50	50	50	50	50
50	50	50	150	50	50

50	50	50	150	50	50
50	72	106	94	83	50
50	72	106	94	83	50
50	72	106	94	83	50
50	50	83	83	83	50
50	50	50	150	50	50

Fig. 3.20   Median vs. mean filtering with border signals unchanged.

Gaussian 3 × 3   Median 3 × 3

Fig. 3.21   Removing the "salt-and-pepper" noise from the input image in Fig. 3.15.

Definition 3.2 (Percentiles). *An αth-percentile, or centile, is a threshold, such that $\alpha\%$ of signals from a given collection (here, from a window at a certain position) are below the threshold.*

The 25th-, 50th-, or 75th-percentile is called the first, second, or third *quartile*, respectively. The second quartile is the median. The percentiles and quartiles are specific types of *quantiles*, or signals taken at regular

3×3 5×5 11×11

Fig. 3.22 Gaussian (top row) versus median (bottom row) filtering.

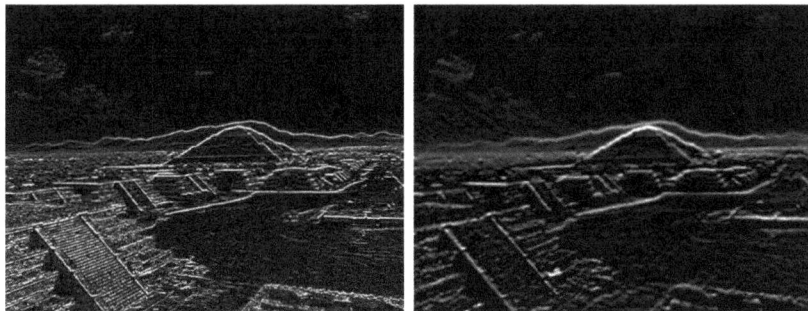

Fig. 3.23 Edge detection before (left) and after (right) Gaussian smoothing.

intervals from the cumulative histogram of signals. Recall that the percentiles, GLHs, and CHs, but in another context, have been already used for nonlinear appearance transformations in Section 2.3 of Chapter 2. Given a CH, $\mathbf{C} = (C(q) : q \in \mathbb{Q} = \{0, 1, \ldots, q_{\max}\})$ of signals in the window, the nonlinear α^{th}-percentile filter selects the output signal, q_α, such that

$$C(q_\alpha) \leq \frac{\alpha}{100} \cdot C(q_{\max})$$

Example 3.16 (Percentiles). *Let the grey levels in a 5×5 window have the GLH, $\mathbf{H} = (H(q) : q \in \{0, 4, \ldots, 95\})$; CH, $\mathbf{C} = (C(q) : q \in$*

$\{0, 4, \ldots, 95\})$, *and percentiles as follows:*

0	12	7	6	90
8	5	9	80	90
5	8	90	70	65
6	5	75	75	70
6	70	90	95	70

$\rightarrow$

q	0	5	6	7	8	9	12	65	70	75	80	90	95
$H(q)$	1	3	3	1	2	1	1	1	4	2	2	3	1
$C(q)$	1	4	7	8	10	11	12	13	17	19	21	24	25
$\alpha\%$	4	16	28	32	40	44	48	52	68	76	84	96	100

Window 5×5

The minimal percentile is $q_4 \equiv q_{min} = 0$, and the quartiles are $q_{25} \equiv q_{28} = 6$; $q_{50} \equiv q_{52} = 65$; $q_{75} \equiv q_{76} = 75$, and $q_{100} \equiv q_{max} = 95$ (see also Fig. 3.24).

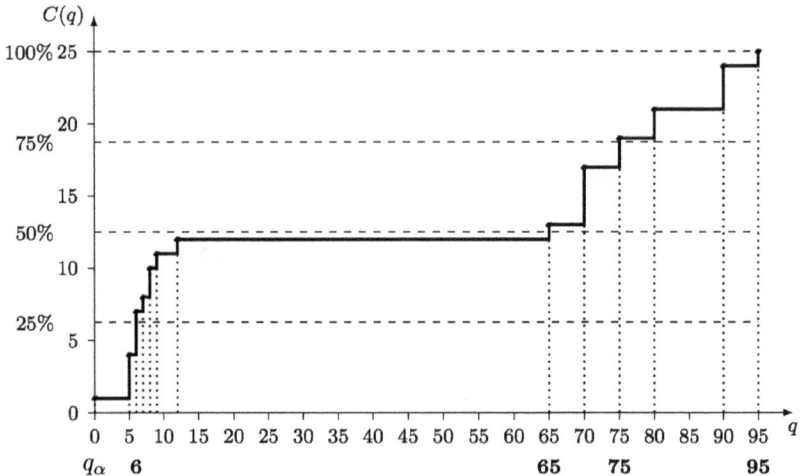

Fig. 3.24   Cumulative histogram and quartiles for Example 3.17.

Definition 3.3 (Rank). *Rank k of a signal q is the position of this signal in an ordered non-decreasing sequence $q_{[1]} \leq q_{[2]} \leq \ldots \leq q_{[K]}$ of K signals.*

Given such a sequence, a nonlinear k-rank filter selects the output signal $q_{[k]}$ of rank k.

Example 3.17 (Ranks vs. percentiles). *For the same 25 signals in the 5×5 window, as in Example 3.16, the ranks, k, and their percentiles* *ranges,* $[\alpha_{[k-1]}, \alpha_{[k]})$*, are as follows:*

0	12	7	6	90
8	5	9	80	90
5	8	90	70	65
6	5	75	75	70
6	70	90	95	70

Window 5×5

$\rightarrow$

q	0	5	6	7	8	9	12	65	70	75	80	90	95
$H(q)$	1	3	3	1	2	1	1	1	4	2	2	3	1
$C(q)$	1	4	7	8	10	11	12	13	17	19	21	24	25
$\alpha_{[k-1]}\%$	0	4	16	28	32	40	44	48	52	68	76	84	96
$\alpha_{[k]}\%$	4	16	28	32	40	44	48	52	68	76	84	96	100
$k_{q:\min}$	1	2	5	8	9	11	12	13	14	18	20	22	25
$k_{q:\max}$	1	4	7	8	10	11	12	13	17	19	21	24	25

Thus, the ranks of and signals for the percentiles $\alpha = 0, 25, 50, 75,$ *and* 100
are here, respectively, $(k \backslash q_{[k]}) = (1 \backslash 0), (7 \backslash 6), (13 \backslash 65), (19 \backslash 75),$ *and* $(25 \backslash 95)$*.*
Figure 3.25 shows the minimum, median, and maximum rank filtering.

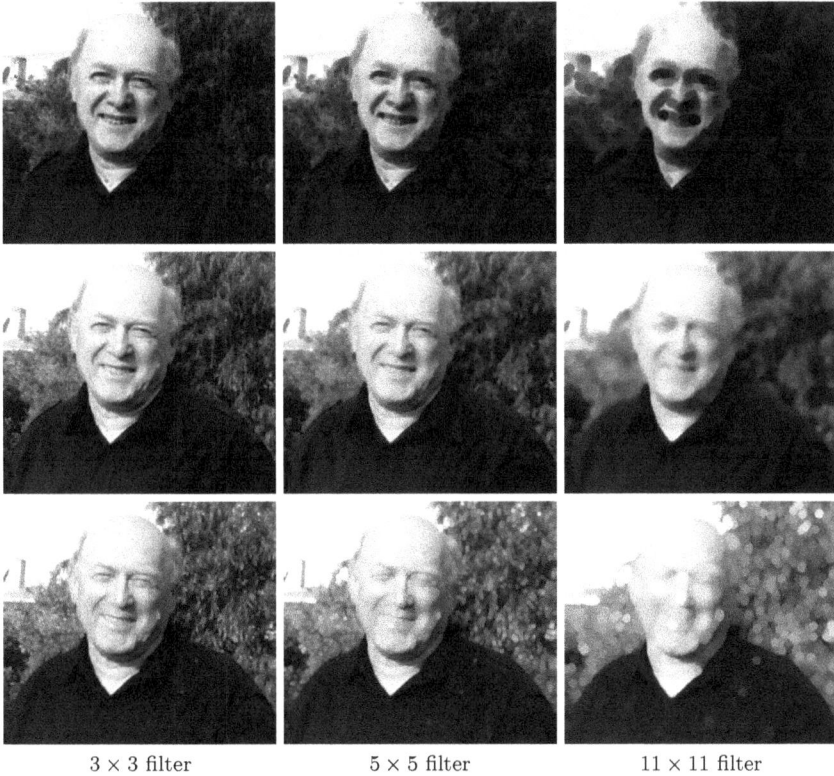

| 3×3 filter | 5×5 filter | 11×11 filter |

Fig. 3.25 MWT of the input image in Fig. 3.5 with $J \times J$ minimum ($k = 1$: row 1);
median ($k = \left\lceil \frac{J^2}{2} \right\rceil$: row 2), and maximum ($k = J^2$: row 3) rank filters.

3.5   Questions and exercises

(1) What is a moving window transform (MWT)?

(2) What is a border effect for an MWT?

(3) How can the border effect be taken into account?

(4) How are the mean and Gaussian filters alike and how do they differ?

(5) How are the linear and nonlinear filters alike and how do they differ?

(6) Why linear filters are called convolution filters?

(7) Are the Laplacian filters linear or not?

(8) Are the rank filters linear or not?

(9) Let an input 1D sequence, $\mathbf{g}$, of size 8 and a kernel, $\mathbf{w}$, of size 3 for the linear MWT producing the output sequence of weighted means be as follows:

$$\mathbf{g} = \left\{ \begin{array}{c|cccccccc} x & 0 & 1 & 2 & 3 & 4 & 5 & 6 & 7 \\ \hline g(x) & 16 & 24 & 24 & 16 & 24 & 16 & 96 & 88 \end{array} \right. \quad \text{and} \quad \mathbf{w} = \left\{ \begin{array}{c|cccc} \xi & -1 & 0 & 1 & 2 \\ \hline w(\xi) & \frac{1}{4} & \frac{1}{2} & \frac{1}{8} & \frac{1}{8} \end{array} \right.$$

(a) Convolve the sequence, $\mathbf{g}$, with the kernel, $\mathbf{w}$, using zero padding to account for border effects.

(b) Convolve the sequence, $\mathbf{g}$, with the kernel, $\mathbf{w}$, using the circular 1D lattice to account for border effects.

(c) Convolve the sequence, $\mathbf{g}$, with the kernel, $\mathbf{w}$, using the mirroring to account for border effects.

(d) Compare the obtained three output sequences and evaluate how much each of them is affected by the assumed outliers $g(6) = 96$ and $g(7) = 88$.

(10) Apply the maximum, median, and minimum rank filtering to the above 1D sequence with the same window coordinate offsets, $\xi = -1, 0, 1, 2$, and three ways of confronting the border effects.

Chapter 4

Filtering to Segment

Segmentation partitions an input image or its dense feature map into non-overlapping regions encoded by numerical or symbolic labels. The input data and output labels are on the same lattice, with each label indicating the region that the lattice site (pixel or voxel) belongs to. An individual region may be disconnected (i.e., contain separate connected parts). Input signals in a region have some similarity, making them distinct from other regions.

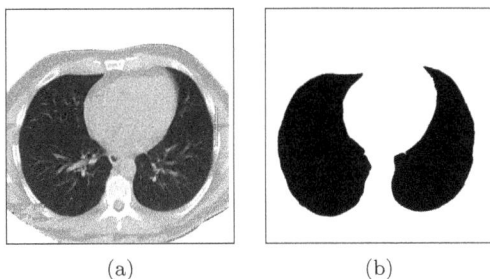

(a) (b)

Fig. 4.1 CT chest slice (a) and its map (b) of black lung and white background labels.

The segmentation is meaningful if at least one of the regions can be associated with a goal object, like, e.g., human lungs on a medical image in Fig. 4.1. The simplest *non-contextual segmentation* assigns a label to every lattice site with no account of the labels at other sites. The input signals are often stratified into clusters by closeness of grey values or other site-wise signal properties irrespective of their locations in the lattice. Such segmentation is similar to *image quantisation*, which replaces each input signal with the closest cluster centre. Unlike quantisation, the segmentation assigns unique labels of clusters to each site of the output region map. The resulting regions may not be contiguous, as well as in many cases they may be meaningless.

Much more powerful *contextual segmentation* labels each image site with due account of its *context*, i.e., its fixed or varying neighbourhood, up to the whole lattice, on the input image. In particular, the region map in Fig. 4.1 differs from a quantised binary image obtained after thresholding the input image, because the grey level histograms for lungs and other chest tissues intersect. Segmenting intricate natural images is out of the scope of this primer. However, even simple contextual segmentation that separates adjacent sites by dissimilarity of signals is sometimes helpful in finding meaningful regions.

What will you find here? Section 4.1 will describe common measures of segmentation accuracy, and Section 4.2 will briefly outline two simple formal models of a region-of-interest (ROI). Each ROI either is associated with one or more intervals of input grey values or other scalar features, or is defined by similarity between the neighbouring input signals.

The first model leads to non-contextual histogram thresholding (Section 4.3) to segment or quantise a greyscale image or a scalar feature map. Thresholds are adapted to input data by relating goal ROIs to prominent peaks of a grey level or feature histogram. Three adaptation scenarios include (*i*) two-region (binary) segmentation in Section 4.3.1 by finding a stationary threshold midway between mean values above and below the threshold; (*ii*) multi-region segmentation in Section 4.3.2 by histogram approximation with a mixture of Gaussians, one per region, and (*iii*) two- or three-region segmentation in Section 4.3.3 by separating tails from a main body of an unimodal histogram. This thresholding is extended onto feature vectors, such as, e.g., colours, in Section 4.4. The second model leads to *connected components labelling*, i.e., to finding and labelling connected uniform ROIs (Section 4.5).

4.1   Measuring segmentation accuracy

Accuracy of segmentation is evaluated experimentally, providing a true region map is available for a test image. Let $\mathbb{S}_{\text{segm}}$, $\mathbb{S}_{\text{true}}$, $\mathbb{S}^{\text{c}}_{\text{segm}}$, and $\mathbb{S}^{\text{c}}_{\text{true}}$ denote, respectively, a region obtained by segmenting the test image, the true region, and their backgrounds that complement each of these regions on the same lattice $\mathbb{S}$:

$$\mathbb{S}_{\text{segm}} \bigcup \mathbb{S}_{\text{segm}}^{c} = \mathbb{S}; \quad \mathbb{S}_{\text{segm}} \bigcap \mathbb{S}_{\text{segm}}^{c} = \emptyset;$$
$$\mathbb{S}_{\text{true}} \bigcup \mathbb{S}_{\text{true}}^{c} = \mathbb{S}; \quad \mathbb{S}_{\text{true}} \bigcap \mathbb{S}_{\text{true}}^{c} = \emptyset.$$

where $\mathbb{A} \bigcup \mathbb{B}$ and $\mathbb{A} \bigcap \mathbb{B}$ denote the union and intersection, respectively, of sets $\mathbb{A}$ and $\mathbb{B}$, and $\emptyset$ is the empty set.

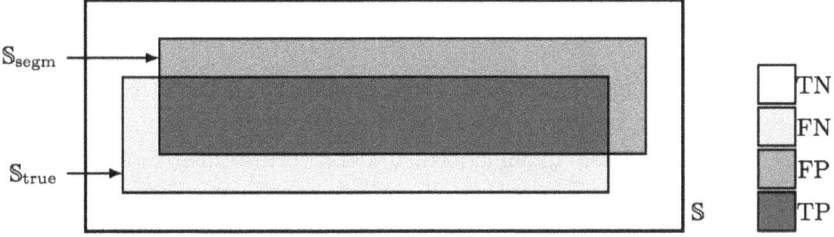

Fig. 4.2 TP, FP, TN, and FN measures of segmentation accuracy.

Definition 4.1 (TP, FP, TN, and FN measures). *The accuracy is measured in terms of total true positive (TP), false positive (FP), true negative (TN) and false negative (FN) areas outlined in Fig. 4.2:*

$$\text{TP} = |\mathbb{S}_{\text{segm}} \bigcap \mathbb{S}_{\text{true}}|; \quad \text{FP} = |\mathbb{S}_{\text{segm}} \bigcap \mathbb{S}_{\text{true}}^{c}|;$$
$$\text{TN} = |\mathbb{S}_{\text{segm}}^{c} \bigcap \mathbb{S}_{\text{true}}^{c}|; \quad \text{FN} = |\mathbb{S}_{\text{segm}}^{c} \bigcap \mathbb{S}_{\text{true}}|.$$

where $|\mathbb{A}|$ is the cardinality of a set $\mathbb{A}$.

Therefore, the following equalities hold: $\text{TP} + \text{FP} + \text{TN} + \text{FN} = |\mathbb{S}|$; $\text{TP} + \text{FP} = |\mathbb{S}_{\text{segm}}|$; $\text{TP} + \text{FN} = |\mathbb{S}_{\text{true}}|$, and $\text{TN} + \text{FP} = |\mathbb{S}_{\text{true}}^{c}|$. The TP area measures the overlap between the true and segmented regions, i.e., the number of their common sites. The FP area measures the difference between the segmented region and its TP part, i.e., the number of common sites in the segmented region and the true background. The TN area measures the overlap between the true and segmented backgrounds, i.e., the number of their common sites. The FN area measures the difference between the true and segmented regions, i.e., the number of common sites in the true region and the segmented background.

Performance of a segmentation algorithm is often characterised by its relative *accuracy; precision*, and *specificity*, being defined, respectively, as

$$\frac{TP + TN}{TP + FP + TN + FN}; \quad \frac{TP}{TP + FP}, \quad \text{and} \quad \frac{TN}{TN + FP}$$

4.2   Modelling image regions

Segmentation is often a first step from low-level processing to high-level analysis of optical images of an observed scene. In particular, an acquired image might be denoised, enhanced, and/or transformed into a map of quantitative features of two or more signals associated with each lattice site. Then the image or feature map is segmented into a region map, and scene descriptions in terms of objects and their properties depend heavily on how accurate and robust to noise are obtained regions-of-interes (ROIs).

Generally, the meaningful segmentation meets with many challenges and involves complicate modelling and optimisation techniques. Most of today's mathematical models of images and their region maps, such as, e.g., probabilistic models involving conditional and joint Markov random fields (MRF) of signals, features, and region labels, are quite complicated and thus are outside of the scope of this primer.

However, quite a few practically important visual objects, such as, e.g., human lungs on CT chest scans in Fig. 4.1, can be segmented, at least, roughly, by separating dominant modes of an 1D GLH or its normed version, an empirical p.d.f. of grey levels. The like segmentation can employ histograms and ranges of values of any site-wise scalar feature that characterises signal co-occurrences in two or more neighbouring lattice sites and is feasible for computing. The only requirement is that feature values should notably differ for the goal regions.

Alternative simple, but still practically useful region models account for homogeneity of, or similarity between site-wise image signals or features. The homogeneity can be tested locally, for the neighbouring sites, or globally, for a whole region. Checking a certain homogeneity score helps to grow a region from a certain initial site, called frequently a *seed*. The growth of each individual region terminates after all its boundary sites have no external neighbours that could be included, without violating the homogeneity.

4.3 Histogram thresholding

Non-contextual histogram thresholding with a single threshold, τ, for all lattice sites $\mathbf{s} \in \mathbb{S}$ is the simplest technique to convert a greyscale image, $\mathbf{g}$, into a binary image that can be considered a binary region map, $\mathbf{g}_{\mathrm{m}}$. The single threshold results in at most two possibly disjoint regions with arbitrarily different labels (typically, 0 and 1), e.g.,

$$g_{\mathrm{m}}(\mathbf{s}) = \begin{cases} 0 \text{ if } g(\mathbf{s}) < \tau \\ 1 \text{ if } g(\mathbf{s}) \geq \tau \end{cases} \quad \text{or} \quad g_{\mathrm{m}}(\mathbf{s}) = \begin{cases} 1 \text{ if } g(\mathbf{s}) < \tau \\ 0 \text{ if } g(\mathbf{s}) \geq \tau \end{cases}$$

Given an input image, the output regions depend on both the threshold and the signal feature to be thresholded.

Generally, two or more thresholds can be used to associate each region with a range of signal values or with several separate ranges, e.g.,

$$g_{\mathrm{m}}(\mathbf{s}) = \begin{cases} 0 \text{ if } \tau_1 \leq g(\mathbf{s}) \leq \tau_2 \\ 1 \text{ if } g(\mathbf{s}) < \tau_1 \text{ OR } g(\mathbf{s}) > \tau_2 \end{cases}$$

Example 4.1 (Simple thresholding). *Figure 4.3 shows object-background maps for hand-picked thresholds between dominant histogram modes at $q = 33, 133, 165,$ and 255. The black-coded label 0 indicates grey levels below the threshold $\tau = 83$ between the first two modes (Map 1), in the range $[\tau_1, \tau_2]$ (Maps 2–5), and above the threshold τ (Maps 6 and 7). In these cases, Map 1 is close to actual lungs in Fig. 4.1, most of other chest parts are in Maps 4 and 5, whereas outer (blank) areas of the CT image are mostly in Maps 6 and 7. Note that separation of individual histogram modes in Maps 2 or 3 does not produce easy-to-interpret regions.*

4.3.1 *Adaptive object-background thresholding*

Example 4.1 demonstrates that selecting an adequate threshold or a few such thresholds manually is a challenging task. However, a meaningful ROI may sometimes relate to a prominent (dominant) mode of an empirical marginal p.d.f., or a normed 1D histogram of signals. Collected over an entire input image, this p.d.f. combines individual distributions over each particular ROI and other areas of the image.

Generally, many of these individual distributions are overlapping, so that a threshold in a valley between two adjacent modes of the mixed distribution might separate main bodies of the related parts of the histogram,

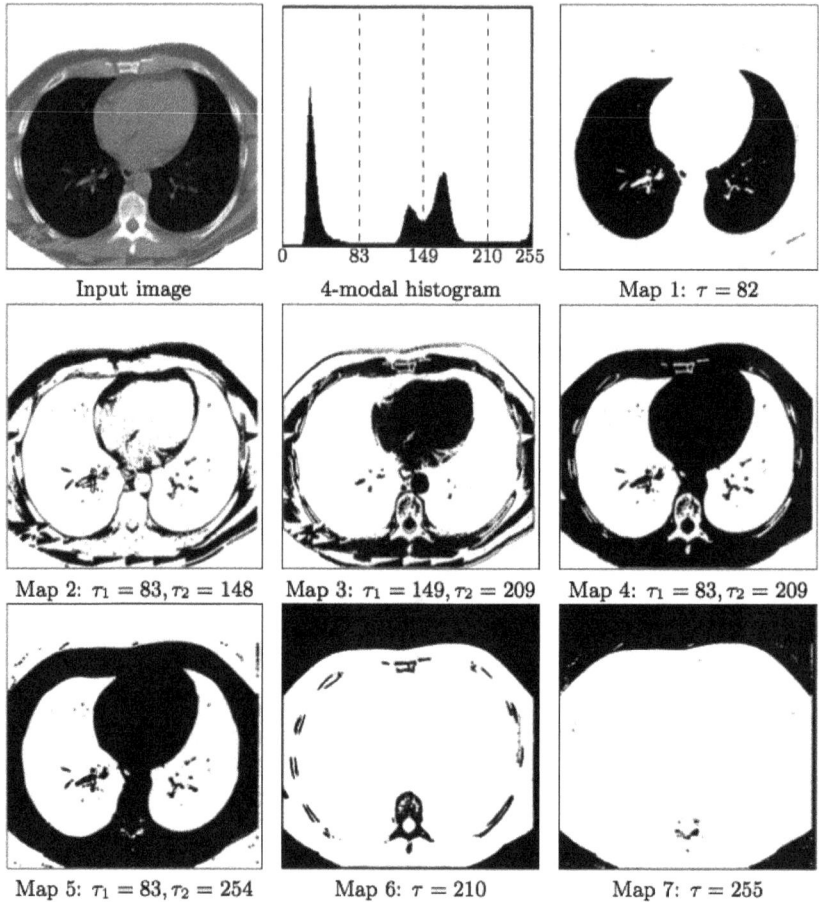

| Input image | 4-modal histogram | Map 1: $\tau = 82$ |

| Map 2: $\tau_1 = 83, \tau_2 = 148$ | Map 3: $\tau_1 = 149, \tau_2 = 209$ | Map 4: $\tau_1 = 83, \tau_2 = 209$ |

| Map 5: $\tau_1 = 83, \tau_2 = 254$ | Map 6: $\tau = 210$ | Map 7: $\tau = 255$ |

Fig. 4.3 Mapping objects (black) with manually chosen signal ranges.

but inevitably accepts or rejects falsely many intermediate signals. To separate an object from its background in a bimodal histogram, a reasonable choice is a threshold that equalises the complementary FP and FN errors.

An adaptive non-contextual object-background separation accounts for empirical marginal p.d.f.s of signals attributed to the goal object and its background (e.g., the darker and brighter pixels, respectively, in Fig. 4.1). Some more complex adaptation schemes vary the threshold in line with the changing local context, e.g., by tracing gradual changes of the background signal distribution (a so-called *background normalisation*).

Algorithm 5 Iterative threshold adaptation.

Input: An image histogram $\mathbf{H} = (H(q) : q \in \mathbb{Q} = \{0, \ldots, Q-1\})$;
the number Q of grey values.

Output: The object-background threshold τ.

Initialisation: $S = \sum_{q=0}^{Q-1} H(q); \; \tau = \frac{1}{S} \sum_{q=0}^{Q-1} q H(q)$.

Iterations: While the threshold τ is changing **do**

$$S_{\text{ob}} = \sum_{q=0}^{\tau} H(q); \qquad S_{\text{bg}} = \sum_{q=\tau+1}^{Q-1} H(q)$$

$$\mu_{\text{ob}} = \frac{1}{S_{\text{ob}}} \sum_{q=0}^{\tau} q H(q); \; \mu_{\text{bg}} = \frac{1}{S_{\text{bg}}} \sum_{q=\tau+1}^{Q-1} q H(q); \; \tau = \frac{1}{2} (\mu_{\text{ob}} + \mu_{\text{bg}})$$

end while

return τ

One of the simplest adaptation techniques (Algorithm 5) inputs only an image histogram and iteratively refines estimated positions of two modes attributed to the object and background. This algorithm assumes similar unimodal and centre-symmetric individual p.d.f.s of object and background signals, their distinct modes being positioned at the relevant empirical means. The probabilities decrease monotonically with a growing absolute deviation from the mean, and the threshold is always placed halfway between the means.

4.3.2 *Gaussian mixture model*

To account for not only means, but also variances of signals for J different ROIs; $1 < J \ll Q = |\mathbb{Q}|$, the J-modal empirical marginal p.d.f. for an input image $\mathbf{g}$:

$$\mathbf{P} = (P(q) : q \in \mathbb{Q}) = \tfrac{1}{S} \mathbf{H}(\mathbf{g}); \; S = \sum_{q \in \mathbb{Q}} H(q)$$

is approximated with a Gaussian mixture, $\widehat{\mathbf{P}}_J = (\widehat{P}(q) : q \in \mathbb{Q})$, such that

$$\widehat{P}(q) = \sum_{j=1}^{J} w_j \varphi(q|\mu_j, \sigma_j); \; w_j \geq 0; \; j \in \{1, \ldots, J\}; \; \sum_{j=1}^{J} w_j = 1$$

The mixture model is usually simplified by assuming continuous signals $q \in \{-\infty, \infty\}$ in the Gaussian densities:

$$\varphi(q|\mu_j, \sigma_j) = \frac{1}{\sigma_j \sqrt{2\pi}} \exp\left(-\frac{1}{2\sigma^2}(q - \mu_j)^2\right)$$

one per each ROI j. Thresholds for separating the histogram are related to so-called *responsibilities*, $\mathbf{\Gamma} = \{\gamma_{q:j} : q \in \mathbb{Q}; j \in \{1, \ldots, J\}\}$, of each Gaussian with the label $j \in \{1, \ldots, J\}$ for each signal $q \in \mathbb{Q}$:

$$0 \leq \gamma_{q:j} \leq 1; \; q \in \mathbb{Q}; \; j \in \{1, \ldots, J\}; \; \sum_{j=1}^{J} \gamma_{q:j} = 1$$

Iterative *Expectation-Maximisation* (EM) process of Algorithm 6 updates successively the responsibilities and the maximum likelihood estimates (MLE) of parameters, (w_j, μ_j, σ_j), of the mixture components. Their number, J, is often selected manually, but it can be also estimated in accord with special informational criteria accounting for both the approximation accuracy and complexity of the mixture.

Algorithm 6 EM estimation of a mixture of the J Gaussians.

Input: The empirical p.d.f. $\mathbf{P} = (P(q) : q \in \mathbb{Q})$; the number J.
Output: The mixture parameters, $\mathbf{\Theta} = \{(w_j, \mu_j, \sigma_j) : j \in \{1, \ldots, J\}\}$.
Initialisation: Select (guess) starting parameters $\mathbf{\Theta}$.
Iterations: While the parameters $\mathbf{\Theta}$ are changing **do**
     [E-step]: Update the responsibilities $\mathbf{\Gamma} = \{\gamma_{q:j} : q \in \mathbb{Q}; j \in \{1, \ldots, J\}\}$:

$$\gamma_{q:j} = \frac{1}{S_q} w_j \varphi(q|\mu_j, \sigma_j) \text{ where } S_q = \sum_{k=1}^{J} w_k \varphi(q|\mu_k, \sigma_k)$$

     [M-step]: Update the MLEs $\mathbf{\Theta}$ using the updated responsibilities $\mathbf{\Gamma}$:

$$w_j = \sum_{q \in \mathbb{Q}} \gamma_{q:j} P(q); \qquad \qquad \mu_j = \frac{1}{w_j} \sum_{q \in \mathbb{Q}} \gamma_{q:j} q P(q);$$
$$\sigma_j^2 = \frac{1}{w_j} \sum_{q \in \mathbb{Q}} \gamma_{q:j} (q - \mu_j)^2 P(q)$$

end while
return $\mathbf{\Theta}$

4.3.3 *Unimodal thresholding*

To form a multimodal histogram, areas of regions related to different signal ranges should be large and comparable. Otherwise, even when the histogram **h**, is unimodal, the image may still contain distinct objects re-lated, e.g., to the main body of the histogram and its left and/or right tails. Figure 4.4 illustrates such a case.

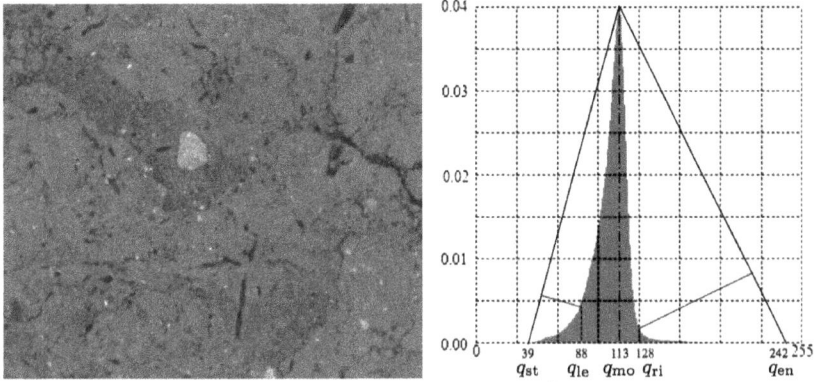

Fig. 4.4   Unimodal thresholding of the histogram of a CT soil image to separate the left and right tails w.r.t. the mode.

Let q_{st}, q_{mo}, and q_{en} denote the start, mode, and end positions of the histogram along the signal axis ($q_{st} = 39$, $q_{mo} = 113$, and $q_{en} = 242$ in Fig. 4.4 with $Q = 256$ grey levels). The Cartesian distances in the $(q, H(q))$-plane from a point $(q^\circ, H^\circ \equiv H(q^\circ))$ to a straight line connecting the mode point, $(q_{mo}, H_{mo} \equiv H(q_{mo}))$, with the start, $(q_{st}, H_{st} \equiv H(q_{st}))$, or the end, $(q_{en}, H_{en} \equiv H(q_{en}))$, point, is, respectively,

$$d_{st}(q^\circ, H^\circ) = \frac{q^\circ(H_{mo} - H_{st}) - H^\circ(q_{mo} - q_{st}) + q_{mo}H_{st} - q_{st}H_{mo}}{\sqrt{(q_{mo} - q_{st})^2 + (H_{mo} - H_{st})^2}}$$

or

$$d_{en}(q^\circ, H^\circ) = \frac{q^\circ(H_{mo} - H_{en}) - H^\circ(q_{mo} - q_{en}) + q_{mo}H_{en} - q_{en}H_{mo}}{\sqrt{(q_{mo} - q_{en})^2 + (H_{mo} - H_{en})^2}}$$

The unimodal thresholding relates borders, q_{le} or q_{ri}, separating the left or right histogram tail in the subsets $\mathbb{Q}_{st} = \{q_{st}, \ldots, q_{mo} - 1\}$ or $\mathbb{Q}_{en} = \{q_{mo} + 1, \ldots, q_{en}\}$ of grey levels, respectively, to the farthest points, $(q_{le}, H(q_{le}))$ or $(q_{ri}, H(q_{ri}))$, from the relevant lines:

$$q_{le} = \arg\max_{q \in \mathbb{Q}_{st}} d_{st}(q, H(q)) \text{ and } q_{ri} = \arg\max_{q \in \mathbb{Q}_{en}} d_{en}(q, H(q))$$

The selected borders specify the 3-region map $\mathbf{g}_m = (g_m(\mathbf{s}) : \mathbf{s} \in \mathbb{S})$ where $g_m(\mathbf{s}) = 0$ if $g(\mathbf{s}) < q_{le}$; 1 if $q_{le} \leq g(\mathbf{s}) < q_{ri}$, and 2 if $q_{ri} \leq g(\mathbf{s})$.

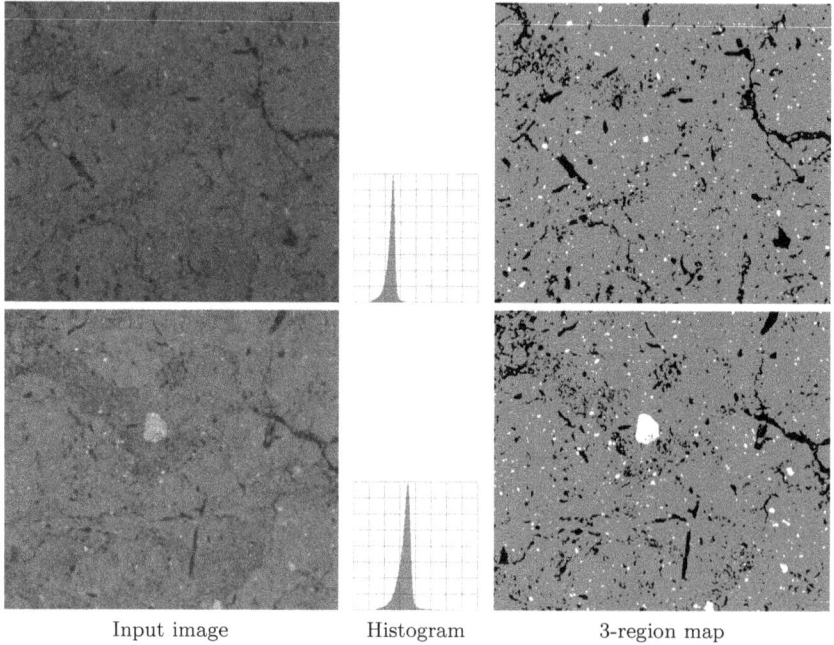

Input image   Histogram   3-region map

Fig. 4.5 Segmentation by unimodal thresholding (regions 0, 1, and 2 are black, grey, and white, respectively); the same image as in Fig. 4.4 and its map in the bottom line.

Example 4.2 (3-region unimodal thresholding). *Figure 4.5 shows two CT soil images with the unimodal histograms. Their segmentation using the above unimodal thresholding produces three disjoint ROIs that could be roughly interpreted as dark "pores", grey "clay+silt", and light grey "sand grains". The thresholds $q_{le} = 88$ and $q_{ri} = 128$ have been selected for the input image in Fig. 4.4.*

4.4   Colour segmentation

Segmenting natural images is often more accurate if each sensed intensity of visible light over the entire range, $[0.38, 0.78]$ μm, of its wavelengths is appended with *chrominance* of the wavelengths. The chrominance is characterised by *hue* and *saturation*, which specify, respectively, a perceived colour, or dominant wavelength(s) of the light, and purity of the colour, i.e., the power of its dominant wavelength with respect to the other wavelengths. Each pure colour has the maximal, i.e. unit saturation, whereas a colourless light has zero saturation.

4.4.1 *RGB–HSI colour representations*

Human colour perception is subjective, but generally each sensed colour combines linearly three primary, or pure red (R), green (G), and blue (B) colours with dominant wavelengths of 0.700 μm, 0.546 μm, and 0.436 μm, respectively. Accordingly, a majority of imaging devices acquire colours as vectors in the RGB space that closely relates to human vision (Fig. 4.6).

However, the R, G, and B components characterise both the intensity and chrominance and thus are interdependent. To reduce this interdependence and obtain more stable and, if necessary, intensity-independent segmentation, the RGB space is usually replaced with the equivalent HSI space of hue (H), saturation (S), and intensity (I) components.

The RGB-to-HSI transformation places the intensity axis, I, along the main diagonal of the RGB cube, $0 \leq R, G, B \leq I_{max} = 255$. The chrominance HS-planes are orthogonal to the intensity axis and have angular hue, H, and radial saturation, S, polar coordinates (Fig. 4.7):

$$I = \frac{R + G + B}{3}; \quad S = 1 - \frac{\min\{R, G, B\}}{I}; \quad H = \begin{cases} \theta & \text{if } G > B \\ 360° - \theta & \text{otherwise} \end{cases}$$

where

$$\theta = \cos^{-1}\left(\frac{R - 0.5(G + B)}{\sqrt{R^2 + G^2 + B^2 - RG - RB - GB}}\right)$$

The inverse HSI-to-RGB transformation is outlined in Algorithm 7.

Further detailing of these colour spaces and multiple other colour representations and transformations, such as, e.g., in colour television or image coding, is out of the scope of this primer.

Example 4.3 (Chrominance mapping). *The chrominance map in Fig. 4.8 is visualised by the HSI-to-RGB-conversion of pixel-wise HS-pairs appended with constant intensities, $I = 85$, in order to keep the points within the RGB-cube for each saturation S; $0 \leq S \leq 1$. The chrominance map leads to intensity-invariant segmentation. However, the colours with too low or high intensities have noisy and sometimes counter-intuitive chrominance, as, e.g., green or pale blue parts of the dark image areas.*

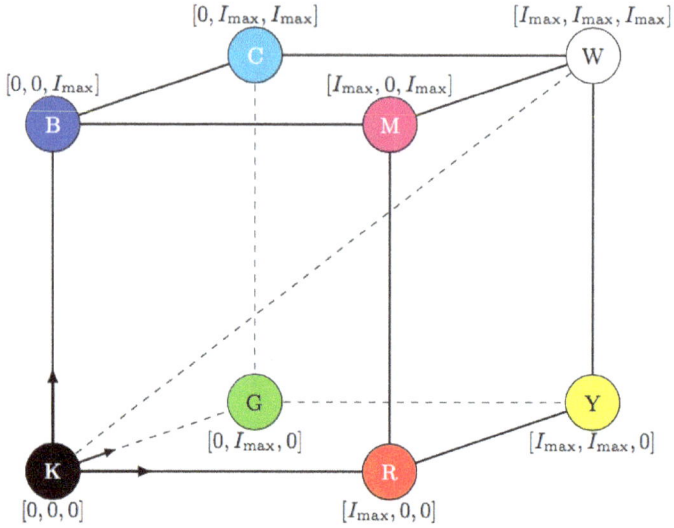

Fig. 4.6   RGB cube of size $I_{max} \times I_{max} \times I_{max}$. Only pure blue (B), cyan (C), green (G), magenta (M), red (R), and yellow (Y) vertices are coloured for clarity. Grey values are along the main black (K) – white (W) diagonal of equal R, G, and B components.

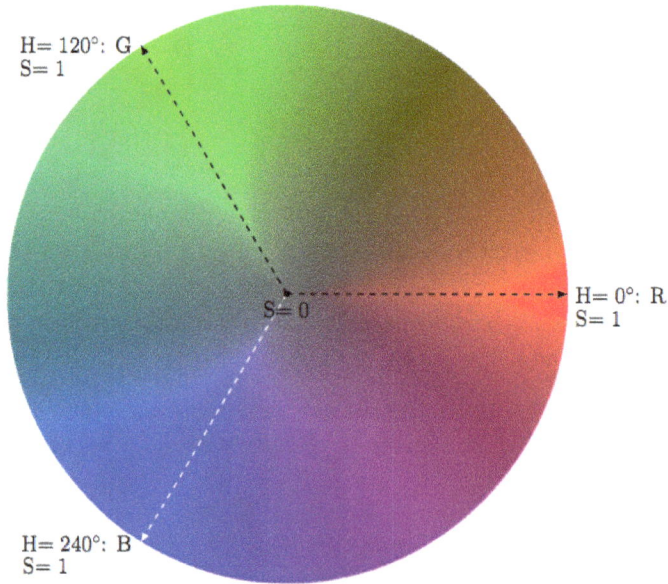

Fig. 4.7   Hue (H) – saturation (S) plane with polar H-S coordinates: $H \in [0, 360°)$ and $S \in [0, 1]$. Here, each (H,S) point has the constant intensity, I = 85.

Algorithm 7 HSI to RGB colour conversion.

Input: an HSI-colour vector with components H, S, I

Output: the RGB-colour vector with components R, G, B

if $0 \leq H \leq 120°$ **then**

$$R = I\left(1 + S\frac{\cos(H)}{\cos(60° - H)}\right); \ B = I(1 - S); \ G = 3I - (R + B)$$

else if $120° < H \leq 240°$ **then**

$$G = I\left(1 + S\frac{\cos(H - 120°)}{\cos(180° - H)}\right); \ R = I(1 - S); \ B = 3I - (R + G)$$

else if $240° < H < 360°$ **then**

$$B = I\left(1 + S\frac{\cos(H - 240°)}{\cos(300° - H)}\right); \ G = I(1 - S); \ R = 3I - (G + B)$$

end if

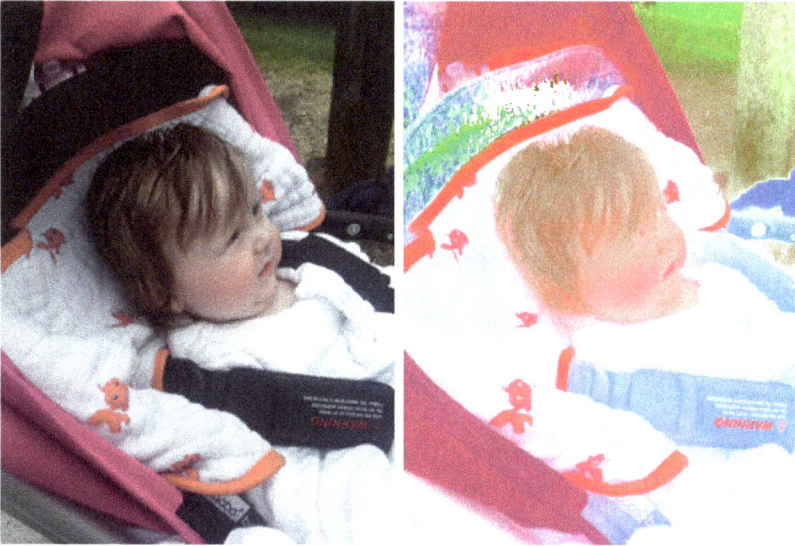

Fig. 4.8 Colour image and its chrominance HS-map with constant intensity I = 85.

4.4.2   Colour thresholding

The simplest colour binary (or foreground-background) segmentation can be performed by thresholding Cartesian distances, $d(\mathbf{q}, \mathbf{q_f})$, from each pixel-wise RGB vector, $\mathbf{q} = [q_R, q_G, q_B]$, to a colour $\mathbf{q_f} = [q_{R:f}, q_{G:f}, q_{B:f}]$, defining the foreground object:

$$g_m(\mathbf{s}) = \begin{cases} 1 & \text{if } d(\mathbf{q}, \mathbf{q_f}) \leq \tau \\ 0 & \text{otherwise} \end{cases}$$

where τ is a given threshold and

$$d(\mathbf{q}, \mathbf{q_f}) = \sqrt{(q_R - q_{R:f})^2 + (q_G - q_{G:f})^2 + (q_B - q_{B:f})^2}$$

The HSI colour space allows for intensity-independent segmentation taking account of chrominance differences between each pixel-wise HSI vector, $\mathbf{q} = [q_H, q_S, q_I]$, and the foreground colour, $\mathbf{q_f} = [q_{H:f}, q_{S:f}, q_{I:f}]$. The polar HS-coordinates result in the following Cartesian distance between the points, $\mathbf{q} = [q_H, q_S]$ and $\mathbf{q_f} = [q_{H:f}, q_{S:f}]$, in the HS-plane (see its derivation in Example 4.4):

$$d(\mathbf{q}, \mathbf{q_f}) = \sqrt{q_S^2 + q_{S:f}^2 - 2q_S q_{S:f} \cos(q_H - q_{H:f})} \qquad (4.1)$$

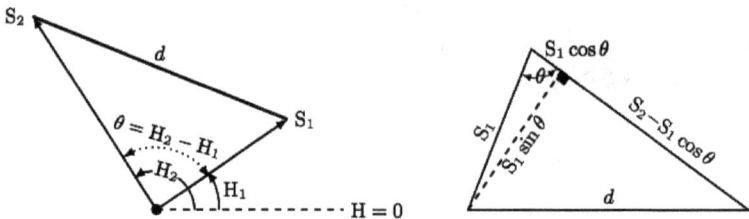

Fig. 4.9   Cartesian distance d in the chrominance plane with the polar (H,S)-coordinates: $H \in [0, 360°)$; $S \in [0, 1]$.

Example 4.4 (Chrominance distance). *Figure 4.9 illustrates deriving the point-to-point Cartesian distance in the chrominance HS-plane. The distance d between two points, $[H_1, S_1]$ and $[H_2, S_2]$, follows from the triangle with two sides of length S_1 and S_2, respectively, and the angle, $\theta = H_2 - H_1$, between these sides. The third side, defining the goal distance, d, is the hypotenuse of the right triangle with the legs of length $S_1 \sin \theta$ and $S_2 - S_1 \cos \theta$, respectively. Therefore,*

$$d^2 = (S_1 \sin \theta)^2 + (S_2 - S_1 \cos \theta)^2 = S_1^2 + S_2^2 + 2S_1 S_2 \cos \theta$$

4.4.3 *Multi-region segmentation*

In a more general case, segmenting an input image into J ROIs of distinct colours, $J \geq 2$, is guided by its dominant colours found by *vector quantisation*. This quantisation maps the input 3D RGB or HSI colour space or its 2D chrominance HS-plane onto a set of J dominant, or characteristic colours, one per ROI. Generally, the quantisation results in a *codebook* of characteristic *codewords*. In application to colours, the codebook is often called a *colour gamut*, or a *palette*. The codebook is either pre-selected, or adapted to an input image by analysing its colour vectors. One of common vector quantisation schemes in Algorithm 8 iteratively doubles the number of codewords until reaching a prescribed codebook size.

Algorithm 8 Iterative vector quantisation.

Input: an input vector set; a codebook size J; a factor ϵ; $0 < \epsilon < 1$.
Initialisation: $t = 0$; $J_0 = 1$:
    Build a single codeword $\mathbf{q}_{1:0}$ from all input vectors.
for $t \leftarrow t + 1$ **until** $(J_t = 2J_{t-1}) \leq J$ **do**
    Double each previous codeword, $q_{j:t-1}$; $j = 1, \ldots, J_{t-1}$:
    (1) Form two initial codewords by multiplicative shifts:

$$\mathbf{q}_{\text{pr}:j:t} = (1 - \epsilon)\mathbf{q}_{j:t-1} \text{ and } \mathbf{q}_{\text{pr}:j+J_{t-1}:t} = (1 + \epsilon)\mathbf{q}_{j:t-1}$$

    or shifts to and from the farthest signal, $\widehat{\mathbf{q}}_{j:t-1}$, in the current ROI j:

$$\mathbf{q}_{\text{pr}:j:t} = (1 - \epsilon)\mathbf{q}_{j:t-1} + \epsilon\widehat{\mathbf{q}}_{j:t-1} \text{ and}$$

$$\mathbf{q}_{\text{pr}:j+J_{t-1}:t} = (1 + \epsilon)\mathbf{q}_{j:t-1} - \epsilon\widehat{\mathbf{q}}_{j:t-1}.$$

    (2) Iteratively build the final J_t codewords:

        while the codewords continue to change **do**

            (2.1) Assign each input vector to its closest codeword.

            (2.2) Update the codewords using their assigned vectors.

        end while
end for

Let $d(\mathbf{q}, \mathbf{q}^\circ)$ be a distance between the colour vectors $\mathbf{q}$ and $\mathbf{q}^\circ$. A codebook $\mathbf{B}_J = \{\mathbf{q}_j : j = 1, \ldots, J\}$ with J codewords is often built by minimising the total squared distance, $D(\mathbf{B}_J)$, between the input vectors and their closest codewords:

$$D(\mathbf{B}_J) = \sum_{\mathbf{s} \in \mathbb{S}} \min_{j=1,\ldots,J} d^2(\mathbf{g}(\mathbf{s}), \mathbf{q}_j) \tag{4.2}$$

To segment an input image, $\mathbf{g}$, each pixel-wise vector, $\mathbf{g}(\mathbf{s})$, is assigned to the closest codeword. In other words, the obtained region map, $\mathbf{g}_\mathrm{m}$, contains labels of these codewords:

$$g_\mathrm{m}(\mathbf{s}) = \arg \min_{j=1,\dots,J} d(\mathbf{g}(\mathbf{s}), \mathbf{q}_j); \quad \mathbf{s} \in \mathbb{S}$$

The vector quantisation allows also to represent the entire original colour space with only J different colours and compress the original image by replacing each signal $\mathbf{g}(\mathbf{s})$ with the corresponding codeword:

$$\mathbf{g}_\mathrm{cmpr} = \big(\mathbf{g}_\mathrm{cmpr}(\mathbf{s}) = \mathbf{q}_{g_\mathrm{m}(\mathbf{s})} : \mathbf{s} \in \mathbb{S}; \ \mathbf{q}_j \in \mathbb{B}_J; \ j = 1, \dots, J\big)$$

For simplicity, each iteration t of Algorithm 8 finds at Step 2 only a local minimum of the distance of Eq. (4.2) with a fast-converging block relaxation. The latter iterates two successive steps: classifying the input vectors into J_t classes, one per codeword (Step 2.1) and building the J_t updated codewords from the vectors of each class (Step 2.2) At each step the distance either decreases, or does not change. The block relaxation terminates after the distances between the codewords at Steps 2.1 and 2.2 become zero or at least reasonably small.

Example 4.5 (Updating the RGB codewords). *The RGB colour vectors, $\mathbf{q} = [q_\mathrm{R}, q_\mathrm{G}, q_\mathrm{B}]^\mathsf{T}$ and $\mathbf{q}^\circ = [q_\mathrm{R}^\circ, q_\mathrm{G}^\circ, q_\mathrm{B}^\circ]^\mathsf{T}$, are often compared with the conventional squared Cartesian distance:*

$$d^2(\mathbf{q}, \mathbf{q}^\circ) = (q_\mathrm{R} - q_\mathrm{R}^\circ)^2 + (q_\mathrm{G} - q_\mathrm{G}^\circ)^2 + (q_\mathrm{B} - q_\mathrm{B}^\circ)^2$$

Let $\mathbb{S}_j$ denote a subset of $S_j = |\mathbb{S}_j|$ pixels supporting colours, $\mathbf{g}(\mathbf{s})$, associated with the jth-codeword. The total squared distance

$$D_j(\mathbf{q}) = \sum_{\mathbf{s} \in \mathbb{S}_j} d^2(\mathbf{g}(\mathbf{s}), \mathbf{q})$$

between these signals and an arbitrary vector $\mathbf{q}$ is minimised by the mean vector, $\mathbf{q}_j = \frac{1}{S_j} \sum_{\mathbf{s} \in \mathbb{S}_j} \mathbf{g}(\mathbf{s})$. This can be derived by equating to zero the first derivative of the scalar function $D_j(\mathbf{q})$ by its vector variable $\mathbf{q}$:

$$\frac{\partial}{\partial \mathbf{q}} D_j(\mathbf{q}) = -2 \sum_{\mathbf{s} \in \mathbb{S}_j} (\mathbf{g}(\mathbf{s}) - \mathbf{q}) = 0$$

Example 4.6 (Updating the HS codewords). *Likewise, the minimiser, $\mathbf{q}_j = [q_{\mathrm{H}:j}, q_{\mathrm{S}:j}]$, of the total squared HS-distance of Eq. (4.1)*

$$\mathbf{q}_j = \arg \min_{\mathbf{q}} \sum_{\mathbf{s} \in \mathbb{S}_j} \big(q_{\mathrm{S}:\mathbf{s}}^2 + q_\mathrm{S}^2 - 2 q_{\mathrm{S}:\mathbf{s}} q_\mathrm{S} \cos (q_{\mathrm{H}:\mathbf{s}} - q_\mathrm{H})\big)$$

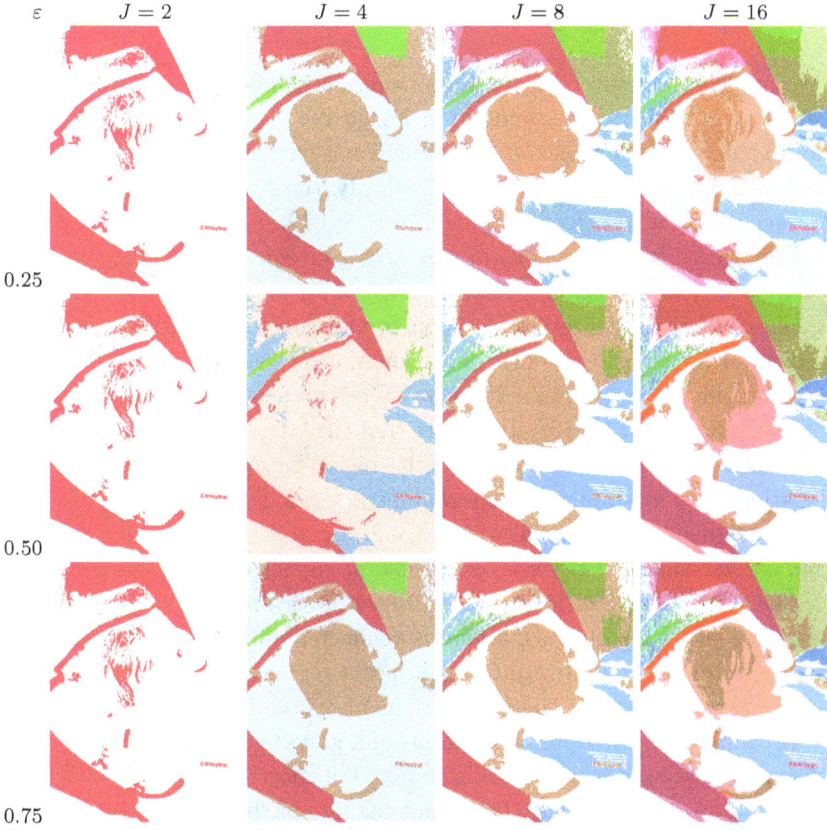

Fig. 4.10   Chrominance-based segmentation with different codebook sizes, J, and shift factors, ϵ (the obtained region labels are visualised with their codewords; note that due to local minimisation the codewords and regions may differ for different factors ϵ).

for a chrominance subset, $(\mathbf{g}(\mathbf{s}) = [q_{\mathrm{H:s}}, q_{\mathrm{S:s}}] : \mathbf{s} \in \mathbb{S}_j)$, *has the components:*

$$q_{\mathrm{H}:j} = \tan^{-1}\left(\frac{V_{\sin:j}}{V_{\cos:j}}\right) \quad \text{and} \quad q_{\mathrm{S}:j} = V_{\cos:j}\cos(q_{\mathrm{H}:j}) + V_{\sin:j}\sin(q_{\mathrm{H}:j})$$

where

$$V_{\sin:j} = \frac{1}{|\mathbb{S}_j|}\sum_{\mathbf{s}\in\mathbb{S}_j} q_{\mathrm{S:s}}\sin(q_{\mathrm{H:s}}) \quad \text{and} \quad V_{\cos:j} = \frac{1}{|\mathbb{S}_j|}\sum_{\mathbf{s}\in\mathbb{S}_j} q_{\mathrm{S:s}}\cos(q_{\mathrm{H:s}})$$

Figure 4.10 illustrates segmentation and compression of the colour image on Fig. 4.8 by applying Algorithm 8 to the chrominance HS-vectors.

4.5   Labelling connected regions

The simplest "grassfire", or wave propagation is labelling connected black regions in a binary black-and-white image by searching sequentially for the first unlabelled pixel and extending each current label to the nearest unlabelled neighbours (Fig. 4.11). Obviously, the 4- and 8-neighbourhoods produce different regions exemplified in Fig. 4.12.

Uniform connected regions in a greyscale or colour image can be specified by a logical condition, called an *uniformity predicate*, being true if all signals in a region possess a common property. In the simplest case, the predicate restricts the absolute deviation of grey levels or colours in a connected region from a certain given value or the absolute signal deviations between the nearest lattice sites. Note that the latter predicate does not restrict their total deviation over the entire region because small neighbouring deviations may accumulate. The total intra-region signal variations have to be constrained in a non-local manner, e.g., by limiting absolute deviations from a given signal or between most distant signals over the region.

The labelling is considered valid if each lattice site is labelled and belongs to a single region; each region is connected and uniform w.r.t. a chosen predicate, and merging any two adjacent regions creates a non-uniform region. However, not all these conditions may hold in practice.

Growing connected uniform regions of a greyscale or colour image from a few given seeds (Algorithm 9) is simple, but mostly is very sensitive to a chosen uniformity predicate, i.e., small changes of the latter may considerably alter the regions found. Different seeds, types of pixel neighbourhoods, routes to find unlabelled pixels in the input image, and modes of exhausting the neighbours of each growing region may also result in very different region maps. Although the regions found are connected and uniform, both the number and locations of the seeds may be insufficient to obtain a region for every pixel. Moreover, if several seeds have been placed within an actually uniform area, the regions grown will have distinct labels.

Algorithm 9 Growing connected regions one-by-one from their seeds.

Initialisation: Manually or automatically defined seed pixels.

Region growth: Sequentially add a pixel to each current region when:

    (1) The pixel has not been assigned to another region.

    (2) The pixel is a neighbour of the current region.

    (3) Adding the pixel leaves the growing region uniform.

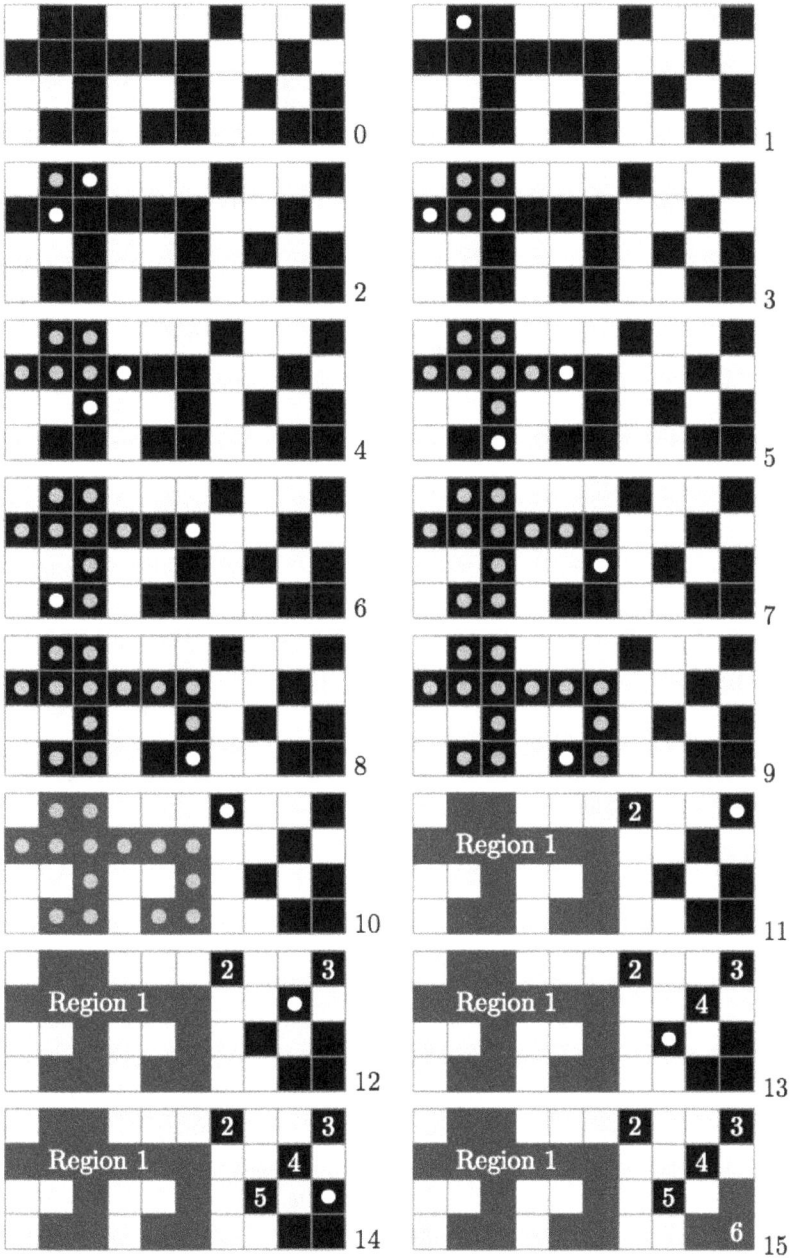

Fig. 4.11   4-connected regions by the grassfire algorithm: propagating (white dots) and already visited (grey dots) pixels at Steps 1–14 and the final region map (15).

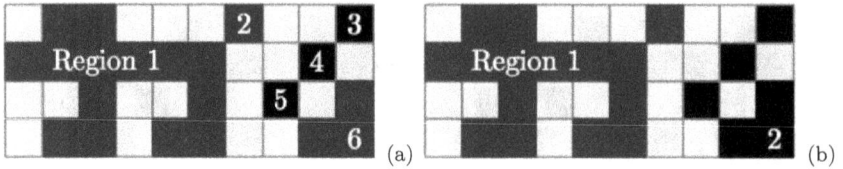

Fig. 4.12   Maps of six 4-connected (a) and two 8-connected (b) regions for the binary image in Fig. 4.11.

To escape manual selection, the seeds can be chosen automatically, e.g., the first unlabelled pixel. For a binary image with several connected components (foreground objects) such a choice is exemplified in Fig. 4.12. An input colour or greyscale image is initially transformed into a binary foreground-background image. The first foreground region begins from an arbitrary foreground pixel and grows while it has foreground neighbours to be added. Then each next region starts from an arbitrary and yet unlabelled foreground pixel.

Algorithm 10 performs region growing by labelling connected components in an input 2D image, $\mathbf{g} = (g(\mathbf{s}) : \mathbf{s} \in \mathbb{S})$. Given a desired K-neighbourhood, e.g., $K = 4$ or 8, the components are built by testing connectedness of each pair of the nearest K-neighbours with a certain uniformity predicate, $U(g(\mathbf{s}), g(\mathbf{s}'))$. If the pixels, $\mathbf{s}$ and $\mathbf{s}'$, belong to foreground in a binary image or support similar signals, $g(\mathbf{s})$ and $g(\mathbf{s}')$, in a greyscale or colour image, then this logical predicate is TRUE, and it is FALSE otherwise.

A *disjoint set*, or *union-find* data structure is efficient for storing and tracing equivalent labels, assigned to the output region map. At every step of region growing, each distinct ongoing, or candidate component is associated with its own disjoint set of labels. The set is indexed with its minimal label, each label in the set referencing to its index.

An input image is scanned sequentially, row-by-row and pixel-by-pixel in a row (such a route is usually called a "TV scan"). At the first pass, each current pixel, $\mathbf{s}$, of the goal region map, $\mathbf{g}_m = (g_m(\mathbf{s}) : \mathbf{s} \in \mathbb{S})$, is labelled in line with its connections to the nearest visited neighbours, i.e., to up to two or four backward connections for the 4- or 8-neighbourhood, respectively. The label, $g_m(\mathbf{s})$, depends on these connections as follows (the explanation below uses a modifiable reference $\rho(l)$ of each region label l to a disjoint set $\Lambda_{\rho(l)}$, containing the label l and indexed with $\rho(l)$):

Algorithm 10 Two-pass connected components labelling.

Input: a 2D binary, greyscale, or colour image, $\mathbf{g}$;

   a pairwise pixel uniformity predicate to test connectedness in $\mathbf{g}$;

   the neighbourhood type, e.g., 4 or 8.

Output: a map, $\mathbf{g}_m$, of connected components.

Initialisation: Empty collection of disjoint sets of labels assigned to the
   same component; zero region label l; $l = 0$.

Pass 1 (assigning one or more own distinct labels to each component):

For each successive image row and each pixel, $\mathbf{s}$, in the row **do**

   Test whether $g(\mathbf{s})$ can be connected to each of its backward neighbours.

   If no connection, begin a new candidate component:

      Increment the label l; $l \leftarrow l + 1$, and assign to the map, $g_m(\mathbf{s}) = l$.

      Form a single-element disjoint set, $\Lambda_l = \{l\}$, indexed with l.

      Refer the label l to the disjoint set Λ_l.

   else if only a single connection, propagate the relevant candidate:

      $g_m(\mathbf{s}) = \lambda$ if this candidate refers to the disjoint set Λ_λ.

   else if two or more connections, merge (if exist) all distinct backward
         candidates and propagate the merged candidate:

      Replace these distinct disjoint sets with their union $\Lambda_{l_{\min}}$ indexed
         with its minimal label, $l_{\min}$, to be propagated.

      $g_m(\mathbf{s}) = l_{\min}$, and refer all labels $\lambda \in \Lambda_{l_{\min}}$ to $l_{\min}$.

   end if

end for

Pass 2 (relabelling): Assign a unique label to each component in $\mathbf{g}_m$ by
   ordering the final disjoint sets and updating their references.

---

(1) (*New candidate*) If there is no backward connection, i.e., the predicate
   is FALSE for all the tested pixel pairs, a new candidate starts at $\mathbf{s}$.
   The ongoing label l is incremented, $l \leftarrow l + 1$, and assigned to the map,
   $g_m(\mathbf{s}) = l$, as well as a new disjoint set, $\Lambda_l = \{l\}$, with a single label, l,
   is created and referenced by this label, $\rho(l) = l$.

(2) (*Candidate propagation*) If $\mathbf{s}$ is connected to only a single backward neighbour, $\mathbf{s}'$, or all backward connections are to the same candidate, i.e., their labels refer to the same disjoint set, then this single candidate propagates: $g_\mathrm{m}(\mathbf{s}) = \rho\left(g_\mathrm{m}(\mathbf{s}')\right)$.

(3) (*Union propagation*) If two or more (for $K = 8$) backward connections are to different candidates, i.e., their labels refer to distinct disjoint sets, all these candidates are merged together and their union propagates from now on as a single candidate. The individual disjoint sets for the merged candidates are united into a set Λ_{l_min}, indexed by its minimal label, l_min; the latter is assigned to the map, $g_\mathrm{m}(\mathbf{s}) = l_\mathrm{min}$, and all the labels in Λ_{l_min} refer to this set, i.e., $\rho(\lambda) = l_\mathrm{min}$ for each $\lambda \in \Lambda_{l_\mathrm{min}}$.

The second pass replaces all the initial labels with their final references, $g_\mathrm{m}(\mathbf{s}) = \rho(g_\mathrm{m}(\mathbf{s}))$, to uniquely label each connected component. The final map is then relabelled to assign an ordered sequence of labels to all the components and, if necessary, remove too small components for "cleaning" the map.

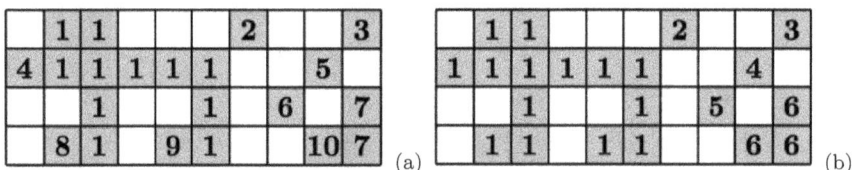

	1	1			2		3
4	1	1	1	1	1		5
		1		1	6		7
	8	1		9	1		10 7

(a)

	1	1			2		3
1	1	1	1	1	1		4
		1		1	5		6
	1	1		1	1		6 6

(b)

Fig. 4.13   Labelled 4-connected foreground regions of the binary image in Fig. 4.11 after Pass 1 (a) and Pass 2 (b) of Algorithm 10.

Example 4.7 (Labelling a binary image of size 4×10). *Figure 4.13 shows the region map for the binary image in Fig. 4.11 after the first and second passes of Algorithm 10. Just as in Fig. 4.11, the 4×10 image lattice $\mathbb{S}$ has the top-to-bottom oriented y-axis, $y = 0, 1, 2, 3$, and the left-to-right-oriented x-axis, $x = 0, 1, \ldots, 9$.*

    Scanning the first row, $y = 0$, produces three referenced disjoint singletons, $(\Lambda_1 = \{1\}; \rho(1) = 1)$; $(\Lambda_2 = \{2\}, \rho(2) = 2)$, and $(\Lambda_3 = \{3\}, \rho(3) = 1)$.

    Scanning the next row, $y = 1$, returns first, for $x = 0$, the self-referenced singleton $\Lambda_4 = \{4\}$ with $\rho(4) = 4$. Then for $x = 1$ the latter set is merged *with the set Λ_1, referenced by the upward connection. The merge results in the union $\Lambda_1 = \{1\}\bigcup\{4\}$ with the minimum index $1 = \min\{1,4\}$. The references to this union are updated as $\rho(1) = 1$ and $\rho(4) = 1$. The upward candidate component, referring to Λ_1, is then propagated along the row. The next new candidate is formed when $x = 8$, i.e., $\Lambda_5 = \{5\}$ with $\rho(5) = 5$.*

Scanning the next row, $y = 2$, only propagates the backward candidate referring to Λ_1 and then forms two new candidates, $\Lambda_6 = \{6\}$ with $\rho(6) = 6$ and $\Lambda_7 = \{7\}$ with $\rho_7 = 7$ for $x = 7$ and $x = 9$, respectively.

Scanning the last row, $y = 3$, creates sequentially three new candidates with the labels 8, 9, and 10 for $x = 1, 4,$ and 8, respectively, but just after incrementing the coordinate x merges the first two candidates with the same upward candidate referring to Λ_1 and the third candidate – with the candidate referring to Λ_7.

The final six disjoint sets and their references from the ten labels assigned to the map during the first pass are as follows:

λ	1	2	3	4	5	6	7	8	9	10
$\rho(\lambda)$	1	2	3	1	5	6	7	1	1	7
Λ_λ	$\{1,4,8,9\}$	$\{2\}$	$\{3\}$		$\{5\}$	$\{6\}$	$\{7,10\}$			
l°	1	2	3		4	5	6			

The second pass replaces the initial labels with their references to, or indices of the six final disjoint sets, $l = 1,2,3,5,6,7$, having been updated to the ordered successive labelling, $l^\circ = 1,2,\ldots,6$, of the components.

Example 4.8 (Labelling a binary image of size $327 \times 245 = 80115$). *Figure 4.14 presents four binary images of black foreground objects on a white background and their colour-coded 4-connected region maps on the 8-connected background, which were formed by Algorithm 10.*

The foreground objects of the input chrominance HS-map in Fig. 4.8 were obtained by selecting the chrominance vectors, $\mathbf{q}(\mathbf{s}) = [q_H(\mathbf{s}), q_S(\mathbf{s})]$, in a fixed interval $0 \leq d(\mathbf{q}(\mathbf{s}), \mathbf{q}_f) \leq \theta_f$ of absolute deviations from a given foreground chrominance, $\mathbf{q}_f = [q_{H:f}, q_{S:f}]$. The interval is defined by a given threshold, τ_f, and the HS-distance is specified in Eq. 4.1.

The region maps shown were cleaned by excluding all regions with areas less than 0.125% of the whole lattice. The chosen uniformity parameters $\mathbf{q}_f$ and τ_f for these binary images, together with the numbers, K_{ini} and K_{fin},

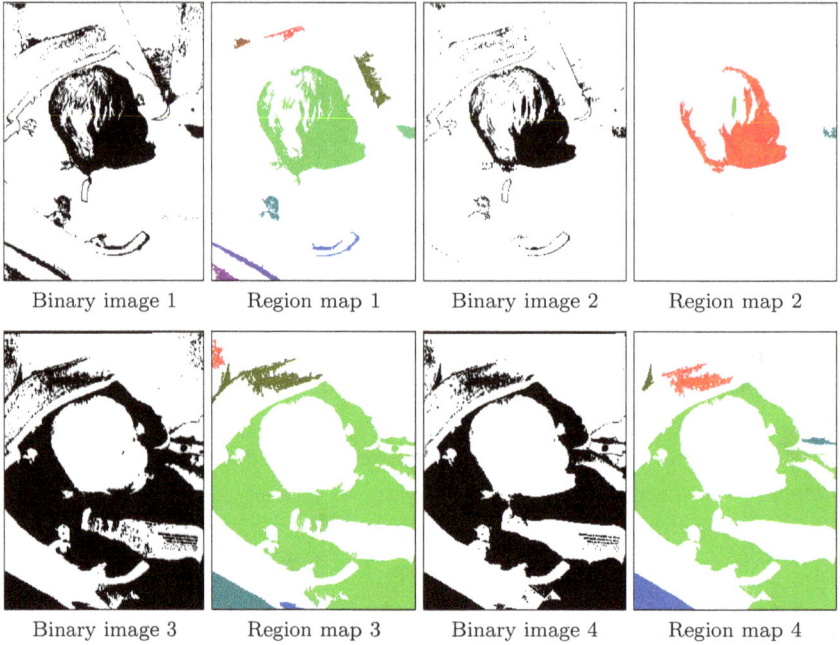

| Binary image 1 | Region map 1 | Binary image 2 | Region map 2 |

| Binary image 3 | Region map 3 | Binary image 4 | Region map 4 |

Fig. 4.14   Binarised HS-images with their colour-coded region maps for Example 4.8.

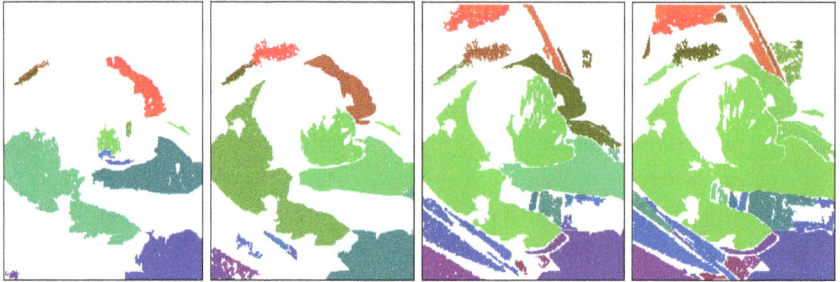

$K = 13$; $\tau_{\mathrm{nei}} = 0.005$ $K = 17$; $\tau_{\mathrm{nei}} = 0.010$ $K = 28$; $\tau_{\mathrm{nei}} = 0.015$ $K = 31$; $\tau_{\mathrm{nei}} = 0.020$

Fig. 4.15   Colour-coded region maps for Example 4.9.

of the obtained 4-connected regions before and after cleaning, respectively, and the relative area, $S_{\max}$, of the largest connected region in the maps $i = 1, 2, 3$ and 4 in Fig. 4.14 are listed below:

i	$q_{H:f}$	$q_{S:f}$	τ_f	K_{ini}	K_{fin}	S_{max}, %
1	90°	0.17	0.15	1003	11	10.4
2	90°	0.17	0.10	934	3	6.8
3	196°	0.03	0.15	787	5	36.5
4	196°	0.03	0.10	645	5	32.7

Example 4.9 (Labelling a colour HS-image of size $327 \times 245 =$ 80115). *Figure 4.15 presents four colour-coded 4-connected region maps formed by Algorithm 10. The uniformity predicate checks here whether the HS-distance of Eq. 4.1 between the nearest pairs of chrominance vectors, $\mathbf{q}(\mathbf{s}) = [q_H(\mathbf{s}), q_S(\mathbf{s})]$, is below a given threshold, τ_{nei}. The maps are cleaned by excluding all regions with areas less than 0.125% of the whole lattice. The cleaning retained 13 regions out of 46,057 for $\tau_{nei} = 0.005$; 17 regions out of 32,474 for $\tau_{nei} = 0.010$; 28 regions out of 23,247 for $\tau_{nei} = 0.015$, and 31 region out of 17,529 for $\tau_{nei} = 0.020$.*

The above examples demonstrate basic shortcomings of simple region models and segmentation techniques, in particular, a host of meaningless small regions and too unstable region shapes under even small changes of uniformity criteria. However, in practice even these techniques can sometimes produce meaningful results.

4.6   Questions and exercises

(1) Let the FP, TN, and FN areas of co-aligned segmented and true region maps be 120000, 5000, 100000, and 25000, respectively. Determine the segmentation accuracy, precision, and specificity.

(2) Which probabilistic models of object and background signals are assumed in the iterative threshold adaptation (Algorithm 5)?

(3) Suppose the object and background signals have different Gaussian p.d.f.s and the object–background threshold is adapted with Algorithm 5 or by estimating a mixture of two Gaussians with Algorithm 6. How are data processing steps of Algorithms 5 and 6 alike and how do they differ in this particular case?

(4) Convert the RGB vector, $\mathbf{q}_{rgb} = [126, 126, 0]$, into the HSI vector.

(5) Convert the HSI vector, $\mathbf{q}_{hsi} = [60°, 1, 84]$, into the RGB vector.

(6) Find the Cartesian distance between two points, $\mathbf{q}_{hs:1} = [60°, 1]$ and $\mathbf{q}_{hs:2} = [180°, 0.5]$, in the chrominance HS-plane.

(7) What is vector quantisation?

(8) How can vector quantisation be used for segmenting colour images?

(9) Find 8-connected dark regions of the binary image in Fig. 4.11 using the grassfire algorithm (Algorithm 9).

(10) Segment 8-connected dark regions of the binary image in Fig. 4.11 by using, as in Example 4.7, the two-pass connected components labelling (Algorithm 10).

Chapter 5

Morphological Filtering

Morphology in general is a study of structures or forms. Morphological processing of a binary image of foreground objects on some background uses a structure, or *structuring element* (SE) of a certain shape or applies several SEs to analyse and reshape the object. Fundamental morphological operations, such as, e.g., *erosion, dilation, closing*, and *opening* in Fig. 5.1, are non-linear MWTs with the SEs as the windows. Specific sequences of these operations may decompose a complex shape into important major and unimportant minor components, separate these groups to reveal essential properties of the object, and exclude its inessential parts. Most of the binary morphological operations can be extended onto greyscale images.

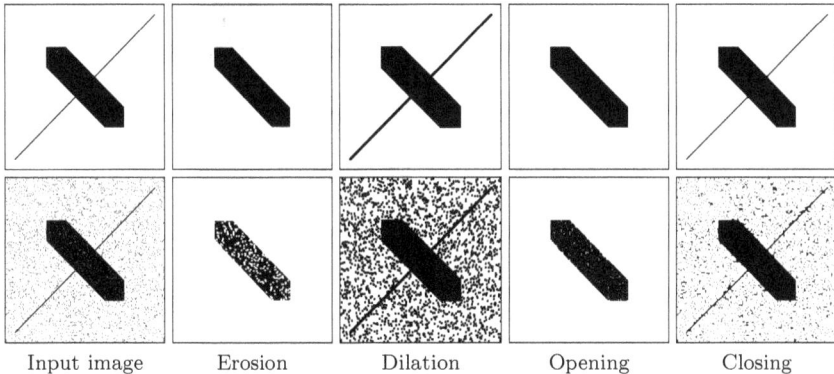

| Input image | Erosion | Dilation | Opening | Closing |

Fig. 5.1   Morphological processing with a square 3×3 SE.

What will you find here? This chapter outlines both the binary (Section 5.1) and greyscale (Section 5.2) morphology. Sections 5.1.1 – 5.1.5 will present the binary SEs and binary erosion, dilation, opening, and closing operations, together with internal, external, and morphological gradients. A combined hit-and-miss transformation, which accounts for both an object and its background to detect specific local shapes and closely resembles non-linear filtering of Chapter 3, will be described in Section 5.1.6.

Greyscale morphological transformations mostly affect visual appearances, rather than shapes of objects in an input image, and extend in part the maximum and minimum filters described in Chapter 3. Sections 5.2.1 – 5.2.3 detail the greyscale SEs and fundamental greyscale erosion, dilation, opening, and closing, together with their relations to conventional non-linear filters. Section 5.2.4 will describe top-hat and dual top-hat image transforms revealing local extremal points of a 3D surface of grey levels.

5.1   Binary morphology

In this case unit (1) and zero (0) labels of a binary image always relate to object (foreground) and background, respectively. Both the regions may be disjoint, and their actual greyscale or colour visualisation is of no concern: e.g., a dark object on a bright background or a bright object on a dark background, as in Fig. 5.2, are equivalent. For definiteness, all further examples in this section will show the dark objects on the bright backgrounds.

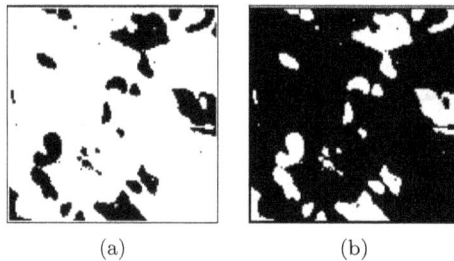

(a)   (b)

Fig. 5.2   Bright (a) / dark (b) background (label 0) vs. dark / bright object (label 1).

Each morphological operation moves an SE across an input image to check at each position to what extent the SE corresponds to image labels.

5.1.1   *Structuring element*

The SE is a relatively small probe or template, characterised by its size, shape, and origin. This template is defined with either a rectangular matrix of zero and unit elements where all zeros are ignored and the origin is specified, or a list of coordinate offsets of the unit elements w.r.t. the origin.

The SE size is either the matrix dimensions, or the list length, respectively, and the SE shape is a spatial pattern of its unit elements. Generally, the *origin* with zero offset, $(0,0)$, can be at any matrix zero and unit element or even outside the matrix.

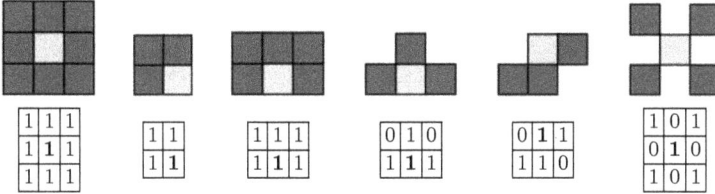

Fig. 5.3   SEs (with light-grey origins) specified by offsets in Table 5.1 and corresponding matrices of zeros and ones with boldfaced origins).

Table 5.1   Coordinate offsets for the SEs in Fig. 5.3 (left-to-right).

SE	J	List $\mathbb{N} = \{\boldsymbol{\nu}_j = (\xi_j, \eta_j) : j = 1, \ldots, J\}$
1	9	$\{(-1,-1), (0,-1), (1,-1), (-1,0), (0,0), (1,0), (-1,1), (0,1), (1,1)\}$
2	4	$\{(-1,0), (0,0), (-1,1), (0,1)\}$
3	6	$\{(-1,0), (0,0), (1,0), (-1,1), (0,1), (1,1)\}$
4	4	$\{(-1,0), (0,0), (1,0), (0,1)\}$
5	4	$\{(-1,-1).(0,-1), (0,0), (1,0)\}$
6	5	$\{(-1,-1), (1,-1), (0,0), (-1,1), (1,1)\}$

Example 5.1 (Symmetric and asymmetric SEs). *Figure 5.3 shows six simple SEs determined by centre-symmetric or asymmetric 3×3, 2×3, and 2×2 $(0,1)$-matrices or by corresponding lists of coordinate offsets of their unit elements in Table 5.1. The symmetric SE (#1 or #6 in Table 5.1) does not change if signs of its coordinate offsets are inverted.*

When the SE origin is positioned at location **s** in an input image, each unit SE component with offset $\boldsymbol{\nu}$ relates to the location $\mathbf{s} + \boldsymbol{\nu}$ or $\mathbf{s} - \boldsymbol{\nu}$, depending on a particular morphological operation. The output of the latter is determined by *fitting* or *hitting* an image object with unit components of the SE (Fig. 5.4).

Definition 5.1 (SE fitting and hitting). *The SE fits an input image if each unit SE element co-aligns with the unit (object) label.*

The SE hits or intersects an input image if at least one of unit SE components co-aligns with the unit (object) label.

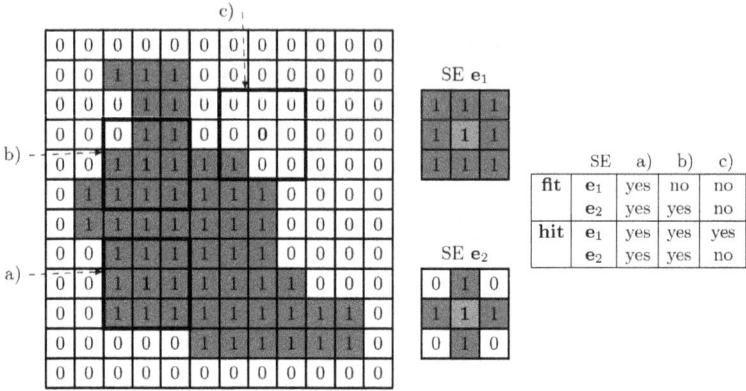

Fig. 5.4   Image hitting and fitting with 3×3 square and cross-like SEs.

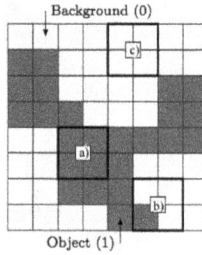

Fig. 5.5   Probing square 2×2 neighbourhoods at locations of fitting (a); hitting (b), and neither fitting, nor hitting the object (c).

Let $\mathbb{N} = \{\boldsymbol{\nu}_j : j = 1, \ldots, J\}$ denote a list of coordinate offsets for unit components of a certain SE of size J. After the SE is placed at an output location, $\mathbf{s}$, the morphological operation tests the corresponding input area, $\mathbb{A}_{\mathbf{s}:+} = \{\mathbf{s} + \boldsymbol{\nu} : \boldsymbol{\nu} \in \mathbb{N}\}$ or $\mathbb{A}_{\mathbf{s}:-} = \{\mathbf{s} - \boldsymbol{\nu} : \boldsymbol{\nu} \in \mathbb{N}\}$, in order to determine whether the SE fits, or hits, or neither fits, nor hits this area. The output location, $\mathbf{s}$, gets the unit (object) label, if testing the input area is successful, and zero label otherwise, as illustrated in Figs. 5.5 and 5.6.

5.1.2   Erosion

Definition 5.2. *Erosion, $\mathbf{g} \ominus \mathbf{e}$, of an input binary image, $\mathbf{g}$, with a SE, $\mathbf{e}$, produces the output binary image, $\tilde{\mathbf{g}} = \mathbf{g} \ominus \mathbf{e}$, with unit labels at all locations, $\mathbf{s}$, where the SE with the origin at $\mathbf{s}$ fits the input, $\mathbf{g}$. The fitting for each $\mathbf{s}$ is tested over the input area $\mathbb{A}_{\mathbf{s}:+}$, i.e., by aligning the SE to the input.*

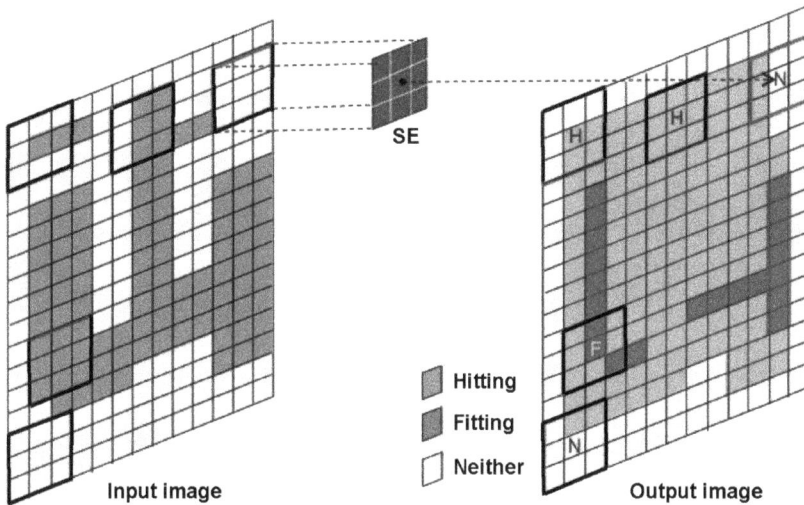

Fig. 5.6   Probing 3×3 square neighbourhoods at all inner input locations.

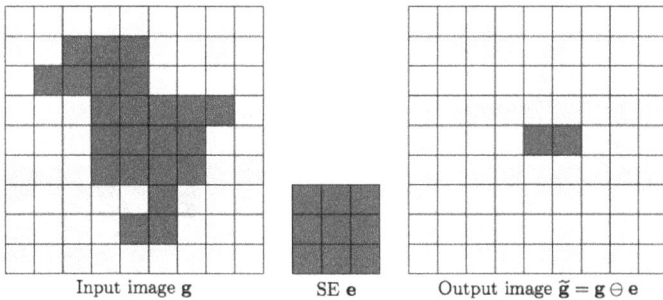

Fig. 5.7   Eroding a zero-padded 9×9 image with the square 3×3 SE.

Eroding with a small, e.g., 2×2 to 5×5, square SE shrinks an input object, or moves its boundaries to enlarge background, including holes and gaps, and removes minor details or imperfections caused by noise. The larger the SE, the more prominent the erosion. The successive erosions with a small SE are similar to a single erosion with a larger SE of the same shape: $\mathbf{g} \ominus \mathbf{e}' \approx (\mathbf{g} \ominus \mathbf{e}) \ominus \mathbf{e}$ where the SEs $\mathbf{e}$ and $\mathbf{e}'$ are of the same shape, but different size: $\mathbf{e}'$ is twice larger than $\mathbf{e}$.

Subtracting from an input image its erosion with the 3×3 square SE produces an **internal boundary**, or *internal gradient* of the object (Fig. 5.8):

$$\nabla_{\text{int:}\mathbf{g}} = \mathbf{g} - (\mathbf{g} \ominus \mathbf{e}) \tag{5.1}$$

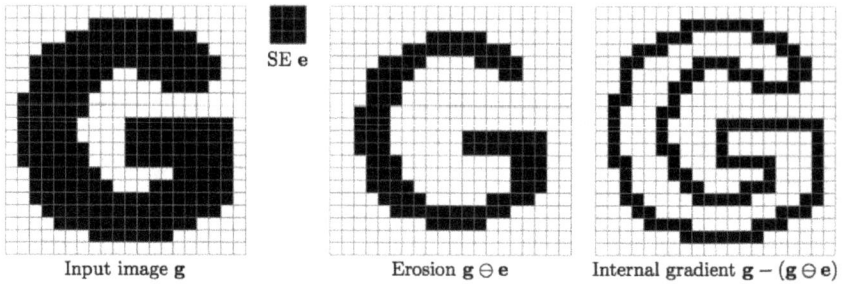

| Input image **g** | Erosion **g** ⊖ **e** | Internal gradient **g** − (**g** ⊖ **e**) |

Fig. 5.8   Internal gradient.

5.1.3   *Dilation*

Definition 5.3. *Dilation,* **g**⊕**e**, *of an input binary image,* **g**, *with a certain SE,* **e**, *produces the output binary image,* $\tilde{\mathbf{g}} = \mathbf{g} \oplus \mathbf{e}$, *with unit labels at all locations,* **s**, *where the SE with the origin at* **s** *hits the input,* **g**, *and with zero labels otherwise. The hitting for each* **s** *is tested over the input area* $\mathbb{A}_{\mathbf{s}:-}$, *i.e., by aligning the SE, rotated by* 180° *w.r.t. its origin, to the input.*

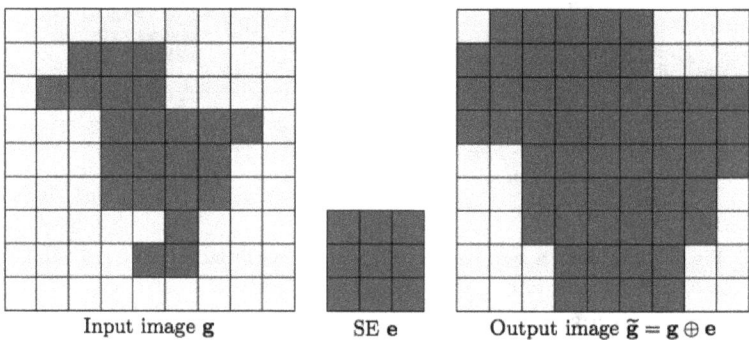

| Input image **g** | SE **e** | Output image $\tilde{\mathbf{g}} = \mathbf{g} \oplus \mathbf{e}$ |

Fig. 5.9   Dilating a zero-padded 9 × 9 image with the square 3 × 3 SE.

The dilation is opposite, or **dual** to the erosion: it extends an input object, i.e., moves boundaries of the object to shrink the background, in particular, fill in holes and gaps of the object. The dilation-erosion duality implies that these operations replace each other for a *complementary* image, **g**^{c}, such that the original labels $g(\mathbf{s}) = 0$ or 1 are converted into the opposite $g^{\text{c}}(\mathbf{s}) = 1$ or 0, respectively: $\mathbf{g} \oplus \mathbf{e} = (\mathbf{g}^{\text{c}} \ominus \mathbf{e}_{\text{rot}})^{\text{c}}$ where the SE $\mathbf{e}_{\text{rot}}$ is the

SE **e** rotated by 180°. The centre-symmetric SE **e** is rotation-invariant: $\mathbf{e}_{\mathrm{rot}} = \mathbf{e}$, and thus is the same in both the cases.

The duality allows for describing both the erosion and dilation in terms of fitting a binary image with a given SE. The erosion fits the SE into the object in the image, while the dilation fits the same symmetric SE or the rotated asymmetric SE into the object in the complementary image, i.e., into the background of the original image, followed by converting the output labels into their opposite values.

The larger the SE, the more prominent the dilation. The successive dilations with a small SE are similar to a single dilation with a larger SE of the same shape: $\mathbf{g} \oplus \mathbf{e}' \approx (\mathbf{g} \oplus \mathbf{e}) \oplus \mathbf{e}$ where the SEs **e** and **e**′ are of the same shape, but different size: **e**′ is twice larger than **e**.

Subtracting an input image from its dilation with the 3×3 square SE produces an **external boundary**, or *external gradient* of the object (Fig. 5.10):

$$\nabla_{\mathrm{ext:g}} = (\mathbf{g} \oplus \mathbf{e}) - \mathbf{g} \qquad (5.2)$$

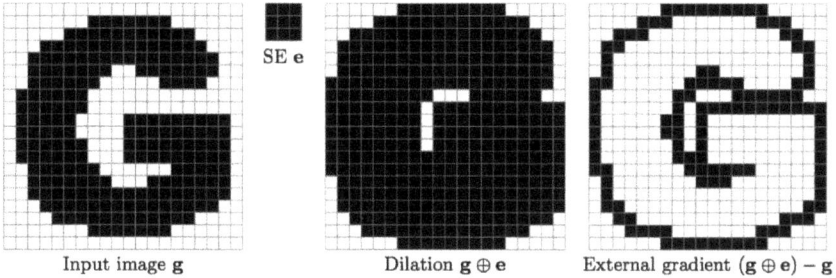

Fig. 5.10   External gradient.

Summing both the internal and external gradients of Eqs. 5.1 and 5.2 gives the entire *morphological gradient*, $\nabla_{\mathbf{g}} = \nabla_{\mathrm{ext:g}} + \nabla_{\mathrm{int:g}}$, being the difference between the dilated and eroded images (Fig. 5.11):

$$\nabla_{\mathbf{g}} = (\mathbf{g} \oplus \mathbf{e}) - (\mathbf{g} \ominus \mathbf{e}) \equiv \underbrace{(\mathbf{g} \oplus \mathbf{e}) - \mathbf{g}}_{\nabla_{\mathrm{ext:g}}} + \underbrace{\mathbf{g} - (\mathbf{g} \ominus \mathbf{e})}_{\nabla_{\mathrm{int:g}}} \qquad (5.3)$$

5.1.4   *Opening*

Definition 5.4. *Opening*, $\mathbf{g} \circ \mathbf{e}$ *of an input binary image,* **g**, *with a certain SE,* **e**, *is the erosion followed by the dilation:* $\mathbf{g} \circ \mathbf{e} = (\mathbf{g} \ominus \mathbf{e}) \oplus \mathbf{e}$.

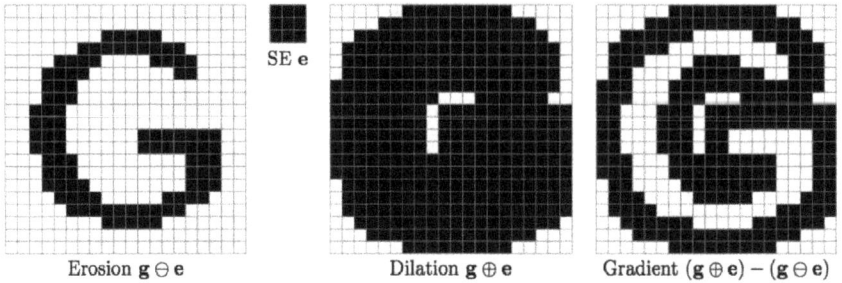

Fig. 5.11   Morphological gradient = dilation − erosion with the square 3×3 SE.

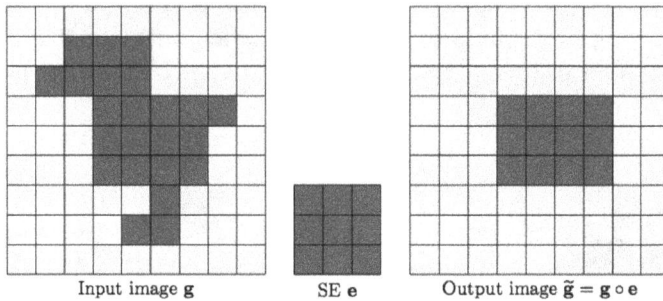

Fig. 5.12   Opening a zero-padded 9×9 image with the square 3×3 SE.

The opening got its name since it excludes fine details of an object within an image, in particular, making open gaps between parts of the object, which are connected by a thin bridge (Figs. 5.12 and 5.13). After opening a binary image, every object's part survived the erosion is restored to its original size by the dilation.

The opening is an *idempotent* operation: $(\mathbf{g} \circ \mathbf{e}) \circ \mathbf{e} = \mathbf{g} \circ \mathbf{e}$, i.e., once an image is opened, next openings with the same SE have no further effect.

5.1.5   *Closing*

Definition 5.5. *Closing,* $\mathbf{g} \bullet \mathbf{e}$ *of an input binary image,* $\mathbf{g}$, *with a certain SE,* $\mathbf{e}$, *is the dilation followed by the erosion:* $\mathbf{g} \bullet \mathbf{e} = (\mathbf{g} \oplus \mathbf{e}) \ominus \mathbf{e}$.

The closing fills holes and thin cracks in an object (Figs. 5.14 and 5.15). After closing a binary image, every object's part extended by the dilation is restored to its original size by the erosion.

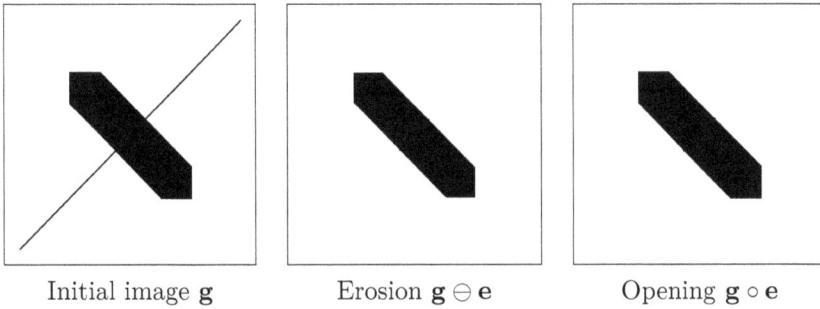

Initial image **g**   Erosion **g** ⊖ **e**   Opening **g** ∘ **e**

Fig. 5.13   Opening with the square 3 × 3 SE.

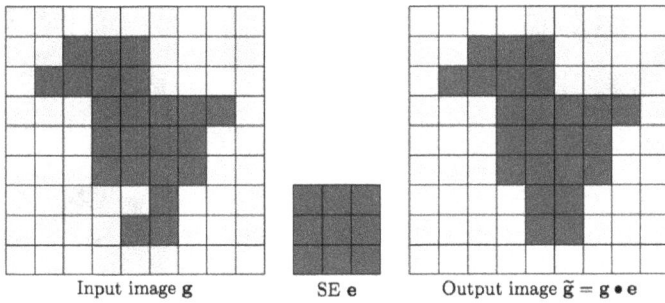

Input image **g**   SE **e**   Output image $\tilde{\mathbf{g}} = \mathbf{g} \bullet \mathbf{e}$

Fig. 5.14   Closing a zero-padded 9 × 9 image with the square 3 × 3 SE.

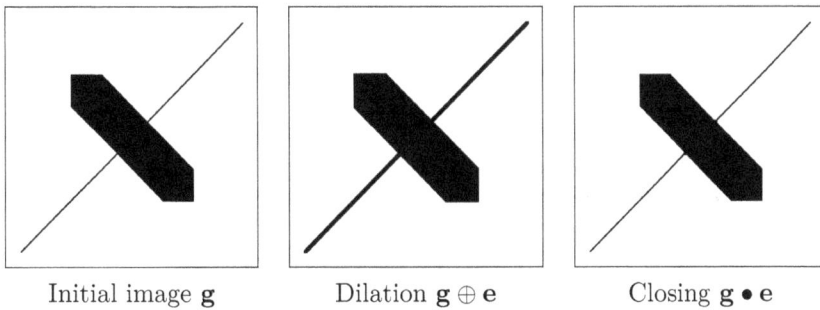

Initial image **g**   Dilation **g** ⊕ **e**   Closing **g** • **e**

Fig. 5.15   Closing with the square 3 × 3 SE.

Just as the opening, the closing is idempotent: once an image is closed, the next closings with the same SE have no further effect: $(\mathbf{g} \circ \mathbf{e}) \circ \mathbf{e} = \mathbf{g} \circ \mathbf{e}$, The closing and opening are dual operations. To close or open a binary image with a certain SE, one might open or close with the same

SE, respectively, the complementary image (i.e., the image with opposite labels: $1/0 \to 0/1$) and take the complement of the result.

The closing with a square or rounded SE excludes smaller holes, gaps, and boundary dents in contiguous parts of the input object, whereas the opening with the like SE excludes smaller isolated parts and thinner bridges between or protrusions of other parts (Figs. 5.16 and 5.17).

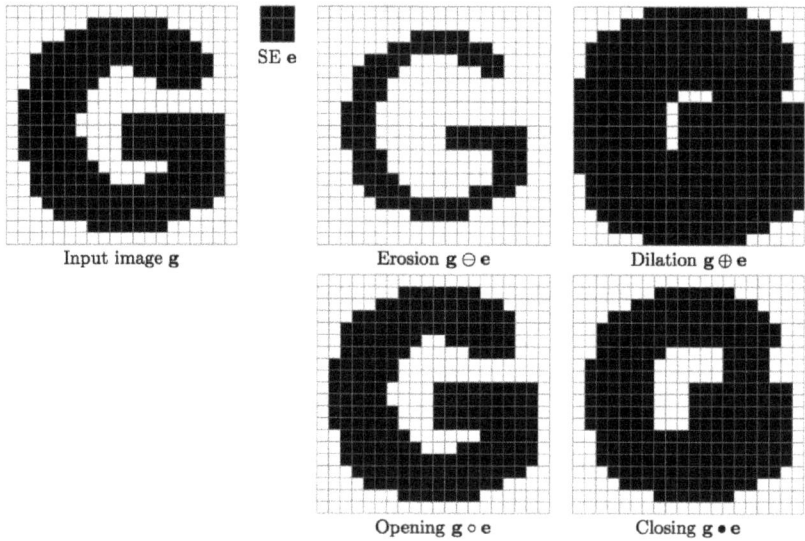

Fig. 5.16   Closing and opening with the square 3×3 SE.

Example 5.2 (Binary morphological operations). *Figure 5.18 illustrates the above transformations of two binarised HS-images in Fig. 4.14 with the square 3×3 SE.*

5.1.6   *Hit-and-miss transform*

Each binary object-background image $\mathbf{g}$ can be considered a set of its object sites: $\mathbb{O}_{\mathbf{g}} = \{\mathbf{s} : \mathbf{s} \in \mathbb{S}; g(\mathbf{s}) = 1\}$. Then its complement, $\mathbf{g}^{\mathrm{c}}$, is represented with a set of remaining sites, $\mathbb{O}_{\mathbf{g}}^{\mathrm{c}} = \mathbb{S} - \mathbb{O}_{\mathbf{g}} \equiv \{\mathbf{s} : \mathbf{s} \in \mathbb{S}; g(\mathbf{s}) = 0\}$, and many important morphological operations combine the MWT for erosion and/or dilation with conventional in the set theory intersection, $\mathbb{O} \cap \mathbb{O}'$,

opening ∘   opening ∘ + closing •

$$\underbrace{\ominus + \oplus}_{\circ} + \underbrace{\oplus + \ominus}_{\bullet}$$

$$\underbrace{\bullet}^{\bullet} \underbrace{\oplus + \ominus}_{} + \underbrace{\ominus + \oplus}_{\circ}$$

closing •   closing • + opening ∘

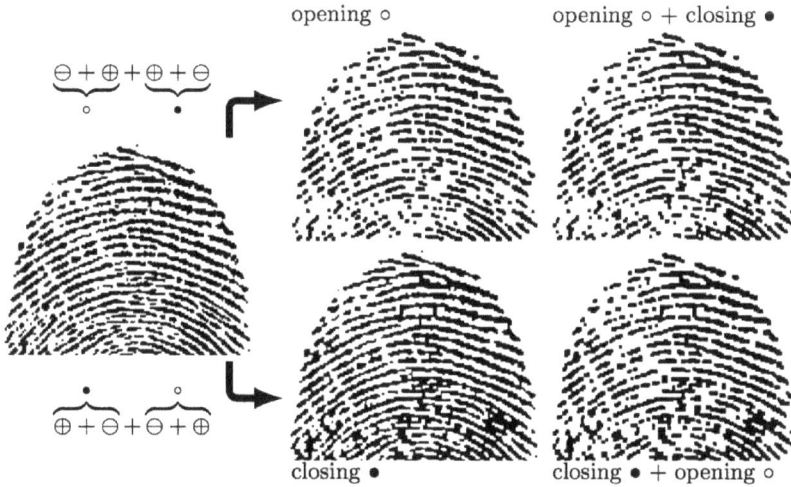

Fig. 5.17   Opening + closing vs. closing + opening with the square 3×3 SE.

and union, $\mathbb{O} \bigcup \mathbb{O}'$, of two sets:

$$\mathbb{O} \bigcap \mathbb{O}' = \{\mathbf{s} : \mathbf{s} \in \mathbb{O} \text{ AND } \mathbf{s} \in \mathbb{O}'\} \text{ and}$$
$$\mathbb{O} \bigcup \mathbb{O}' = \{\mathbf{s} : \mathbf{s} \in \mathbb{O} \text{ OR } \mathbf{s} \in \mathbb{O}'\}$$

These set representations have to be kept in mind when the operations $\bigcup$ and $\bigcap$ are applied directly to the images in order to simplify the notation.

Definition 5.6. *The hit-and-miss transform,* $\mathbf{g} \otimes (\{\mathbf{e}_1, \mathbf{e}_2\})$, *probes bilateral object-background relationships in a binary image simultaneously inside and outside the object by a moving pair of non-intersecting SEs,* $\{\mathbf{e}_1, \mathbf{e}_2\}$, *with the same origin:* $\mathbf{g} \otimes \{\mathbf{e}_1, \mathbf{e}_2\} = (\mathbf{g} \ominus \mathbf{e}_1) \bigcap (\mathbf{g}^c \oplus \mathbf{e}_2)$.

The hit-and-miss transform assigns the object label to a site $\mathbf{s}$ if and only if the SE $\mathbf{e}_1$ with the origin placed at that site fits inside the object AND the SE $\mathbf{e}_2$ with the origin at the same site fits outside the object (Fig. 5.19), i.e., fits the complementary object. Both the SEs do not intersect to make possible the simultaneous fittings to the object and its background.

The hit-and-miss transform is easier to consider an MWT with a single probing template that combines both the SEs and contains ones and zeros for the components of the SE $\mathbf{e}_1$ and $\mathbf{e}_2$, respectively. An output label at the site $\mathbf{s}$ is set to 1 only if the ones and zeros of the template with the origin at $\mathbf{s}$ match exactly the labels in the input image. Otherwise, this output label is set to 0. When a spatial pattern of the object (1) and background

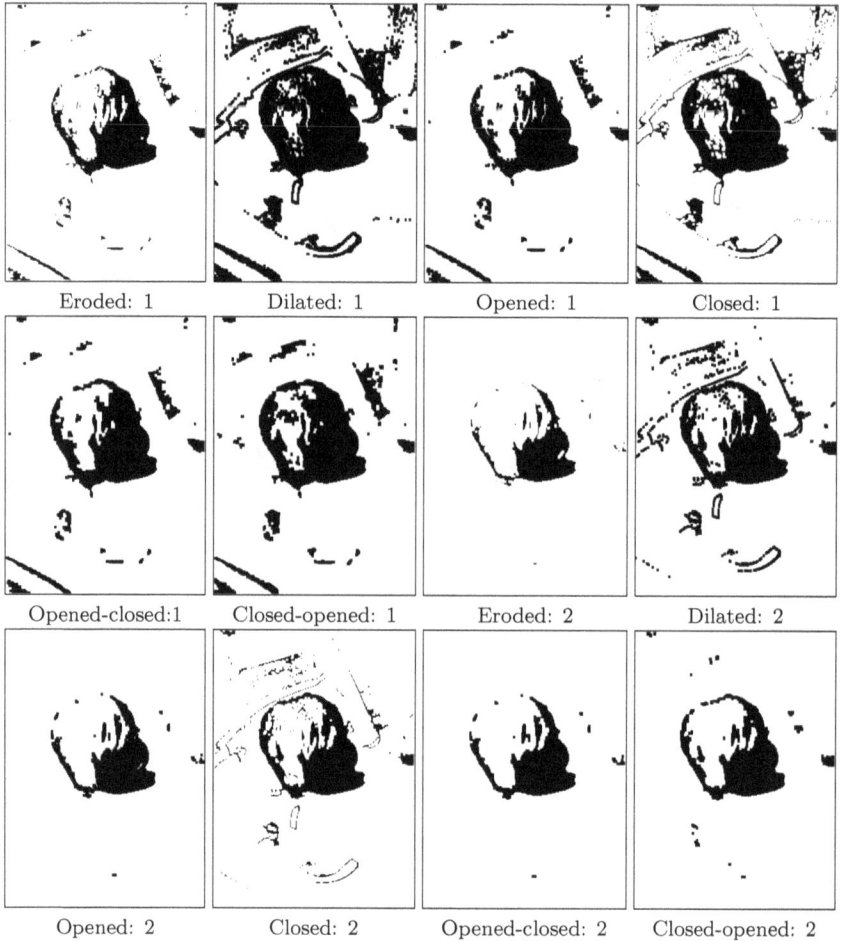

| Eroded: 1 | Dilated: 1 | Opened: 1 | Closed: 1 |

| Opened-closed:1 | Closed-opened: 1 | Eroded: 2 | Dilated: 2 |

| Opened: 2 | Closed: 2 | Opened-closed: 2 | Closed-opened: 2 |

Fig. 5.18   Morphological transformations of the binary images 1 and 2 in Fig. 4.14.

(0) labels in the template has a specific shape, the hit-and-miss transform detects places occupied by these local shapes in the entire input object.

5.2   Greyscale morphology

Greyscale morphology transforms visual appearance, rather than shape of depicted objects. Its fundamental operations, which are called, just as in the binary case, erosion, dilation, opening, and closing (Fig. 5.20), account for and produce grey levels.

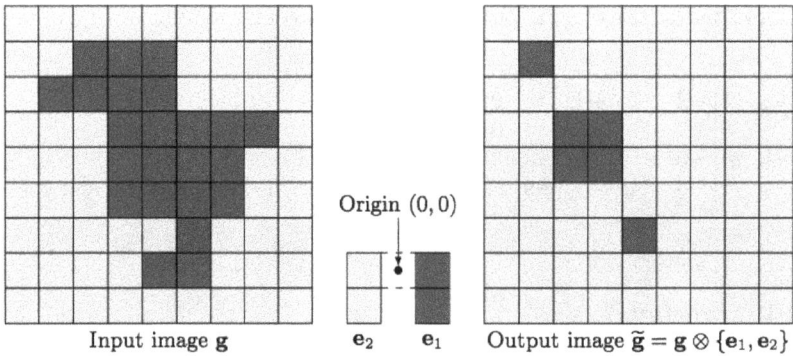

Fig. 5.19 Hit-and-miss transform of zero-padded input by the SEs $\mathbf{e}_1 = \{(1,0),(1,-1)\}$ and $\mathbf{e}_2 = \{(-1,0),(-1,-1)\}$ with the origin $(0,0)$.

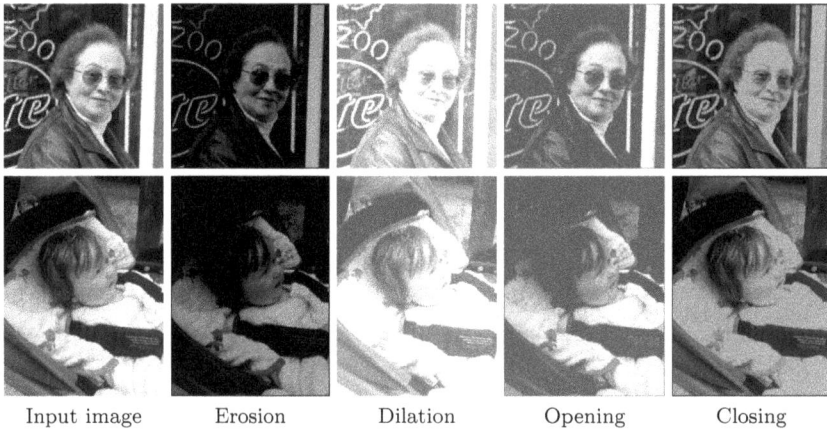

| Input image | Erosion | Dilation | Opening | Closing |

Fig. 5.20 Greyscale morphology with a 3×3 SE detailed in the text.

An image has non-negative integer grey levels, $g(\mathbf{s})$, at each lattice site, $\mathbf{s} \in \mathbb{S}$, whereas components of a SE on a certain set, $\mathbb{N}$, of relative coordinate offsets: $\mathbf{e} = (e(\boldsymbol{\nu}) : \boldsymbol{\nu} \in \mathbb{N})$, take any positive, negative, or zero integer values. Sometimes such a SE is called a *structuring function*.

Because zero grey levels are now significant, relative locations, which have to be excluded from a morphological operation, are indicated by other means, e.g., by using an explicit list of coordinate offsets, $\mathbb{N}$, defining the SE. The SEs with all zero components are called *flat*: $\mathbf{e} = (e(\boldsymbol{\nu}) = 0 : \boldsymbol{\nu} \in \mathbb{N})$.

Two symmetric 3×3 SEs, which are used in Fig. 5.20 and Examples 5.3 and 5.4 below have the same offsets $\mathbb{N} = \{\boldsymbol{\nu} = (\xi, \eta) : \xi = -1, 0, 1; \eta =$

$-1, 0, 1\}$ w.r.t. the origin, $(0,0)$, but different components:

ξ	1	1	-1	0	0	0	1	1	1	
η	-1	0	1	-1	0	1	-1	0	1	
$e(\xi, \eta)$	-10	-10	-10	-10	90	-10	-10	-10	-10	in Fig. 5.20
	-1	11	-1	-9	11	-9	-1	11	-1	in Examples 5.3 and 5.4

5.2.1 *Erosion*

Definition 5.7 (Greyscale erosion). *Greyscale erosion,* $\mathbf{g} \ominus \mathbf{e}$*, of an image,* $\mathbf{g}$*, with a certain SE,* $\mathbf{e}$*, assigns to each lattice site,* $\mathbf{s}$*, that the SE origin is aligned with, the minimum difference between the input grey level and the corresponding SE component:*

$$\tilde{g}(\mathbf{s}) = \min_{\boldsymbol{\nu} \in \mathbb{N}} \{g(\mathbf{s} + \boldsymbol{\nu}) - e(\boldsymbol{\nu})\} \qquad (5.4)$$

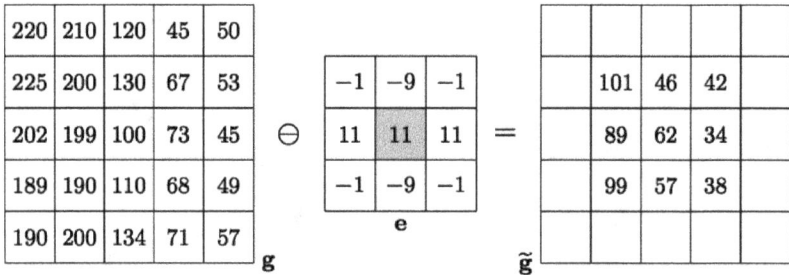

Fig. 5.21   Eroding the inner part of a 5×5 test image with a 3×3 SE.

Example 5.3 (Greyscale erosion). *Figure 5.21 details the greyscale erosion of the inner* 3×3 *part of an artificial input* 5×5 *image with a given symmetric* 3×3 *SE. When the SE origin is aligned with the location* $(x = 1, y = 3)$*, the output signal in accord with Eq. (5.4) is:*

$$\tilde{g}(1,4) = \min \left\{ \begin{array}{lll} 220 + 1, & 210 + 9, & 120 + 1, \\ 225 - 11, & 200 - 11, & 130 - 11, \\ 202 + 1, & 199 + 9, & 100 + 1 \end{array} \right\}$$
$$= \min\{221, 219, 121, 214, 189, 119, 203, 208, 101\} = 101$$

The greyscale erosion with a flat SE is equivalent to the least-rank, or minimum filtering, $\tilde{g}(\mathbf{s}) = \min\{g(\mathbf{s}+\boldsymbol{\nu}) : \boldsymbol{\nu} \in \mathbb{N}\}$, by the MWT with the SE window $\mathbb{N}$.

5.2.2 Dilation

Definition 5.8 (Greyscale dilation). *Greyscale dilation,* $\mathbf{g} \oplus \mathbf{e}$, *of an image,* $\mathbf{g}$*, with a certain SE,* $\mathbf{e}$*, assigns to each lattice site,* $\mathbf{s}$*, aligned with the origin of the SE, the maximum pairwise sum of the input grey level and the corresponding component of the SE rotated by 180° degrees:*

$$\tilde{g}(\mathbf{s}) = \max_{\boldsymbol{\nu} \in \mathbb{N}}\{g(\mathbf{s}-\boldsymbol{\nu}) + e(\boldsymbol{\nu})\} \tag{5.5}$$

The greyscale dilation is dual to the erosion.

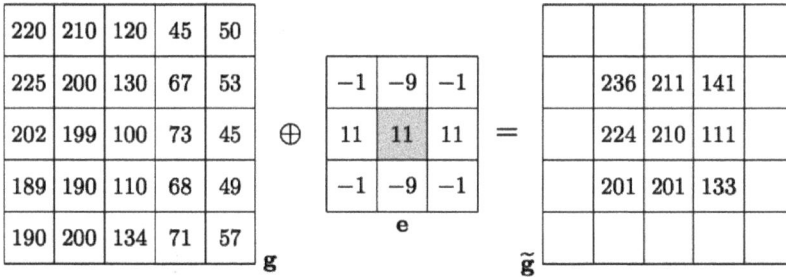

220	210	120	45	50
225	200	130	67	53
202	199	100	73	45
189	190	110	68	49
190	200	134	71	57

$\mathbf{g}$

$\oplus$

−1	−9	−1
11	11	11
−1	−9	−1

$\mathbf{e}$

$=$

	236	211	141	
	224	210	111	
	201	201	133	

$\tilde{\mathbf{g}}$

Fig. 5.22   Dilating the inner area of a 5 × 5 test image with a 3 × 3 SE.

Example 5.4 (Greyscale dilation). *Figure 5.22 details the greyscale dilation of the inner* 3×3 *part of an artificial input* 5×5 *image with a given symmetric* 3×3 *SE. When the SE origin is aligned with the location* $(1,3)$*, the output signal in accord with Eq. (5.5) is:*

$$\tilde{g}(1,4) = \max \left\{ \begin{array}{ccc} 220-1, & 210-9, & 120-1, \\ 225+11, & 200+11, & 130+11, \\ 202-1, & 199-9, & 100-1 \end{array} \right\}$$
$$= \max\{219, 201, 119, 236, 211, 141, 201, 190, 99\} = 236$$

The greyscale dilation with a flat SE is equivalent to the top-rank, or maximum filtering, $\tilde{g}(\mathbf{s}) = \max\{g(\mathbf{s}-\boldsymbol{\nu}) : \boldsymbol{\nu} \in \mathbb{N}\}$, by the MWT with the rotated by 180° SE window $\mathbb{N}$.

5.2.3   *Opening and closing*

The greyscale opening and closing are defined just as in the binary case: $\mathbf{g} \circ \mathbf{e} - (\mathbf{g} \ominus \mathbf{e}) \oplus \mathbf{e}$ and $\mathbf{g} \bullet \mathbf{e} = (\mathbf{g} \oslash \mathbf{e}) \oslash \mathbf{e}$, respectively. With an appropriate SE, these operations smooth an input image, i.e., blur its appearance, rather than only object boundaries, as the binary morphology.

| Input image | Erosion | Dilation | Opening | Closing |

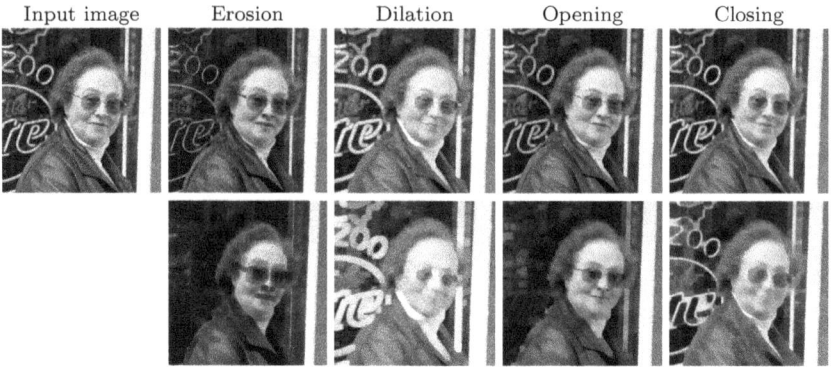

Fig. 5.23   Morphology with the flat 3×3 (upper row) and 7×7 (bottom row) SE.

| Input image | Erosion | Dilation | Opening | Closing |

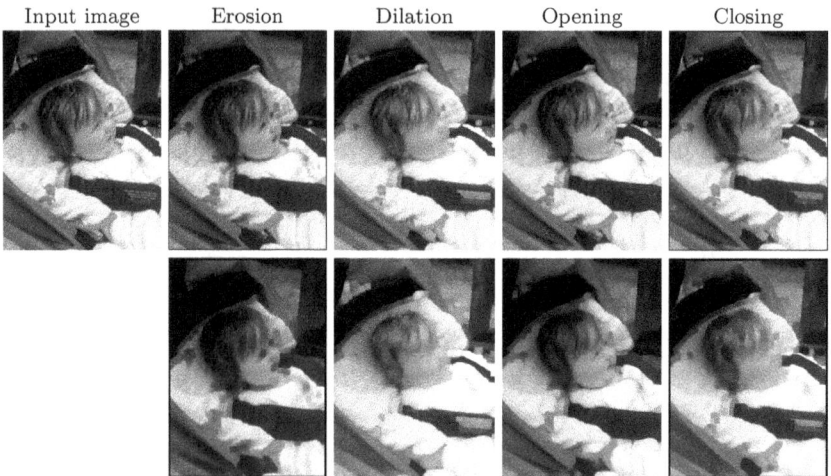

Fig. 5.24   Morphology with the flat 3×3 (upper row) and 7×7 (bottom row) SE.

As shown in Figs. 5.20, 5.23, and 5.24, the opening and closing tend to suppress small-scale input bright and dark details, respectively.

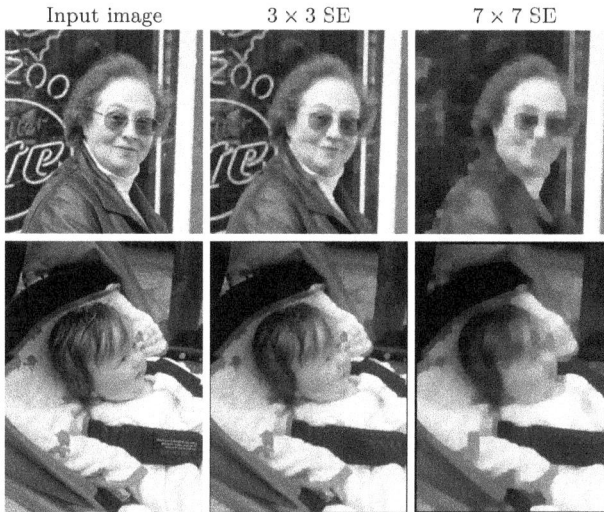

Input image   3 × 3 SE   7 × 7 SE

Fig. 5.25   Morphological smoothing with the flat 3 × 3 and 7 × 7 SE.

The greyscale erosion–opening and dilation–closing pairs resemble the like binary cases. The erosion decreases bright and increases dark areas, while the opening suppresses bright, but does not emphasise dark details. Conversely, the dilation decreases dark and increases bright areas, while the closing suppresses dark, but does not emphasise bright ones.

Opening followed by closing with the same flat SE results in *morphological smoothing* of bright and dark details, like median filtering (Fig. 5.25).

5.2.4   *Top-hat and dual top-hat transforms*

The greyscale opening, $\mathbf{g} \circ \mathbf{e}$, and closing, $\mathbf{g} \bullet \mathbf{e}$, make bright image signals darker and dark signals brighter, respectively. The *top-hat transform*, $\mathbf{g} - (\mathbf{g} \circ \mathbf{e})$, and its dual version, $(\mathbf{g} \bullet \mathbf{e}) - \mathbf{g}$, return only the signals portions removed. In other words, the top-hat transform returns a pattern of grey-level peaks and ridges, whereas the dual one returns a pattern of pits and valleys on the image lattice.

Example 5.5 (Patterns of local greyscale extrema). *Figure 5.26 shows results of the top-hat and dual top-hat transforms with the flat* 3×3 *square SE. These difference images have been negated, and their contrast was considerably enhanced for better visibility.*

Input image   Top-hat transform   Dual transform

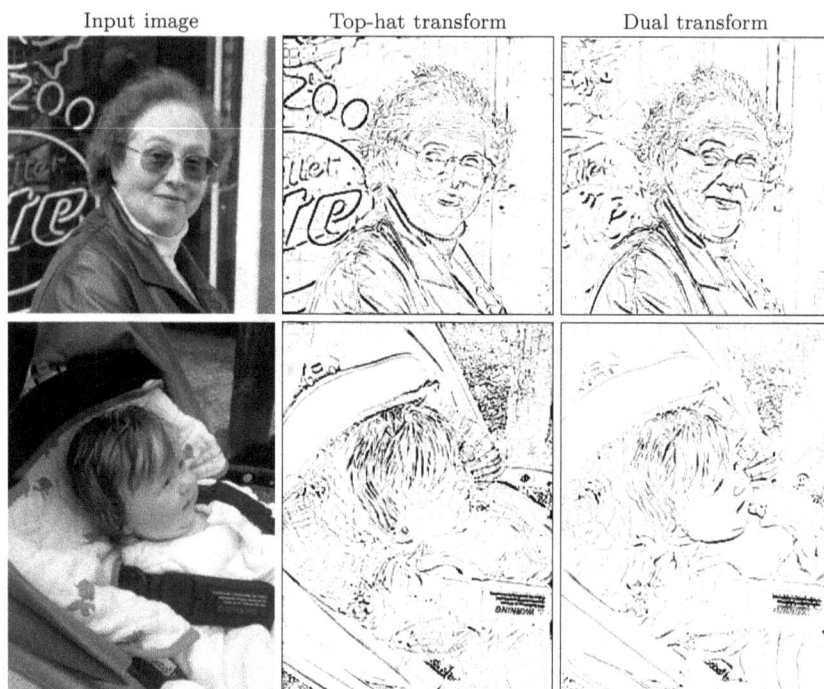

Fig. 5.26   Negated and enhanced top-hat and dual top-hat transforms.

5.3   Questions and exercises

(1) How do fitting and hitting an input image with a certain SE differ?
(2) How do the binary erosion and dilation differ w.r.t. aligning the SE to an input image?
(3) Let the 12×12 binary image in Fig. 5.4 have the left-to-right x- and bottom-up y-coordinate axes; $x, y = 0, 1, \ldots, 11$. Determine binary erosion and dilation outputs at locations $s_a = [3, 3]$ and $s_b = [3, 7]$ of the origin of the asymmetric 2×2 SE #2 in Table 5.1 and Fig. 5.3.
(4) What are the binary internal, external, and morphological gradients?
(5) What are the binary opening and closing?
(6) Which operations among the binary erosion, dilation, opening, and closing are idempotent?
(7) Which spatial pattern does the hit-and-miss transform detect?
(8) Which rank filters are extended by the greyscale morphology?
(9) Which properties do the top-hat and dual top-hat transforms detect?

Chapter 6

Deforming Boundaries to Segment

Extracting boundaries from objects or regions of interests (ROI) in images or videos is a fundamental problem in image processing. Objects can usually be extracted from an image using either a region or boundary separation paradigm. Direct region segmentation, based on (global) histogram information or (local) pixel neighbourhood properties, mostly fails for areas with complex colour patterns. Evolving fitted boundaries towards objects has become a more useful solution in many applications (notably, in medical image analysis) where ROIs have complex colour or grey-scale patterns (eliminating segmentation by direct pixel labelling), but well defined or expected shapes or edges (e.g., for human organs). The fitted boundary curve is typically formulated as a closed loop with established "inside" and "outside" positions, i.e., inner and outer areas.

The technique may require an initialisation close to the goal object(s) and some level of manual fitting of parameters governing the boundary evolution. Typically, a deformable boundary, a.k.a. an active contour (AC) or a snake, evolves under the influence of a set of (internal and external) forces, which constrain its shape and tend to maximise differences between distinctive signal features of its inner and outer areas.

Energy minimisation (or negative energy maximisation) frameworks are typically employed to converge ACs towards ROIs. Energy functions account for grey values and their gradients, as well as restrict either (*i*) curvature and spacing of discrete points for the ACs; or (*ii*) zeros of level sets defining geodesic ACs (GACs), or (*iii*) variations of control points in active shape models (ASMs). The latter are found from a given training database of ROIs and encode an expected shape of a ROI to be segmented.

What will you find here? Detailed descriptions of these segmentation tools are outside of the scope of this primer. Section 6.1 will outline AC formulations that allow for continuous and discrete implementations. In particular, Sections 6.1.1 and 6.1.2 will sketch explicit (parametric) and implicit (level-sets based) ACs, respectively. One popular level-sets-based AC, a.k.a. the Chan-Vese AC, in Section 6.1.2.2 uses a stopping function that evaluates differences between average grey values or colours of its inner and outer areas. Finally, Section 6.2 describes the ASM using statistical constraints of allowed contour deformations to define its internal energy.

6.1   Evolving an AC

Deformable boundaries are outline templates for regions to be found in the image. Fitting ACs to target ROIs is achieved through matching known traits that are encoded into the AC definition.

The first step is to define an energy function, which equates the fitting to energy minimisation. The energy functions are typically non-linear, and thus are optimised through a sequence of evolutionary steps. An optimal fit is found if the refinement process converges onto a single solution that cannot be improved further.

The energy functions are normally non-convex, thus iterative refinement risks convergence onto a nearest local minimum. To overcome this, the ACs should be initialised close to the target ROI. In some cases it is possible to do this automatically, otherwise it must be done manually.

6.1.1   *Parametric ACs*

The most popular examples of ACs to segment a target ROI are based on an explicitly defined parametric AC model (ACM). While there exist several formulations of the ACM, this primer focuses on convergence towards region edges, i.e., on the ACMs that perform edges selection for the purpose of segmentation.

The ACM is defined as a parametric curve, $\mathbb{B} = (\mathbf{b}(s) = [x(s), y(s)]^\mathsf{T} : s \in [0,1])$ where $\mathbf{b}(s)$ represents 2D image coordinates parameterised by the scalar s. The degree to which an evolving curve fits to the image ROI is defined by an energy function:

$$E = \int_0^1 [E_{\text{int}}(\mathbf{b}(s)) + E_{\text{ext}}(\mathbf{b}(s))] \, ds \equiv E_{\text{int}} + E_{\text{ext}} \qquad (6.1)$$

The energy function of Eq. (6.1) consists of two terms representing constraints imposed on the curve. The external energy, E_{ext}, integrates point-wise differences, $E_{\text{ext}}(\mathbf{b}(s))$, between certain inner and outer image properties w.r.t the curve and is minimised when the curve is located on the boundary of the ROI. The internal energy, E_{int}, integrates first- and second-order point-wise continuity and curvature characteristics, $E_{\text{int}}(\mathbf{b}(s))$, of the curve and enforces the desired smoothness and continuity of the curve.

6.1.1.1 *External AC energy*

The point-wise external energy across an AC $\mathbb{B}$ is often defined as:

$$E_{\text{ext}}(\mathbf{b}(s)) = -|\nabla_{g_\sigma}(\mathbf{b}(s))|^2 \tag{6.2}$$

where $g_\sigma(\mathbf{b}(s))$ are pixel-wise signals of a Gaussian-filtered image that the curve $\mathbb{B}$ is being fitted against. Filtering by convolving an original image, $\mathbf{g}$, with the Gaussian blur operator (Section 3.3.3) with the std σ is for noise reduction. Edges are found through the gradient filter (Section 7.1), ∇, quantifying gradients of grey values in both the x- and y-directions of the image. Within the ACM context, this type of energy is usually referred to as a *stopping function*, since it causes the AC to stop evolving at edges within the target image. The combined gradient extraction and Gaussian blur are most common means for removing high frequency noise, which may be associated to spurious edges.

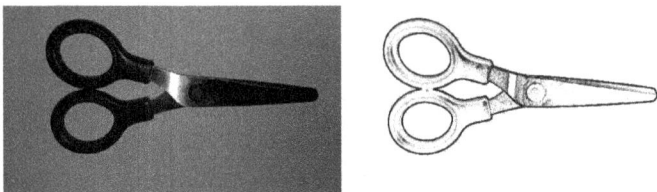

Fig. 6.1   Original image of scissors (left) and its grey-coded pixel-wise external energies, $E_{\text{ext}}(\mathbf{s})$ (the lowest and highest energies are encoded black and white, respectively).

6.1.1.2 *Internal AC energy*

The point-wise internal energy along an AC, $\mathbb{B}$, is usually defined by using the first and second derivatives of the curve w.r.t. its parameter s, the curvilinear arc length ($s \in [0,1]$):

$$E_{\text{int}}(\mathbf{b}(s)) = \alpha(s)\left|\frac{d\mathbf{b}(s)}{ds}\right|^2 + \beta(s)\left|\frac{d^2\mathbf{b}(s)}{ds^2}\right|^2 \tag{6.3}$$

where the coefficients $\alpha(s)$ and $\beta(s)$ determine weights of each continuity term at various points within the curve.

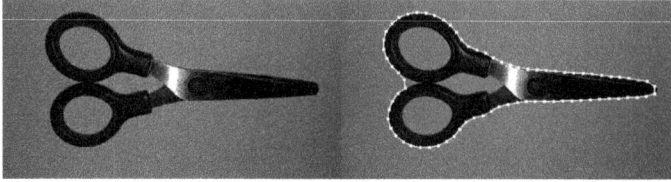

Fig. 6.2   Original scissors (left) and the overlaid converged AC (right) in white.

6.1.1.3   *AC evolution*

The overall energy, E, of Eq. (6.1) can be used to fit an AC to a given image, g. This process begins with placing an initial boundary, $\mathbb{B}_0 = (\mathbf{b}_0(s) :\ s \in [0,1])$, within the image through some automated means or manually. Let E_0 denote the energy associated with the boundary $\mathbb{B}_0$. Fitting the boundary to the image is equivalent to finding a new placement of the boundary, $\mathbb{B}_t$, such that it corresponds to the local minimum, E_t, of its energy. This is classically done with an iterative *gradient descent*. It determines the energy gradient w.r.t. localising parameters of the AC $\mathbb{B}$ and advances small steps in the gradient direction to decrease the energy until no further improvements can be made.

Focusing on a single iteration within this algorithm, the first goal is to derive the energy gradient w.r.t. shifts of each point, $\mathbf{b}(s)$, of the current AC along the x- and y-direction within the image. One of most popular parametric AC is a polygon with a given number, n, of nodes, i.e., a piecewise-linear closed curve specified with n control points, $\{\mathbf{b}_j = [x_j, y_j]^{\mathsf{T}};\ j \in \{0, 1, \ldots, n-1\}\}$ for equispaced values of the control parameter, s:

$$\mathbb{B} = \left(\mathbf{b}(s) = \sum_{j=0}^{n-1} (\mathbf{b}_j + (ns - j)(\mathbf{b}_{j+1} - \mathbf{b}_j)) U\left(s : \frac{j}{n}; \frac{j+1}{n} \right) \right)$$

where $\mathbf{b}(0) \equiv \mathbf{b}_0 = \mathbf{b}(1) \equiv \mathbf{b}_n$ and $U\left(s : s_{\text{beg}}; s_{\text{end}}\right)$ denotes the boxcar function with unit values over the semi-open interval $(s_{\text{beg}}, s_{\text{end}})$:

$$U\left(s : s_{\text{beg}}; s_{\text{end}}\right) = \begin{cases} 1 \text{ if } s_{\text{beg}} < s \leq s_{\text{end}} \\ 0 \text{ otherwise} \end{cases}$$

Inference of the first- and second-order derivatives along the polygonal AC in Eq. (6.3) involves the mathematical theory of generalised functions and thus is outside the scope of this primer. As can be shown, the internal energy of Eq. (6.3) is represented with a sum of nodal terms, $E_{\text{int}:j}$; $j = 0, 1, \ldots, n - 1$, such that

$$E_{\text{int}:j} = \alpha_j |\mathbf{b}_j - \mathbf{b}_{j-1}|^2 + \beta_j |\mathbf{b}_{j-1} - 2\mathbf{b}_j + \mathbf{b}_{j+1}|^2 \qquad (6.4)$$

The point-wise external energy term, $E_{\text{ext}:j}$, is approximated as in Eq. (6.2):

$$E_{\text{ext}:j} = -|\nabla_{g_\sigma}(\mathbf{b}_j)|^2 \qquad (6.5)$$

where $\nabla_{g_\sigma}(\mathbf{b}_j)$ denotes a point-wise discrete approximate gradient of the Gaussian-filtered original image (Section 7.1). Examples of most widely used gradient approximations include the 3×3 Prewitt filters (Section 7.3) or any other edge filters. Then, an iterative gradient descent can be applied to minimize the AC energy to make sure that the boundary $\mathbb{B}$ converges towards the image edges. A flat (constant intensity) image would produce the null external energy term. Minimizing the remaining internal energy of the AC would push the discrete boundary $\mathbb{B}$ to iteratively reduce the distance between its consecutive points while minimizing the local curvature. Starting from any initial shape, the AC would quickly evolve towards a shrinking circular shape stopping once all boundary points have collapsed at the shape centre.

Example 6.1 (Evolving a polygonal AC). *Let us, for simplicity, assume the unit-valued internal energy parameters in Eq. (6.4) : $\alpha_j = \beta_j = 1$. Let a goal object to be segmented be a small black 0.2×0.2 square with nodes*

$$\mathbf{s}_0 = [0.4, 0.4]^\mathsf{T}; \; \mathbf{s}_1 = [0.4, 0.6]^\mathsf{T}; \; \mathbf{s}_2 = [0.6, 0.6]^\mathsf{T}; \; \mathbf{s}_3 = [0.6, 0.4]^\mathsf{T}$$

on a 2D 1.0×1.0 image ($x \in [0,1]$ and $y \in [0,1]$) with white background. The black and white points have zero and unit grey values, respectively.

Let a closed quadrangular AC, $\mathbb{B} = (\mathbf{b}(s) : s \in [0,1]; \mathbf{b}(0) = \mathbf{b}(1))$, be specified by its four nodes, $\{\mathbf{b}_j = \mathbf{b}(0.25j) : j = 0, 1, 2, 3\}$, connected by straight edges: for $0.25j < s \leq 0.25(j + 1); j = 0, 1, 2, 3$, and $\mathbf{b}_4 \equiv \mathbf{b}_0$:

$$\mathbf{b}(s) = (j + 1 - 4s)\mathbf{b}_j + (4s - j)\mathbf{b}_{j+1}$$

Let the following nodes initialise the AC:

$$\mathbf{b}_0 = [0.1, 0.2]^\mathsf{T}; \; \mathbf{b}_1 = [0.2, 0.9]^\mathsf{T}; \; \mathbf{b}_2 = [0.8, 0.8]^\mathsf{T}; \; \mathbf{b}_3 = [0.9, 0.1]^\mathsf{T}$$

Then its internal energy, $E_{\text{int}} = 3.07$, is a sum of four terms:

$$E_{\text{int:0}} = \| \mathbf{b}_0 - \mathbf{b}_3 \|^2 + \| \mathbf{b}_3 - 2\mathbf{b}_0 + \mathbf{b}_1 \|^2$$
$$= \left((0.1 - 0.9)^2 + (0.2 - 0.1)^2\right) +$$
$$\left((0.9 - 2 \cdot 0.1 + 0.2)^2 + (0.1 - 2 \cdot 0.2 + 0.9)^2\right) = 1.82$$

$$E_{\text{int:1}} = \| \mathbf{b}_1 - \mathbf{b}_0 \|^2 + \| \mathbf{b}_0 - 2\mathbf{b}_1 + \mathbf{b}_2 \|^2$$
$$= \left((0.2 - 0.1)^2 + (0.9 - 0.2)^2\right) +$$
$$\left((0.1 - 2 \cdot 0.2 + 0.8)^2 + (0.2 - 2 \cdot 0.9 + 0.8)^2\right) = 1.39$$

$$E_{\text{int:2}} = \| \mathbf{b}_2 - \mathbf{b}_1 \|^2 + \| \mathbf{b}_1 - 2\mathbf{b}_2 + \mathbf{b}_3 \|^2$$
$$= \left((0.8 - 0.2)^2 + (0.8 - 0.9)^2\right) +$$
$$\left((0.2 - 2 \cdot 0.8 + 0.9)^2 + (0.9 - 2 \cdot 0.8 + 0.1)^2\right) = 0.98$$

$$E_{\text{int:3}} = \| \mathbf{b}_3 - \mathbf{b}_2 \|^2 + \| \mathbf{b}_2 - 2\mathbf{b}_3 + \mathbf{b}_0 \|^2$$
$$= \left((0.9 - 0.8)^2 + (0.1 - 0.8)^2\right) +$$
$$\left((0.8 - 2 \cdot 0.9 + 0.1)^2 + (0.8 - 2 \cdot 0.1 + 0.2)^2\right) = 1.95$$

The external energy integrating absolute increments of grey values separated by the AC points is equal to zero when the AC is within the white or black area with zero increments of grey values (like the above initial AC position). The total initial AC energy is equal to the internal one: $E = 6.14$.

After the AC coincides with the edge of the black square, its internal energy is $E_{\text{int}} = 0.64$, while the external energy integrates negated absolute increments along the edges. The assumed unit increments give the external energy equal to the total length of edges, $E_{\text{ext}} = -1.60$, decreasing the entire AC energy to $E = 0.64 - 1.60 = -0.96$. It is the local minimum because a small move of any node inside or outside the black square only slightly affects the internal energy, but simultaneously reduces to zero the increments at all the points along the corresponding incident edges. Then the integral absolute increments are reduced almost twice, and the entire AC energy grows considerably ($E \approx 0.64 - 0.80 = -0.16 \gg -0.96$), thus stopping the AC evolution.

6.1.2   Geometric (level-set) ACs

Explicit definitions of deformable boundaries (Section 6.1.1) limit their flexibility to evolve. Explicit boundaries can be effective tools for simple regions, however, they perform poorly when having to adapt to complex regions such as those with holes or those that are fragmented into multiple subregions. To overcome this limitation, a new formulation of the ACM taking advantage of the implicit representation of a boundary using the level-set approach was introduced.

A zero-level set, $\Gamma = \{s = (x, y) \in \mathbb{S} \mid d(x, y) = 0\}$ encodes the curve as the set of zero points of a signed distance function (SDF), $d(x, y)$, where each $d(x, y)$ represents the signed distance to the nearest point of the curve, so that $d(x, y) = 0$ represents the curve itself. The sign indicates whether a point is inside or outside the curve.

The challenge of the level-set representation is to update it in a way that retains distance relationships, as well as preserves smooth implicit curve representation with similar continuity constraints as those applied to the explicit representation.

6.1.2.1 *Geodesic ACs*

Energy functions of geometric geodesic AC (GAC), like the parametric AC in Section 6.1.1, have an internal term enforcing curve smoothness and an external term favouring proximity to edges. The GAC energy may be expressed in terms of the explicit boundary $\mathbb{B} = (\mathbf{b}(s) : s \in [0, 1])$ as follows:

$$E = \alpha \int_0^1 \left| \frac{d\mathbf{b}(s)}{ds} \right|^2 ds + \int_0^1 h(|\nabla g_\sigma(\mathbf{b}(s))|)^2 ds \qquad (6.6)$$

where $h(t)$ is a strictly decreasing function typically defined as:

$$h(t) = \frac{1}{1 + t^\gamma} \qquad (6.7)$$

where the scalar γ is typically equal to 1 or 2. Minimizing the GAC energy is equivalent to finding the boundary $\mathbb{B}$, which sits at the minima of function h, hence at the maxima of the image gradient or edges. This representation slightly differs from the previous parametric AC energy of Eq. (6.1). The edge function in Eq. (6.7) is selected to be consistent with the typical level-set formulation. The internal term is reduced to first-order smoothing, with the global to the curve weight α. These simplifications help to avoid obscuring key ideas with unnecessary complex second-order derivatives.

It can be shown that the smoothing term of Eq. (6.6) effectively biases the energy function to favour curves of a shorter length. This can be intuitively understood since a smooth curve will have a shorter length than a jagged curve when both enclose a similar area. This leads to a new energy function:

$$E = \int_0^1 h(|\nabla g_\sigma(\mathbf{b}(s))|) \left| \frac{d\mathbf{b}(s)}{ds} \right| ds \qquad (6.8)$$

The GAC owes its "geodesic" name to its evolving along the shortest route between iso-gradient lines, given a topography of image signals. This evolution is achieved by advancing the curve with respect to its normal vectors at each point within the curve. The evolution of the curve naturally has an effect on the energy function, which can be determined by taking the derivative of the energy function in Eq. (6.8) with respect to time step. In order to model implicit curve evolution embedded, the level-set framework has to be reformulated in terms of the signed distance function, $d(x, y)$. As shown in Fig. 6.3, the implicit representation allows the GAC for segmenting multiple disjoint subregions of a goal ROI.

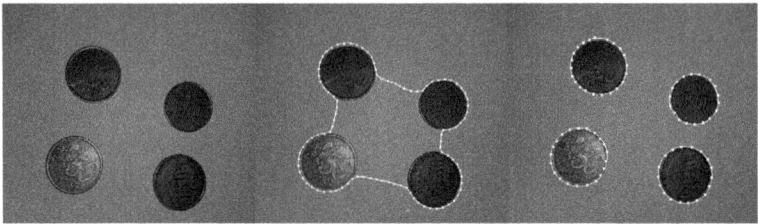

Fig. 6.3 Original image of coins (left) and the converged explicit (middle) and implicit boundary (right) in white. Note the latter was able to split into multiple boundaries to accommodate the coins.

6.1.2.2 *Chan-Vese AC*

So far, the ACs considered have stopped on edges. However, it is possible to account instead for all grey values or colours that are expected in image regions to be segmented. The main objective is to acquire a smooth boundary around a region of a clearly distinct colour, but with an ill-defined boundary.

Chan-Vese ACs introduced two decades ago by L. Vese and T. Chan are also called "ACs without edges" due to their centring around region colours, rather than edges. Like the above GACs, the Chan-Vese AC is defined in terms of an implicit level-set representation.

The Chan-Vese level sets are similar to those from the GACs in using the signed distances of all image pixels, $\mathbf{s} = (x, y) \in \mathbb{S}$, to each current boundary, $\mathbb{B}$. The latter is a set of all the pixels with zero signed distance, $\mathbb{B} = \{\mathbf{s} = (x, y) : d(x, y) = 0\}$. Locations $(x, y) \in \mathbb{S}$ that do not fall on the boundary have non-zero signed distance to the closest boundary point. The sign indicates whether the location is on the interior $(d(x,y) < 0)$ or exterior $(d(x,y) > 0)$ of the boundary:

$$\mathbb{S}_{\text{int}} = \{(x,y): (x,y) \in \mathbb{S}; d(x,y) < 0\};$$
$$\mathbb{S}_{\text{ext}} = \{(x,y): (x,y) \in \mathbb{S}; d(x,y) > 0\}, \text{ and}$$
$$\mathbb{S} = \mathbb{S}_{\text{int}} \bigcup \mathbb{S}_{\text{ext}} \bigcup \mathbb{B}$$

Obviously, each particular level-set allows for defining average interior, $\bar{g}_{\text{int}}$, and exterior, $\bar{g}_{\text{ext}}$, grey values or colours. These averages lead to an explicit energy definition of the boundary:

$$E = \alpha|\mathbb{B}| + \sum_{\mathbf{s} \in \mathbb{S}_{\text{int}}} |g(\mathbf{s}) - \bar{g}_{\text{int}}|^2 + \sum_{\mathbf{s} \in \mathbb{S}_{\text{ext}}} |g(\mathbf{s}) - \bar{g}_{\text{ext}}|^2 \qquad (6.9)$$

The first term of Eq. 6.9 enforces smoothness by favouring short curves. The second and third terms penalise signal variances at the internal or external locations w.r.t. the boundary, respectively.

The derivative of Eq. (6.9) with respect to evolution time step t, is then combined with the signal variances to code changes in the level-set energy while the deformable boundary evolves. Figure 6.4 exemplifies the resulting segmentation.

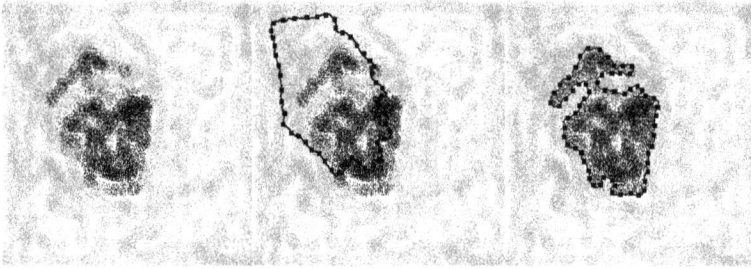

Fig. 6.4 Original image (left) epicting a fuzzy region in the centre; an edge-based AC (middle; in black) failed to converge due to the abundances of image edges, and a colour based Chan-Vese AC (right; in black) having found the defined region.

6.2 Active shape models

The above ACs converged to a solution based exclusively on initial placement and image data. However, image segmentation is complicated by occlusions, clutter, imaging artefacts, and noise. Additional constraints may reduce chances of the incorrect results due to image outliers, thereby favouring the successful convergence. An active shape model (ASM) restricts the potential solutions to certain general parametrised shapes. How to represent an AC using the ASM, derive and model the shape, as well as match such ACs to a given image will be outlined below.

In an ASM, the AC is a set of n 2D points $\mathbb{B} = \{\mathbf{b}_0, \mathbf{b}_1, ..., \mathbf{b}_{n-1}\}$, each point representing a well-defined characteristic element of the goal shape that all these points collectively form. The location of each point should be chosen in such a way that the same point is always identifiable across all shape variants. A tangible example of the good choice could be corner points of the eye in the case of eye segmentation on a facial image.

Legal variants of the shape are often encoded by a point distribution model (PDM), being controlled by four global scale (γ), translation (Δ_x, Δ_y), and orientation (θ) parameters (see Chapter 8), along with an additional set of k parameters, $(\alpha_0, \alpha_1, ..., \alpha_{k-1})$ that locally alter the shape to within an allowable domain. Shape consistency is achieved by constantly enforcing the PDM on the ASM point-set, $\mathbb{B}$, during the matching process.

Fig. 6.5 Nine training images for lip segmentation using the ASM. Here, the AC (in white) consists of seven characteristic points.

6.2.1 *Derivation of the PDM*

The PDM is derived from a collection of K training images ideally covering the full range of shapes that could be encountered during segmentation. Each training image should contain a relevant set of points, $\mathbb{B}_k$; $k = 0, 1, \ldots, K - 1$, demarcating the shape. Typically, these points are placed by hand (e.g., with $n = 40$ for early work in lip segmentation).

The first step in deriving an ASM is to align (register, or superpose) the training images by minimizing a weighted sum of squared deviations between the corresponding points across the training collection. Such a registration derives a set of translation, rotation and scaling operations to be applied to each image in order to create a fixed reference frame across the images and meaningfully analyse relative variations of of the target shape points.

After the registration, a distribution for each 2D point $\mathbf{b}_{k:j}$ in the point sets $\mathbb{B}_0, \ldots, \mathbb{B}_{K-1}$ can be determined. Ideally this distribution has an elliptical form, the major ellipse axis indicating the dominant point's motion across the K variants of the target shape. Well-known in statistics, Principal Component Analysis (PCA) is typically applied to the co-aligned training point sets in order to model the shape and find suitable parameters to define its variants. PCA is able to represent both variations of the individual points across the training set and common relationships between these points.

6.2.2 *Registration of training images*

The registration has to find the translations $(\Delta_{k:x}, \Delta_{k:y})$, rotation angles, θ_k, and scales, γ_k; $k = 0, 1, \ldots, K - 1$, that minimise the squared weighted distances between all corresponding points across all K training shapes. These transformations are detailed in Chapter 8. The point-wise weights depend on stability of each point across the training collection.

The co-aligned training sets of points allow for calculating an average shape, $\bar{\mathbb{B}}$. In order to register the images, a reference frame is also required. Its choice is flexible, however the following process works well:

- The translation, (Δ_x, Δ_y), is derived to match the centre of gravity of a given training image with the centre of gravity of the average shape.
- The orientation, θ, is derived to place a given feature in the shape always at the top.

- The scale, γ, is derived to set the distance between two points in the point set, $\mathbb{B}_k$, to a fixed length in pixels.

The above results lead to the registration Algorithm 11.

Algorithm 11 Training image registration.

1: **procedure** REGISTER
2:     **repeat**
3:         $\bar{\bar{\mathbb{B}}} \leftarrow$ FindMeanShape()
4:         **for each** $\mathbb{B}_k \in$ Training Collection **do**
5:             $(\Delta_x, \Delta_y) \leftarrow$ MoveCentroidToAverageCentroid$(\mathbb{B}_k, \bar{\bar{\mathbb{B}}})$
6:             $\theta \leftarrow$ RotateUpright()
7:             $\gamma \leftarrow$ MeanShapeSize$(\mathbb{B}_k, \bar{\bar{\mathbb{B}}})$
8:             Transforming $\mathbb{B}_k$ with $(\Delta_x, \Delta_y), \theta, \gamma$
9:         **end for**
10:     **until** no more changes
11: **end procedure**

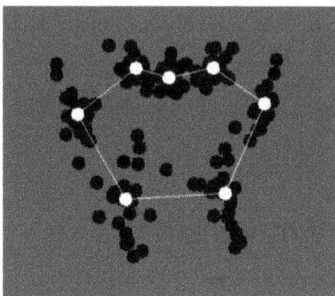

Fig. 6.6 Distribution of training points from a 7-point lip model (in black), white points and lines showing the average shape of the lip. The top three points are clearly more stable than the bottom two, as per the point clusters.

6.2.3 *Using PCA to determine a PDM*

After co-aligning the training images, the next step is to derive the PDM defining a deformable shape to be taken by each point set, $\mathbb{B}$, as well as parameters enumerating various valid variations of this shape. After the average training shape, $\bar{\bar{\mathbb{B}}}$, is found, deviations of each image in the training set from the mean, $\mathbb{B}_k - \bar{\bar{\mathbb{B}}}$; $k = 0, \ldots, K - 1$, allow for constructing a covariance matrix. The latter encodes relationships between deviations of the points across the training collection. Each covariance measures the joint variability of two points, the larger positive or negative values suggesting similar or opposite behaviour, respectively. The covariances close to zero indicate low or no correlation.

PCA, which is outside the scope of this primer, finds so-called eigenvectors and eigen-values of the covariance matrix revealing its principle axes and their associated magnitudes of variations, respectively. The full set of eigenvalue-eigenvector pairs can prove to be rather unwieldy. Fortunately, this collection can be dramatically reduced. Each eigenvalue-eigenvector pair of the covariance matrix characterises deviations from the average shape. Due to the ordering, the first pair represents the largest change and then each subsequent contribution gets successively smaller. Since the contribution tends to drop off quite quickly, leaving the remaining pairs with almost negligible contribution, the collection of pairs might be considerably reduced by defining a cut-off proportion of the total variance.

Then, the final PDM may contain the mean shape vector and a reduced number of eigenvectors. Their linear combinations produce all the allowable shapes determined with the training collection, and thus present a natural way towards parametric shape variants. For robustness sake, in the simplest case, the range of absolute deviations of each point from its mean location could be restricted to three stds.

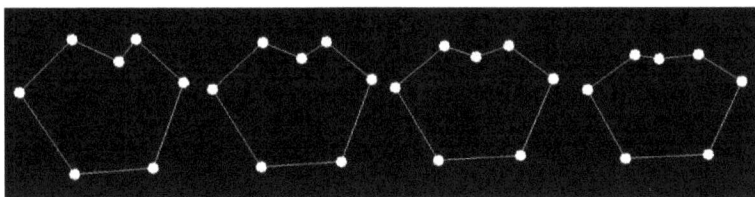

Fig. 6.7   Four different lip shapes acquired by altering the weight of the first eigenvector of the covariance matrix.

6.2.4   *Matching an ASM to an unseen image*

Once the ASM has been defined, it may be used to segment similar regions to those that were in the training collection. Fitting an ASM to an image is equivalent to finding their relative translation, rotation and scale, along with the shape parameters, or a linear combination of the chosen eigen-vectors to best fit the image data. Matching the ASM is similar to the AC evolution in Section 6.1.1.3 with an additional step to enforce the PDM on the point set $\mathbb{B}$.

Generally, the process begins with the initial placement of the point set, $\mathbb{B}$, within the image either by some automated algorithm, or simply by hand. Next an iterative process is invoked that advances each of points in $\mathbb{B}$ towards the closest edge and then regularises the point positions by finding the global registration parameters $(\Delta_x, \Delta_y, \theta, \gamma)$ and coefficients of the linear combination of the eigen-vectors to best fit the new locations of the points. This process continues until no point in $\mathbb{B}$ changes its location.

6.3 Questions and exercises

(1) Which forces affect an evolving AC?
(2) What is the behaviour of an AC if the coefficients α, respectively β, are set to zero?
(3) What happens to an AC set to evolve in an image with constant intensity level?
(4) Sometimes an additional internal force, which is proportional to the normal vector to the contour, is added. What is the purpose of such force?
(5) Which of the introduced deformable boundaries methods would perform better on an image where edges are not continuous?
(6) What are, for each of the introduced deformable boundaries methods, their main weakness and strength?

Chapter 7

Filtering to Find Points-of-Interest

To match and co-align different views of a scene or recognise its objects, an image is often described in terms of local spatial features. Each feature characterises a detectable and locatable pattern of grey values, colours, or other pixel-wise signals, such as, e.g., distinctive boundaries and their details. Informally, an outer object-background or inner intra-object boundary is, in the simplest case, a continuous path via locations of rapid signal changes between relatively uniform regions in an image plane. However, these changes also may be caused by irrelevant sensor noise and uneven imaging conditions, e.g., shadows and non-uniform illumination.

To formally define a boundary, a 2D image is usually considered a scalar real-valued function of continuous planar coordinates. Then a number of meaningful straight boundary elements, called sometimes elementary edges or *edgels*, and other points-of-interest (POIs), representing, e.g., sharp bends (corners) and intersections (junctions) of a boundary, are associated with differential properties of the function, in particular, with extremal points of first spatial derivatives and zero crossings of second spatial derivatives. Many conventional POI detectors rely on differential models, together with additional formal or heuristic criteria for suppressing spurious (noise-caused) extrema, selecting reasonable candidate POIs, and localising proper POIs among multiple candidates.

What will you find here? Section 7.1 will outline most popular differential properties of a continuous image, which are used to describe signal variations and define the POIs. The most important properties include point-wise gradients (gradient vectors), structure matrices, and Hessians (Hessian matrices), as well as their finite difference estimates for a digital image. Because signal noise is amplified by differentiation, the latter is usually combined with noise suppression, e.g., with filtering to denoise the

131

images. Section 7.1.2 will detail popular noise-suppressing differential filters, such as Difference of Gaussians (DoG), Difference of Offset Gaussians (DoOG), and Laplacian of Gaussian (LoG) MWTs. Some pixel-wise descriptors, such as, e.g., the Local Binary Pattern (LBP), outlined earlier in Section 1.3.2 of Chapter 1 and the *Smallest Univalue Segment Assimilating Nucleus* (SUSAN) in Section 7.1.3 below, do not perform the differentiation, but still allow for specifying edges and corners.

Classical gradient-based edge detectors in Section 7.2, including the most popular Canny detector, produce a list of oriented edgels for an input image. Such a description is easily made invariant to global translations and rotations of the input image, but repeatability and stability of the edges found are quite low, especially, in the presence of noise and uneven contrast changes. Section 7.3 outlines the quest of more stable POIs, starting from Harris-Stephens edge–corner detector and Förstner interest operator (Section 7.3.1). More effective recent translation-, rotation-, and scale-invariant POI detectors, such as SIFT (Scale Invariant Feature Transform) and its accelerated and enhanced version, SURF (Speeded Up Robust Features), will be detailed in Section 7.3.2. The SIFT and SURF detectors produce distinctive image descriptors that combine histograms of signal gradients around each POI and are stable under translations, rotations, scaling, and contrast variations. However, the descriptors will be only sketched in brief because feature-based image recognition is outside of the scope of this primer.

7.1   Differential image properties: Gradients and Hessians

For ease of formalising notions of a POI, such as, e.g., an edge or a corner, a 2D greyscale image, $\mathbf{g} = (g(\mathbf{s}) : \mathbf{s} \in \mathbb{S})$, is conveniently considered a 3D plot of a non-negative and differentiable scalar function, $g : \mathbb{S} \to \mathbb{Q}$. It assigns values, $g(\mathbf{s})$, from an interval, $\mathbb{Q} = [q : 0 \le q \le Q]; Q \ge 1$, to points, $\mathbf{s}$, of a rectangular plane, $\mathbb{S} = [(x, y) : 0 \le x \le X; 0 \le y \le Y]$. Cartesian point coordinates will be considered below a vector-column, $\mathbf{s} = [x, y]^\mathsf{T}$.

Candidate POIs often relate to specific shapes prevailing in the vicinity of each location, $\mathbf{s}_c$; $\mathbf{s}_c \in \mathbb{S}$, and reflecting differential properties of the plotted surface. To determine a local shape, the function is usually decomposed into a Taylor's series, truncated to its second-order (quadratic) term:

$$\widetilde{g}(\mathbf{s}_\nu) = \widetilde{g}(\mathbf{s}_c) + \boldsymbol{\nu}^\mathsf{T} \boldsymbol{\nabla}_g(\mathbf{s}_c) + \frac{1}{2} \boldsymbol{\nu}^\mathsf{T} H_g(\boldsymbol{s}_c) \boldsymbol{\nu} \qquad (7.1)$$

Here, $\boldsymbol{\nabla}_g(\mathbf{s}_c)$ is a *gradient vector* of first spatial derivatives; $H_g(\mathbf{s}_c)$ is a

Hessian matrix of second derivatives, and $\boldsymbol{\nu} = [\xi, \eta]^\mathsf{T}$ denotes coordinate variations. The Hessian matrix is sometimes replaced with a singular *structure matrix* built from the first derivatives, as well as the decomposition may use only the first-order (linear) term:

$$\widetilde{g}(\boldsymbol{\nu}) = g(\mathbf{s}_c) + \boldsymbol{\nu}^\mathsf{T} \boldsymbol{\nabla}_g(\mathbf{s}_c) \qquad (7.2)$$

or only the second-order term:

$$\widetilde{g}(\boldsymbol{\nu}) = g(\mathbf{s}_c) + \frac{1}{2} \boldsymbol{\nu}^\mathsf{T} H_g(\mathbf{s}_c) \boldsymbol{\nu} \qquad (7.3)$$

Definition 7.1 (Gradient vector). *The gradient,* $\boldsymbol{\nabla}_g(\mathbf{s}_c)$, *at location* $\mathbf{s}_c \in \mathbb{S}$ *is a vector-column of first partial derivatives:*

$$\boldsymbol{\nabla}_g(\mathbf{s}_c) = \begin{bmatrix} g_x(\mathbf{s}_c) \\ g_y(\mathbf{s}_c) \end{bmatrix} \text{ where } g_x(\mathbf{s}_c) \equiv \left. \frac{\partial g(\mathbf{s})}{\partial x} \right|_{\mathbf{s}=\mathbf{s}_c} \text{ and } g_y(\mathbf{s}_c) \equiv \left. \frac{\partial g(\mathbf{s})}{\partial y} \right|_{\mathbf{s}=\mathbf{s}_c}$$

Definition 7.2 (Structure matrix). *The* 2×2 *structure matrix,* $H_{\mathrm{str}:g}(\mathbf{s}_c)$, *at location* $\mathbf{s}_c \in \mathbb{S}$ *is a singular matrix of squares and mutual products of the gradient components:*

$$H_{\mathrm{str}:g}(\mathbf{s}_c) = \begin{bmatrix} g_x^2(\mathbf{s}_c) & g_x(\mathbf{s}_c)g_y(\mathbf{s}_c) \\ g_x(\mathbf{s}_c)g_y(\mathbf{s}_c) & g_y^2(\mathbf{s}_c) \end{bmatrix} \equiv \boldsymbol{\nabla}_g(\mathbf{s}_c) \boldsymbol{\nabla}_g^\mathsf{T}(\mathbf{s}_c)$$

Definition 7.3 (Hessian matrix). *The* 2×2 *Hessian matrix, or simply a Hessian,* $H_g(\mathbf{s}_c)$, *at location* $\mathbf{s}_c \in \mathbb{S}$, *is a matrix of second partial derivatives:*

$$H_g(\mathbf{s}_c) = \begin{bmatrix} g_{xx}(\mathbf{s}_c) & g_{xy}(\mathbf{s}_c) \\ g_{xy}(\mathbf{s}_c) & g_{yy}(\mathbf{s}_c) \end{bmatrix}$$

where

$$g_{xx}(\mathbf{s}_c) \equiv \left. \frac{\partial^2 g(\mathbf{s})}{\partial x^2} \right|_{\mathbf{s}=\mathbf{s}_c} \text{ ; } g_{xy}(\mathbf{s}_c) \equiv \left. \frac{\partial^2 g(\mathbf{s})}{\partial x \partial y} \right|_{\mathbf{s}=\mathbf{s}_c}, \text{ and } g_{yy}(\mathbf{s}_c) \equiv \left. \frac{\partial^2 g(\mathbf{s})}{\partial y^2} \right|_{\mathbf{s}=\mathbf{s}_c}$$

For completeness, Statements 7.1 and 7.2 below summarise basic descriptors of an arbitrary 2×2 matrix with real-valued elements.

Statement 7.1 (Eigenvalues and eigenvectors). *A* 2×2 *matrix* A *is completely characterised with its eigenvalues,* λ_i, *and eigenvectors,* $\mathbf{e}_i$; $i = 1, 2,$

$$A = \begin{bmatrix} a_{11} & a_{12} \\ a_{21} & a_{22} \end{bmatrix} = \sum_{i=1}^{2} \lambda_i \mathbf{e}_i \mathbf{e}_i^\mathsf{T} \equiv \sum_{i=1}^{2} \lambda_i \begin{bmatrix} e_{i:1} \\ e_{i:2} \end{bmatrix} [e_{i:1}, \ e_{i:2}] \qquad (7.4)$$

such that for $i, j \in \{1, 2\}$; $i \neq j$, *the following relationships hold:*

$$A\mathbf{e}_i = \lambda_i \mathbf{e}_i; \ \mathbf{e}_i^\mathsf{T} \mathbf{e}_i = 1, \text{ and } \mathbf{e}_i^\mathsf{T} \mathbf{e}_j = 0 \qquad (7.5)$$

Statement 7.2 (Determinant and trace). *The determinant,* Det_A, *and the trace,* Tr_A *of a* 2×2 *matrix A:*

$$\text{Det}_A = a_{11}a_{22} - a_{12}a_{21} \text{ and } \text{Tr}_A = a_{11} + a_{22}$$

specify its eigenvalues:

$$\lambda_1 = \frac{\text{Tr}_A}{2} + \sqrt{\frac{\text{Tr}_A^2}{4} - \text{Det}_A} \text{ and } \lambda_2 = \frac{\text{Tr}_A}{2} - \sqrt{\frac{\text{Tr}_A^2}{4} - \text{Det}_A} \qquad (7.6)$$

Proof. The eigenvalues of Eq. (7.6) solve the equality $\text{Det}_{A-\lambda U} = 0$ where U is the diagonal unit 2×2 matrix: $u_{11} = u_{22} = 1$ and $u_{12} = u_{21} = 0$, i.e., solve the quadratic equation

$$\text{Det}_{A-\lambda U} \equiv (a_{11} - \lambda)(a_{22} - \lambda) - a_{12}a_{21} = \lambda^2 - \lambda\text{Tr}_A + \text{Det}_A = 0$$

$\square$

Substituting the eigenvalues of Eq. (7.6) to Eq. (7.5) results in the corresponding eigenvectors, $\mathbf{e}_i$; $i = 1, 2$, with the components:

$$e_{i:1} = \frac{a_{12}}{\sqrt{a_{12}a_{21} + (\lambda_i - a_{11})^2}} \text{ and } e_{i:2} = \frac{\lambda_i - a_{11}}{\sqrt{a_{12}a_{21} + (\lambda_i - a_{11})^2}}$$

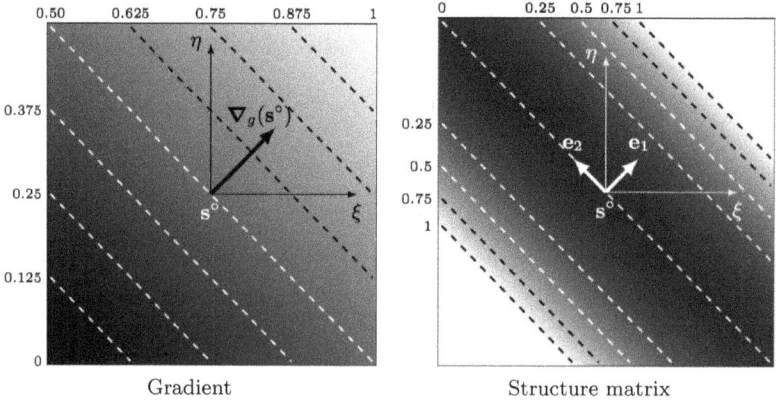

Fig. 7.1 1st-order gradient and 2nd-order structure matrix approximations with dashed grey-value isolines.

Gradient-based approximations of Eqs. (7.2) and (7.3). The magnitude, $\mu(\mathbf{s}_c)$, and orientation angle, $\theta(\mathbf{s}_c)$, of a gradient at a point $\mathbf{s}_c$:

$$\mu(\mathbf{s}_c) = \sqrt{g_x^2(\mathbf{s}_c) + g_y^2(\mathbf{s}_c)} \text{ and } \theta(\mathbf{s}_c) = \tan^{-1}\left(\frac{g_y(\mathbf{s}_c)}{g_x(\mathbf{s}_c)}\right)$$

specify speed and direction, respectively, of the dominant spatial variation of the function, g, i.e., the slope and orientation of the planar surface, $\widetilde{g}(\boldsymbol{\nu})$, in Eq. (7.2). Straight isolines (lines of equal values) of the function $\widetilde{g}$ in Eq. 7.2 are perpendicular to the gradient, i.e., are inclined by the angle $90° + \theta(\mathbf{s}_c)$ to the x-axis, as shown in Fig. 7.1.

A special quadratic approximation of Eq. (7.3) uses the singular (zero-determinant) *structure matrix* depending on the gradient. Its eigenvalues, λ_i and eigenvectors, $\mathbf{e}_i$; $i = 1, 2$, are easily derived, as in Statements 7.1 and 7.2, due to zero determinant:

$$\mathbf{e}_1 = \frac{1}{\mu(\mathbf{s}_c)} \boldsymbol{\nabla} g(\mathbf{s}_c) \equiv \frac{1}{\mu(\mathbf{s}_c)} \begin{bmatrix} g_x(\mathbf{s}_c) \\ g_y(\mathbf{s}_c) \end{bmatrix} ; \; \lambda_1 = \mu(\mathbf{s}_c);$$

$$\mathbf{e}_2 = \frac{1}{\mu(\mathbf{s}_c)} \begin{bmatrix} -g_y(\mathbf{s}_c) \\ g_x(\mathbf{s}_c) \end{bmatrix} ; \qquad \lambda_2 = 0$$

In this case the approximation $\widetilde{g}$ in Eq. (7.3) varies quadratically along the eigenvector $\mathbf{e}_1$, i.e., the normed gradient, while its isolines in Fig. 7.1 are parallel to the perpendicular eigenvector $\mathbf{e}_2$.

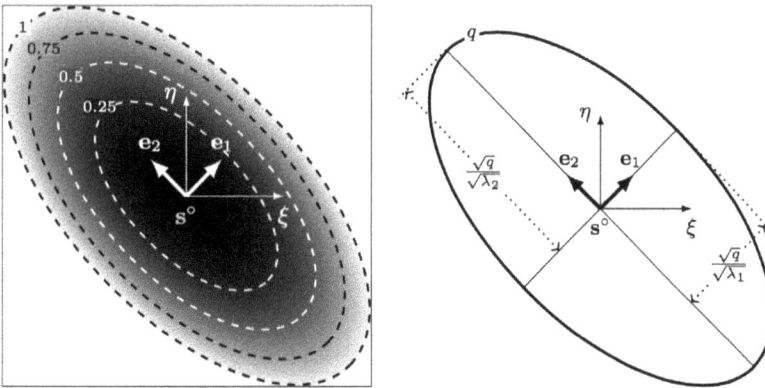

Fig. 7.2   2nd-order Hessian approximation with dashed grey-value isolines.

The **Hessian-based approximation of Eq. (7.3)** depends on the eigenvalues and eigenvectors specified in Statements 7.1 and 7.2. When the Hessian is positive definite ($\lambda_1 > 0$ and $\lambda_2 > 0$, i.e., $\text{Det}_H(\mathbf{s}_c) > 0$ and $g_{xx}(\mathbf{s}_c) > 0$) or negative definite ($\lambda_1 < 0$ and $\lambda_2 < 0$, i.e., $\text{Det}_H(\mathbf{s}_c) > 0$ and $g_{xx}(\mathbf{s}_c) < 0$), the plotted approximation is of concave or convex ellipsoidal shape, respectively, a concave surface of grey values being exemplified in Fig. 7.2. Otherwise, it is of saddle or inconclusive shape, which is not considered a candidate POI.

The eigenvectors of a positive or negative definite Hessian determine orientations of the major and minor axes of ellipsoidal isolines. Given a certain value q of the function, $\tilde{g}$, the half-axes of its elliptic isoline, which are oriented along the eigenvectors, are inversely proportional to the corresponding eigenvalues: $\rho_{q:i} = \sqrt{q/\lambda_i}$; $i = 1, 2$. These relationships are detailed in Fig. 7.2 and Table 7.1 (note also the infinite major axis in Fig. 7.1 for a singular structure matrix with $\lambda_2 = 0$).

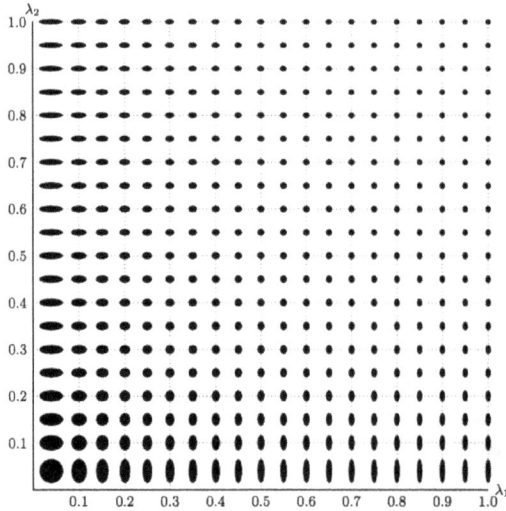

Fig. 7.3   Isolines $q \leq 1$ for the Hessian eigenvalues, $0.05 \leq \lambda_1, \lambda_2 \leq 1.0$.

Table 7.1   Half-axis lengths $\rho = 1/\sqrt{\lambda}$ of the elliptic isoline for $q = 1$ and eigenvalue λ.

λ	0	0.0001	0.0005	0.001	0.005	0.01	0.05	0.10	0.5	1.0
ρ	∞	100.0	44.7	31.6	14.4	10.0	4.5	3.2	1.4	1.0

If the quadratic surface of Eq. 7.3 is ellipsoidal, the eigenvalues, or equivalently, the trace and determinant of its Hessian, help to roughly determine whether the candidate location is featureless or might belong to an edge or a corner. Figure 7.3 and Table 7.1 illustrate gradual changes of the ellipse in Fig. 7.2 when both the eigenvalues vary over the interval $0.05 \leq \lambda_i \leq 1.0$; $i = 1, 2$.

The larger the ratio between the eigenvalues, the longer the major axis is in comparison to the more inclined the surface along the minor axis of the

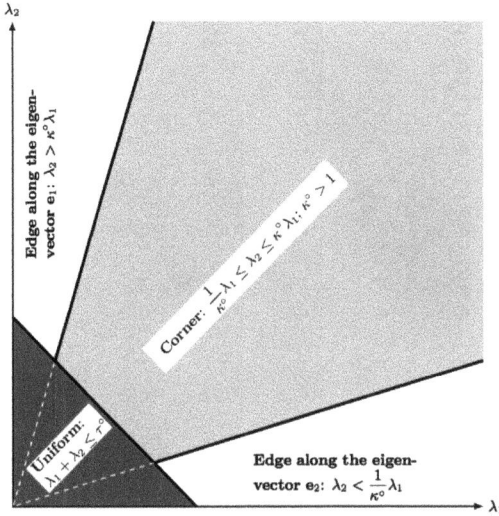

Fig. 7.4   Uniform regions, edges, and corners via the Hessian eigenvalues.

ellipse. The smaller the eigenvalues are, the larger both the axes and the flatter the surface, i.e., the more uniform the signals approximated. The latter points are often considered featureless when the sum of eigenvalues, i.e., the trace of the Hessian, is below a certain positive threshold, $\tau^\circ > 0$, i.e., $\lambda_1 + \lambda_2 \equiv \text{Tr}_H(\mathbf{s}_c) \le \tau^\circ$. Then the remaining points are associated with edges and corners as follows (Fig. 7.4):

$$\text{Corner POI: } \tfrac{1}{\kappa^\circ}\lambda_1 \le \lambda_2 \le \kappa^\circ\lambda_1;$$
$$\text{Edge POI: } \quad \lambda_2 < \tfrac{1}{\kappa^\circ}\lambda_1 \text{ OR } \lambda_2 > \kappa^\circ\lambda_1 \tag{7.7}$$

where a fixed positive ratio, $\kappa^\circ > 1$, of the eigenvalues separates the "edge-like" and "corner-like" ellipsoidal surfaces.

The **gradient-Hessian representation** of Eq. (7.1) shifts a candidate POI to the location, $\mathbf{s}_c + \boldsymbol{\nu}^*$, of zero first derivatives, i.e., of the extremum of the ellipsoidal shape, $\tilde{g}(\boldsymbol{\nu})$. Such a shift is illustrated in Fig. 7.5 and conveniently derived by differentiating Eq. (7.1) in the matrix-vector form:

$$\frac{d\tilde{g}(\boldsymbol{\nu})}{d\boldsymbol{\nu}} = \boldsymbol{\nabla}_g(\mathbf{s}_c) + H_g(\mathbf{s}_c)\boldsymbol{\nu} = 0, \text{ so that } \boldsymbol{\nu}^* = -H_g^{-1}(\mathbf{s}_c)\boldsymbol{\nabla}_g(\mathbf{s}_c) \tag{7.8}$$

As can be shown (the derivation is simple, but is out of the scope of this primer), if the Hessian, $H_g(\mathbf{s}_c)$, in Eq. (7.1) is singular, but non-null (i.e., $\text{Det}_H(\mathbf{s}_c) = 0$, but $\text{Tr}_H(\mathbf{s}_c) \ne 0$), or it is replaced with the singular structure

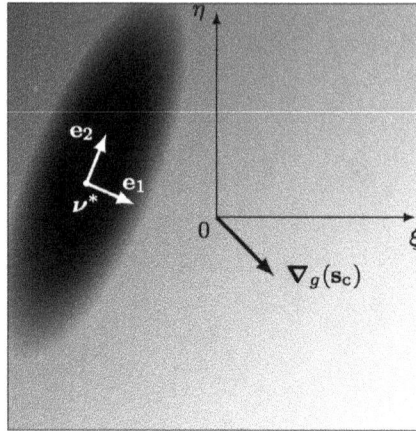

Fig. 7.5   Biased candidate POI for the shape representation of Eq. (7.1).

matrix, $H_{\text{str}:g}(\mathbf{s}_c)$, the POI is shifted along the gradient:

$$\boldsymbol{\nu}^* = -\frac{1}{\text{Tr}_H(\mathbf{s}_c)}\nabla_g(\mathbf{s}_c) \text{ or } \boldsymbol{\nu}^* = -\frac{1}{\mu^2(\mathbf{s}_c)}\nabla_g(\mathbf{s}_c), \text{ respectively.}$$

7.1.1   *Gradients and Hessians in a digital image*

To analyse differential properties of a discrete 2D function, g, on a finite 2D lattice, $\mathbb{S}$, with integer pixel coordinates, the original continuous function, $\widetilde{g}$, has to be restored in the vicinity of each pixel, $\mathbf{s}_c \in \mathbb{S}$. The simplest straightforward restoration replaces unknown pixel-wise spatial derivatives in Eqs. (7.1) – (7.3) with their conventional backward, forward, or symmetric finite difference estimates, such as the first finite differences in Table 7.2. Diagonal (directional) first derivatives can be also represented with similar

Table 7.2   Finite difference analogues of the first spatial derivatives.

	Forward	Backward	Symmetric
$\frac{\partial g(x,y)}{\partial x}$	$g(x+1,y) - g(x,y)$	$g(x,y) - g(x-1,y)$	$\frac{1}{2}\big(g(x+1,y) - g(x-1,y)\big)$
$\frac{\partial g(x,y)}{\partial y}$	$g(x,y+1) - g(x,y)$	$g(x,y) - g(x,y-1)$	$\frac{1}{2}\big(g(x,y+1) - g(x,y-1)\big)$

finite differences, e.g., $g(x,y) - g(x-1,y-1)$ and $g(x,y) - g(x-1,y+1)$ in the backward case. The first finite differences lead to the like estimates of the second derivatives, e.g.,

$$\frac{\partial^2 g(\mathbf{s})}{\partial x^2} \approx g(x-1,y) - 2g(x,y) + g(x+1,y)$$

$$\frac{\partial^2 g(\mathbf{s})}{\partial x \partial y} \approx g(x-1,y-1) - g(x-1,y) - g(x,y-1) + g(x,y)$$

$$\frac{\partial^2 g(\mathbf{s})}{\partial y^2} \approx g(x,y-1) - 2g(x,y) + g(x,y+1)$$

to mention just a few (Fig. 7.6 shows their respective 1×3, 2×2, and 3×1 windows and pixel-wise weights).

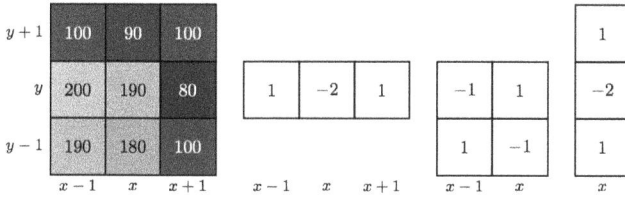

$y+1$	100	90	100
y	200	190	80
$y-1$	190	180	100
	$x-1$	x	$x+1$

| 1 | -2 | 1 |
| | $x-1$ | x | $x+1$ |

-1	1
1	-1
	$x-1$	x

| | | 1 |
| -2 |
| 1 |
| x |

Fig. 7.6   Finite-difference representations of the second derivatives for a 3×3 window.

Example 7.1 (Approximate spatial derivatives). *Finite difference estimates of the first and second derivatives at the centre of a 3×3 window in Fig. 7.6 are as follows:*

$$\frac{\partial g(x,y)}{\partial x} \approx g(x+1,y) - g(x,y) = 80 - 190 = -110$$

$$\frac{\partial g(x,y)}{\partial y} \approx g(x,y+1) - g(x,y) = 90 - 190 = -100$$

$$\frac{\partial^2 g(x,y)}{\partial x^2} \approx 80 - 2 \cdot 190 + 200 = -100$$

$$\frac{\partial^2 g(x,y)}{\partial x \partial y} \approx 80 - 190 - 100 + 90 = -120$$

$$\frac{\partial^2 g(x,y)}{\partial y^2} \approx 90 - 2 \cdot 190 + 180 = -110$$

More adequate finite-difference estimates of the point-wise gradient, $\nabla_g(\mathbf{s}_c)$, and Hessian, $H_g(\mathbf{s}_c)$, follow from the least-square approximation of a 3×3 window centred at each pixel, $\mathbf{s}_c$, with the closest linear or quadratic surface of Eqs. (7.1) – (7.3) with parameters $\Theta = \{g_0, g_x, g_y, g_{xx}, g_{xy}, g_{yy}\}$; $\{g_0, g_x, g_y\}$, or $\{g_0, g_{xx}, g_{xy}, g_{yy}\}$, respectively:

$$\widetilde{g}(\xi, \eta | \Theta) = \begin{cases} g_0 + g_x\xi + g_y\eta & \text{for Eq. (7.2)} \\ g_0 + \frac{1}{2}g_{xx}\xi^2 + g_{xy}\xi\eta + \frac{1}{2}g_{yy}\eta^2 & \text{for Eq. (7.3)} \\ g_0 + g_x\xi + g_y\eta + \frac{1}{2}g_{xx}\xi^2 + g_{xy}\xi\eta + \frac{1}{2}g_{yy}\eta^2 & \text{for Eq. (7.1)} \end{cases}$$

The minimiser of the total approximation error:

$$\widehat{\Theta} = \arg\min_{\Theta} \sum_{\xi=-1}^{1} \sum_{\eta=-1}^{1} (g(x^\circ + \xi, y^\circ + \eta) - \widetilde{g}(\xi, \eta | \Theta))^2 \qquad (7.9)$$

defines the estimated central signal, gradient, or/and Hessian:

$$\tilde{g}(\mathbf{s}_c) = \widehat{g}_0; \quad \nabla_g(\mathbf{s}_c) = \begin{bmatrix} \widehat{g}_x \\ \widehat{g}_y \end{bmatrix}, \text{ and } H_g(\mathbf{s}_c) = \begin{bmatrix} \widehat{g}_{xx} & \widehat{g}_{xy} \\ \widehat{g}_{xy} & \widehat{g}_{yy} \end{bmatrix}$$

It can be shown that pixel-wise minimisers of Eq. (7.9) are obtained with 3×3 linear filters in Table 7.3 that differ only for the central signals. Both the gradient filters are historically called *Prewitt filters*.

Table 7.3 3×3 linear filters for the least-square approximation of Eqs. (7.1)–(7.3).

Eq.	$\tilde{g}(\mathbf{s}_c)$	$g_x(\mathbf{s}_c)$	$g_y(\mathbf{s}_c)$	$g_{xx}(\mathbf{s}_c)$	$g_{xy}(\mathbf{s}_c)$	$g_{yy}(\mathbf{s}_c)$
7.2	$\frac{1}{9}\begin{bmatrix}1&1&1\\1&1&1\\1&1&1\end{bmatrix}$	$\frac{1}{6}\begin{bmatrix}-1&0&1\\-1&0&1\\-1&0&1\end{bmatrix}$	$\frac{1}{6}\begin{bmatrix}1&1&1\\0&0&0\\-1&-1&-1\end{bmatrix}$			
7.3	$\frac{1}{9}\begin{bmatrix}-1&2&-1\\2&5&2\\-1&2&-1\end{bmatrix}$			$\frac{1}{3}\begin{bmatrix}1&-2&1\\1&-2&1\\1&-2&1\end{bmatrix}$	$\frac{1}{4}\begin{bmatrix}-1&0&1\\0&0&0\\1&0&-1\end{bmatrix}$	$\frac{1}{3}\begin{bmatrix}1&1&1\\-2&-2&-2\\1&1&1\end{bmatrix}$
7.1	$\frac{1}{9}\begin{bmatrix}-1&2&-1\\2&5&2\\-1&2&-1\end{bmatrix}$	$\frac{1}{6}\begin{bmatrix}-1&0&1\\-1&0&1\\-1&0&1\end{bmatrix}$	$\frac{1}{6}\begin{bmatrix}1&1&1\\0&0&0\\-1&-1&-1\end{bmatrix}$	$\frac{1}{3}\begin{bmatrix}1&-2&1\\1&-2&1\\1&-2&1\end{bmatrix}$	$\frac{1}{4}\begin{bmatrix}-1&0&1\\0&0&0\\1&0&-1\end{bmatrix}$	$\frac{1}{3}\begin{bmatrix}1&1&1\\-2&-2&-2\\1&1&1\end{bmatrix}$

Example 7.2 (Linear and quadratic approximation). *Figure 7.7 illustrates the least-square approximation of the same 3×3 window as in Fig. 7.6 centred at $\mathbf{s}_c = \mathbf{0}$ with the surfaces of Eqs. (7.1) – (7.3). Linear filters of Table 7.3 provide the following parameter estimates:*

$$\tilde{g}(\mathbf{0}) = \begin{cases} \frac{190+180+100+200+190+80+100+90+100}{9} = \frac{1230}{9} = 136.7 \approx 137 \text{ or} \\ \frac{-190+360-100+400+950+160-100+180-100}{9} = \frac{1560}{9} = 173.3 \approx 173; \end{cases}$$

$$g_x(\mathbf{0}) = \frac{-190+100-200+80-100+100}{6} = \frac{-210}{6} = -35;$$

$$g_y(\mathbf{0}) = \frac{-190-180-100+100+90+100}{6} = \frac{-180}{6} = -30;$$

$$g_{xx}(\mathbf{0}) = \frac{190-360+100+200-380+80+100-180+100}{3} = \frac{-150}{3} = -50;$$

$$g_{xy}(\mathbf{0}) = \frac{190-100-100+100}{4} = \frac{90}{4} = 22.5;$$

$$g_{yy}(\mathbf{0}) = \frac{190+180+100-400-380-160+100+90+100}{3} = \frac{-180}{3} = -60$$

Therefore, the continuous function restored around the window centre is:

$$\tilde{g}(\boldsymbol{\nu}) = \begin{cases} 137 - 35\xi - 30\eta & \text{for Eq. (7.2)} \\ 173 - 25\xi^2 + 22.5\xi\eta - 30\eta^2 & \text{for Eq. (7.3)} \\ 173 - 35\xi - 30\eta - 25\xi^2 + 22.5\xi\eta - 30\eta^2 & \text{for Eq. (7.1)} \end{cases}$$

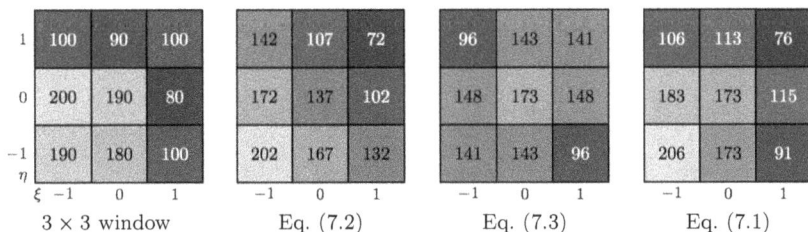

Fig. 7.7   Least-square approximation of the 3 × 3 window in Fig. 7.6.

When the transitional regions are wide, the edges could be associated with ridges of a surface of gradient magnitudes, the ridges being determined by zero crossings of directional first-order signal derivatives along the gradients or of second-order signal derivatives (Hessians).

7.1.2 DoG, DoOG, and LoG

Spatial differentiation considerably amplifies noise affecting image regions with constant or slowly varying signals. Thus, computing the gradients and Hessians is usually accompanied with noise reduction by linear or nonlinear MWT, called image *denoising* or smoothing. Each original pixel-wise signal is corrected depending on the signals in a fixed or, generally, adaptive (signal-guided) window centred on the pixel.

Definition 7.4 (Linear operation). *A math operation $L(\mathbf{g})$ on a set $\mathbb{G}$ of images $\mathbf{g}$ is linear if $L(\mathbf{g} + \mathbf{g}') = L(\mathbf{g}) + L(\mathbf{g}')$ and $L(\gamma \mathbf{g}) = \gamma L(\mathbf{g})$ for all $\mathbf{g}, \mathbf{g}' \in \mathbb{G}$ and any scalar factor γ.*

Because the differentiation is linear operation, it can be integrated with any linear denoising MWT, e.g., the weighted mean in Section 3.3, into a joint linear filter computing the gradient or Hessian component for a smoothed image:

$$\frac{d}{d\mathbf{s}} \tilde{g} \equiv \frac{d}{d\mathbf{s}} (w * g) = \left(\frac{dw}{d\mathbf{s}} * g \right)$$

Given a separable square $(2m + 1) \times (2m + 1)$ Gaussian smoothing filter,

$$w(\xi, \eta) = \frac{1}{2\pi\sigma^2} \exp\left(-\frac{\xi^2 + \eta^2}{2\sigma^2} \right); \quad \xi \in \{-m, \ldots, m; \ \eta \in \{-m, \ldots, m\}$$

the gradient and Hessian components of the smoothed image are obtained by convolving the original image $\mathbf{g}$ with the respective linear filters, ($w_{\mathrm{gr:x}}$,

$w_{\text{gr:y}}$) and ($w_{\text{he:xx}}$, $w_{\text{he:xy}}$, $w_{\text{he:yy}}$), with the following weights at the positions $\boldsymbol{\nu} = (\xi, \eta)$:

$$w_{\text{gr:x}}(\xi, \eta) = \frac{\partial}{\partial \xi} w(\xi, \eta) = -\frac{\xi}{2\pi\sigma^4} \exp\left(-\frac{\xi^2 + \eta^2}{2\sigma^2}\right)$$

$$w_{\text{gr:y}}(\xi, \eta) = \frac{\partial}{\partial \eta} w(\xi, \eta) = -\frac{\eta}{2\pi\sigma^4} \exp\left(-\frac{\xi^2 + \eta^2}{2\sigma^2}\right)$$

$$w_{\text{he:xx}}(\xi, \eta) = \frac{\partial^2}{\partial \xi^2} w(\xi, \eta) = \frac{1}{\pi\sigma^4} \left(\frac{\xi^2}{\sigma^2} - 1\right) \exp\left(-\frac{\xi^2 + \eta^2}{2\sigma^2}\right)$$

$$w_{\text{he:xy}}(\xi, \eta) = \frac{\partial^2}{\partial \xi \partial \eta} w(\xi, \eta) = \frac{\xi\eta}{2\pi\sigma^6} \exp\left(-\frac{\xi^2 + \eta^2}{2\sigma^2}\right)$$

$$w_{\text{he:yy}}(\xi, \eta) = \frac{\partial^2}{\partial \eta^2} w(\xi, \eta) = \frac{1}{\pi\sigma^4} \left(\frac{\eta^2}{\sigma^2} - 1\right) \exp\left(-\frac{\xi^2 + \eta^2}{2\sigma^2}\right)$$

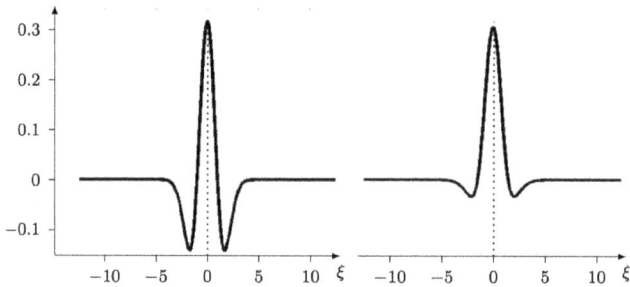

Fig. 7.8   2D section; $\eta = 0$, of the negated LoG (left); $\sigma^2 = 1$, vs. the DoG (right); $\sigma_1^2 = 2/3$ and $\sigma_2^2 = 2$.

The **difference of Gaussians** (DoG) filter:

$$w(\xi, \eta) = \frac{1}{\pi\sigma_1^2} \exp\left(-\frac{\xi^2 + \eta^2}{2\sigma_1^2}\right) - \frac{1}{\pi\sigma_2^2} \exp\left(-\frac{\xi^2 + \eta^2}{2\sigma_2^2}\right)$$

approximates a so-called Mexican hat filter or wavelet in Fig. 7.8, which represents the **Laplacian of Gaussian** (LoG):

$$w(\xi, \eta) = -\frac{1}{\pi\sigma^4} \left(1 - \frac{\xi^2 + \eta^2}{2\sigma^2}\right) \exp\left(-\frac{\xi^2 + \eta^2}{2\sigma^2}\right)$$

Example 7.3 (The nearest-neighbour 1D and 2D LoG filters). *The 1D filter of size 3, $[1 \quad -2 \quad 1]$, provides a finite-difference approximation of the second spatial derivative. The non-separable 2D 3×3 filters combine either two horizontal and vertical partial second derivatives, or four directional second derivatives (adding also the diagonals):*

$$\begin{bmatrix} 0 & 1 & 0 \\ 1 & -4 & 1 \\ 0 & 1 & 0 \end{bmatrix} \quad or \quad \begin{bmatrix} 1 & 1 & 1 \\ 1 & -8 & 1 \\ 1 & 1 & 1 \end{bmatrix}$$

The separable 2D LoG filter is a product of the 1D filters

$$\begin{bmatrix} 1 \\ -2 \\ 1 \end{bmatrix} \begin{bmatrix} 1 & -2 & 1 \end{bmatrix} = \begin{bmatrix} 1 & -2 & 1 \\ -2 & 4 & -2 \\ 1 & -2 & 1 \end{bmatrix}$$

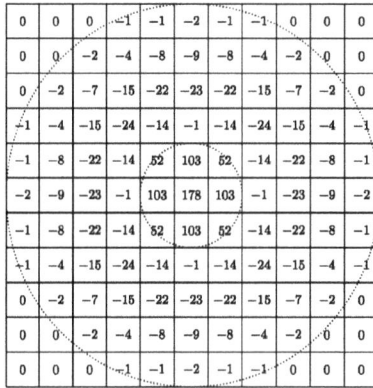

0	0	0	-1	-1	-2	-1	-1	0	0	0
0	0	-2	-4	-8	-9	-8	-4	-2	0	0
0	-2	-7	-15	-22	-23	-22	-15	-7	-2	0
-1	-4	-15	-24	-14	-1	-14	-24	-15	-4	-1
-1	-8	-22	-14	52	103	52	-14	-22	-8	-1
-2	-9	-23	-1	103	178	103	-1	-23	-9	-2
-1	-8	-22	-14	52	103	52	-14	-22	-8	-1
-1	-4	-15	-24	-14	-1	-14	-24	-15	-4	-1
0	-2	-7	-15	-22	-23	-22	-15	-7	-2	0
0	0	-2	-4	-8	-9	-8	-4	-2	0	0
0	0	0	-1	-1	-2	-1	-1	0	0	0

Fig. 7.9 The scaled-up LoG ("Mexican hat") 11×11 linear filter.

Example 7.4 (The 11×11 LoG filter). *The finite-difference approximation (Fig. 7.9) of the non-separable rotation-invariant 11×11 LoG filter is scaled up to obtain the integer coefficients.*

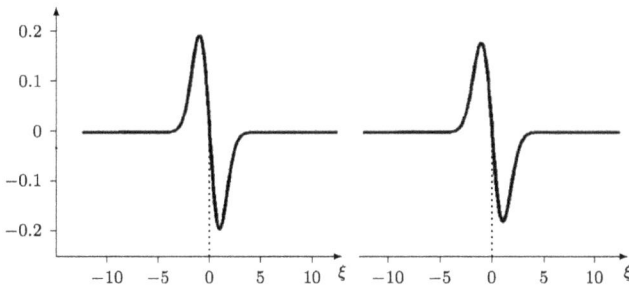

Fig. 7.10 2D section; $\eta = 0$, of the Gaussian ξ-derivative (left) vs. the DoOG (right); $\sigma^2 = 1$ and the DoOG ξ-offsets of $\pm\sigma$.

The **difference of offset Gaussians** (DoOG) filter approximates the directional first derivative after Gaussian smoothing along the offset

(Fig. 7.10). The offsets along the x- or y-axes relate the DoOG to the gradient components. In particular, for the 1D Gaussian along the ξ-axis it holds that:

$$\frac{\partial}{\partial \xi}\left(\frac{1}{\sqrt{2\pi}\sigma}\exp\left(-\frac{\xi^2}{2\sigma^2}\right)\right) = -\frac{\xi}{\sqrt{2\pi}\sigma^2}\exp\left(-\frac{\xi^2}{2\sigma^2}\right)$$

$$\approx \frac{1}{\sqrt{2\pi}\sigma}\frac{\left(\exp\left(-\frac{1}{2\sigma^2}(\xi+\sigma)^2\right)-\exp\left(-\frac{1}{2\sigma^2}(\xi-\sigma)^2\right)\right)}{2\sigma}$$

To estimate differential properties of a noiseless continuous image from its discrete noisy versions is one of the main tasks of filtering and other MWTs. Alternatively, the meaningful POI descriptors are sometimes found by segmenting an image into regions, being homogeneous w.r.t. some pixel-wise features (Chapter 4).

7.1.3   *Inverse USAN areas*

These pixel-wise descriptors emphasise borders between almost uniform areas in an image or its dense feature map. Each pixel is considered a *nucleus*, and a set of locations in a fixed window around the pixel, which support the same or approximately the same signal as the nucleus, is called the *univalue segment assimilating nucleus* (USAN).

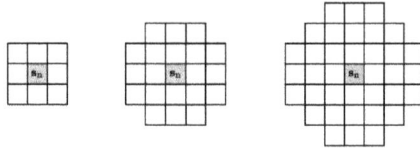

Fig. 7.11   Typical rounded USAN masks with the nuclei $\mathbf{s}_n$.

Given a nucleus $\mathbf{s}_n$, the USAN area is found using a fixed "round" mask $\mathbb{W}_n$, centred at the nucleus and covering either 9, or 21, or 37 pixels (Fig. 7.11). Each pixel is included to the USAN with either an exact "on-off" membership indicator, $u_\varepsilon(\mathbf{s}, \mathbf{s}_n)$, accounting for a given threshold, ε, of admissible deviations between the central and peripheral signals:

$$u_\varepsilon(\mathbf{s}, \mathbf{s}_n) = \begin{cases} 1 \text{ if } |g(\mathbf{s}) - g(\mathbf{s}_n)| \le \varepsilon \\ 0 \text{ otherwise} \end{cases} ; \quad \mathbf{s} \in \mathbb{W}_n$$

or a fuzzy membership function, which has been specially derived to minimise an expected total number of detected false and missed true edge

Test image   Contrasted grey-coded maps

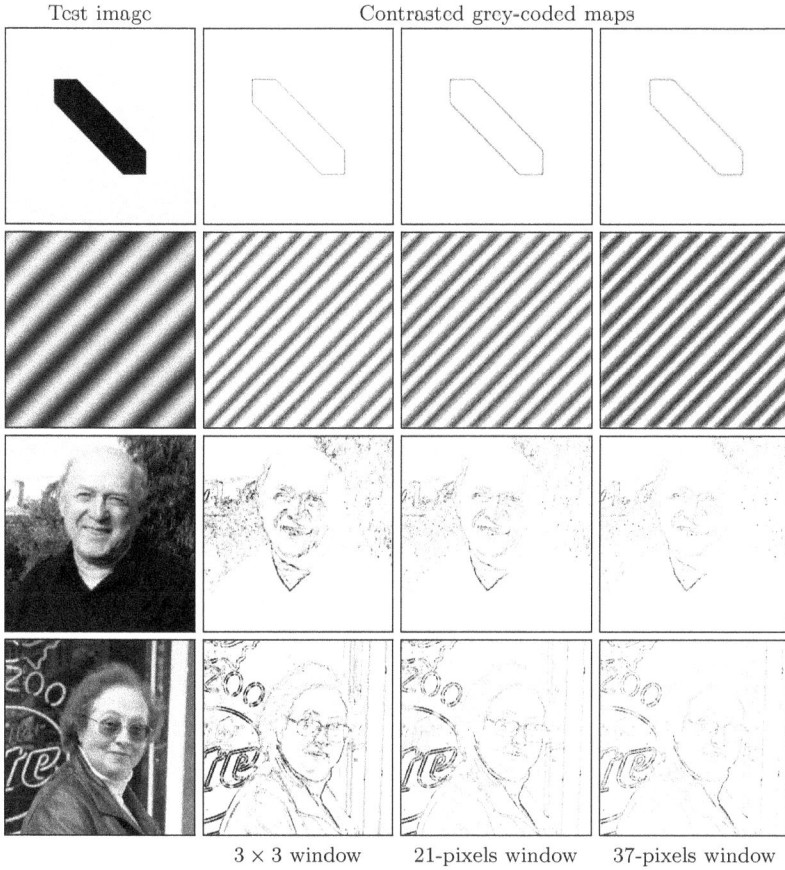

3 × 3 window   21-pixels window   37-pixels window

Fig. 7.12   White-to-black encoding of inverse pixel-wise USAN areas for $\varepsilon = 10$.

locations in the presence of Gaussian signal noise:

$$u_\varepsilon(\mathbf{s}, \mathbf{s}_\mathrm{n}) = \exp\left(-\left(\frac{g(\mathbf{s}) - g(\mathbf{s}_\mathrm{n})}{\varepsilon}\right)^6\right) ; \quad \mathbf{s} \in \mathbb{W}_\mathrm{n}$$

The USAN area, the nucleus-to-centroid (centre of gravity) distance, and second-order spatial moments can be associated with some prominent image locations, such as, e.g., edges, corners, or junctions (intersections) of several edges. In particular, the USAN area:

$$A_\varepsilon(\mathbf{s}_\mathrm{n}) = \sum_{\mathbf{s} \in \mathbb{W}_\mathrm{n}} u_\varepsilon(\mathbf{s}, \mathbf{s}_\mathrm{n})$$

decreases towards an edge and becomes minimal at the exact location of a step-wise edge, as well as the same area decreases further near a corner, up to a deeper minimum at the corner location. That the inverse USAN areas amplify both the features leads to the smallest USAN (abbreviated SUSAN) principle: the inverted USAN areas, $A_\varepsilon^{-1}(\mathbf{s}_\mathrm{n})$, enhance a single edge less than a junction of two edges, or corners, as illustrated in Fig. 7.12. Because computing the USAN areas involves no derivatives, these statistics are more robust to a pixel-wise random noise, than the conventional gradients, Hessians, or Laplacians. As a result, denoising by image filtering in Chapter 3 can be replaced with SUSAN-based image smoothing.

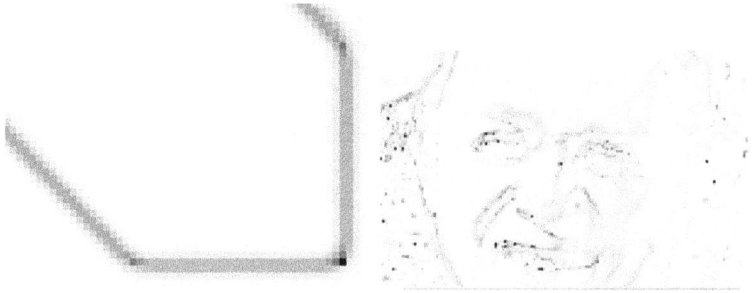

Fig. 7.13   Scaled-up fragments of grey-coded maps of inverse USAN areas for the test images in Fig. 7.12. Note that in the facial image, unlike the synthetic black-white one, almost no local maxima of the inverse USAN areas can be associated with corners.

7.2   Edge detection

Let pixel-wise grey values or other scalar signals in a continuous image be almost constant for each object, but differ significantly in the neighbouring objects. Then an ideal object boundary is a concatenation of *edgels*.

Definition 7.5 (Edge element, or edgel). *Let a small circular window radius ρ_w be centred on a candidate point, $\mathbf{s}_\mathrm{c}$. Then a step edgel is a straight line separating two uniform regions with distinct constant signals q_0 and q_1 (Fig. 7.14). The line is at some distance, ρ; $\rho_\mathrm{w} > \rho \geq 0$, from the centre, $\mathbf{s}_\mathrm{c}$, and rotated about some angle, α, w.r.t. the x-axis.*

Two parallel edgels in the same window specify a straight line element.

Definition 7.6 (Line element). *Given the window of Definition 7.5, a line element is an uniform region between two parallel edgels (Fig. 7.14). Generally, it separates distinct uniform regions, i.e., their signals, q_0 and*

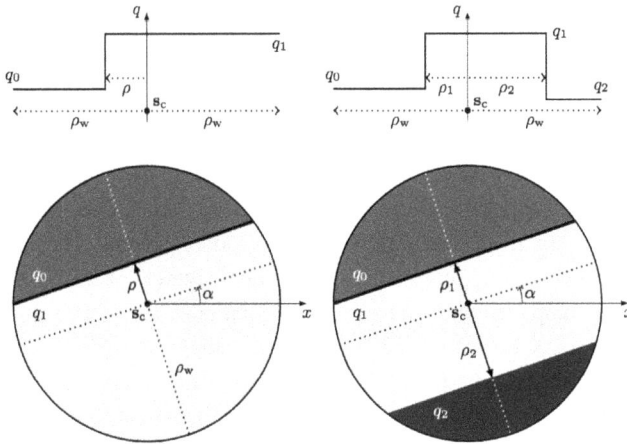

Fig. 7.14   Edgel (left) and line element(right) in a circular window.

q_2, *may be different. The window centre may be in either the line or the neighbouring region, the line width being $\rho_1 + \rho_2$, or $|\rho_1 - \rho_2|$, respectively.*

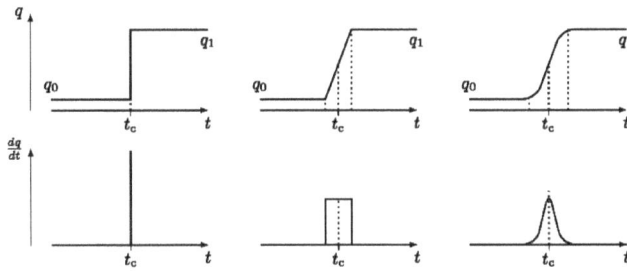

Fig. 7.15   Signals and their first derivatives across ideal step and ramp edgels.

A step edgel makes signals discontinuous, i.e., their absolute directional first derivative across this edge is infinite. More realistic *ramp edgels* (Fig. 7.15) that could be considered smoothed step edgels preserve signal continuity and sometimes have continuous first and even second directional derivatives, too. A ramp edgel should be not only detected, but also localised, e.g., associated with its centre, t_c, within the ramp in Fig. 7.15.

Because general-purpose line detectors are rare, this section will focus on only edge detection.

7.2.1   *Thresholding gradients*

Many known edge detectors separate edgels from featureless background points by comparing magnitudes of pixel-wise gradients of image signals with one or more fixed or adaptive (data-driven) thresholds. However, the straightforward thresholding usually produces too noisy edge maps with thick, or multiple-pixels-wide edges. Generally, edge detection errors in a real-world noisy image are threefold: (*i*) inaccuracies, or missed true and labelled false edgels, comprising false negative (FN) and false positive (FP) outputs, respectively; (*ii*) incorrect localisations of the labelled true edgels, e.g., a bias between the found and true centres of a ramp edgel, and (*iii*) non-unique, or multiple labels for the same true edgel, e.g., across the same ramp. Any practical edge detector has to decrease the errors, in particular, incorporate noise reduction (cleaning) and edge thinning. However, the more accurate the detection due to denoising, the less precise the localisation.

The images are either cleaned with a certain MWT before spatial differentiation, or both the denoising and differentiation are combined into a single MWT, like, e.g., the DoG, DoOG, or LoG filters in Section 7.1.2. A few such MWTs have been detailed earlier, in Chapter 3 and Section 7.1.1.

To decrease non-uniqueness, the edgels are often associated with local maxima of gradient magnitudes across the boundary. Each local maximum relates in turn to *zero crossing* of the second directional spatial derivative, which can be approximated, e.g., with the 2D Laplacian. The LoG filters in Section 7.1.2 combine image denoising with zero-crossing detection. Due to searching for only zero crossings, the filter coefficients are scaled-up to integers, as, e.g., in Example 7.3 and Fig. 7.9. Zero crossings often occur between the lattice sites and are indicated by adjacent positive and negative LoG responses.

A simpler alternative way to decrease the non-uniqueness is *non-maxima suppression*. The gradient magnitude, $\mu_c \equiv \mu(x_c, y_c)$, at a candidate edge pixel, (x_c, y_c), is compared to the magnitudes, $\mu_n \equiv \mu(x_n, y_n)$ and $\mu_p \equiv \mu(x_p, y_p)$, for its next, (x_n, y_n), and preceding, (x_p, y_p), points, respectively, along the gradient line:

$$(x - x_c)\cos\theta_c + (y - y_c)\sin\theta_c$$

where $\theta_c \equiv \theta(x_c, y_c)$ is the gradient orientation angle. The candidate is preserved only if its magnitude forms a local directional maximum: $\mu_c > \mu_n$ and $\mu_c > \mu_p$. The next and preceding points are either just the nearest

8-neighbours:

(x_p, y_p)	(x_n, y_n)	Condition
$(x_c - 1, y_c)$	$(x_c + 1, y_c)$	$0 \le \theta_c < \frac{\pi}{8}$ OR $\frac{7\pi}{8} \le \theta_c < \frac{9\pi}{8}$ OR $\frac{15\pi}{8} \le \theta_c < 2\pi$
$(x_c - 1, y_c - 1)$	$(x_c + 1, y_c + 1)$	$\frac{\pi}{8} \le \theta_c < \frac{3\pi}{8}$ OR $\frac{9\pi}{8} \le \theta_c < \frac{11\pi}{8}$
$(x_c, y_c - 1)$	$(x_c, y_c + 1)$	$\frac{3\pi}{8} \le \theta_c < \frac{5\pi}{8}$ OR $\frac{11\pi}{8} \le \theta_c < \frac{13\pi}{8}$
$(x_c - 1, y_c + 1)$	$(x_c + 1, y_c - 1)$	$\frac{5\pi}{8} \le \theta_c < \frac{7\pi}{8}$ OR $\frac{13\pi}{8} \le \theta_c < \frac{15\pi}{8}$

where angles are measured in radians (π *rad* $= 180°$), or are linearly interpolated from the closest to the gradient line 8-neighbours.

7.2.2 *Canny edge detector*

This very popular and efficient detector detailed in Algorithm 12, was developed to meet all the requirements of Section 7.2.1, i.e., attain the best edge detection and localisation for expected signal-to-noise ratios, along with a single label for a true edgel. The real edgel was modelled with an ideal step edgel corrupted with an additive "white" Gaussian noise affecting each pixel-wise signal independently of other signals.

Optimal linear filters restoring x- and y-components of the gradient depend on expected displacements between the true edges. Each filter resembles the difference of offset boxcar functions for very close local gradient maxima, but becomes similar to the first derivative of Gaussian, or, equally, the DoOG for the more distant maxima. For simplicity, the detector implements only the DoOG (as multiple experiments had shown, its standard deviation, σ, should be in the interval $1.0 \le \sigma \le 2.0$).

To label edge points after the non-maxima suppression detailed in Section 7.2.1, each remaining gradient magnitude is compared to two thresholds, τ_e and τ_c, such that $\tau_e > \tau_c$. The magnitudes above the higher threshold indicate strong (unconditional) edge points, whereas the magnitudes between the thresholds indicate weaker, or candidate points. Each candidate is considered the edge only if its 8-neighbourhood contains at least one strong edge point.

Example 7.5 (Canny edge detection). *Figure 7.16 shows edges detected in the images of Fig. 7.12 with the DoOG's standard deviation $\sigma = 1.0$ or 2.0 and the edge thresholds $(\tau_e; \tau_c) = (0.2, 0.08)$ or $(0.1; 0.04)$.*

Algorithm 12 Canny edge detector.

Input: a greyscale digital image, $\mathbf{g}$;
   a standard deviation, σ, of the DoOG filter;
   an edge threshold, τ_e; a candidate edge threshold, τ_c; $\tau_c < \tau_e$.
Output: the map, $\mathbf{m}$, of edge/background labels.

(1) Find DoOG approximations of the pixel-wise gradient components, e.g., smooth $\mathbf{g}$ with Gaussian filtering and compute the pixel-wise gradients.
(2) **Non-maxima suppression** to preserve only local magnitude maxima along each gradient direction:

   - Compare each gradient magnitude, $\mu(\mathbf{s})$, to two adjacent values along the approximate or actual gradient line (see Section 7.2.1).
   - Set to zero each $\mu(\mathbf{s})$, being less than one of these two neighbours.

(3) Label edge, candidate, and "non-edge" (background) pixels:

$$m(\mathbf{s}) = \begin{cases} \text{edge} & \text{if } \mu(\mathbf{s}) > \tau_e \\ \text{candidate} & \text{if } \tau_c \leq \mu(\mathbf{s}) \leq \tau_e \\ \text{background} & \text{if } \mu(\mathbf{s}) < \tau_c \end{cases}$$

(4) Assign edge labels to the candidates, being 8-connected to the edge pixels, and background labels to all other candidates.

7.3 Detecting POIs

Mutually similar edgels along boundaries are insufficient for establishing correspondences between different views of a scene or an object. More distinct POIs should be detected to match and co-align two or more images under spatially variant contrast/offset deviations and noise, together with geometric deformations caused by multiple sensors at different positions, uneven illumination, partial occlusions, and other nuisance factors.

Descriptive POIs are often associated with easily-localised areas where differential signal properties are rapidly changing in all directions and form local extrema. Such small and less elongated "blobs" along the main diagonal in Figs. 7.3 and 7.4, relate, in particular, to corners (rapid bends) and T-junctions of boundaries between uniform signal regions. Early POI detectors, such as the Harris-Stephens edge–corner detector and Förstner interest operator, strived for invariance to rotations of a 2D depicted scene, whereas more recent POI detectors, such as the SIFT and SURF, added also invariance to scaling, which is even more common in practice.

Inverted grey-coded maps of edge POIs

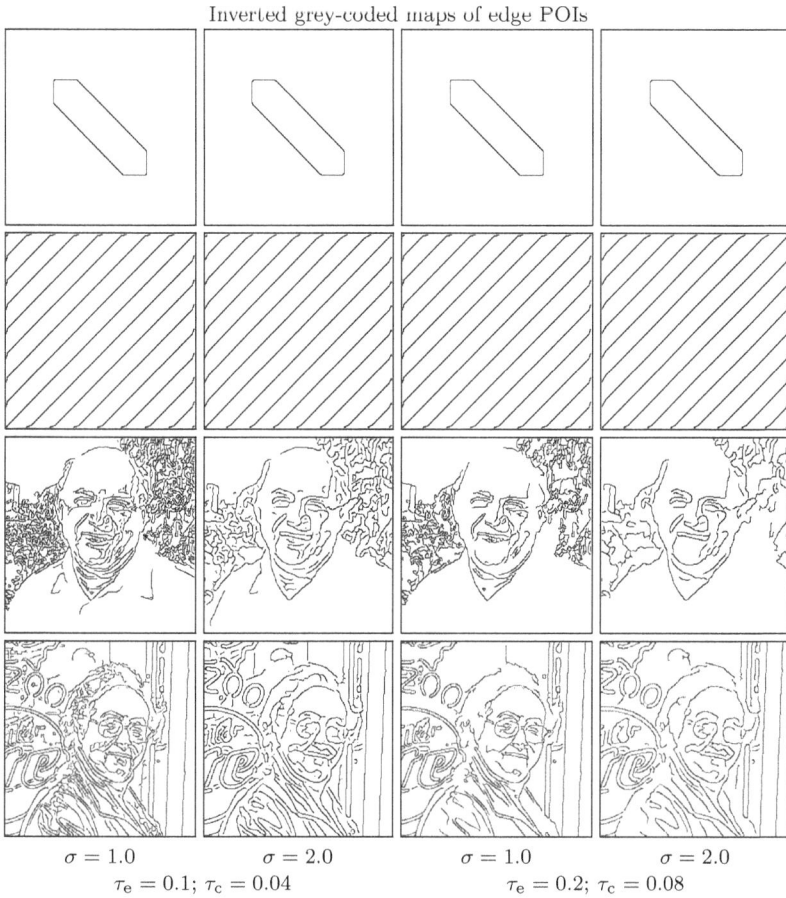

$\sigma = 1.0 \qquad\qquad \sigma = 2.0 \qquad\qquad\qquad \sigma = 1.0 \qquad\qquad \sigma = 2.0$

$\tau_e = 0.1;\ \tau_c = 0.04 \qquad\qquad\qquad \tau_e = 0.2;\ \tau_c = 0.08$

Fig. 7.16   Applying the Canny edge detector to the input images of Fig. 7.12.

7.3.1   *Rotation-invariant POIs*

The **Harris-Stephens edge–corner detector** separates POIs from featureless background pixels by approximating signal variations at small shifts, $\boldsymbol{\nu} = [\xi, \eta]^{\mathsf{T}}$, around each pixel, $\mathbf{s}_c = [x_c, y_c]^{\mathsf{T}}$, with a quadratic surface (see Section 7.1),

$$e(\mathbf{s}_c + \boldsymbol{\nu}) = \boldsymbol{\nu}^{\mathsf{T}} H_g(\mathbf{s}_c)\boldsymbol{\nu} \equiv \boldsymbol{\nu}^{\mathsf{T}} \begin{bmatrix} \widehat{g}_{xx}(\mathbf{s}_c) & \widehat{g}_{xy}(\mathbf{s}_c) \\ \widehat{g}_{xy}(\mathbf{s}_c) & \widehat{g}_{yy}(\mathbf{s}_c) \end{bmatrix} \boldsymbol{\nu} \qquad (7.10)$$

depending on the approximate pixel-wise Hessian, $H_g(\mathbf{s}_c)$, obtained by averaging adjacent structure matrices. Components of the matrix $H_g(\mathbf{s}_c)$ are sums of weighted squares and products of finite difference estimates of the pixel-wise gradient components in a centred on $\mathbf{s}_\text{c}$ Gaussian window:

$$\widehat{g}_{xx}(\mathbf{s}_\text{c}) = \sum_{k=-K}^{K} \sum_{l=-K}^{K} w_{\sigma:k,l} g_x^2(x+k,y+l)$$

$$\widehat{g}_{xy}(\mathbf{s}_\text{c}) = \sum_{k=-K}^{K} \sum_{l=-K}^{K} w_{\sigma:k,l} g_x(x+k,y+l) g_y(x+k,y+l)$$

$$\widehat{g}_{yy}(\mathbf{s}_\text{c}) = \sum_{k=-K}^{K} \sum_{l=-K}^{K} w_{\sigma:k,l} g_y^2(x+k,y+l)$$

Here, the gradient x- and y-components are estimated with symmetric finite differences:

$$g_x(x+k,y+l) = g(x+k+1,y+l) - g(x+k-1,y+l)$$
$$g_y(x+k,y+l) = g(x+k,y+l+1) - g(x+k,y+l-1)$$

and $w_{\sigma:k,l}$; $k,l \in \{-K,\ldots,0,1,\ldots,K\}$, are coefficients of the $(2K+1) \times (2K+1)$ Gaussian filter with the empirical st.d, σ, and half-size, K:

$$w_{\sigma:k,l} = \frac{1}{w_0}\exp\left(-\frac{k^2+l^2}{2\sigma^2}\right); \quad w_0 = \sum_{k=-K}^{K}\sum_{l=-K}^{K}\exp\left(-\frac{k^2+l^2}{2\sigma^2}\right)$$

The POIs are separated from the background by thresholding the matrix trace to guarantee the ellipsoidal surface of Eq. (7.10). Then the edge- and corner-like POIs are classified with a heuristic discriminant function depending on the matrix trace and determinant:

$$\Xi(\mathbf{s}_\text{c}) = \text{Det}_H(\mathbf{s}_\text{c}) - \tau^\circ \cdot \text{Tr}_H^2(\mathbf{s}_\text{c}) \tag{7.11}$$

Its control parameter, τ°; $0 < \tau^\circ < 0.25$, specifies the edge/corner threshold, κ°, in Eq. (7.7). Table 7.4 illustrates relationships between these parameters:

$$\tau^\circ = \frac{\kappa^\circ}{(1+\kappa^\circ)^2} \quad \text{and} \quad \kappa^\circ = \frac{1}{2\tau^\circ}\left(1 - 2\tau^\circ + \sqrt{1-4\tau^\circ}\right)$$

The pixel, $\mathbf{s}_\text{c}$, is considered featureless if the matrix trace is below an empirical positive threshold, $\tau_{\text{tr}} > 0$, i.e., if $\text{Tr}_H(\mathbf{s}_\text{c}) < \tau_{\text{tr}}$. Otherwise,

Table 7.4   Threshold, κ°, for the eigenvalues ratio vs. the control parameter, τ°, of the Harris-Stephens detector.

τ°	0.25	0.1	0.07	0.06	0.05	0.04	0.03	0.02	0.01
κ°	1.0	7.9	12.2	14.6	17.9	22.9	31.3	48.0	98.0

this pixel is the corner-like or edge-like candidate if the discriminant function is non-negative, $\Xi(\mathbf{s}_c) \geq 0$, or negative, $\Xi(\mathbf{s}_c) < 0$, respectively. The selected candidates correspond to local extrema of the discriminant function. Each output corner relates to a local maximum w.r.t. the nearest 8-neighbourhood of that pixel, whereas each output edgel relates to a directional local minimum along the gradient in the like 8-neighbourhood. The empirical control parameter, τ°, of the discriminant function, $0.04 \leq \tau^\circ \leq 0.06$, is equivalent to the border ratio, $14.6 \leq \kappa^\circ \leq 22.9$, between the principal axes of ellipsoids associated with the edgels and corners (see Table 7.4).

Continuity of the output edges can be enhanced, as in the Canny edge detector (see Section 7.2.2), using two thresholds, k_l° and k_h°; $k_h^\circ > k_l^\circ$, to discriminate between weak and strong candidates. The strong ones and the weak candidates with the nearest strong 8-neighbours become the edgels.

The **Förstner interest operator** enhanced the Harris-Stephens detector by Gaussian filtering of the input image, $\mathbf{g}$, before estimating its pixel-wise gradients, Gaussian or fast mean filtering to form the pixel-wise matrices, $H_{\mathrm{str}:g}(\mathbf{s}_c)$, accounting for possible shifts of the candidate POIs; see Eq. (7.8), and analysing quadratic approximations of local signal variations in more detail. Elongated, small round, and large round ellipsoidal shapes, associated with edgels, well-localised POIs, and featureless pixels, respectively, are labelled on the basis of the matrix eigenvalues, λ_1 and λ_2. To be ellipsoidal, the shape should be of a positive size, or, what is the same, positive inverse size,

$$\frac{1}{\lambda_1} + \frac{1}{\lambda_2} = \frac{\mathrm{Tr}_H(\mathbf{s}_c)}{\mathrm{Det}_H(\mathbf{s}_c)} > 0$$

Then the shape roundness,

$$\rho(\mathbf{s}_c) = 1 - \left(\frac{\lambda_1 - \lambda_2}{\lambda_1 + \lambda_2}\right)^2 \equiv \frac{4\mathrm{Det}_H(\mathbf{s}_c)}{\mathrm{Tr}_H^2(\mathbf{s}_c)} = \frac{4\kappa}{(1+\kappa)^2}; \quad 0 \leq \rho(\mathbf{s}_c) \leq 1, \quad (7.12)$$

is compared to a heuristic threshold, τ°, to label the edgel if $\rho(\mathbf{s}_c) < \tau^\circ$ or the POI otherwise. The threshold specifies the border ratio, κ°, of the eigenvalues (see also Table 7.5):

$$\tau^\circ = \frac{4\kappa^\circ}{(1+\kappa^\circ)^2} \quad \text{and} \quad \kappa^\circ = \frac{1}{\tau^\circ}\left(2 - \tau^\circ + \sqrt{4\tau^\circ(1-\tau^\circ)}\right)$$

Example 7.6 (Harris-Stephens POI detection). *Figures 7.17 – 7.20 show edgels and corners detected in the four input images of Fig. 7.12 with the control parameter $\tau^\circ = 0.04$ and different hand-picked windows and background thresholds (K, σ, τ°).*

Table 7.5   Threshold, $\kappa°$, for the eigenvalues ratio vs. the roundness limit, $\tau°$, of the Förstner interest operator.

$\tau°$	1.0	0.9	0.8	0.7	0.6	0.5	0.4	0.3	0.2	0.1
$\kappa°$	1.0	1.9	2.6	3.4	4.4	5.8	7.9	11.2	17.9	38.0

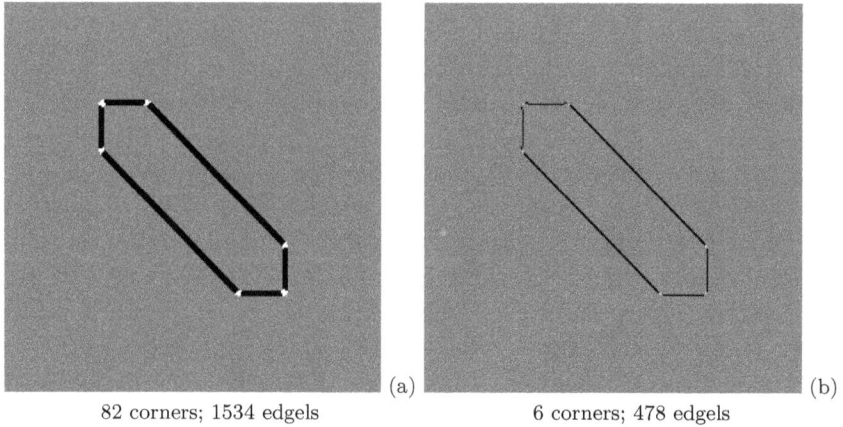

(a)   (b)

82 corners; 1534 edgels   6 corners; 478 edgels

Fig. 7.17   White corners and black edgels detected in the top 256×256 image of Fig. 7.12 before (a) and after (b) non-extrema suppression: $K = 3$; $\sigma = 1.0$; $\tau° = 0.2$.

The detected edgels and corners can be easily interpreted for artificial objects, such as in Figs. 7.17 and 7.18. However, the corners look less meaningful for realistic scenes, like, e.g., facial images in Figs. 7.19 and 7.20. Moreover, edgel locations detected along straight or slowly bending boundaries are too unstable to establish accurate correspondences between various images of the same scene. To co-align such images, the more diverse transformations, than only rotations, should be taken into account. Most popular today's POI detectors/descriptors allow for image rotations and scaling.

7.3.2 *Scale-rotation invariance: SIFT and SURF*

Scale-rotation-invariant POIs are associated with local extrema of differential properties of a 3D *scale space* for a 2D image.

Definition 7.7 (Continuous scale space). *A continuous scale space for a continuous image, g, is built by convolving the image with a continuous 2D Gaussian kernel, φ, of variable scale, i.e., with a standard deviation, σ,*

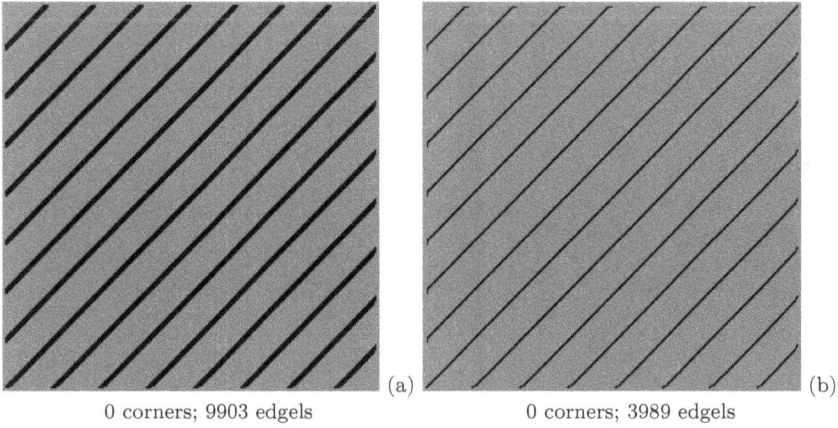

0 corners; 9903 edgels   0 corners; 3989 edgels

Fig. 7.18   White corners and black edgels in the second top 256×256 image of Fig. 7.12 before (a) and after (b) non-extrema suppression: $K = 3$; $\sigma = 1.0$; $\tau^\circ = 0.01$.

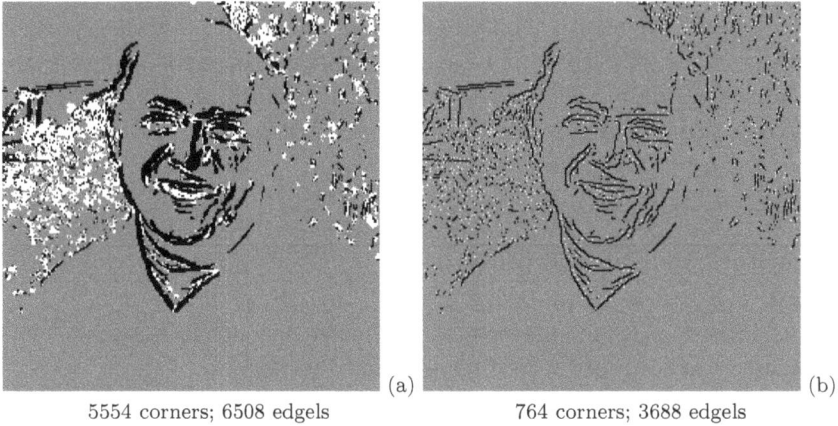

5554 corners; 6508 edgels   764 corners; 3688 edgels

Fig. 7.19   White corners and black edgels in the third top 256×256 image of Fig. 7.12 before (a) and after (b) non-extrema suppression: $K = 2$; $\sigma = 0.5$; $\tau^\circ = 0.01$.

in Eq. (3.10) that varies within a certain interval, $\sigma_{\min} \leq \sigma \leq \sigma_{\max}$:

$$g_{\mathrm{ss}}(x, y, \sigma) = \varphi(x, y, \sigma) * g(x, y); \quad (x, y) \in \mathbb{S} \qquad (7.13)$$

The 3D scale space has two spatial axes, (x, y), of 2D image coordinates and the third scale axis, σ.

Discrete approximations of the continuous scale space are built in accord with the scale-space theory, which is omitted in this primer.

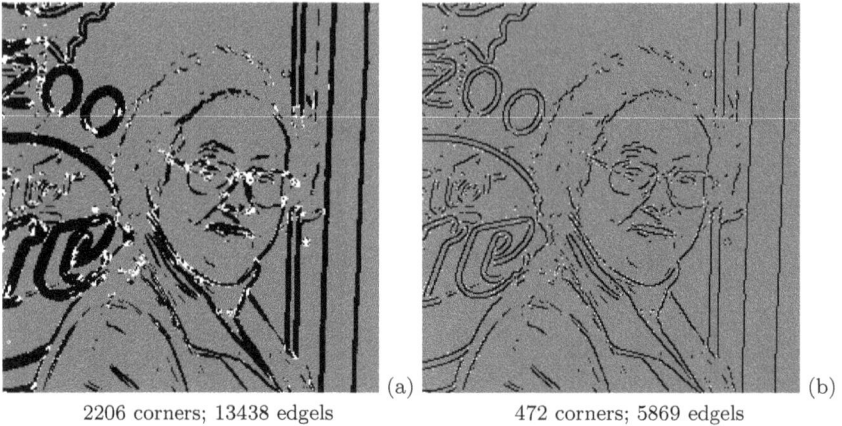

(a)   (b)
2206 corners; 13438 edgels   472 corners; 5869 edgels

Fig. 7.20   White corners and black edgels in the bottom 256×256 image of Fig. 7.12 before (a) and after (b) non-extrema suppression: $K = 2$; $\sigma = 0.5$; $\tau^\circ = 0.02$.

The **Scale Invariant Feature Transform** (SIFT) detects the POIs that mostly are repetitive and have stable intra-scene locations under scaling, rotations, limited contrast variations, and additive noise. Main detection steps listed in Algorithm 13 will be detailed below. The SIFT forms also a distinctive image descriptor based on distributions of signal gradients around the POIs.

Algorithm 13 SIFT POI detector.

Input: a greyscale digital image, $\mathbf{g} = (g(x,y) : (x,y) \in \mathbb{S})$;
    a number, $n_{\max}$, of octaves with five image or four DoG layers.
Output: a list of POIs; a POI-based image descriptor.

(1) Form a scale-space Gaussian image pyramid with $n_{\max}$ 5-layer octaves:

   (a) Double the size of and pre-smooth the input image, $\mathbf{g}$.
   (b) Form each octave by Gaussian filtering with a growing st.d.
   (c) Halve the layer size for each next octave w.r.t. the preceding one.

(2) Form a scale-space DoG pyramid with $n_{\max}$ 4-layer octaves.
(3) Detect well-defined local scale-space DoG extrema as POIs.
(4) Form the descriptor by analysing signal gradients for the POIs.

Building the scale-space Gaussian pyramid. To facilitate fast POI detection, the SIFT forms a discrete scale space for a digital input image, $\mathbf{g}$, as a multilayer pyramidal structure divided into *octaves*. Each initial octave consists of five layers, containing the image **g** after Gaussian filtering with scales, growing bottom-up with a constant factor, $\gamma = \sqrt{2} \approx 1.414$.

Let i and j be ordinal numbers of an octave and a layer, respectively. Layers of a single octave, i, have the same spatial resolution and size. Each next octave, $i + 1$, doubles scales of the layers w.r.t. the preceding octave, i. To accelerate the SIFT, the next octave has also twice coarser spatial resolution and halved numbers of columns and rows in its lattice, $\mathbb{S}_{i+1}$, that in the previous one, $\mathbb{S}_i$.

The first layer, $j = 1$, of each higher octave, $i + 1$, is produced by sampling even rows and even columns of the middle layer, $j = 3$, in the preceding octave, i, followed by Gaussian smoothing with the empirically justified st.d., $\sigma = 1.6$. To detect more POIs and enhance their repeatability, the first octave, $i = 1$, is of twice larger size and finer resolution along the spatial axes, than the input image. This enlarged image is formed by bilinear interpolation (see Section 8.1 of Chapter 8), sampling with halved inter-pixel spacings, and preliminary smoothing of the input image. Therefore, the lattice $\mathbb{S}_1$ has twice more rows and columns than the image lattice, $\mathbb{S}$; the lattice $\mathbb{S}_2 = \mathbb{S}$; the lattice $\mathbb{S}_3$ has twice less rows and columns than $\mathbb{S}_2$, and so forth (see Example 7.7).

The five layers of the first octave are formed by Gaussian filtering of the enlarged image with scales $\gamma_j \sigma$ where $\gamma_j = 1.0; 1.414; 2.0; 2.828;$ and 4 for $j = 1, \ldots, 5$, respectively. To accelerate the SIFT, the 2D filtering is performed by successive row- and then column-wise 1D filtering (see Section 3.3.3 of Chapter 3). Also, due to the chosen octaves' resolutions and layers' scales, just the same 2D Gaussian filter of scale σ is applied sequentially to form each next layer, $j + 1$, from the current layer, j, of the same octave; $j = 1, \ldots, 4$, in accord with Eq. (3.9).

Example 7.7 (Space-scale octaves). *Given an input image of size* 384×256, *the image sizes and the successive Gaussian scales for the four-octave scale space are as follows:*

Octave	Layer size	Scale factors γ_j
1	768×512	1.0; 1.4; 2.0; 2.8; 4.0
2	384×256	2.0; 2.8; 4.0; 5.7; 8.0
3	192×128	4.0; 5.7; 8.0; 11.3; 16.0
4	96×64	8.0; 11.3; 16.0; 22.6; 32.0

Building the scale-space DoG pyramid. Each octave, i, of the DOG pyramid contains four layers, j; $j = 1, \ldots, 4$, of differences between successive images of Eq. (7.13) in the Gaussian octave,

$$\Delta(x, y, \sigma_{i:j}) = g_{ss}\left(x, y, \sigma_{i:j+1} = \sigma_{i:j}\sqrt{2}\right) - g_{ss}\left(x, y, \sigma_{i:j}\right); \; (x, y) \in \mathbb{S}_i;$$
$$\sigma_{i:j} = 2^{i-2}\sqrt{2^{j-1}} : \; j = 1, 2, 3, 4; \; i = 1, 2, \ldots, i_{max}$$

Each difference layer is the enlarged, original, or reduced input image after the DoG filtering with successive pairs of scales, $\sigma_{i:j}$ and $\sigma_{i:j+1} = \sigma_{i:j}\sqrt{2}$.

Detecting the POIs. The candidate POIs correspond to well-defined local extrema of the differences, $\Delta(x, y, \sigma_{i:j})$, in the 3D DoG pyramid. For input signals in the range $0 \le g(x, y) \le 1$, the extremum is considered well-defined if its absolute value is greater than an empirical noise threshold: $|\Delta(x, y, \sigma_{i:j})| > 0.03$. To select the extrema, each 3D signal $\Delta(x, y, \sigma_{i:j})$ is compared with its nearest 26-neighbourhood. To accelerate the SIFT, the non-extrema are eliminated first by comparing with the nearest 8-neighbours at the same-scale layer. Then, if still necessary, the $2 \times 9 = 18$ neighbours in the nearest previous- and next-scale layers take part in elimination.

To more accurately localise the remaining candidate POIs, the 3D scale-space DoG signal is approximated in the vicinity of each found extremum with a truncated to the quadratic term Taylor's series. Much as for the like 2D approximations in Section 7.1, three x-, y-, and σ-components of the gradients and six xx-, xy-, $x\sigma$-, yy-, $y\sigma$-, and $\sigma\sigma$-components of the symmetric 3×3 Hessians are estimated with simple finite differences. Along the scale axis, the estimates account for the multiplicative scale changes. Then inter-nodal shifts of the POIs in the discrete 3D scale space are evaluated using a 3D analogue of Eq. (7.8).

If the evaluated shift exceeds the axial half-distance between the nearest 3D scale-space nodes, the candidate is transferred to the closest node, and the same approximations and evaluations continue until the shift of the extremum is acceptable. The extremal DoG value for the shifted candidate is then replaced with its Taylor's approximation.

Poorly localised edge-like candidates are eliminated after evaluating, as in Sections 7.1 and 7.3.1, the eigenvalues ratios, κ, for each spatial 2×2 Hessian, $H_g(\mathbf{s}_c)$, in the DoG layer for the scale, σ_c, of the candidate, $(\mathbf{s}_c, \sigma_c)$. To simplify computations, the inverse of the roundness in Eq. (7.12) is compared in the SIFT with a heuristic threshold, $\tau^\circ = 12.1$, corresponding to the ratio $\kappa^\circ = 10$:

$$\frac{\mathrm{Tr}^2_{H(\mathbf{s}_c)}}{\mathrm{Det}_{H(\mathbf{s}_c)}} \equiv \frac{(\kappa + 1)^2}{\kappa} \ge \tau^\circ = \frac{(\kappa^\circ + 1)^2}{\kappa^\circ}$$

Fig. 7.21   POIs (small bright areas) detected by the SIFT.

Example 7.8 (POIs by the SIFT). *Figure 7.21 shows the POIs detected by the SIFT on two realistic scenes. Typical numbers of the POIs are quite large due to selecting both small- and large-scale distinctive areas.*

Example 7.9 (Robustness of the SIFT). *Repeatability and stability of the POIs w.r.t. rotation, scaling, and contrast changes are demonstrated in Figs. 7.22 – 7.24. Note that considerable numbers of the POIs are detected at the same or almost the same locations w.r.t. the depicted scene.*

Forming the image descriptor. The descriptor combines histograms of magnitude-weighted relative orientations of gradients of the scale-space images of Eq. (7.13) around the location and at the scale of each detected POI. Measuring all the orientations for a single POI w.r.t. their dominant orientation, together with subsequent normalisation of the histograms, make the descriptor rotation and partially contrast invariant.

The **Speeded-up Robust Features (SURF)** POI detector and descriptor accelerates the SIFT by replacing the DoG scale space with an approximate scale space components of spatial 2×2 Hessians at different scales (i.e., of second-order Gaussian spatial derivatives). This part of the SURF is called the *Fast-Hessian* detector because the approximation uses fast-computable *box filters* (see Section 3.3.2 of Chapter 3).

Fig. 7.22   POIs detected by the SIFT in the transformed image from Fig. 7.21.

The lowest-scale, $\sigma_{1:1} = 1.2$, first layer, $j = 1$, of the first octave, $i = 1$, of the scale space is formed by smoothing the input image of finest resolution with the 5×9, 7×7, and 9×5 filters, consisting each of three or four boxes (Fig. 7.25). The whole scale space is built by changing only filter sizes in this triad, while keeping the input image resolution, because computational complexity of box filtering does not depend on the box size. Each triad roughly approximates pixel-wise second spatial derivatives (Hessian components), $\widehat{g}_{xx}(\mathbf{s}, \sigma_{i:j})$, $\widehat{g}_{xy}(\mathbf{s}, \sigma_{i:j})$, and $\widehat{g}_{xx}(\mathbf{s}, \sigma_{i:j})$, respectively, for a pixel, $\mathbf{s}$, after Gaussian filtering with the scale, $\sigma_{i:j}$.

The above Hessian components for all the layers, $j = 1, 2, 3, 4$, of each octave, $i = 1, \ldots, i_{\max}$, are computed with the respective filter sizes, $K_{1:i,j} \times K_{3:i,j}$; $K_{3:i,j} \times K_{2:i:j}$, and $K_{3:i,j} \times K_{1:i,j}$, where

$$K_{1:i,j} = 2^{i+1}j + 1; \quad K_{2:i,j} = 2^{i+1}j + 3, \text{ and } K_{3:i,j} = 3(2^i j + 1)$$

Fig. 7.23   POIs detected by the SIFT in original and transformed facial images.

Fig. 7.24   POIs detected by the SIFT in original and transformed facial images.

The Gaussian scales grow according to the maximal linear size:

$$\sigma_{i:j} = \sigma_{1:1} \frac{K_{3:i:j}}{K_{3:1:1}}, \text{ e.g., } \sigma_{1:3} = 1.2\frac{21}{9} = 2.8 \text{ or } \sigma_{1:4} = 1.2\frac{27}{9} = 3.6$$

Table 7.6 details these filters for the first three octaves.

The candidate POIs relate to the local scale-space maxima of the discriminant function depending on the Hessian determinant corrected in accord with the chosen filters:

$$\Xi(\mathbf{s}, \sigma) = \widehat{g}_{xx}(\mathbf{s}, \sigma)\widehat{g}_{yy}(\mathbf{s}, \sigma) - 0.81\widehat{g}_{xy}^2(\mathbf{s}, \sigma)$$

To select the POIs, the non-maxima are suppressed by analysing the nearest 26-neighbourhoods of each scale-space site. Just as in the SIFT, only two

$K_{2:i,j}$

1	1	1		-1	-1	-1
1	1	1		-1	-1	-1
1	1	1		-1	-1	-1

1	1	1	1	1
1	1	1	1	1
1	1	1	1	1
-2	-2	-2	-2	-2
-2	-2	-2	-2	-2
-2	-2	-2	-2	-2
1	1	1	1	1
1	1	1	1	1
1	1	1	1	1

$K_{3:i,j}$

1	1	1	-2	-2	-2	1	1	1
1	1	1	-2	-2	-2	1	1	1
1	1	1	-2	-2	-2	1	1	1
1	1	1	-2	-2	-2	1	1	1
1	1	1	-2	-2	-2	1	1	1
1	1	1	-2	-2	-2	1	1	1

$K_{1:i,j}$

$$\approx \frac{\partial^2 \varphi(\xi,\eta,\sigma_{1:1})}{\partial \xi^2}$$

-1	-1	-1		1	1	1
-1	-1	-1		1	1	1
-1	-1	-1		1	1	1

$$\approx \frac{\partial^2 \varphi(\xi,\eta,\sigma_{1:1})}{\partial \xi \partial \eta}$$

$$\approx \frac{\partial^2 \varphi(\xi,\eta,\sigma_{1:1})}{\partial \eta^2}$$

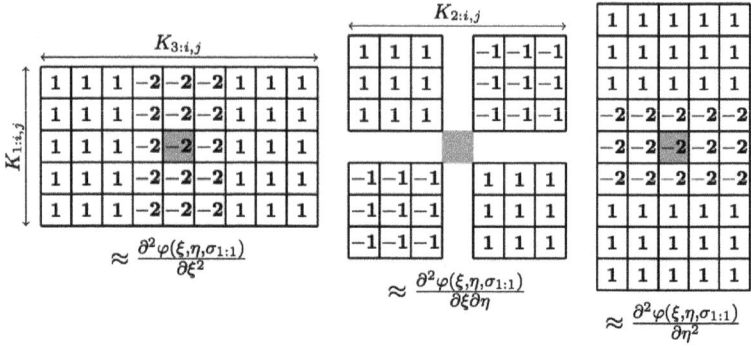

Fig. 7.25   Filters in the SURF (centres are highlighted).

Table 7.6   Sizes and scales of the rectangular SURF filters.

Octave	$i=1$				$i=2$				$i=3$			
Layer j	1	2	3	4	1	2	3	4	1	2	3	4
$K_{1:i,j}$	5	9	13	17	9	17	25	33	17	33	49	65
$K_{2:i,j}$	7	11	15	19	11	19	27	35	19	35	51	67
$K_{3:i,j}$	9	15	21	27	15	27	39	51	27	51	75	99
$\sigma_{i:j}$	1.2	2.0	2.8	3.6	2.0	3.6	5.2	6.8	3.6	6.8	10.0	13.2

layers, $j = 2, 3$, of each octave, forming the sequence of growing scales:

$$\sigma_{1:2} = 2.0 < \sigma_{1:3} = 2.8 < \sigma_{2:2} = 3.6 < \sigma_{2:3} = 5.2 < \sigma_{2:3} = 6.8 < \ldots$$

facilitate the selection, and the POIs are accurately localised by quadratic approximation of the discriminant function with a truncated Taylor's series and shift to the maximiser of this quadric.

The SURF and SIFT descriptors resemble each other to some extent (both are based of local distributions of spatial gradients). However, the SURF descriptor is computed faster due to approximating image gradients using symmetrised Haar wavelets (see Section 9.4.2 of Chapter 9).

Example 7.10 (SIFT vs. SURF POIs). *Figures 7.26 – 7.28 compare POIs detected with the SIFT and SURF on the artificial and two realistic facial greyscale images. Note that many of the POIs coincide for both the detectors.*

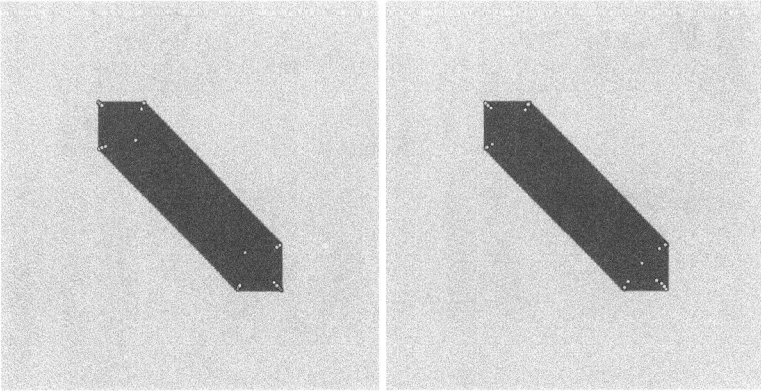

Fig. 7.26   POIs detected by the SIFT (left) vs. the SURF (right).

Fig. 7.27   POIs detected by the SIFT (left) vs. the SURF (right).

7.4   Questions and exercises

(1) Which differential properties of a continuous image, which is restored approximately around a certain pixel of a digital image, are used to detect edgels, POIs, or featureless points?

(2) How does the Canny edge detector estimate pixel-wise signal gradients?

(3) Each gradient magnitude is compared in the Canny edge detector with two different thresholds. Why?

Fig. 7.28 POIs detected by the SIFT (left) vs. the SURF (right).

(4) Find whether the input 3×3 window in Fig. 7.7 is corner- or edge-like by performing the following computations:

 (a) Find eigenvalues λ_1 and λ_2; $\lambda_1 \geq \lambda_2$, of the 2×2 Hessian in Example 7.2.

 (b) Compare the ratio, $\kappa = \lambda_2/\lambda_1$, with the value of the discriminant function in Eq. (7.11) for the corner-edge Harris-Stephens detector, provided that the control parameter $\tau^\circ = 0.04$.

 (c) Compare the same ratio, κ, with the shape roundness of Eq. (7.12) for the Förstner interest operator.

(5) Find the POI shift of Eq. (7.8) for Example 7.2.

(6) Which differential properties do the POIs detected by the SIFT or SURF possess?

(7) How are scale-related differential image properties evaluated in the SIFT?

(8) Which processing steps are accelerated in the SURF w.r.t. the SIFT?

Chapter 8

Transforming Image Plane

Geometric spatial relationships between pixels or groups of pixels follow from sampling a continuous image plane to acquire a digital image. Geometric operations change these relationships by moving pixels to new locations while preserving (at least, to some extent) their near neighbourhoods in order to keep visual appearance of depicted objects.

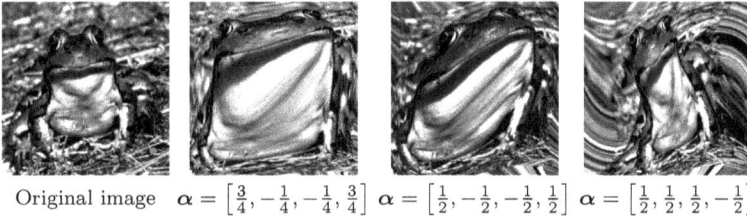

Original image $\quad \boldsymbol{\alpha} = \left[\frac{3}{4}, -\frac{1}{4}, -\frac{1}{4}, \frac{3}{4}\right] \quad \boldsymbol{\alpha} = \left[\frac{1}{2}, -\frac{1}{2}, -\frac{1}{2}, \frac{1}{2}\right] \quad \boldsymbol{\alpha} = \left[\frac{1}{2}, \frac{1}{2}, \frac{1}{2}, -\frac{1}{2}\right]$

Fig. 8.1   Initial and distorted images for Example 8.1.

Example 8.1 (Cubic coordinate transformations). *Both the original,* $\mathbf{g}$, *and transformed continuous images,* $\widetilde{\mathbf{g}}$, *in Fig. 8.1 have planar coordinates* $(x, y) \in \mathbb{S} = [-1, 1] \times [-1, 1]$. *A transformation,* $\widetilde{\mathbf{g}} = \mathbf{T}_{\boldsymbol{\alpha}} \mathbf{g}$, *with control parameters* $\boldsymbol{\alpha} = [a_1, a_2, b_1, b_2]$, *makes each signal,* $\widetilde{g}(x, y)$, *equal to the original signal at the closest to the real-valued back-transformed location:*

$$\widehat{x} = \max\left\{-1,\ \min\left\{1,\ x + a_1 x(x^2 - 1) + a_2 y(y^2 - 1)\right\}\right\};$$
$$\widehat{y} = \max\left\{-1,\ \min\left\{1,\ y + b_1 x(x^2 - 1) + b_2 y(y^2 - 1)\right\}\right\}$$

What will you find here? This chapter presents basic geometric transformations of a 2D planar image that might be used, e.g., to correct images of the same scene acquired by various sensors, or align an image to its template. Geometric manipulations just with a digital image encounter difficulties even in the simplest cases, such as scaling up by replicating each pixel or scaling down by replacing several pixels with a single pixel. Information losses due to such scaling become evident after a reduced image is enlarged to its previous size because of resulting "blocky" appearance and/or overlaid interference patterns that cause spatial *aliasing*, called a *Moiré effect*, in rescaled repetitive textures (Fig. 8.2).

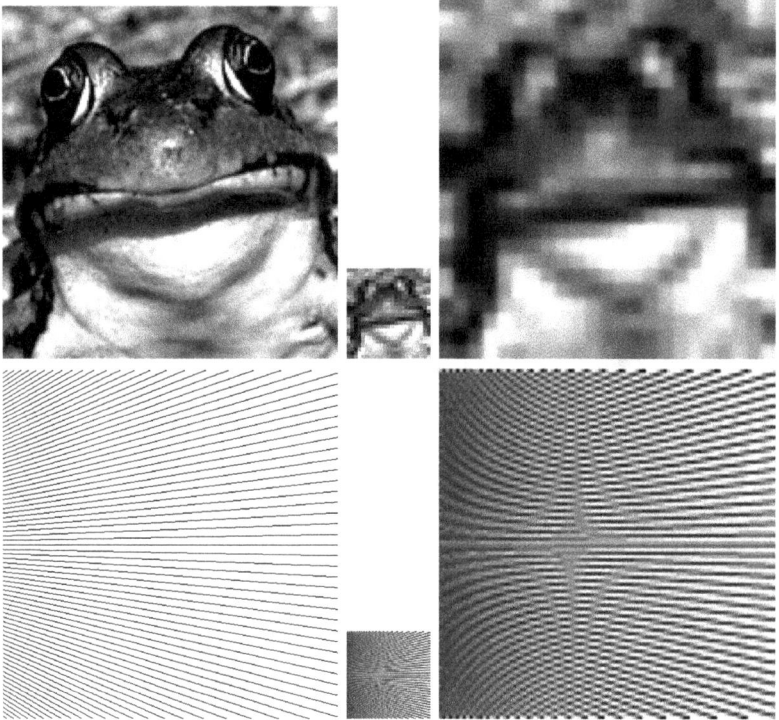

Fig. 8.2   Original vs. scaled down, rescaled, and enhanced digital images.

To partly circumvent these problems, geometric transformations of a digital image are applied to a restored continuous image, which is then resampled into the goal digital image. Section 8.1 will detail signal interpolation to restore a continuous image from its lattice-supported digital version. Section 8.2 will outline forward and backward direction of a transformation (Section 8.2.1); basic rigid affine transformations (Section 8.2.2), combining translation, rotation, scaling, and shearing, and simple non-rigid polynomial transformations (Section 8.2.3) of a 2D image plane.

8.1   Signal interpolation for restoring continuous images

Restoration of a continuous image from a digital one is an inverse transformation to the direct sampling of signals from the continuous image in
order to create the digital image. Given locations of the sampled signals,
all other signals at any location of the original continuous image have to be
restored from the available ones. Generally, the non-sampled signals can
be restored exactly only when the original images are band-limited, i.e.,
contain no spatial frequencies above certain thresholds, and their sampling
intervals account for the maximal spatial frequencies.

Common rectangular $M \times N$ lattices supporting digital images are so-
called *arithmetic lattices* with unit-step integer coordinates:

$$\mathbf{g} = (g(m,n) : m = 0, 1, \ldots, M - 1; \ n = 0, 1, \ldots, N - 1)$$

Signals in all non-integer locations (x, y) of a continuous plane, $\mathbb{S} = \{(x, y) : 0 \le x \le M - 1; 0 \le y \le N - 1\}$, are restored by summing special interpolation functions, weighted with available sampled signals:

$$g(x, y) = \sum_{m=0}^{M-1} \sum_{n=0}^{N-1} g(m,n)\phi_{2\mathrm{D}}(x - m, y - n) \qquad (8.1)$$

Usually, the bivariate interpolation employs a separable function

$$\phi_{2\mathrm{D}}(\xi, \eta) = \phi_{1\mathrm{D}}(\xi)\phi_{1\mathrm{D}}(\eta)$$

with the same univariate factor, $\phi_{1\mathrm{D}}(\ldots)$, for each coordinate offset, $\xi = x - m$ or $\eta = y - n$. This factor has unit value for zero offset and zero
values for all other integer offsets:

$$\phi_{1\mathrm{D}}(\nu) = \begin{cases} 1 \text{ if } \nu = 0; \\ 0 \text{ if } \nu = \pm 1, \pm 2, \ldots, \pm \infty \end{cases}$$

Therefore, the interpolation preserves all the sampled signals of the digital
image.

In principle, a band-limited 1D signal with the upper spatial frequency,
$\omega_{\max} < 0.5$, in the inverse pixel units, i.e., with the minimum wavelength
above 2 pixels, can be restored exactly if the factor is a so-called *sinc
function*:

$$\phi_{1\mathrm{D}}(\nu) = \mathrm{sinc}(\nu) \equiv \frac{1}{\pi\nu} \sin(\pi\nu); \quad -\infty < \nu < \infty$$

However, this interpolation is totally impractical, and the sinc function
is usually replaced by zero-, first-, or third-order polynomials. These functions, which gradually approach the sinc function and provide computationally efficient and sufficiently accurate approximation of continuous signals,
are illustrated in Fig. 8.3 and detailed below.

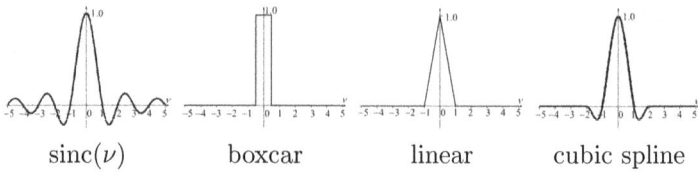

sinc(ν)   boxcar   linear   cubic spline

Fig. 8.3   1D interpolation functions.

Zero-order, or *nearest-neighbour* interpolation rounds real-valued co-ordinates to their nearest integer values: $m = \lfloor x + 0.5 \rfloor$ and $n = \lfloor y + 0.5 \rfloor$ where $\lfloor t \rfloor$ is the integer part of the real number t, i.e. the maximum integer below than or equal to t. The corresponding boxcar 1D interpolation function is:

$$\phi_{1D}(\nu) = U_{0.5}(\nu) \equiv \begin{cases} 1 & \text{if } 0 \leq |\nu| \leq 0.5 \\ 0 & \text{otherwise} \end{cases} \tag{8.2}$$

Zero-order interpolation is the easiest to compute, but it restores piecewise-constant discontinuous signals that might make a transformed image "blocky".

First-order, or *linear* 1D and *bilinear* 2D interpolation is summing weighted signals from the nearest integer locations. In this case the corresponding linear 1D interpolation function is:

$$\phi_{1D}(\nu) = \begin{cases} 1 - |\nu| & \text{if } 0 \leq |\nu| \leq 1 \\ 0 & \text{otherwise} \end{cases} \tag{8.3}$$

Let $m = \lfloor x \rfloor$ and $n = \lfloor y \rfloor$ be the closest integers, being smaller than or equal to the real-valued coordinates x and y, respectively. Then the nearest integer locations around the location (x, y) are (m, n); $(m + 1, n)$, $(m, n+1)$, and $(m + 1, n + 1)$, and the 2D weights depend bilinearly on the offsets $\xi = x - m$ and $\eta = y - n$:

$$\begin{aligned} g(x, y) &= q_{00}(1 - \xi)(1 - \eta) + q_{10}\xi(1 - \eta) + q_{01}(1 - \xi)\eta + q_{11}\xi\eta \\ &= q_{00} + \xi(q_{10} - q_{00}) + \eta(q_{01} - q_{00}) + \xi\eta(q_{00} - q_{10} - q_{01} + q_{11}); \\ & \quad 0 \leq \xi, \eta < 1 \end{aligned}$$

where for brevity $q_{00} = g(m, n)$; $q_{10} = g(m + 1, n)$; $q_{01} = g(m, n + 1)$, and $q_{11} = g(m + 1, n + 1)$. The restored continuous (piecewise-bilinear) signals result in better appearance of the transformed images. However, there might be false boundaries due to discontinuous first spatial derivatives of the restored signals.

Third-order, or *bicubic spline* interpolation is visually even more appealing, and the resulting continuous image has also continuous first derivatives. But it is more complex computationally because of using a 4×4

neighbourhood to restore each signal. The corresponding cubic-spline 1D interpolation function is in this case as follows:

$$\phi_{1D}(\nu) = \begin{cases} 1 - 2\nu^2 + |\nu|^3 & \text{if } 0 \leq |\nu| < 1 \\ 4 - 8|\nu| + 5\nu^2 - |\nu|^3 & \text{if } 1 \leq |\nu| < 2 \\ 0 & \text{otherwise} \end{cases} \qquad (8.4)$$

8.2 Basic geometric transformations

Any geometric transformation, $T = (T_x, T_y)$, transfers each location (x, y) of a continuous 2D image to a new location, $(\widehat{x}, \widehat{y})$ on the image plane:

$$(\widehat{x}, \widehat{y}) = T(x, y) \equiv \left(T_x(x, y), T_y(x, y)\right)$$

Both the transformational relationships, $T_x(x, y)$ and $T_y(x, y)$, are typically low-degree polynomials in x and y. This section will focus on linear affine transformations and non-linear quadratic or cubic warping.

8.2.1 *Forward and backward coordinate mapping*

An input image is geometrically transformed by using either forward, or backward coordinate mapping.

Definition 8.1 (Forward mapping). *The* forward mapping *transfers each input pixel with integer coordinates, (m, n), to its new output planar location, $(\widehat{x}, \widehat{y}) = T(m, n)$, and copies the input signal, $g(m, n)$, to that location.*

Definition 8.2 (Backward mapping). *The* backward mapping *transfers each output pixel, $(\widehat{m}, \widehat{n})$, to the input image by the inverse coordinate transformation, $(x, y) = T^{-1}(\widehat{m}, \widehat{n})$, and copies the corresponding input signal to that output location.*

In both the cases the goal locations might have non-integer coordinates or be outside the target image. In the latter case the input signals to be copied are absent and have to be prescribed. The former problem might be solved in the forward mapping by shifting this location to the closest site with integer coordinates. However, then each output site might correspond to either several input locations with different signals, or no location at all leaving a "gap" in the output image. Because the backward mapping escapes the gaps, it remains the main tool of geometric transformations.

8.2.2 Affine transformations

The forward and backward affine transformations are specified as:

$$\left.\begin{array}{l} \widehat{x} = a_{10}x + a_{01}y + a_{00} \\ \widehat{y} = b_{10}x + b_{01}y + b_{00} \end{array}\right\} \longleftrightarrow \left\{\begin{array}{l} x = \alpha_{10}\widehat{x} + \alpha_{01}\widehat{y} + \alpha_{00} \\ y = \beta_{10}\widehat{x} + \beta_{01}\widehat{y} + \beta_{00} \end{array}\right. \tag{8.5}$$

where coefficients for non-singular cases, such that $a_{10}b_{01} - a_{01}b_{10} \neq 0$ and $\alpha_{10}\beta_{01} - \alpha_{01}\beta_{10} \neq 0$ are interrelated:

$$\alpha_{10} = \frac{b_{01}}{a_{10}b_{01} - a_{01}b_{10}}; \quad \alpha_{01} = \frac{-a_{01}}{a_{10}b_{01} - a_{01}b_{10}};$$

$$\alpha_{00} = \frac{a_{01}b_{00} - a_{00}b_{01}}{a_{10}b_{01} - a_{01}b_{10}}; \quad \beta_{10} = -\frac{-b_{10}}{a_{10}b_{01} - a_{01}b_{10}}; \tag{8.6}$$

$$\beta_{01} = \frac{a_{10}}{a_{10}b_{01} - a_{01}b_{10}}; \quad \beta_{00} = \frac{-a_{10}b_{00} + a_{00}b_{10}}{a_{10}b_{01} - a_{01}b_{10}}$$

and

$$a_{10} = \frac{\beta_{01}}{\alpha_{10}\beta_{01} - \alpha_{01}\beta_{10}}; \quad a_{01} = \frac{-\alpha_{01}}{\alpha_{10}\beta_{01} - \alpha_{01}\beta_{10}};$$

$$a_{00} = \frac{\alpha_{01}\beta_{00} - \alpha_{00}\beta_{01}}{\alpha_{10}b_{01} - \alpha_{01}b_{00}}; \quad b_{10} = -\frac{-\beta_{10}}{\alpha_{10}\beta_{01} - \alpha_{01}\beta_{10}}; \tag{8.7}$$

$$b_{01} = \frac{\alpha_{10}}{\alpha_{10}\beta_{01} - \alpha_{01}\beta_{10}}; \quad b_{00} = \frac{-\alpha_{10}\beta_{00} + \alpha_{00}\beta_{10}}{\alpha_{10}b_{01} - \alpha_{01}\beta_{10}}$$

Two or more successive affine transformations combine into a single affine transformation.

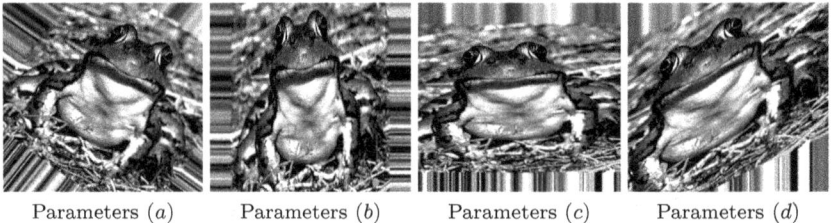

Parameters (a)   Parameters (b)   Parameters (c)   Parameters (d)

Fig. 8.4   Affine transformations of Example 8.2 applied to the original image in Fig. 8.1.

Example 8.2 (Affine transformations). *Figure 8.4 shows affine transformed output images for the input image in Fig. 8.1 and the following* *backward and forward mapping parameters in accord with Eqs. (8.6) and (8.7):*

	α_{10}	α_{01}	α_{00}	β_{10}	β_{01}	β_{00}
(a)	0.800	−0.600	0.100	0.600	0.800	−0.100
(b)	0.800	0.000	0.000	0.000	1.250	0.000
(c)	1.250	0.000	0.000	0.000	0.800	0.000
(d)	1.000	0.500	0.100	0.000	0.800	0.100

	a_{10}	a_{01}	a_{00}	b_{10}	b_{01}	b_{00}
(a)	0.800	0.600	−0.020	−0.600	0.800	0.140
(b)	1.250	0.000	0.000	0.000	0.800	0.000
(c)	0.800	0.000	0.000	0.000	1.250	0.000
(d)	1.000	−0.625	0.525	0.000	1.250	−0.100

Translational parameters α_{00}, β_{00}, a_{00}, and b_{00} in Example 8.2 are measured in fractions of the image width in pixels.

If 2D points are considered column vectors, $\mathbf{s} = [x, y]^{\mathsf{T}}$, the affine transformation consists of a left multiplication by a 2×2 matrix followed by adding a vector:

$$\begin{bmatrix} \widehat{x} \\ \widehat{y} \end{bmatrix} = \begin{bmatrix} a_{10} & a_{01} \\ b_{10} & b_{01} \end{bmatrix} \begin{bmatrix} x \\ y \end{bmatrix} + \begin{bmatrix} a_{00} \\ b_{00} \end{bmatrix} \longleftrightarrow \begin{bmatrix} x \\ y \end{bmatrix} = \begin{bmatrix} \alpha_{10} & \alpha_{01} \\ \beta_{10} & \beta_{01} \end{bmatrix} \begin{bmatrix} \widehat{x} \\ \widehat{y} \end{bmatrix} + \begin{bmatrix} \alpha_{00} \\ \beta_{00} \end{bmatrix}$$

It is convenient to make an arbitrary affine transformation linear by introducing *homogeneous coordinates.*

Definition 8.3 (Homogeneous 2D coordinates). *Each 2-element vector of 2D Cartesian coordinates, $\mathbf{s} = [x, y]^{\mathsf{T}}$, can be represented with a 3-element vector, $[cx, cy, c]^{\mathsf{T}}$ of equivalent homogeneous coordinates having an arbitrary real-valued factor c; $-\infty \leq c \leq \infty$, as their third element. Given a homogeneous vector, $[v_1, v_2, v_3]^{\mathsf{T}}$, the corresponding Cartesian x- and y-coordinates are obtained as ratios, $x = v_1/v_3$ and $y = v_2/v_3$, respectively.*

Planar affine transformations use only unit factor, $c = 1$. Any such transformation of an (x, y)-pixel multiplies a 3×3 matrix to the homogeneous $[x, y, 1]$-vector:

$$\begin{bmatrix} \widehat{x} \\ \widehat{y} \\ 1 \end{bmatrix} = \begin{bmatrix} a_{10} & a_{01} & a_{00} \\ b_{10} & b_{01} & b_{00} \\ 0 & 0 & 1 \end{bmatrix} \begin{bmatrix} x \\ y \\ 1 \end{bmatrix} \longleftrightarrow \begin{bmatrix} x \\ y \\ 1 \end{bmatrix} = \begin{bmatrix} \alpha_{10} & \alpha_{01} & \alpha_{00} \\ \beta_{10} & \beta_{01} & \beta_{00} \\ 0 & 0 & 1 \end{bmatrix} \begin{bmatrix} \widehat{x} \\ \widehat{y} \\ 1 \end{bmatrix} \quad (8.8)$$

the matrix representing relationships in Eqs. (8.5) – (8.7). This matrix-vector representation proves the same affine form of a sequence of affine transformations one after another, because their individual 3×3 matrices are left-multiplied into a single combined 3×3 matrix.

Table 8.1   Elementary affine transformations.

	a_{10}	a_{01}	a_{00}	b_{10}	b_{01}	b_{00}
Identity (no transformation)	1	0	0	0	1	0
Translation by (Δ_x, Δ_y)	1	0	Δ_x	0	1	Δ_y
Uniform scaling by a factor γ	γ	0	0	0	γ	0
Non-uniform scaling by γ_x and γ_y	γ_x	0	0	0	γ_y	0
Clockwise rotation by an angle θ	$\cos(\theta)$	$\sin(\theta)$	0	$-\sin(\theta)$	$\cos(\theta)$	0
Horizontal shear by a factor γ	1	γ	0	0	1	0
Vertical shear by a factor γ	1	0	0	γ	1	0

Because any sequence of affine transformations is also an affine transformation, any arbitrary affine transformation can be combined from the sequential elementary translation, scaling, rotation, and shearing operations in Table 8.1. A sequence of these forward elementary operations is easy to implement due to their easy-to-compute inversions for the backward mapping (Table 8.2). Common in practice rigid *Euclidean transformations* consist of only translations and rotations, preserving angles between straight lines and point-to-point distances in a transformed object.

Table 8.2   Inverses of the elementary affine transformations in Table 8.1.

	a_{10}	a_{01}	a_{00}	b_{10}	b_{01}	b_{00}
Identity (no transformation)	1	0	0	0	1	0
Translation by (Δ_x, Δ_y)	1	0	$-\Delta_x$	0	1	$-\Delta_y$
Uniform scaling by a factor γ	γ^{-1}	0	0	0	γ^{-1}	0
Non-uniform scaling by γ_x and γ_y	γ_x^{-1}	0	0	0	γ_y^{-1}	0
Clockwise rotation by an angle θ	$\cos(\theta)$	$-\sin(\theta)$	0	$\sin(\theta)$	$\cos(\theta)$	0
Horizontal shear by a factor γ	1	$-\gamma$	0	0	1	0
Vertical shear by a factor γ	1	0	0	$-\gamma$	1	0

An inverse, T^{-1}, of an arbitrary affine transformation, T, returns every transformed pixel to its original location. However, signal interpolations during both the transformations might affect the original grey values.

Example 8.3 (Sequential execution of elementary operations). *Let an affine transformation consist of four sequential steps:*

(1) the horizontal shear by factor $\gamma = 0.5$;
(2) the clockwise rotation by angle $\theta = -53°.13$, or what is the same, the counterclockwise rotation by angle $53°.13$ (in this case $\cos(\theta) = 0.6$ and $\sin(\theta) = -0.8$);
(3) the uniform scaling by factor $\gamma = 2$, and
(4) the translation by offsets $(3, -2)$ in pixels.

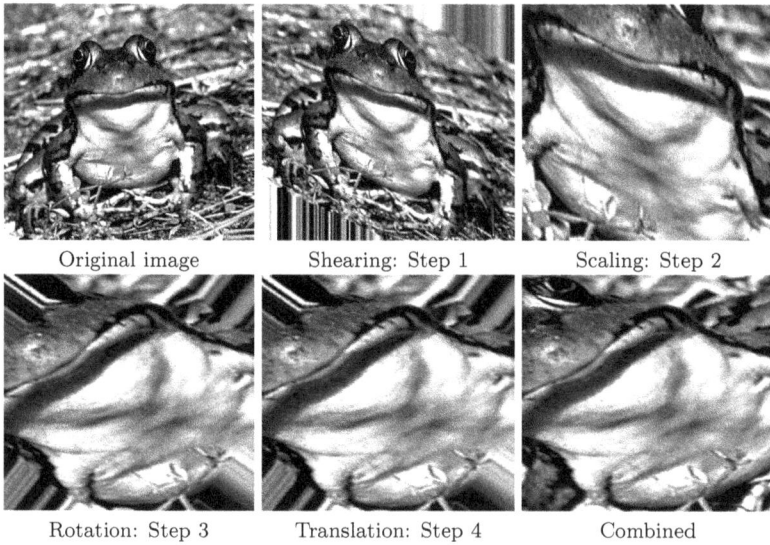

Original image	Shearing: Step 1	Scaling: Step 2
Rotation: Step 3	Translation: Step 4	Combined

Fig. 8.5   Affine transformations of Example 8.3.

The transformation is described with the following 3×3 matrices:

$$\underbrace{\begin{bmatrix} 1 & 0 & 3 \\ 0 & 1 & -2 \\ 0 & 0 & 1 \end{bmatrix}}_{Translation} \underbrace{\begin{bmatrix} 0.6 & -0.8 & 0 \\ 0.8 & 0.6 & 0 \\ 0 & 0 & 1 \end{bmatrix}}_{Rotation} \underbrace{\begin{bmatrix} 2 & 0 & 0 \\ 0 & 2 & 0 \\ 0 & 0 & 1 \end{bmatrix}}_{Scaling} \underbrace{\begin{bmatrix} 1 & 0.5 & 0 \\ 0 & 1 & 0 \\ 0 & 0 & 1 \end{bmatrix}}_{Shearing} = \underbrace{\begin{bmatrix} 1.2 & -1 & 3 \\ 1.6 & 2 & -2 \\ 0 & 0 & 1 \end{bmatrix}}_{Combined}$$

Figure 8.5 compares the sequentially executed elementary operations with the combined simultaneous transformation. Obviously, the latter preserves the original image data better than the equivalent sequence of operations.

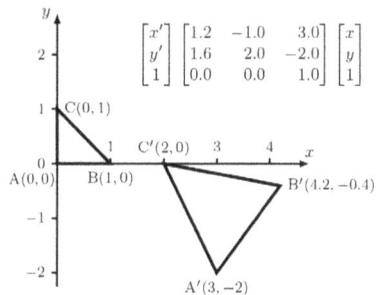

Fig. 8.6   Affine transformation of a triangle.

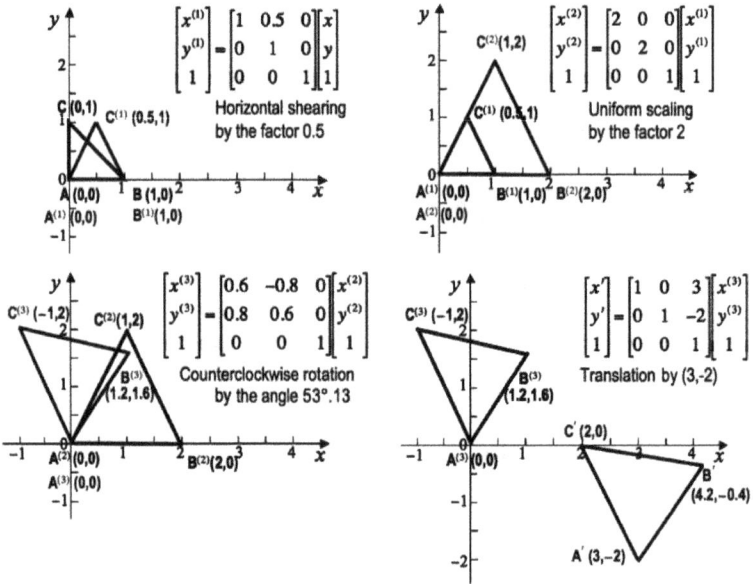

Fig. 8.7   Affine transformation of a triangle: sequential steps.

The transformation in Example 8.3 maps a triangle ABC with the vertices A $=$ $(0,0)$, B $=$ $(1,0)$, and C $=$ $(0,1)$ to the triangle A′B′C′ where A′ $=$ $(3, -2)$, B′ $=$ $(4.2, -0.4)$, and C′ $=$ $(2,0)$ (Figs. 8.6 and 8.7). Each affine transformation T can be viewed as a triangle-to-triangle mapping because its six parameters solve six linear equations for the vertex coordinates before and after the transformation:

$$\underbrace{\begin{bmatrix} a_{10} & a_{01} & a_{00} \\ b_{10} & b_{01} & b_{00} \\ 0 & 0 & 1 \end{bmatrix}}_{\text{Unknown } T} \underbrace{\begin{bmatrix} x_1 & x_2 & x_3 \\ y_1 & y_2 & y_3 \\ 1 & 1 & 1 \end{bmatrix}}_{\text{Known coordinates}} = \begin{bmatrix} \widehat{x}_1 & \widehat{x}_2 & \widehat{x}_3 \\ \widehat{y}_1 & \widehat{y}_2 & \widehat{y}_3 \\ 1 & 1 & 1 \end{bmatrix}$$

$$\rightarrow \underbrace{\begin{bmatrix} x_1 & y_1 & 1 \\ x_2 & y_2 & 1 \\ x_3 & y_3 & 1 \end{bmatrix} \begin{bmatrix} a_{10} & b_{10} \\ a_{01} & b_{01} \\ a_{00} & b_{00} \end{bmatrix}}_{\text{Six linear equations for } a_{10}, a_{01}, \ldots, b_{00}} = \begin{bmatrix} \widehat{x}_1 & \widehat{y}_1 \\ \widehat{x}_2 & \widehat{y}_2 \\ \widehat{x}_3 & \widehat{y}_3 \end{bmatrix}$$

Actually this system consists of the two linear subsystems for the three unknown parameters each: (a_{10}, a_{01}, a_{00}) and (b_{10}, b_{01}, b_{00}).

8.2.3 *Polynomial warping*

Non-linear mapping of coordinates is generally expressed by low-order polynomials in x and y. Most popular transformation to introduce more complex geometric distortions than an affine transformation is a *quadratic warp* with 12 forward or backward mapping parameters:

$$\begin{cases} \widehat{x} = a_{20}x^2 + a_{11}xy + a_{02}y^2 + a_{10}x + a_{01}y + a_{00} \\ \widehat{y} = b_{20}x^2 + b_{11}xy + b_{02}y^2 + b_{10}x + b_{01}y + b_{00} \end{cases}$$
$$\longleftrightarrow \begin{cases} x = \alpha_{20}\widehat{x}^2 + \alpha_{11}\widehat{x}\widehat{y} + \alpha_{02}\widehat{y}^2 + \alpha_{10}\widehat{x} + \alpha_{01}\widehat{y} + \alpha_{00} \\ y = \beta_{20}\widehat{x}^2 + \beta_{11}\widehat{x}\widehat{y} + \beta_{02}\widehat{y}^2 + \beta_{10}\widehat{x} + \beta_{01}\widehat{y} + \beta_{00} \end{cases} \tag{8.9}$$

Note that cubic (with 20 coefficients) or higher-degree polynomial warps are relatively rare in practice.

Original image · Parameter set 1 · Parameter set 2 · Parameter set 3

Parameter set 4 · Parameter set 5 · Parameter set 6 · Parameter set 7

Fig. 8.8   Quadratic transformations with parameters of Example 8.4.

Example 8.4 (Quadratic warping). *Figure 8.8 shows results of the backward quadratic warps of Eq. (8.9). The control parameters have the following settings in Fig. 8.8:*

Set	α_{20}	α_{11}	α_{02}	α_{10}	α_{01}	α_{00}	β_{20}	β_{11}	β_{02}	β_{10}	β_{01}	β_{00}
1	0.1	0.1	0.1	1.0	0.1	0.0	0.1	0.1	0.1	0.1	1.0	0.0
2	0.1	0.3	0.1	1.0	0.2	0.0	0.1	0.3	0.1	0.2	1.0	0.0
3	0.2	0.4	0.2	1.0	0.2	0.0	0.2	−0.4	0.2	−0.2	1.0	0.0
4	0.2	0.0	0.2	1.0	−0.5	0.0	−0.2	0.0	−0.2	−0.5	1.0	0.0
5	−0.1	0.2	−0.1	1.0	−0.3	0.0	−0.1	0.2	−0.1	−0.3	1.0	0.0
6	−0.2	−0.2	−0.2	1.0	−0.2	0.0	0.3	0.1	0.3	0.3	1.0	0.0
7	−0.3	−0.6	−0.3	1.0	−0.3	0.0	0.3	0.6	0.3	0.3	1.0	0.0

In practice, any polynomial warp can be defined by prescribing locations of control points before and after the transformation, e.g., of at least six control points for a quadratic warp to get a linear system of 12 equations for the unknown 12 coefficients. If more point-to-point correspondences are specified than their minimum number to find the mapping parameters, the resulting overdetermined system of linear equations has an approximate least-square solution. The latter minimises the total squared Cartesian distance between the initial and transformed control points.

A more practical *piecewise warping* uses a control grid, or mesh of x- and y-oriented lines to guide warping an input image. Intersections of the grid lines are considered vertices of rectangles (or, generally, quadrangles) on the input image to be placed to new locations in the transformed image. The piecewise quadrangle-to-quadrangle warping is uniquely determined with the bilinear 8-parameter transformation:

$$\begin{cases} \widehat{x} = a_{11}xy + a_{10}x + a_{01}y + a_{00} \\ \widehat{y} = b_{11}xy + b_{10}x + b_{01}y + b_{00} \end{cases} \longleftrightarrow \begin{cases} x = \alpha_{11}\widehat{x}\widehat{y} + \alpha_{10}\widehat{x} + \alpha_{01}\widehat{y} + \alpha_{00} \\ y = \beta_{11}\widehat{x}\widehat{y} + \beta_{10}\widehat{x} + \beta_{01}\widehat{y} + \beta_{00} \end{cases}$$

$$\underbrace{\qquad\qquad\qquad\qquad}_{\text{Forward mapping}} \qquad\qquad \underbrace{\qquad\qquad\qquad\qquad}_{\text{Backward mapping}}$$

The four vertices are sufficient to find the above eight parameters for each corresponding pair of the input and output quadrangles. Generally, the lines need not be only straight, like, e.g., in the piecewise warping of a rectangular grid to a polar grid.

8.3 Questions and exercises

(1) Which coordinate mapping does not create gaps in the output image?
(2) What is an affine transformation of a 2D image?
(3) What is a polynomial warping of a 2D image?
(4) Given the digital 1D sequence **g** from Example 3.1 (Chapter 3), restore the continuous signal $g(x)$ for $x = 2.5$ by linear and cubic interpolation.
(5) Why are homogeneous coordinates more convenient in representing affine transformations?
(6) Build the affine matrix that rotate each 2D coordinate vector by the angle $\theta = 45°$, then scale it uniformly by the factor $\gamma = 1.5$, and then translate it by the offsets ($\Delta_x = 2.5$, $\Delta_y = -1.0$).
(7) How many point-to-point correspondences between input and output 2D images should be given to determine the unique quadratic warp that will co-align these pairs?

Chapter 9

Spectra and Spectral Filtering

Information about an observed scene is encoded in spatial variations of image signals over a supporting plane or volume. To explore these variations and reveal their informative properties, an image is often decomposed into a weighted sum, or linear combination of specific basis functions:

$$g(\mathbf{s}) = w_0\psi_0(\mathbf{s}) + w_1\psi_1(\mathbf{s}) + \ldots + w_{J-1}\psi_{J-1}(\mathbf{s}); \ \mathbf{s} \in \mathbb{S}; \ J \geq 1$$

Both the images, $g : \mathbb{S} \to \mathbb{Q}$, and basis functions, $\psi_j : \mathbb{S} \to \mathbb{U}; \ \mathbb{Q} \subseteq \mathbb{U}$, are elements of a certain set, $\mathbf{\Psi}$, of functions with a defined scalar *inner*, or *dot product*, $\langle \psi, \phi \rangle$, of every pair of its functions, $\psi, \phi \in \mathbf{\Psi}$. The decomposition is considerably simplified for an *orthonormal* (abridged "orthogonal" and "normed") basis, such that $\langle \psi_j, \psi_k \rangle = \delta(j - k); \ j, k = 0, \ldots, J - 1$, where $\delta(u)$ is the Kronecker's function of integer arguments ($\delta(0) = 1$ and 0 otherwise) With such a basis, the J weights follow directly from the dot products: $w_j = \langle g, \psi_j \rangle; \ j = 0, \ldots, J - 1$.

What will you find here? This chapter will outline two common linear decompositions: the *Fourier transform* (FT) and the *wavelet transform* (WT). The FT basis functions are periodic (co)sinusoidal oscillations, or waves, called simply *harmonics*. For completeness, Sections 9.1 and 9.2 will detail the 1D and 2D spatial harmonics, respectively. Both the sections may be skipped if this mathematical background is already known.

Each harmonic is a complex-valued exponential function (here, of spatial coordinates), which combines real-valued cosine and sine functions. Note that the imaginary unit in a complex number will be denoted i such that $i^2 = -1$ below. That spatial differentiation does not change the exponential, except of a constant scaling factor, makes the FT very useful for analysing variations of both the signals and their spatial derivatives as a whole.

Section 9.3 will outline the *discrete FT* (DFT) on rectangular lattices. For brevity, only square $N \times N$ lattices will be considered, but changing to rectangular $M \times N$ lattices is straightforward. Computed complex-valued weights of harmonics for an image form its *Fourier spectrum* (Section 9.3.1) with basic properties sketched in Section 9.3.2. Section 9.3.3 will detail the most accurate DFT, called the *discrete cosine transform* (DCT), and Section 9.3.4 will describe in brief the famous *fast FT* (FFT), being among the today's "Top Ten" computational algorithms. Fourier spectra and spectral filtering have gained wide-spread acceptance in computational signal processing due to "linearithmic" ($N \log N$) FFT complexity for 1D sequences of N signals, which is considerably lower than quadratic (N^2) complexity of the straightforward DFT.

That all images in practice have finite supports and limited spatial resolution calls for constrained spans and upper frequencies of the decomposition bases. However, the harmonics and Fourier spectra are unconstrained in space. Because wavelets (Section 9.4) have finite supports, the WT not only captures, but also localises characteristic oscillations. Due to these capabilities, the wavelets are widely used for image compression (coding) and denoising. Section 9.4.1 will outline the WT-based multi-resolution analysis (MRA) of images, and Sections 9.4.2 and 9.4.3 will sketch the discontinuous Haar and continuous (smooth) wavelets, respectively.

Section 9.5 will consider image filtering in the (Fourier) frequency, or spectral domain. The extremely useful relationships derived for convolution filtering in the signal and spectral domains will be detailed in Section 9.5.1, and Section 9.5.2 will outline simple high-, low-, and band-pass spectral filtering. More intricate homomorphic and cepstral filters for specific types of image noise will be described in brief in Section 9.5.4. Note that the word "cepstr..." is the permuted "spectr..." and should be read [s·e·p·s·t·r···] or [k·e·p·s·t·r···].

9.1 1D complex exponentials

To study the FT, let us begin from an integrable complex-valued 1D function, which is periodic on a certain interval of positional coordinates t.

Definition 9.1 (1D harmonic). *A harmonic unit-amplitude 1D wave, or a 1D harmonic, is a periodic 1D complex-valued exponential function:*

$$\psi(t) = \exp(2\pi i f t) \equiv \exp(i\omega t) = \cos(\omega t) + i \cdot \sin(\omega t) \qquad (9.1)$$

where f is its frequency and $\omega = 2\pi f$ is its angular frequency.

The cosine wave, $\cos(\omega t)$, is the real part of the exponential, whereas the sine wave, $\sin(\omega t)$, is its imaginary part.

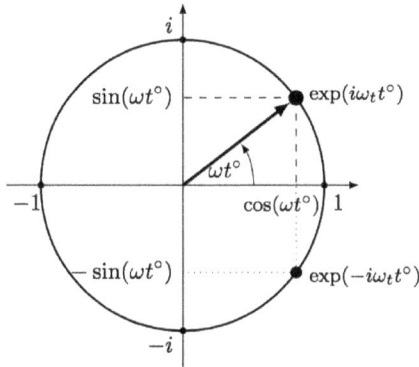

Fig. 9.1   Values of a periodic complex-valued exponential $\psi(t) = e^{i\omega t}$ of Eq. (9.1) and its conjugate $\overline{\psi(t)} = e^{-i\omega t}$ for $t = t^\circ$ as points in the complex $(1, i)$-plane.

Definition 9.2 (Complex conjugate). *Each complex function, $h(t) = h_{\mathrm{re}}(t) + ih_{\mathrm{im}}(t)$, with scalar real, $h_{\mathrm{re}}(t)$, and imaginary, $h_{\mathrm{im}}(t)$, parts has the conjugate function indicated below by the upper bar: $\overline{h(t)} = h_{\mathrm{re}}(t) - ih_{\mathrm{im}}(t)$, e.g., $\overline{\exp(i\omega t)} = \exp(-i\omega t)$.*

Each value of the exponential, $\exp(i\omega t^\circ)$, and its conjugate, $\exp(-i\omega t^\circ)$, are represented by points of the complex $(1, i)$-plane in Fig. 9.1, which sit on the unit circle centred at the origin of perpendicular real (1) and imaginary (i) axes. When the positional coordinate, t°, is increasing from $-\infty$ to $+\infty$, these mirror-symmetric points are rotating counter-clockwise and clockwise, respectively, along the circle. Each individual value of the exponential in Eq. (9.1) or its conjugate is repeating infinitely many times with a constant coordinate step, called a *period*, or cycle of this function.

Definition 9.3 (Frequency and angular frequency). *A frequency, f, is the number of periods in the unit coordinate interval, i.e., the number of complete turns of the point in Eq. (9.1) along the unit circle in Fig. 9.1, when the position t is growing from 0 to 1. An angular frequency, $\omega = 2\pi f$, is the total rotation angle for these turns because one complete turn covers 2π radians, or 360 degrees (360°).*

Statement 9.1 (Frequency vs. period). *The angular frequency, ω, frequency, f, and the period, Λ, are inversely dependent, $\Lambda = f^{-1} \equiv 2\pi\omega^{-1}$.*

Proof. For any angular frequency, ω; $0 \leq \omega < 2\pi$, and any integer factor $j = 0, \pm1, \pm2, \ldots$, the equality:

$$\exp(i(\omega t \pm 2\pi j)) = \exp(i\omega t)\,(\exp(2\pi i))^j = \exp(i\omega t)$$

holds due to the obvious equality, $\exp(2\pi i) = 1$, from Eq. (9.1). Therefore,

$$\exp(i(\omega t \pm 2\pi j)) = \exp\left(2\pi i f\left(t \pm jf^{-1}\right)\right) \equiv \exp\left(2\pi i f\left(t \pm j\Lambda\right)\right)$$

$\square$

Definition 9.4 (Dot product of complex-valued functions). *Dot product, $\langle h(t), h'(t) \rangle$, of two integrable complex-valued 1D functions, $h(t)$ and $h'(t)$, on the unit interval, $0 \leq t < 1$, is defined as*

$$\langle h(t), h'(t) \rangle = \int_0^1 h(t)\overline{h'(t)}dt$$

Statement 9.2 (Orthonormal basis). *Complex 1D exponentials of Eq. (9.1) with integer frequencies:*

$$\phi_j(t) = \exp(2\pi i j t); \quad j = 0, 1, 2, \ldots; \ 0 \leq t \leq 1 \qquad (9.2)$$

form an orthonormal basis of all integrable complex-valued 1D functions on the unit interval.

Proof. The orthonormality condition:

$$\langle \phi_j(t), \phi_k(t) \rangle = \delta(j - k) \equiv \begin{cases} 1 \text{ if } j = k; \\ 0 \text{ otherwise} \end{cases} ; \ j, k = 0, 1, 2, \ldots$$

is derived by direct integration:

$$\int_0^1 \exp\left(2\pi i(j - j)t\right) dt = \int_0^1 1 \cdot dt = 1;$$

$$\int_0^1 \exp\left(2\pi i(j - k)t\right) dt = \tfrac{1}{2\pi i(j-k)} \exp\left(2\pi i(j - k)t\right)\big|_0^1 = 0; \ j \neq k,$$

because $\exp(2\pi i t) = 1$ for each integer $t = 0, \pm1, \pm2, \ldots, \pm\infty$. $\square$

Definition 9.5 (Fourier series). *Let $g(t)$ be an 1D periodic signal with an integer period N, i.e., $g(t) = g(t + N)$ for any positional coordinate t. Then its repetitive part, $g(t)$; $0 \le t < N$ can be decomposed into a* Fourier series, *or a weighted sum of the scaled basis functions of Eq. (9.2):*

$$g(t) = G(0) + \sum_{n=1}^{N-1} G(n)\psi_n(t); \ 0 \le t < N \tag{9.3}$$

where

$$\psi_n(t) = \frac{1}{\sqrt{N}}\phi_n\left(\frac{t}{N}\right) \equiv \frac{1}{\sqrt{N}}\exp\left(2\pi i \frac{n}{N}t\right) \tag{9.4}$$

Definition 9.6 (Fourier spectrum). *Complex weights, $G(n)$; $n = 0, 1, \ldots, N - 1$, of the basis functions, $\psi_n(t)$, in Eqs. (9.3) and (9.4) form a discrete* Fourier spectrum *of the scalar function, $g(t)$; $0 \le t < N$, from Definition 9.5.*

The weights, called often *spectral components* or *Fourier coefficients*, are computed by integration:

$$G(0) = \int_0^N g(t)\overline{\psi_0(t)}dt = \frac{1}{\sqrt{N}}\int_0^N g(t)dt;$$
$$G(n) = \int_0^N g(t)\overline{\psi_n(t)}dt = \frac{1}{\sqrt{N}}\int_0^N g(t)\exp\left(-2\pi i \frac{n}{N}t\right)dt; \ n = 1, \ldots, N - 1$$

The real, $G_{re}(n)$, and imaginary, $G_{im}(n)$, scalar parts of each complex spectral component, $G(n) = G_{re}(n) + iG_{im}(n)$, of $g(t)$ can be computed individually using scalar orthonormal cosine and sine bases:

$$G_{re}(n) = \frac{1}{\sqrt{N}}\int_0^N g(t)\cos\left(2\pi \frac{n}{N}t\right)dt$$
$$G_{im}(n) = \frac{1}{\sqrt{N}}\int_0^N g(t)\sin\left(2\pi \frac{n}{N}t\right)dt$$

However, an equivalent exponential magnitude-phase representation, $G(n) = A(n)\exp(i\theta(n))$, of the spectral component where

$$A(n) = \sqrt{G_{re}^2(n) + G_{im}^2(n)} \text{ and } \theta(n) = \tan^{-1}\left(\frac{G_{im}(n)}{G_{re}(n)}\right)$$

denote the magnitude (amplitude) and phase, respectively, is more informative for visual assessments of the Fourier spectrum.

9.2   2D/3D exponentials

2D and 3D images have the like FTs. This primer will consider only so-called *separable* 2D/3D FTs, such that their basis functions are products of the coordinate-wise 1D exponentials:

$$\exp(i\mathbf{s}^{\mathsf{T}}\boldsymbol{\omega}_{\mathbf{s}}) \equiv \begin{cases} \exp(i(x\omega_{\mathrm{x}} + y\omega_{\mathrm{y}})) & \text{(2D)} \\ \exp(i(x\omega_{\mathrm{x}} + y\omega_{\mathrm{y}} + z\omega_{\mathrm{z}})) & \text{(3D)} \end{cases} \qquad (9.5)$$

where components of the vectors $\mathbf{s}$ and $\boldsymbol{\omega}_{\mathbf{s}}$ are planar pixel, (x, y), or spatial voxel, (x, y, z), coordinates and corresponding angular frequencies, $(\omega_{\mathrm{x}}, \omega_{\mathrm{y}})$ or $(\omega_{\mathrm{x}}, \omega_{\mathrm{y}}, \omega_{\mathrm{z}})$, respectively.

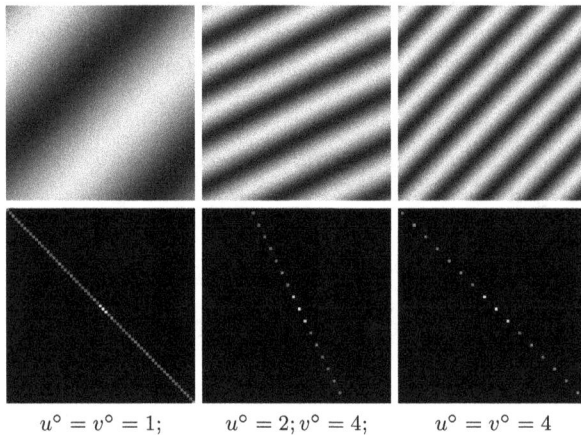

$$u^{\circ} = v^{\circ} = 1; \qquad u^{\circ} = 2; v^{\circ} = 4; \qquad u^{\circ} = v^{\circ} = 4$$

Fig. 9.2   Synthetic 2D sinusoids $g(x, y) = 96 \sin\left(\pi(u^{\circ}x + v^{\circ}y)/128\right) + 127$; $0 \leq x, y \leq 255$; and enlarged central parts, $-32 \leq u, v \leq 32$, of their log-magnitude spectra in the entire frequency range $-127 \leq u, v \leq 128$.

Both the direct (image-to-spectrum) and inverse (spectrum-to-image) FT are lossless, i.e., they preserve all image information, provided that numerical values of spectral components are not rounded off. Note that dynamic range of the spectral components is considerably larger than the range $[0 - 255]$ of the ordinary 8-bit grey values, e.g., up to $[0 - 8{,}300{,}000]$ for the magnitudes of spectral components of synthetic waves in Fig. 9.2. In contrast to the above waves, spatial variations of grey values in a vast majority of realistic images are non-periodic. However, spectral representations and transformations notably facilitate solutions of many image processing and analysis problems.

9.3 Discrete Fourier transform (DFT)

Separable 2D/3D exponentials of Eq. (9.5) simplify the FT of images on rectangular lattices. The forward DFT of a 2D digital image, $\mathbf{g} = (g(x, y) : x, y \in \{0, 1, \ldots, N - 1\})$, supported, for brevity, by a square $N \times N$ lattice, forms a discrete spectrum, $\mathbf{G} = (G(u, v) : u, v = 0, 1, \ldots, N - 1)$, of the complex Fourier coefficients:

$$G(u, v) = \frac{1}{N} \sum_{x=0}^{N-1} \sum_{y=0}^{N-1} g(x, y) \exp\left(-\frac{2\pi i}{N}(ux + vy)\right) \qquad (9.6)$$

Each coefficient $G(u, v)$ evaluates a contribution of the related periodic basis exponential, i.e., the individual contributions of its real (cosine) and imaginary (sine) parts, into the image g. Because the N-component vectors sampled from the complex exponentials of Eq. (9.6):

$$\left[\exp\left(-\frac{2\pi i j}{N}\right) : j = 0, 1, \ldots, N - 1\right]$$

are orthonormal, the inverse DFT converting a spectrum back into its initial image differs from the forward DFT only by the sign of the exponent:

$$g(x, y) = \frac{1}{N} \sum_{u=0}^{N-1} \sum_{v=0}^{N-1} G(u, v) \exp\left(\frac{2\pi i}{N}(ux + vy)\right)$$

The $N \times N$ array of complex Fourier coefficients obtained by the forward DFT of a greyscale $N \times N$ image provides a complete dual representation of the image and allows for reconstructing it back by the inverse DFT.

Transformations and analysis of an image $\mathbf{g}$ in the signal or spectral domain deal with its pixel-wise grey values, $g(x, y)$, or Fourier coefficients, $G(u, v)$, respectively. Switching from one domain to another by the forward or inverse DFT loses, by itself, no information, except for possible negative impacts of limited accuracy of computations.

Example 9.1 (Computational accuracy impacts). *Figure 9.3 illustrates restoring a black-white synthetic image with the inverse DFT after encoding with 8-, 16-, and 32-bit integers both the real and imaginary parts of spectral components produced by the forward DFT.*

9.3.1 Amplitude, phase, and power spectra

As mentioned in Section 9.1, each complex Fourier coefficient, $G(u, v)$, for a 2D image is equivalently represented by its amplitude, $A(u, v)$, denoted

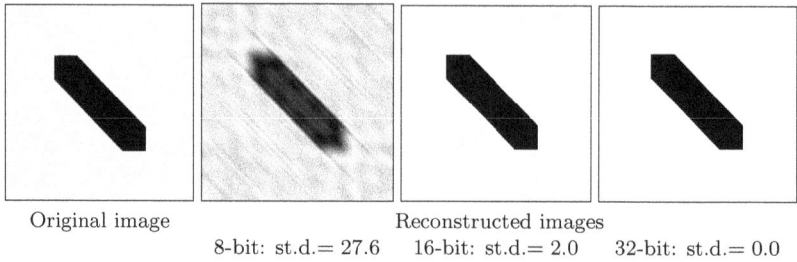

Original image   Reconstructed images
8-bit: st.d.= 27.6   16-bit: st.d.= 2.0   32-bit: st.d.= 0.0

Fig. 9.3   Image reconstruction after integer encoding of spectral components.

often $|G(u,v)|$, and phase, $\theta(u,v)$:

$$A(u,v) = \sqrt{G_{\text{re}}^2(u,v) + G_{\text{im}}^2(u,v)} \text{ and } \theta(u,v) = \tan^{-1}\left[\frac{G_{\text{im}}(u,v)}{G_{\text{re}}(u,v)}\right]$$

Definition 9.7 (Amplitude and phase spectra). *The amplitudes,* $\mathbf{A} = (A(u,v) : 0 \le u,v \le N-1)$, *and phases,* $\boldsymbol{\theta} = (\theta(u,v) : 0 \le u,v \le N-1)$, *of Fourier coefficients obtained by the DFT of an image form, respectively, the* amplitude spectrum *and* phase spectrum *of the image.*

Definition 9.8 (Power spectra). *The* power spectrum, *called also the* spectral density *of an image, is the squared amplitude spectrum,* $\mathbf{F} = (F(u,v) : 0 \le u,v \le N-1)$ *where* $F(u,v) = A^2(u,v) = G_{\text{re}}^2(u,v) + G_{\text{im}}^2(u,v)$.

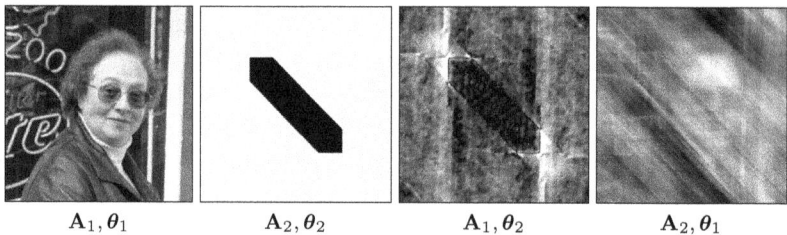

A_1, θ_1 A_2, θ_2 A_1, θ_2 A_2, θ_1

Fig. 9.4   Images before and after exchanging their phase spectra.

Peaks in the amplitude and power spectra indicate dominant harmonics. The phase spectrum encodes relative mutual shifts of harmonics. When the phase information is lost, the depicted objects are completely destroyed. However, when only the amplitudes are lost, the actual pixel brightness cannot be restored, but most prominent object boundaries still can be seen to some extent, as shown in Fig. 9.4. Because the phases preserve visual appearance, image processing in the spectral domain affects for the most part only the amplitudes.

9.3.2 Some properties of the DFT

In our simplified case an image is supported by a finite $N \times N$ lattice, $\mathbb{S} = \{(x, y) : x = 0, \ldots, N-1; y = 0, \ldots, N-1\}$, or, equivalently, the image is on the infinite lattice, $\mathbb{S}_{\text{inf}} = \{(x, y) : x = 0, \pm1, \ldots, \pm\infty; y = 0, \pm1, \ldots, \pm\infty\}$, but has only zero signals outside its $N \times N$ block $\mathbb{S}$; $\mathbb{S} \subset \mathbb{S}_{\text{inf}}$. However, the Fourier spectrum produced by the DFT is infinite, periodic, and symmetric due to mirror symmetry and periodicity of complex-valued exponentials and their conjugates along the spatial axes:

$$\exp\left(\pm\frac{2\pi i f}{N}t\right) = \cos\left(\frac{2\pi f}{N}t\right) \pm i \cdot \sin\left(\frac{2\pi f}{N}t\right); \quad -\infty \leq t \leq \infty \quad (9.7)$$

Centring the DFT. When the integer index f in Eq. (9.7) increases from 0 to $N/2$, the angular frequency of this harmonic is increasing from zero to the maximum value of π. Then, while the index f continues to increase from $N/2$ to N, the angular frequency is actually decreasing back to zero due to the mirror symmetry:

$$\exp\left(2\pi i \tfrac{f}{N}\right) = \exp\left(-2\pi i \tfrac{N-f}{N}\right), \text{ or}$$
$$\cos\left(\tfrac{2\pi f}{N}\right) = \cos\left(\tfrac{2\pi(N-f)}{N}\right); \sin\left(\tfrac{2\pi f}{N}\right) = -\sin\left(\tfrac{2\pi(N-f)}{N}\right)$$

Therefore, the $N \times N$ array of Fourier coefficients, $G(u, v)$, after the 2D DFT is actually a core of the infinite spectrum, replicating the core infinitely many times with the period of N along both the u- and v-axes:

$$G(u, v) = G(u + nN, v + mN); \ m, n \in \{0, \pm1, \pm2, \ldots, \pm\infty\}$$

Non-negative real-valued images have most prominent spectral amplitudes for zero spatial frequencies, so that centring their spectra at the origin, $(u = 0, v = 0)$, facilitates visual assessment. The centred spectrum, $\mathbf{G} = (G(u, v) : -N/2 \leq u, v \leq N/2)$, can be built by rotating quadrants of the initial spectrum after the DFT, as illustrated in Fig. 9.5.

A more elegant alternative way to the same centring is suggested by the *shift theorem*, which is beyond the scope of this primer. To sketch this way, spectral coefficients of Eq. (9.6) for the centred spectral coordinates, $u' = u - N/2$ and $v' = v - N/2$, should be rewritten using the equality $\exp(-i\pi) = -1$ for the complex-valued exponentials:

$$G(u', v') = \tfrac{1}{N} \sum_{x=0}^{N-1}\sum_{y=0}^{N-1} g(x, y) \exp\left(-i\tfrac{2\pi}{N}\left(\left(u - \tfrac{N}{2}\right)x + \left(v - \tfrac{N}{2}\right)y\right)\right)$$
$$= \tfrac{1}{N} \sum_{x=0}^{N-1}\sum_{y=0}^{N-1} (-1)^{x+y} g(x, y) \exp\left(-i\tfrac{2\pi}{N}\left(ux + vy\right)\right)$$

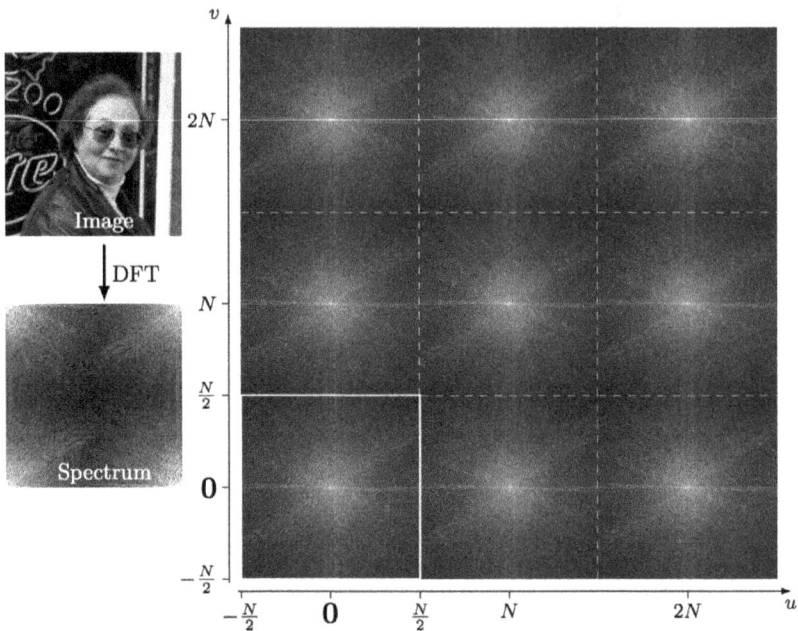

Fig. 9.5   Greyscale $N \times N$ image with its $N \times N$ amplitude spectrum (left) and the centred spectrum in a portion of the entire infinite periodic spectrum (right).

Therefore, to shift the origin to the centre of the DFT spectrum of Eq. (9.6), the adjacent signals $g(x,y)$ should be made sign-alternate by multiplying by $(-1)^{x+y}$, i.e., negating for the odd sums, $x + y$, of pixel coordinates.

Example 9.2 (Visualising amplitude spectra). *Synthetic 2D sinusoids in Fig. 9.2 have the simplest dot-like spectra consisting of a few basis harmonics. Generally, typical low frequency amplitudes are considerably larger than the high frequency ones. To visualise characteristic details, the original amplitudes are nonlinearly (mostly, logarithmically) mapped onto the 8-bit greyscale range, $[0, 255]$, or linearly scaled down and truncated to this range. Figure 9.6 exemplifies these transformations of the same spectrum as in Fig. 9.5. For logarithmic mapping the amplitudes are biased up by adding 1 to exclude negative outputs.*

Windowing to reduce distortions. The Fourier spectrum of a finite $N \times N$ image in Fig. 9.5 is infinite and periodic, its finite $N \times N$ core formed by the DFT being repeated infinitely many times in both directions. To restore the finite image, the inverse DFT should have added up infinitely

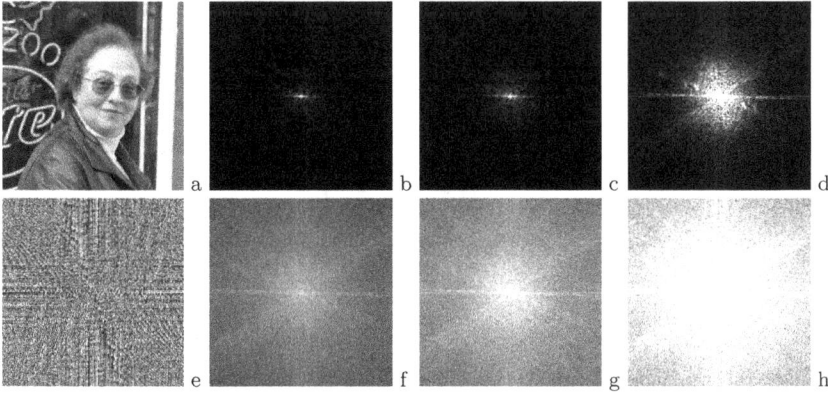

Fig. 9.6 Test image (a) with its centred grey-coded amplitude spectrum truncated at 10% (b), 5% (c), and 0.5% (d) of the maximal amplitude (here, the amplitude range is $[4, 6.7 \cdot 10^6]$); its centred phase spectrum (e), and the log-amplitude spectrum (f) together with versions truncated at 75% (g) and 50% (h) of the maximal logarithmic amplitude.

many terms, but fortunately no infinite sums are needed. Considering the $N \times N$ core an infinite spectrum with zero amplitudes at all other points of the (u, v)-plane leads to an infinitely replicated restored $N \times N$ image, like in Fig. 9.7. Equivalently, a planar $N \times N$ image lattice may be considered toroidal by joining its left and top sides with the right and bottom sides, respectively, as was shown, e.g., in Chapter 3 (Fig. 3.2). Both the considerations suggest that any mismatch along the joining lines, i.e., any border discontinuity in the periodic image, distorts the Fourier spectrum of the core image at high frequencies.

These distortions are often reduced by *windowing* an image before the DFT. Pixel-wise signals are gradually scaled down to zero outside a circular window of a given radius, $\rho_{\max}$, around the image centre, $\mathbf{s}_c = (x_c, y_c)$. Scale factors for the pixels, $\mathbf{s} = (x, y)$, are specified by a *windowing function*, $w_{\mathbf{s}}$; $0 \leq w_{\mathbf{s}} \leq 1$, depending on relative closeness, $\zeta_{\mathbf{s}}$; $0 \leq \zeta_{\mathbf{s}} \leq 1$, to the image centre:

$$\zeta_{\mathbf{s}} = \begin{cases} 1 - \frac{1}{\rho_{\max}} d(\mathbf{s}, \mathbf{s}_c) \text{ if } d(\mathbf{s}, \mathbf{s}_c) \leq \rho_{\max}; \\ 0 \qquad\qquad\qquad \text{otherwise} \end{cases}$$

where $d(\mathbf{s}, \mathbf{s}_c) = \sqrt{(x - x_c)^2 + (y - y_c)^2}$ is the inter-pixel Cartesian distance. Table 9.1 presents three efficient windowing functions proposed by M. S. Bartlett, J. van Hann (it is traditionally called the Hanning window), and R. S. Blackman. Figure 9.8 illustrates the Hanning windowing.

Mirroring to reduce distortions. Spectral distortions due to border

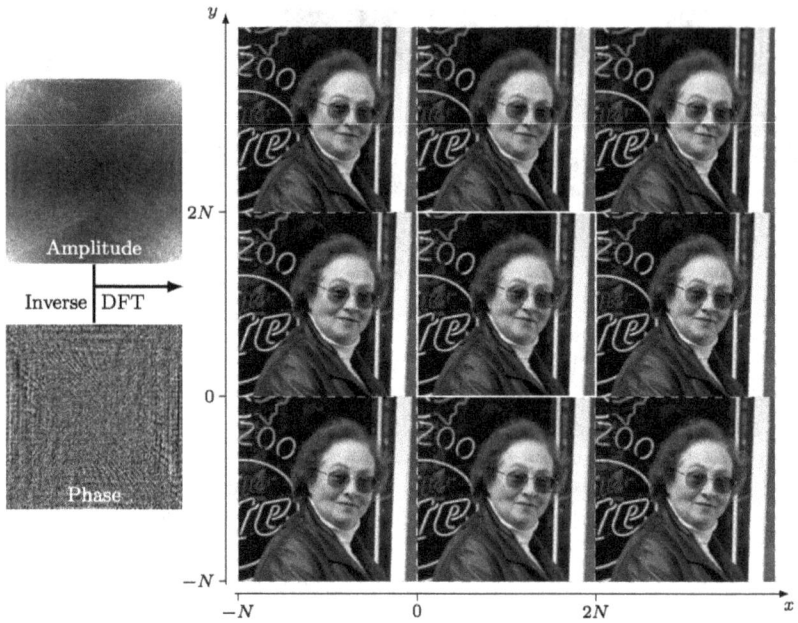

Fig. 9.7   Periodic image restored from the finite $N \times N$ spectrum with the inverse DFT.

Table 9.1   2D windowing functions $w_{\mathbf{s}}$ in relation to $\zeta_{\mathbf{s}}$.

Window	Bartlett's	Hanning	Blackman's
$w_{\mathbf{s}} =$	$\zeta_{\mathbf{s}}$	$0.5 - 0.5 \cos (\pi \zeta_{\mathbf{s}})$	$0.42 - 0.5 \cos (\pi \zeta_{\mathbf{s}}) + 0.08 \cos (2\pi \zeta_{\mathbf{s}})$

discontinuities are reduced more efficiently if an input image is mirrored at its borders (see Fig. 3.2 in Chapter 3).

Replacing the DFT with the *discrete cosine transform* (DCT) detailed below, in Section 9.3.3, makes a finite $N \times N$ spectrum of an infinite periodic image (its small part is exemplified in Fig. 9.9). Because each replicated $2N \times 2N$ block contains vertically and horizontally mirrored $N \times N$ input images, no extra discontinuities appear at borders of all the replicas.

9.3.3   *Discrete cosine transform (DCT)*

Mirroring a sequence, $\mathbf{g} = (g(t) : t = 0, 1, \ldots, N - 1)$, of N 1D signals produces a sequence, $\mathbf{g}_{\mathrm{p}} = (g(t) : t = 0, 1, \ldots, 2N - 1)$, of length $2N$, such that $g(t) = g(2N - 1 - t)$ for $t = 0, 1, \ldots, N - 1$. Infinitely many repetitions of the latter sequence result in an infinite periodic sequence with no extra

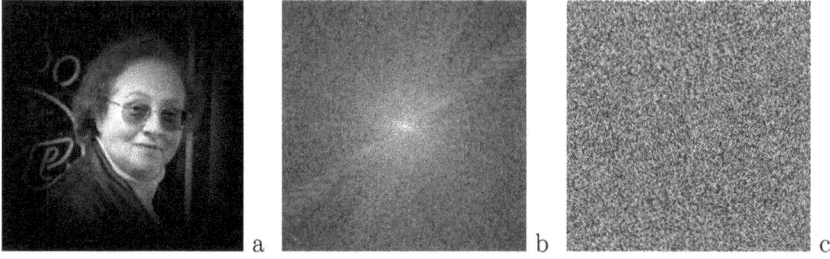

a   b   c

Fig. 9.8 Image from Fig. 9.6 after the Hanning windowing (a) and its log-amplitude (b) and phase (c) spectra. Note that high-frequency areas are now more uniform.

discontinuities at borders of its half-periods of length N.

Statement 9.3 (DCT spectra). *The DFT spectrum of the mirrored sequence,* $\mathbf{g}_p$, *is the DCT spectrum of the initial sequence,* $\mathbf{g}$, *of length* N.

Proof. Components of the DFT $G = (G(u) : u = 0, 1, \ldots, 2N - 1)$ of the mirrored sequence $\mathbf{g}_p$:

$$G(u) = \sum_{t=0}^{2N-1} g(t) \exp\left(-i\frac{2\pi u}{2N} t\right) = \sum_{t=0}^{2N-1} g(t) \exp\left(-i\frac{\pi u}{N} t\right)$$

can be rewritten as

$$G(u) = \sum_{t=0}^{N-1} g(t) \exp\left(-i\frac{\pi u}{N} t\right) + \sum_{t=N}^{2N-1} g(t) \exp\left(-i\frac{\pi u}{N} t\right)$$

By substituting a new index, $s = 2N - 1 - t$, into the second sum and using the equality, $\exp(-2\pi i s) = 1$, for any integer s, $G(u)$ is transformed as follows:

$$G(u) = \sum_{t=0}^{N-1} g(t) \exp\left(-i\frac{\pi u}{N} t\right) + \sum_{s=0}^{N-1} g(s) \exp\left(-i\frac{\pi u}{N}(2N - 1 - s)\right)$$

$$= \sum_{t=0}^{N-1} g(t) \exp\left(-i\frac{\pi u}{N} t\right) + \exp(-i2\pi u) \sum_{s=0}^{N-1} g(s) \exp\left(i\frac{\pi u}{N}(1 + s)\right)$$

$$= \sum_{t=0}^{N-1} g(t) \left(\exp\left(-i\frac{\pi u}{N} t\right) + \exp\left(i\frac{\pi u}{N}\right) \exp\left(i\frac{\pi u}{N} t\right)\right)$$

$$= \exp\left(i\frac{\pi u}{2N}\right) \sum_{t=0}^{N-1} g(t) \left(\exp\left(-i\frac{\pi u}{N}\left(t + \tfrac{1}{2}\right)\right) + \exp\left(i\frac{\pi u}{N}\left(t + \tfrac{1}{2}\right)\right)\right)$$

$$\equiv 2 \exp\left(i\frac{\pi u}{2N}\right) \sum_{t=0}^{N-1} g(t) \cos\left(\frac{\pi u}{N}\left(t + \tfrac{1}{2}\right)\right)$$

Fig. 9.9   Mirrored infinite image with less border discontinuities w.r.t. Fig. 9.7.

The obtained relationship leads to the forward and inverse real-valued DCT:

$$G_{\mathrm{DCT}}(u) = \gamma_u \sum_{t=0}^{N-1} g(t) \cos\left(\tfrac{\pi u}{N}\left(t + \tfrac{1}{2}\right)\right); \ u = 0, 1, \ldots, N-1$$

$$g(t) \quad = \gamma_t \sum_{u=0}^{N-1} G_{\mathrm{DCT}}(u) \cos\left(\tfrac{\pi u}{N}\left(t + \tfrac{1}{2}\right)\right); \ t = 0, 1, \ldots, N-1$$

with the following scaling factors:

$$\gamma_0 = \frac{1}{\sqrt{N}} \text{ and } \gamma_1 = \gamma_2 = \ldots = \gamma_{N-1} = \frac{\sqrt{2}}{\sqrt{N}}$$

$\square$

The above relationships confirm that the DCT spectrum, $\mathbf{G} = (G(u) : u = 0, 1, \ldots, N-1)$, of an original 1D sequence, $\mathbf{g}$, is less affected by border discontinuities, than the DFT spectrum of the original sequence. The same is true for the 2D DCT of a rectangular $N \times N$ image, which is the 2D DFT spectrum of an infinite periodic image repeating the $2N \times 2N$ blocks of the mirrored $N \times N$ images.

9.3.4 Fast Fourier transform (FFT)

The 2D DFT or DCT computes a single spectral component, $G(u, v)$, by summing complex-valued products over all the pixels of a square $N \times N$ image. This quadratic time complexity, $O(N^2)$, suggests the $O(N^4)$ complexity of forming the entire $N \times N$ Fourier spectrum. In practice, such computations are too slow, as will be shown below, in Table 9.2.

Separability of the complex-valued 2D exponentials suggests the faster two-stage 2D DFT: (i) the 1D DFT is applied to each row of an input $N \times N$ image to form an intermediate $N \times N$ array of complex-valued spectral components of the row-wise 1D image signals and (ii) the 1D DFT is then applied to each column of the intermediate array to form the $N \times N$ 2D spectral components $G(u, v)$. These $2N^3$, rather than N^4, complex-valued multiplications reduce the DFT complexity to $O(N^3)$, but even the cubic complexity is still impractical (see Table 9.2 below).

Table 9.2 DFT vs. FFT for 10^{-9} sec per complex-valued multiplication.

Size ($N \times N$)	DFT (N^4 ops)	DFT ($2N^3$ ops)	FFT ($2N^2 \log_2 N$ ops)
256×256	43 *sec*	0.34 *sec*	0.01 *sec*
512×512	690 *sec*	2.7 *sec*	0.05 *sec*
1024×1024	11,000 *sec*	22 *sec*	0.21 *sec*

The recursive 1D FFT (Algorithm 14) computing a Fourier spectrum of an 1D sequence of N signals has *linearithmic*, $O(N \log N)$, time complexity. Assuming the length, N, is a power of two, $N = 2^n$, the DFT of this sequence is considered a sum of two DFTs of twice shorter subsequences, and such partitioning continues down to the shortest subsequences of length two. Then the overall amount of computations is proportional to $N \log_2 N$, rather than N^2 for the conventional 1D DFT.

Due to time complexity $O(N^2 \log N)$, i.e., only $2N^2 \log_2 N$ complex-valued multiplications for an image of size $N \times N$, the separable 2D FFT considerably outperforms the separable 2D DFT (see Table 9.2). Both the direct and inverse FFTs of the complex-valued inputs in Algorithm 14 are

---

Algorithm 14 1D FFT for an input sequence of size $N = 2^n$.

Input: Direction γ: -1 (direct FFT) or 1 (inverse FFT);
    a signal or spectral sequence $\mathbf{a} = (a(t) : t = 0, 1, \ldots, N-1)$;
    complex-valued work arrays $A_1[0..N-1]$ and $A_2[0..N-1]$.
Initialisation: $A_1 = \mathbf{a}$; $\lambda = \gamma \frac{2\pi i}{2^n}$
Iterations:
for $j = 1$ **step** $j \leftarrow j+1$ **until** n **do**
    $\Lambda = 2^{n-j}$
    for $k = 0$ **step** $k \leftarrow k+1$ **until** $2^{j-1} - 1$ **do**
        $t_{2p} = k\Lambda$; $t_{2n} = t_{2p} + 2^{n-1}$
        for $l = 0$ **step** $l \leftarrow l+1$ **until** $2^{n-k} - 1$ **do**
            $A_2[l + t_{2p}] = A_1[l + 2k\Lambda] + \exp\left(\lambda k 2^{n-k}\right) A_1[l + (2k+1)\Lambda]$
            $A_2[l + t_{2n}] = A_1[l + 2k\Lambda] - \exp\left(\lambda k 2^{n-k}\right) A_1[l + (2k+1)\Lambda]$
        end for
    end for
    $A_1 = A_2$
end for
return $\frac{1}{\sqrt{N}} A_1$

---

normed symmetrically:

$$G(u) = \frac{1}{\sqrt{N}} \sum_{x=0}^{N-1} g(x) \exp\left(-\frac{2\pi i}{N} xu\right) ; \; u = 0, \ldots, N-1$$

$$g(x) = \frac{1}{\sqrt{N}} \sum_{u=0}^{N-1} G(u) \exp\left(\frac{2\pi i}{N} xu\right) ; \quad x = 0, \ldots, N-1$$

and differ only by their negative or positive exponential factors. The above classical FFT requires the input data size, N, being a power of two. More complex today's FFT algorithms accept much more diverse inputs.

9.4 Wavelets and wavelet decompositions

Fourier spectra of spatially localised signals provide weights of the basis complex-valued exponentials. The latter combine real-valued sine and cosine waves that spread with no change over an infinite supporting line, plane, or volume. Thus, actually the weights characterise an infinite and periodic repetition of the same localised signal, as, e.g., in Fig. 9.7.

    The narrower the span of spectral energy, the wider the span of spatial signal energy and vice versa, due to a so-called *uncertainty principle*,

$\sigma_g \sigma_G \geq 0.5$. It states that standard deviations, σ_g and σ_G, of the signal and spectral energies, respectively, are inversely proportional.

Replacing the infinite waves by *wavelets* with constrained both spatial and spectral supports leads to linear decompositions, which are in many cases more suitable, than the Fourier spectra, for describing, analysing, and encoding local signal variations.

Like the FT, a *wavelet transform* (WT) decomposes a signal into a linear combination of specific basis functions of the same shape and different scales. But unlike the FT, the basis functions are localised in both the signal and frequency domains, so that the same-scale components are also placed at different locations. Also, unlike the FT, the wavelet basis functions are not prescribed and can be tailored to a problem under consideration.

9.4.1 Multi-resolution analysis (MRA)

A wavelet family is formed by scaling and shifting a single *mother wavelet*.

Definition 9.9 (Basis wavelets). *If $\psi(t)$ is a mother wavelet for 1D signals $g(t)$, the basis function of scale κ and at location s is defined as*

$$\psi_{\kappa,s}(t) = \frac{1}{\sqrt{|\kappa|}} \psi\left(\frac{t-s}{\kappa}\right)$$

Many wavelet families are orthonormal, e.g., the most common families of scale $\kappa = 2$ and with integer shifts, ν, where $\psi_{0,0}(t) = \psi(t)$ and

$$\psi_{r,\nu}(t) = \frac{1}{(\sqrt{2})^r} \psi\left(\frac{t}{2^r} - \nu\right); \quad \nu = 0, \pm 1, \pm 2, \ldots$$

Given an 1D signal sequence, $\mathbf{g} = (g(t) : t = 0, 1, \ldots, N-1)$, and its maximal resolution, R, it is most convenient to consider and implement the WT:

$$g(t) = \sum_{r \leq R} \sum_{\nu=0,\pm 1,\ldots} w_{r,\nu} \psi_{r,\nu}(t)$$

in terms of *multi-resolution analysis* (MRA). At each successive resolution stage, r, the MRA iterates two operations:

(1) Reduce the resolution by scaling the current signal down and
(2) Decompose differences between the current and scaled signals.

Generally, in addition to the mother wavelet, the WT-based MRA employs a certain *scaling function* to cover the entire Fourier spectrum of the input signal. However, these details are omitted in this primer. Similarly to the FT, the WT is easily generalised to 2D/3D images because a number of typical 2D/3D wavelets are products of the 1D functions.

9.4.2 *Haar wavelets*

One of the most prominent 1D mother wavelets and apparently the simplest one, called the *Haar function*, is localised on a line segment with positional coordinates t in the unit interval $0 \le t < 1$:

$$\psi(t) = \begin{cases} 1 \text{ if } 0 \le t < 0.5 \\ -1 \text{ if } 0.5 \le t < 1 \\ 0 \text{ if } t < 0 \text{ or } t \ge 1 \end{cases}$$

It produces the following orthogonal Haar wavelets on the same segment:

$$\psi_{r,\nu}(t) = \left(\sqrt{2}\right)^r \psi(2^r t - \nu) = \begin{cases} \left(\sqrt{2}\right)^r \text{ if } \frac{\nu}{2^r} \le t < \frac{\nu+0.5}{2^r} \\ -\left(\sqrt{2}\right)^r \text{ if } \frac{\nu+0.5}{2^r} \le t < \frac{\nu+1}{2^r} \\ 0 \text{ otherwise} \end{cases} \quad (9.8)$$

where, as can be easily shown, exactly 2^r shifts, $\nu = 0, \ldots, 2^r - 1$, exist for each resolution $r = 0, 1, 2, \ldots, n$.

The single starting Haar wavelet, $\psi_{0,0}$, coincides with the mother function in Eq. (9.8), $\psi_{0,0}(t) = \psi(t)$. The two wavelets at the next resolution ($r = 1$ and $\nu = 0$ or 1), are listed in Eq. (9.9):

$$\psi_{1,0}(t) = \begin{cases} \sqrt{2} \text{ if } 0 \le t < \frac{1}{4} \\ -\sqrt{2} \text{ if } \frac{1}{4} \le t < \frac{1}{2} \\ 0 \text{ otherwise} \end{cases} ; \quad \psi_{1,1}(t) = \begin{cases} \sqrt{2} \text{ if } \frac{1}{2} \le t < \frac{3}{4} \\ -\sqrt{2} \text{ if } \frac{3}{4} \le t < 1 \\ 0 \text{ otherwise} \end{cases} \quad (9.9)$$

Let a sequence **g** of $N = 2^n$ signals with integer coordinates $t = 0, 1, \ldots, 2^n - 1$ be considered a vector-column. Then its discrete Haar decomposition (DHT) can be represented by the orthonormal $N \times N$ matrix H, such that its rows are vectors of the orthonormal Haar wavelets.

Example 9.3 (8×8 **DHT matrix**). *The DHT matrix for the maximal* *resolution $n-3$ is as follows:*

$$H = \begin{bmatrix} \mathbf{u}^{\mathsf{T}} \\ \boldsymbol{\psi}_{0,0}^{\mathsf{T}} \\ \boldsymbol{\psi}_{1,0}^{\mathsf{T}} \\ \boldsymbol{\psi}_{1,1}^{\mathsf{T}} \\ \boldsymbol{\psi}_{2,0}^{\mathsf{T}} \\ \boldsymbol{\psi}_{2,1}^{\mathsf{T}} \\ \boldsymbol{\psi}_{2,2}^{\mathsf{T}} \\ \boldsymbol{\psi}_{2,3}^{\mathsf{T}} \end{bmatrix} \equiv \begin{bmatrix} \frac{1}{\sqrt{8}} & \frac{1}{\sqrt{8}} & \frac{1}{\sqrt{8}} & \frac{1}{\sqrt{8}} & \frac{1}{\sqrt{8}} & \frac{1}{\sqrt{8}} & \frac{1}{\sqrt{8}} & \frac{1}{\sqrt{8}} \\ \frac{1}{\sqrt{8}} & \frac{1}{\sqrt{8}} & \frac{1}{\sqrt{8}} & \frac{1}{\sqrt{8}} & -\frac{1}{\sqrt{8}} & -\frac{1}{\sqrt{8}} & -\frac{1}{\sqrt{8}} & -\frac{1}{\sqrt{8}} \\ \frac{1}{2} & \frac{1}{2} & -\frac{1}{2} & -\frac{1}{2} & 0 & 0 & 0 & 0 \\ 0 & 0 & 0 & 0 & \frac{1}{2} & \frac{1}{2} & -\frac{1}{2} & -\frac{1}{2} \\ \frac{1}{\sqrt{2}} & \frac{1}{\sqrt{2}} & 0 & 0 & 0 & 0 & 0 & 0 \\ 0 & 0 & \frac{1}{\sqrt{2}} & -\frac{1}{\sqrt{2}} & 0 & 0 & 0 & 0 \\ 0 & 0 & 0 & 0 & \frac{1}{\sqrt{2}} & -\frac{1}{\sqrt{2}} & 0 & 0 \\ 0 & 0 & 0 & 0 & 0 & 0 & \frac{1}{\sqrt{2}} & -\frac{1}{\sqrt{2}} \end{bmatrix} \tag{9.10}$$

Weights $\mathbf{w} = [w, w_{0,0}, w_{1,0}, \ldots]^{\mathsf{T}}$ of the linear signal decomposition, $\mathbf{g} = H\mathbf{w}$, with the DHT matrix, H, of Example 9.3 are easily found as $\mathbf{w} = H^{\mathsf{T}}\mathbf{g}$ due to orthonormality of this matrix.

Example 9.4 (Haar wavelet decomposition). *Let $n = 3$, i.e., $N = 2^3 = 8$, as in Example 9.3, and $\mathbf{g}° = [10, 20, 30, 20, 50, 40, 30, 40]^{\mathsf{T}}$. Then the decomposition weights are*

$$\mathbf{w}° = H^{\mathsf{T}}\mathbf{g}° = \left[\frac{240}{\sqrt{8}}, \frac{-80}{\sqrt{8}}, \frac{-20}{2}, \frac{20}{2}, \frac{-10}{\sqrt{2}}, \frac{10}{\sqrt{2}}, \frac{10}{\sqrt{2}}, \frac{-10}{\sqrt{2}} \right]^{\mathsf{T}}$$

for the DHT matrix H in Eq. 9.10. The decomposition $\mathbf{g}° = H^{\mathsf{T}}\mathbf{w}°$ is lossless:

$$\mathbf{g}° = \begin{bmatrix} 30 & -10 & -5 & & -5 & \\ 30 & -10 & -5 & & +5 & \\ 30 & -10 & +5 & & +5 & \\ 30 & -10 & +5 & & -5 & \\ 30 & +10 & +5 & & +5 & \\ 30 & +10 & +5 & & -5 & \\ 30 & +10 & -5 & & -5 & \\ 30 & +10 & -5 & & +5 & \end{bmatrix} = \begin{bmatrix} 10 \\ 20 \\ 30 \\ 20 \\ 50 \\ 40 \\ 30 \\ 40 \end{bmatrix}$$

Multi-scale DHT At different scales, $r = 0, 1, \ldots, n$, and shifts, $\nu = 0, 1, \ldots, 2^r - 1$, the Haar wavelets decompose in a similar way the successive groups of $2^r = 2, 4, \ldots, 2^n$ adjacent signals. This property calls for replacing the fixed-resolution DHT using the 2^n wavelets with a multi-scale, or multi-resolution DHT. Starting from an original high-resolution signal sequence of length $N = 2^n$, the multi-scale DHT builds a binary tree of height n.

The original sequence. $\mathbf{g}°$, is associated with the tree root (the node at level $r = 0$), and gives rise at the next level, $r = 1$, to the scaled down sequence $\mathbf{g}_1$ of length 2^{n-1} and its same-length complement, $\mathbf{\Delta}_1$, helping to restore the original sequence, $\mathbf{g}° \equiv \mathbf{g}_0$.

The same partitioning is then applied to the node associated with the lower-resolution sequence, $\mathbf{g}_1$. Each decomposition step, $r = 0, 1, \ldots, n-1$ of the lossless multi-scale DHT replaces the successive signal pairs, $\big(g_\nu(2s), g_\nu(2s+1)\big)$, with their means, or halved sums, $g_{r+1}(s)$, and halved differences, $\Delta_{r+1}(s)$:

$$g_{r+1}(s) = \tfrac{1}{2}\left(g_r(2s) + g_r(2s+1)\right); \; \Delta_{r+1}(s) = \tfrac{1}{2}\left(g_r(2s) - g_r(2s+1)\right);$$
$$s = 0, \ldots, 2^{n-r-1}$$

The original signal sequence at step $r = 0$, $\mathbf{g}_0 = \mathbf{g}°$, is converted at the last step, $r = n-1$, into the sequence $\mathbf{w}°$ of the Haar weights, comprising the 1D Haar spectrum of $\mathbf{g}°$.

Example 9.5 (Multi-scale Haar wavelet decomposition). *Given the same signal sequence,* $\mathbf{g}° = [10, 20, 30, 20, 50, 40, 30, 40]^\mathsf{T}$, *as in Example 9.4, the multi-scale direct DHT for obtaining the Haar spectrum, or the weights* $\mathbf{w}°$, *and the inverse restoration of the initial signal sequence from the spectrum are detailed in Table 9.3.*

Table 9.3   Multi-scale DHT of a sequence of length $N = 2^3 \equiv 8$ (3 stages).

Stage	Original and transformed signal sequences								
	10	20	30	20	50	40	30	40	$\mathbf{g}_0 = \mathbf{g}°$
$1 \rightarrow$	15	25	45	35	-5	5	5	-5	$\mathbf{g}_1;\ \mathbf{\Delta}_1$
$2 \rightarrow$	20	40	-5	5	-5	5	5	-5	$\mathbf{g}_2;\ \mathbf{\Delta}_2;\ \mathbf{\Delta}_1$
$3 \rightarrow$	30	-10	-5	5	-5	5	5	-5	$\mathbf{g}_3;\ \mathbf{\Delta}_3;\ \mathbf{\Delta}_2;\ \mathbf{\Delta}_1$
	w	$w_{0,0}$	$w_{1,0}$	$w_{1,1}$	$w_{2,0}$	$w_{2,1}$	$w_{2,2}$	$w_{2,3}$	
				Haar spectrum $\mathbf{w}°$					

Generally, this decomposition tree embraces both the lossless and lossy multi-scale decompositions, separating at each step a current signal sequence into its compressed lower-resolution version and its complement for exact or approximate restoration of the higher-resolution sequence. In the lossless DHT both the compressed and complementary parts have no quantisation errors and allow for restoring the exact original sequence.

2D DHT. The 2D multi-scale DHT of a square $2^n \times 2^n$ greyscale image performs at each next tree level, r, a 2D pyramidal image compression with three complements corresponding to horizontal, vertical, and diagonal pairs

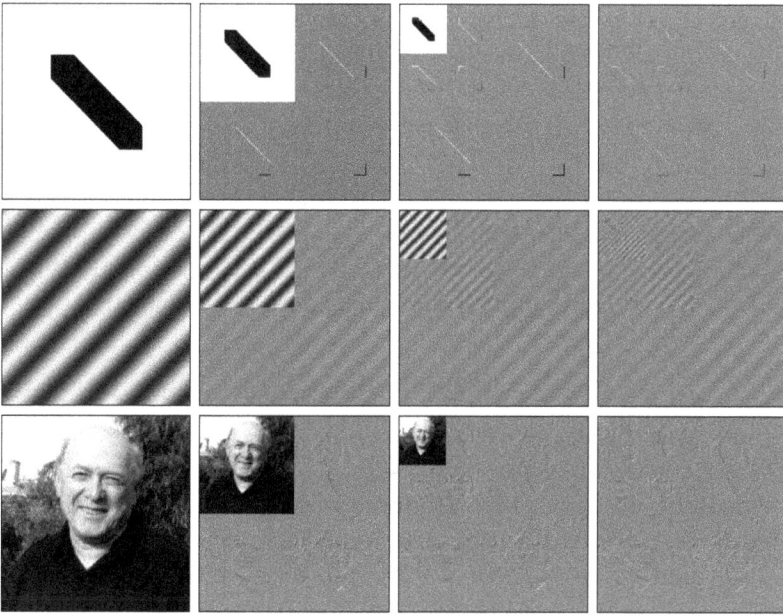

Fig. 9.10 $2^8 \times 2^8$ images and stages 1, 2, and 8 (spectrum) of their multi-scale DHT.

of pixels:

$$
\begin{aligned}
g_{r+1}(x,y) &= \tfrac{(g_r(2x,2y)+g_r(2x+1,2y)+g_r(2x,2y+1)+g_r(2x+1,2y+1))}{4} \\
\Delta_{x:r+1}(x,y) &= \tfrac{(g_r(2x,2y)-g_r(2x+1,2y))}{2} \\
\Delta_{y:r+1}(x,y) &= \tfrac{(g_r(2x,2y)-g_r(2x,2y+1))}{2} \\
\Delta_{xy:r+1}(x,y) &= \tfrac{(g_r(2x,2y)-g_r(2x+1,2y+1))}{2} \\
x &= 0,\ldots,2^{n-r-1}; \ y = 0,\ldots,2^{n-r-1}
\end{aligned}
\tag{9.11}
$$

Figure 9.10 shows two stages of the multi-scale DHT, together with the obtained at the last step 2D Haar spectra of two synthetic images and a realistic facial image of size $2^8 \times 2^8$. The larger the uniform image regions, the lesser the number of non-zero components in the Haar wavelet spectrum, e.g., 468 out of 65536 components, or 0.71% for the bi-level synthetic image, comparing to 69.2% for the facial image in Fig. 9.10.

9.4.3   *Smooth wavelets*

The Haar basis functions are discontinuous (non-differentiable) and therefore have little to offer for continuous signals, especially, if the latter have continuous first- or even higher-order derivatives. Moreover, the Hair function is poorly localised in the spectral domain:

$$\Psi(\omega) = \int\limits_{-\infty}^{\infty} \psi(t)\exp(-i\omega t)dt = i\exp(-0.5i\omega)\frac{\sin^2(0.25t)}{0.25t}$$

so that its spectral amplitude is inversely proportional to the absolute angular frequency, $|\Psi(\omega)| \leq 4|\omega|^{-1}$ when $|\omega| \to \infty$.

A continuous *Mexican hat* wavelet (a second derivative of an 1D Gaussian) is localised tighter in both the signal and spectral domains:

$$\psi(t) = \frac{2}{\sqrt{3}}\pi^{-0.25}(t^2 - 1)\exp\left(-0.5t^2\right)$$
$$\Psi(\omega) = -2\frac{\sqrt{2}}{\sqrt{3}}\pi^{0.25}\omega^2\exp\left(-0.5\omega^2\right)$$

This and other continuous wavelets made the MRA by wavelet decompositions most common in image compression.

Wavelets via low-/high-frequency separation. The 1D Haar wavelets can be derived as two orthonormal 2-component vectors: $\mathbf{w}_l = [w_{l:0}, w_{l:1}]$ and $\mathbf{w}_h = [w_{h:0}, w_{h:1}]$ with special properties of their Fourier spectra, $W_l(\omega) = w_{l:0} + w_{l:1}\exp(i\omega)$ and $W_h(\omega) = w_{h:0} + w_{h:1}\exp(i\omega)$:

$$W_h(0) = w_{l:0} + w_{l:1} = 0, \text{ or } w_{l:1} = -w_{l:0}$$

The orthonormality adds three more relationships:

$$\sum_{k=0}^{1} w_{l:k}^2 = 1; \sum_{k=0}^{1} w_{h:k}^2 = 1; \sum_{k=0}^{1} w_{l:k}w_{h:k} = 0$$

to be solved with the two-component Haar wavelets: $\mathbf{w}_l = [1/\sqrt{2}, 1/\sqrt{2}]$ and $\mathbf{w}_h = [1/\sqrt{2}, -1/\sqrt{2}]$. In this case two-step shifts of the successive wavelets exclude partial overlaps and thus guarantee the orthonormality.

But more general K-component wavelets; $K > 2$, have to account for partial overlaps between the shifted wavelets. Also, their spectral properties are constrained for $\omega = 0$ and $\omega = \pi$. If necessary, the constraints are applied also to the first and sometimes even higher-order derivatives of the low-pass wavelet in the spectral space (see Example 9.6 below):

$$\frac{d}{d\omega}W_l(\omega) \equiv W_l'(\omega) = w_{l:1}\exp(i\omega) + 2w_{l:2}\exp(2i\omega) + 3w_{l:3}\exp(3i\omega)$$

Example 9.6 (4-component Daubechies orthonormal wavelets).
Let $\mathbf{w}_l = [w_{l:0}, w_{l:1}, w_{l:2}, w_{l:3}]$ and $\mathbf{w}_h = [w_{h:0}, w_{h:1}, w_{h:2}, w_{h:3}]$, so that the spectral components are as follows:

$$W_l(\omega) = w_{l:0} + w_{l:1}\exp(i\omega) + w_{l:2}\exp(2i\omega) + w_{l:3}\exp(3i\omega)$$
$$W_h(\omega) = w_{h:0} + w_{h:1}\exp(i\omega) + w_{h:2}\exp(2i\omega) + w_{h:3}\exp(3i\omega)$$

The eight unknowns are constrained with six orthonormality conditions ac-counting for partial overlaps after the two-step shifts:

$$w_{l:0}^2 + w_{l:1}^2 + w_{l:2}^2 + w_{l:3}^2 = w_{h:0}^2 + w_{h:1}^2 + w_{h:2}^2 + w_{h:3}^2 = 1$$

$$w_{l:0}w_{h:0} + w_{l:1}w_{h:1} + w_{l:2}w_{h:2} + w_{l:3}w_{h:3} = 0$$

$$w_{l:0}w_{l:2} + w_{l:1}w_{l:3} = w_{h:0}w_{h:2} + w_{h:1}w_{h:3} = w_{h:0}w_{l:2} + w_{h:1}w_{l:3} = 0$$

In addition, there are two constraints on the spectrum, $W_1(\pi) = 0$, and its first derivative, $W_1'(\pi) = 0$, i.e.,

$$w_{l:0} - w_{l:1} + w_{l:2} - w_{l:3} = 0 \quad and \quad -w_{l:1} + 2w_{l:2} - 3w_{l:3} = 0$$

Both the constraints force the spectral magnitude $|W_1'(\omega)|$ to approach zero tangentially near the highest angular frequency $\omega = \pi$.

Under these constraints, the following pair of the 4-component Daubechies wavelets is derived: $w_{h:k} = (-1)^k w_{l:3-k}$; $k = 0, 1, 2, 3$, and

$$w_{l:0} = \frac{1 + \sqrt{3}}{4\sqrt{2}}; \ w_{l:1} = \frac{3 + \sqrt{3}}{4\sqrt{2}}; \ w_{l:2} = \frac{3 - \sqrt{3}}{4\sqrt{2}}; \ w_{l:3} = \frac{1 - \sqrt{3}}{4\sqrt{2}}$$

Lossless or lossy image compression and denoising are main applications of the today's *discrete wavelet transforms* (DWT) using a rich variety of much more general wavelet families, than the above examples.

9.5 Filtering in the spectral domain

Impacts of any MWT in the signal (spatial) domain onto spatial oscillations comprising an input image are assessed and evaluated more naturally in the spectral, or (Fourier) frequency domain. Moreover, linear filtering in the frequency domain replaces multiple convolutions of an image with a moving window (filter kernel) with the equivalent single component-wise multiplication of the image and kernel spectra.

Definition 9.10 (OTF). *The optical transfer function (OTF) of a linear filter is the Fourier spectrum of the filter kernel.*

If degradation of a sensed image is modelled as linear filtering of an ideal (noiseless) image, the filter kernel is called a *point spread function* (PSF). Let an ideal image, $\mathbf{g}_{id}$, of a point-wise light source contain a single bright point on a dark background, i.e., $g_{id}(\mathbf{s}) = 1$ at a single location, $\mathbf{s} = \mathbf{s}^\circ$, and 0 at all other locations. The PSF describes an area of non-zero signals in a degraded real image, i.e., it shows to what extent the ideal single point is scattered. The OTF of this filter is the Fourier spectrum of its PSF.

Definition 9.11 (MTF and PhTF). *The magnitude and phase parts of the OTF are called the modulation transfer function (MTF) and the phase transfer function (PhTF), respectively.*

A so-called "white", or uniform noise has equal amplitudes at all frequencies. When the amplitudes vary, the noise is often called "coloured" by analogy with light and its optical spectrum.

To preserve shapes of objects, mainly *zero-phase-shift filters*, affecting no phases and changing only amplitudes, are used in the spectral domain. Restoration (at least, approximate) of an ideal image by *deconvolving* its degraded version presumes the degrading PSF and OTF are either known, or can be estimated from available training images.

9.5.1 *Convolution in the spectral domain*

In line with Eq. (3.4) (Chapter 3), the convolution, $\widetilde{\mathbf{g}} = \mathbf{g} * \mathbf{w}$, of an image, $\mathbf{g} = (g(x, y) : (x, y) \in \mathbb{S})$, with a filter kernel, $\mathbf{w} = (w(\xi, \eta) : (\xi, \eta) \in \mathbb{W})$, forms the filtered image, $\widetilde{\mathbf{g}} = (\widetilde{g}(x, y) : (x, y) \in \mathbb{S})$, such that:

$$\widetilde{g}(x, y) = \sum_{(\xi, \eta) \in \mathbb{W}} g(x - \xi, y - \eta) w(\xi, \eta)$$

Let the images, the kernel, and their spectra, $\widetilde{\mathbf{G}} = (\widetilde{G}(u, v) : (u, v) \in \mathbb{U})$; $\mathbf{G} = (G(u, v) : (u, v) \in \mathbb{U})$, and $\mathbf{W} = (W(u, v) : (u, v) \in \mathbb{U})$, respectively, be, for simplicity, on the same toroidal square $N \times N$ lattice,

$$\mathbb{S} = \mathbb{U} = \mathbb{W} = \{0, 1, \ldots, N - 1\}^2 \equiv \{(0, 0), (0, 1), \ldots, (N - 1, N - 1)\}$$

Theorem 9.1 (Convolution in the spectral domain). *The image-kernel convolution, $\widetilde{\mathbf{g}} = \mathbf{g} * \mathbf{w}$, is equivalent to the component-wise product, $\widetilde{\mathbf{G}} = \mathbf{G}\mathbf{W}$, of their Fourier spectra:*

$$\widetilde{G}(u, v) = G(u, v)W(u, v); \quad (u, v) \in \mathbb{U}$$

The output image, $\widetilde{\mathbf{g}}$, is obtained by the inverse DFT of the product, $\widetilde{\mathbf{G}}$.

Proof. Let, for brevity, $\iota_N = -\frac{2\pi i}{N}$. Then

$$
\begin{aligned}
\tilde{G}(u,v) &= \sum_{x=0}^{N-1}\sum_{y=0}^{N-1} \tilde{g}(x,y)\exp\left(\iota_N(ux+vy)\right) \\
&= \sum_{x=0}^{N-1}\sum_{y=0}^{N-1}\left(\sum_{\xi=0}^{N-1}\sum_{\eta=0}^{N-1} g(x-\xi,y-\eta)w(\xi,\eta)\right)\exp\left(\iota_N(ux+vy)\right) \\
&= \underbrace{\left(\sum_{x-\xi=0}^{N-1}\sum_{y-\eta=0}^{N-1} g(x-\xi,y-\eta)\exp\left(\iota_N(x-\xi)u+(y-\eta)v\right)\right)}_{G(u,v)}
\end{aligned}
$$

$$
\times \underbrace{\left(\sum_{\xi=0}^{N-1}\sum_{\eta=0}^{N-1} w(\xi,\eta)\exp\left(\iota_N(\xi u+\eta v)\right)\right)}_{W(u,v)} \equiv G(u,w)\cdot W(u,w)
$$

$\square$

Although this chapter considers, for simplicity, a square infinite and periodic 2D image with a period N in both directions, the duality of Theorem 9.1 between the spatial convolution and spectral multiplication holds for all continuous and discrete rectangular images and filter kernels. Due to this duality, the signal or spectral domain can be chosen according to which of them ensures faster and easier-to-implement linear filtering.

Image degradation, caused by imaging devices, lighting conditions, object movements etc., is often modelled by convolving an ideal image, $\mathbf{g}_{\mathrm{id}}$, with a linear blurring filter, $\mathbf{w}$, and corrupting further with an additive random noise, ε:

$$
\mathbf{g} = \mathbf{g}_{\mathrm{id}} * \mathbf{w} + \varepsilon; \text{ or}
$$
$$
g(x,y) = \sum_{(\xi,\eta)\in\mathbb{N}} g_{\mathrm{id}}(x-\xi,y-\eta)w(\xi,\eta)+\varepsilon(x,y) \tag{9.12}
$$

Generally, both the filter, $\mathbf{w}$, and noise, ε, may vary spatially. But considerably simpler spatially invariant models are more common in practice.

9.5.2 Low-, high-, and band-pass spectral filtering

Low-pass filtering suppresses high frequency components to produce smooth (blurred) images. The MTF of a simple circular or square *cutoff filter* excludes all input spatial frequencies at distances above a fixed threshold, τ, from the origin, $(0,0)$, or along the u- and v-axes, respectively, and changes no other spectral components:

$$W(u,v) = \begin{cases} 1 \text{ if } \sqrt{u^2 + v^2} \leq \tau \\ 0 \text{ otherwise} \end{cases} \quad \text{or} \quad \begin{cases} 1 \text{ if } |u| \leq \tau \text{ AND } |v| \leq \tau \\ 0 \text{ otherwise} \end{cases} \quad (9.13)$$

The cut-off MTF causes damped oscillations around edges in an input image because the corresponding PSF (obtained by the inverse DFT) is a wavy *sinc function*, $\text{sinc}(t) = \sin(t)/t$. To suppress such oscillations, the low-pass MTF should approach its zero domain smoothly, i.e., together with, at least, first partial derivatives, while keeping its unit domain as close to the frequency threshold, τ, as possible. Two popular centre-symmetric filters with the MTFs of such type, namely, the Gaussian and K^{th}-order Butterworth low-pass filters are listed in Table 9.4.

Table 9.4 Butterworth and Gaussian low-pass filters.

K^{th}-order Butterworth	Gaussian
$W(u,v) = \dfrac{1}{1 + \left(\frac{u^2+v^2}{\tau^2}\right)^K}$	$W(u,v) = \exp\left(-2\pi^2 \frac{u^2+v^2}{\tau^2}\right)$

The Butterworth filter components, $W(u,v) = 1/(1 + \rho^{2K})$ at the distance $\sqrt{u^2 + v^2} = \rho\tau$ from the origin, tend to the unit value, $W(u,v) \to 1$, for $\rho < 1$; are equal to 0.5, i.e., $W(u,v) = 0.5$ for $\rho = 1$, and tend to zero, $W(u,v) \to 0$, for $\rho > 1$. The larger the order K, the closer the smooth Butterworth filter to the discontinuous circular cut-off one. The MTF for the Gaussian filter is not only smooth, but also yields the Gaussian PSF:

$$w(\xi, \eta) = \frac{\tau^2}{2\pi} \exp\left(-\frac{1}{2}\tau^2(\xi^2 + \eta^2)\right); \quad (\xi, \eta) \in \mathbb{N}$$

High-pass filtering complements the low-pass one in suppressing uniform image areas and enhancing edges. The cut-off high-pass filter excludes all input frequencies at distances below a fixed threshold, τ, from the origin, $(0,0)$, or along the u- and v-axes:

$$W(u,v) = \begin{cases} 1 \text{ if } \sqrt{u^2 + v^2} > \tau \\ 0 \text{ otherwise} \end{cases} \quad \text{or} \quad \begin{cases} 1 \text{ if } |u| > \tau \text{ AND } |v| > \tau \\ 0 \text{ otherwise} \end{cases} \quad (9.14)$$

The cut-out high-pass images might be corrupted by oscillating signal transitions, too. These oscillations could be suppressed by using filters with the smoother MTFs, e.g., the Kth-order Butterworth high pass filter with

$$W(u,v) = \frac{1}{1 + \left(\frac{\tau^2}{u^2+v^2}\right)^K}$$

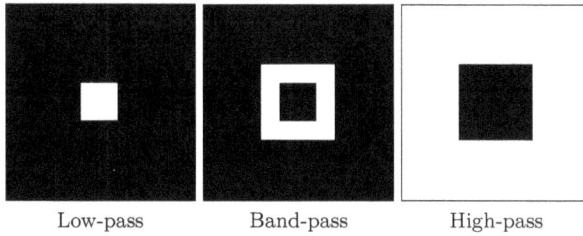

| Low-pass | Band-pass | High-pass |

Fig. 9.11 Cut-off rectangular MTFs for filtering in the frequency domain.

The high-pass Butterworth filter approaches the ideal cutoff one, too, if its order, K, increases. One of the popular high-pass schemes is *unsharp masking*: $\widetilde{\mathbf{g}} = \mathbf{g} - (\mathbf{g} * \mathbf{w})$ where $\mathbf{w}$ is a low-pass kernel.

Band pass filtering preserves a certain range of frequencies and suppresses all others, whereas **band stop filtering** suppresses a range of frequencies and preserves all other frequencies. A band-pass filter may combine a cut-off high-passing of radius τ_{hi}, followed by a cut-off low-passing of radius τ_{lo}, such that $\tau_{\mathrm{lo}} > \tau_{\mathrm{hi}}$. More intricate filtering edits only selected frequencies, e.g., to remove periodic noise by suppressing narrow peaks in the input spectrum.

Example 9.7 (Low-, band-, and high-pass filtering). *Figures 9.11 and 9.12 show the cut-off spectral filters and their application to the test image.*

9.5.3 *Inverse and Wiener filters*

Restoring a degraded, e.g., blurred image is most obvious in the spectral domain. In line with Eq. (9.12) and Theorem 9.1, the spectra G_{id}, G, and E of the ideal image, degraded image, and noise, respectively, and the OTF W relate as:

$$G(u, v) = G_{\mathrm{id}}(u, v)W(u, v) + E(u, v); \quad (u, v) \in \mathbb{U}$$

For a negligibly small noise, the simplest way to restore the ideal image is *inverse filtering*:

$$G_{\mathrm{id}}(u, v) \approx \widetilde{G}(u, v) = \frac{G(u, v)}{W(u, v)}; \quad (u, v) \in \mathbb{U} \qquad (9.15)$$

where $W^{-1}(u, v)$ is an OTF component of the inverse filter suppressing the degradation. This straightforward deconvolution has serious drawbacks:

(1) The ratios in Eq. (9.15) become infinite or undefined for zero MTF components, $W(u, v) = 0$, relating to non-zero or zero spectral amplitudes $G(u, v)$, respectively, of the degraded image.

(2) The omitted noise-dependent ratios, $E(u,v)/W(u,v)$, may be large even for a small noise if the MTF components are close to zero.

As a result, the restored by inverse filtering spectral components, $\widetilde{G}(u,v)$, might differ much from the desired ideal ones, $G_{\text{id}}(u,v)$. This problem has a simple heuristic solution, which sometimes decreases the degradation and equates any ratio in Eq. (9.15) to zero if the MTF amplitude is below some threshold, τ, i.e., $\widehat{G}(u,v) = 0$ if $|W(u,v)| \leq \tau$.

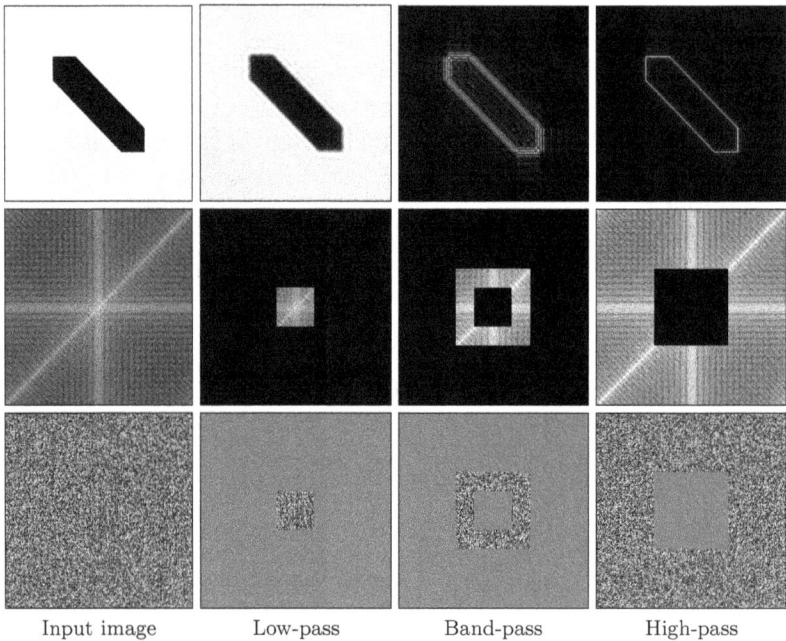

| Input image | Low-pass | Band-pass | High-pass |

Fig. 9.12   Cut-off filtering of the test image in the frequency domain (images and their magnitude/phase spectra; note ringing around the boundaries).

| Blurring: $\sigma = 2$ | Restored image | Blurring: $\sigma = 4$ | Restored image |

Fig. 9.13   Inverse filtering after Gaussian low-pass blurring.

Example 9.8 (Inverse filtering). *Figure 9.13 shows the test image of Fig. 9.6, blurred with two low-pass Gaussian filters ($\sigma = 2$ and $\sigma = 4$), and results of its restoration by inverse filtering with the threshold $\tau = 0.05$. Note that the wider the blurring, the more corrupted the restored image.*

Wiener filtering solves the above problem on a theoretical footing of the minimum expected total squared error between the restored and ideal images. The underlying theory assumes the known variances of noise, σ_{n}^2, and of ideal image signals, σ_{id}^2, around their mean values. Under a few additional simplifying assumptions, the derived Wiener filter accounts for a scaled by factor κ ratio between the variances:

$$G_{\mathrm{id}}(u, v) \approx \widehat{G}(u, v) = \frac{G(u, v)}{W(u, v)} \frac{|W(u, v)|^2}{|W(u, v)|^2 + \kappa \sigma_{\mathrm{n}}^2 / \sigma_{\mathrm{id}}^2}; \quad (u, v) \in \mathbb{U} \quad (9.16)$$

If $\sigma_{\mathrm{n}}^2 = 0$ (no noise), the Wiener and inverse filtering coincide. If $|W(u, v)| \ll \kappa \sigma_{\mathrm{n}}^2 / \sigma_{\mathrm{id}}^2$, the growth of its inverse, $W^{-1}(u, v)$, in the first cofactor of Eq. (9.16) is limited by the rapidly decreasing second cofactor.

9.5.4 *Homomorphic and cepstral filters*

Multiplicative noise, $g(\mathbf{s}) = a_{\mathbf{s}} g_{\mathrm{id}}(\mathbf{s})$, scales image signals with respect to their ideal (noiseless) values, $g_{\mathrm{id}}(\mathbf{s})$. For an observed 3D scene, all grey values acquired are products of illumination and reflection of surface elements. Thus, the ideal signal, $g_{\mathrm{id}}(\mathbf{s})$, and its noise factor, $a_{\mathbf{s}}$, relate to the point-wise reflectance and incident light, respectively.

Homomorphic filtering assumes the illumination-related multiplicative noise is changing much slower, than the reflectance. Then logarithms of the sensed signals separate the illumination and reflectance in the spectral domain:

$$\log g(\mathbf{s}) = \log (a_{\mathbf{s}} g_{\mathrm{id}}(\mathbf{s})) = \log a_{\mathbf{s}} + \log g_{\mathrm{id}}(\mathbf{s}); \quad \mathbf{s} \in \mathbb{S}$$

The Fourier spectrum of the log-signal is then transformed to partly exclude the illumination-caused variations by suppressing its lower frequencies relative to the higher ones. After the high-pass filtering in the spectral domain, the goal output of homomorphic filtering is formed by the inverse Fourier transform, followed by exponentiation.

Example 9.9 (Homomorphic Gaussian filtering). *Algorithm 15 and Fig. 9.14 illustrate a particular case of filtering a 2D $N \times N$ input image $\mathbf{g}$, such that a three-parametric Gaussian high-pass spectral mask is applied to the log-image in the spectral domain.*

Algorithm 15 Homomorphic filtering of a 2D $N \times N$ image $\mathbf{g}$.

Input: the image $\mathbf{g} = (g(x,y) : (x,y) \in \mathbb{S} = \{0, 1, \ldots, N-1\}^2)$;
    parameters σ, α, and β of a high-pass Gaussian filter.

(1) Build the log-image, $\mathbf{g}_l = (\log g(x,y) : (x,y) \in \mathbb{S})$.
(2) Find its centred Fourier spectrum:

$$\mathbf{G}_{\log} = \left(G(u,v) : (u,v) \in \mathbb{U} = \left\{ -\frac{N}{2}, \ldots, \frac{N}{2} \right\}^2 \right)$$

(3) Build the spectral mask, $\mathbf{W} = (W(u,v) : (u,v) \in \mathbb{U})$, combining two
complementary high- and low-pass Gaussian masks having the same
standard deviation, σ, with the weights, α and β; $\alpha \geq \beta$, respectively:

$$W(u,v) = (\alpha - \beta) \underbrace{\left(1 - \frac{1}{2\pi\sigma^2} \exp\left(-\frac{u^2 + v^2}{2\sigma^2} \right) \right)}_{\text{high-pass Gaussian mask}} + \beta$$

(4) Apply the mask to the centred spectrum,

$$\widehat{G}_{\log}(u,v) = W(u,v)G_{\log}(u,v)$$

(5) Find the filtered log-image, $\widehat{\mathbf{g}}_{\log}$, by the inverse FT of $\widehat{\mathbf{G}}_{\log}$.
(6) Perform the exponentiation:

$$\widetilde{\mathbf{g}} = (\widetilde{g}(x,y) = \exp(\widehat{g}_{\log}(x,y)) : (x,y) \in \mathbb{S})$$

Cepstral filtering assumes a more complex noise model, such that
an input image is obtained by transmitting an ideal image through a noisy
linear channel with a slow changing PSF. In other words, the image to be
restored is an ideal image convolved with a randomly varying spatial linear
filter: $\mathbf{g} = \mathbf{g}_{\text{id}} * \mathbf{w}_{\text{ch}}$, so that the image and channel spectra are multiplied
in the spectral domain: $\mathbf{G} = \mathbf{G}_{\text{id}} \mathbf{W}_{\text{ch}}$.

Basic ideas behind the homomorphic and cepstral filtering resemble each
other. The cepstral filter decreases channel-caused noise by taking the
logarithm of the corrupted spectrum, $\mathbf{G}$, and high-pass filtering of the log-
spectrum. The inverse Fourier transform of the filtered log-spectrum,

$$\log \mathbf{G} = \log \mathbf{G}_{\text{id}} + \log \mathbf{W}_{\text{ch}}$$

forms a so-called *complex cepstrum* where dominant lower-frequency spectral components attributed to the PSF are separated from higher-frequency
components of the ideal image and thus can be filtered out. The term

| Input image | $\alpha = 1.9, \beta = 0.1$ | $\alpha = 1.5, \beta = 0.5$ | $\alpha = 1.1, \beta = 0.9$ |

Fig. 9.14 Homomorphic filtering of two 256×256 facial images ($\sigma = 10$).

"cepstrum" reflects these component-wise permutations of the original spectrum. However, the cepstral filters are outside the scope of this primer because their implementation has to account for multiplicity of logarithms of a spectral component due to periodic phases of any complex value.

9.6 Questions and exercises

(1) What is an image according to the FT?
(2) Given a 10×10 image **g** such that $g(0,0) = 255$ and $g(x,y) = 0$ for all other pixels $(x,y) \neq (0,0)$, find its discrete Fourier spectrum.
(3) Given a 10×10 image **g** such that $g(x,y) = 255$ for all the pixels x, y, find its discrete Fourier spectrum.
(4) Apply the inverse DFT to the spectrum $G(0,0) = 255$ and $G(u,v) = 0$ for all other components with $(u,v) \neq (0,0)$.
(5) How can you centre an image spectrum produced by the DFT?
(6) How can you visualise an amplitude spectrum?
(7) Why does the DCT produce less distorted spectra, than the DFT?
(8) What is a mother wavelet and how does it produce a family of wavelets?
(9) What is the main advantage of smooth wavelets over the Haar wavelet?
(10) What is the OTF of a linear filter?
(11) How will you perform spatial convolution in the Fourier frequency domain?

(12) Let the cut-off filter, $\mathbf{W} = (W(u, v) : (u, v) \in \{-10, -9, \ldots, 10\}^2$ possess the following components:

$$W(u, v) = \begin{cases} 1 \text{ if } 10 \leq |u| + |v| \leq 40 \\ 0 \text{ otherwise} \end{cases}$$

Which spectral filtering does it perform?

(13) How are the inverse and Wiener filters alike and how do they differ?

(14) Which type of noise can the homomorphic filter suppress?

Appendix A

Further Reading

A.1 More diverse sources

Initial knowledge provided by the primer should be considerably extended and deepened for dealing with important image processing and analysis applications, such as, e.g., vision-guided robotics, biometrics, or computer-aided medical diagnostics to mention just a few. A rich variety of monographs, textbooks, and handbooks, including [Bovik (2009); Burger and Burge (2009, 2013); Chan and Shen (2006); Efford (2000); Fisher (2014); Gonzales *et al.* (2004); Nixon (2008); Petrou and Petrou (2010); Pratt (2014); Russ and Neal (2016); Sonka *et al.* (2015)], and many others, will help you in further studying, implementing, and advancing modern techniques for transforming and describing greyscale and colour imagery. More informative multi-spectral and hyper-spectral images are frequent in remote sensing applications [Bovik (2005); Petrou and Petrou (2010); Schowengerdt (2007)].

Advanced image processing and analysis techniques can be also found in various popular Internet-based tutorials or specialised web pages, such as, e.g., `http://www.tutorialspoint.com/dip/` or `http://www.imageprocessingbasics.com/` among many others, as well as in a multitude of journal and conference papers. The most influential professional journals in these research fields include *IEEE Transactions on Pattern Analysis and Machine Intelligence*, *IEEE Transactions on Image Processing*, and *International Journal of Computer Vision*, and the most important conferences are *International IEEE Conference on Computer Vision* (ICCV), *International IEEE Conference on Computer Vision and Pattern Recognition* (CVPR), *European Conference on Computer Vision* (ECCV), and *International IEEE Conference on Image Processing* (ICIP).

A.2   Bibliographical and historical notes

Digital images. The primer only touches upon interrelations between continuous and digital images, as well as their global and local features. These interrelations have been considered important and explored from the very first steps of digital image processing [Rosenfeld (1969); Rosenfeld and Kak (1976)]. Interplays between shapes, sizes, and locations of continuous planar or spatial objects and their discrete representations are studied in depth in special branches of mathematics, called digital, discrete, or computational geometry: see, e.g., [Berg *et al.* (2008); Chen (2014)]. **Mathematical morphology** for image processing and analysis can be explored further in [Shih (2009); Soille (2004)].

Image features. Quantitative descriptions of entire images or their regions with computable quantitative features constitute a broad domain of image analysis. Each feature is a scalar or low-dimensional vector function of multiple image signals. The primer considered only simple features obtained by filtering grey levels or colour vectors in a moving window to analyse their statistical or differential properties. However, even these features and derived from them image descriptors still are useful for image enhancement or segmentation, especially, in conjunction with more advanced techniques. For example, statistics of a local GLCH [Haralick *et al.* (1973)], which are more than four decades old, but appear partly in this primer, can be often found in many modern image analysis frameworks. This primer also touches upon a few more special higher-order features, including the LBP [Ojala *et al.* (2002); Pietikäinen *et al.* (2011)], characterising contrast-invariant signal properties, and the USAN/SUSAN areas [Smith and Brady (1997)], which help in detecting prominent edges and corner-like POIs in a greyscale image.

Histogram thresholding. A large number of such techniques can be found in almost any aforementioned textbook. For simplicity, this primer omits the popular Otsu thresholding [Otsu (1979)] to search for J; $J \geq 1$ thresholds that separates the signal range into $J + 1$ intervals, one per a goal region. This thresholding performs a dynamic-programming-like global maximisation of the total weighted squared distance between the mean signals for the successive signal intervals. Algorithm 5 in Section 4.3.1 (Chapter 4) can be considered a local-maximisation-based approximation of the Otsu thresholding for $J = 1$. The EM based maximum likelihood estimates (MLE) of Gaussian mixture parameters appeared first in the 1950s–1960s. But the EM received its current name and gained general acceptance after the pivotal generalising paper [Dempster *ct al.* (1977)]. At present, a large number of the EM and more advanced algorithms exist to deal with mixtures of p.d.f.s; see, e.g., [McLachlan and Krishnan (2008)].

Edge and POI detection. This primer presents only a few of the most popular edge and POI detectors, including the rotation-invariant Canny edge detector [Canny (1986)], Förstner interest operator [Förstner and Gülch (1987)], and Harris-Stephens edge-corner detector [Harris and Stephens (1988)], as well as scale-rotation-invariant SIFT [Lowe (2004)] and SURF [Bay *et al.* (2008)]. However, many other efficient POI detectors and descriptors have been omitted, but can be explored using the aforementioned textbooks and original publications. The omitted POI detectors include, e.g., BRIEF (Binary Robust Independent Elementary Features) [Calonder *et al.* (2010)], BRISK (Binary Robust Invariant Scalable Keypoints) [Leutenegger *et al.* (2011)], FAST [Rosten and Drummond (2006)], FREAK (Fast Retina Keypoint) [Alahi *et al.* (2012)], ORB (Oriented FAST and Rotated BRIEF) [Rublee *et al.* (2011)], SBRISK (Speedup BRISK) [Yang *et al.* (2016)], scale-rotation-invariant Förstner operator [Förstner *et al.* (2009)], and so forth.

FT, WT, and spectral filtering. These topics are detailed in a host of books and textbooks (see, e.g., [Burger and Burge (2009); Gonzales *et al.* (2004)]). The theory of wavelets can be found in [Mallat (1999)], and their applications to image processing, including practical computations of various wavelets, are detailed in [Broughton and Bryan (2009); Van Fleet (2008)]. The FFT, which belongs to ten most influential algorithms of the 20th century, was invented more than five decades ago [Cooley and Tukey (1965)] (its history was detailed in [Cooley *et al.* (1967)]). The 1D FFT algorithm in Chapter 9 highlighting the simplicity of this recursive computation follows closely the early C-program in [Ulrich (1969)]. Signal filtering in the Fourier frequency space, including homomorphic filtering, is detailed in [Oppenheim *et al.* (1968)], as well as in many other publications.

Deforming boundaries to segment. Extracting boundaries from objects or regions of interests in images or videos is a fundamental problem in image processing. The original MPEG-4 committee intended to base the MPEG-4 compression standard on the detection, extraction and separate encoding of objects within an image or video sequence [Richardson (2004)]. While MPEG-4 is still prevalent today as a go-to compression format, the detection, segmentation and extraction of separate objects within an image/video sequence, which was the original foundation of MPEG-4 standards for image data description, is still an open problem. Parametric active contours were introduced three decades ago in [Kass *et al.* (1988)]. A comprehensive overview of these tools in application to medical images can be found in [McInerney and Terzopoulos (1996)]. As a more stable in practice solution, [Caselles *et al.* (1997)] proposed an implicit representation of deformable boundaries, achieved by embedding them into a level-sets framework [Osher and Fedkiw (2006)]. The (external) energy terms appearing in most variations of the deformable models are an extension of the Marr-Hidreth's [Marr and Hildreth (1980)] approach, which was first introduced to detect edges in images. Deformable models with internal constraints are either statistically based ASMs [Cootes *et al.* (1995); Caplier *et al.* (1999)], or geometrically constrained with deformable templates [Yuille (1991)], or based on a truncated representation of the regularising Tikhonov operators [Tikhonov and Arsenin (1977)] of the first order for GACs or the second order for ACs. Adding the Tikhonov operators of the infinite order to any specific function would allow the associated problem to converge, thus transforming an ill-posed (non-convex) problem into a well-posed (convex) one that converges to its optimal solution. Further proof of mathematical equivalence between the level set representation and the second order finite difference approach of the AC was developed in [Aubert and Blanc-Féraud (1999)]. The Chan-Vese edgeless ACs were first proposed in [Chan and Vese (1999)].

Markov random fields. The MRF models of images and region maps are widely used at present to accurately segment or enhance complex textured images. However, for simplicity, these models and related image processing and analysis algorithms are completely omitted in this primer. Initial information about these models and techniques can be found, e.g., in [Blake *et al.* (2011); El-Baz *et al.* (2016); Li (2009); Winkler (2012)].

Appendix B

Symbols and Math Notation

B.1 Latin symbols

$\mathbb{A}$	Probing area (a subset of pixels).
A	Gain; amplitude; USAN area; array.
a	Gain; accumulator; cosine; coefficient.
$\mathbb{B}$	Set of image points.
$\mathbf{B}$	Codebook.
B, b	Bias.
B, b	Blue component in the RGB colour model.
b	Bit-length; sine; coefficient.
C	Component of a cumulative histogram $\mathbf{C}$.
$\mathbf{C}$	Cumulative histogram.
c	Contrast.
d, D	Distance.
E	Noise spectrum.
e	Base of natural logarithms: ≈ 2.7182818283.
$\mathbf{e}$	Structuring element.
F	Power spectrum.
f	Focal distance; feature; frequency.
G	Fourier spectrum of a greyscale image.
G, g	Green component in the RGB colour model.
$\mathbf{g}$	Greyscale image.
$\hat{g}$	Hessian component.
$g(\mathbf{s})$	Grey level at site $\mathbf{s}$.
$\mathbf{g}(\mathbf{s})$	K–band, $K \geq 2$, or colour ($K = 3$) vector signal at site $\mathbf{s}$.

H	Haar matrix.
$H(q\|\mathbf{g})$	Component of a GLH for a signal q in an image $\mathbf{g}$.
$\mathbf{H}$	Grey-level histogram (GLH).
H	Hue component in the HSI colour model.
h	Function.
I	Intensity component in the HSI colour model.
i	Complex unit, $i = \sqrt{-1}$.
J	Linear size of a rectangular window.
j	Index.
K	Number of elements; order of a filter.
k	Size; half-filter size, index.
L	Number of distinct regions.
$\mathbb{L}$	Set of region labels.
l	Region label; half-filter size.
ℓ_i	A line indexed by the counter i.
M	Height (number of rows) of a rectangular lattice.
m	Integer height coordinate.
$\mathbb{N}$	Neighbourhood.
N	Width (number of columns) of a rectangular lattice; period.
n	Integer width coordinate; index.
$\mathbf{O}$	Optical centre.
$\mathbb{O}$	Set of object's sites.
$\mathbf{P}$	Probability distribution function; co-occurrence matrix.
$P(q\|\mathbf{g})$	Component of a p.d.f. for a signal q in an image $\mathbf{g}$.
p	Probability density.
Q	Number of signal values (grey levels).
$\mathbb{Q}$	Set of signal values.
q	Image signal (grey value, or level; intensity).
$q_{\max}$	The brightest image signal.
R	Maximal resolution.
R, r	Red component in the RGB colour model.
r	Signal range; resolution.
$\mathbb{S}$	Continuous or discrete set of image sites.
S	Size (cardinality) of $\mathbb{S}$; area.
S	Saturation component in the HSI colour model.
$\mathbf{s}, \mathbf{S}$	Image site (pixel or voxel).
s	Signal; location; index.

T	Transposition of a vector or a matrix.
T	LUT mapping; transformation.
t	Spatial 1D coordinate; iteration.
$\mathbb{U}$	Set of spectrum sites.
U	Uniformity predicate; unit diagonal matrix; boxcar function.
u	Vector.
$\mathbf{S}^\circ = (X^\circ, Y^\circ, Z^\circ)$	A spatial point.
u	Spatial frequency in x direction; membership function.
V	Function of chrominance.
v	Spatial frequency in y-direction.
$\mathbb{W}$	Set of window sites.
W	Weight matrix; spectrum.
w	Weight; windowing function.
x, X	Cartesian 2D/3D coordinate (width).
y, Y	Cartesian 2D/3D 3D coordinate (height).
z, Z	Cartesian 3D coordinate (depth).

B.2   Greek symbols

α	Collection of parameters.
α	Probability; percentile; coefficient.
β	Percentile; coefficient.
Γ	Level set.
$\mathbf{\Gamma}$	Collection of responsibilities.
γ	Variable; coefficient; responsibility.
$\mathbf{\Delta}$	Complementary sequence.
Δ	Components of $\mathbf{\Delta}$; difference of signals.
$\delta(t)$	Kronecker's delta-function: $\delta(0) = 1$ and 0 otherwise.
ϵ	Factor.
ε	Spatial or signal resolution; noise.
ζ	Closeness.
η	y-coordinate or offset.
Θ	Collection of parameters.
θ	Phase of a sinusoidal pattern; angle.

ι	Shorthand notation.
κ	Ratio of eigenvalues; scale.
Λ	Disjoint set of labels; period (cycle length).
λ	LBP value; label; factor.
μ	Mean, or average value.
μm	Micrometer, a.k.a. micron.
$\boldsymbol{\nu}$	Vector of coordinate offsets.
ν	Shift.
∇	Gradient.
Ξ	Discriminant function.
ξ	x-coordinate or offset.
π	≈ 3.1415926536 (circle circumference-to-diameter ratio).
ρ	Reference; radius; relative distance.
σ	St.d. (σ^2 – variance).
τ	Threshold.
Φ	Gaussian blur operator.
ϕ	Interpolation function; periodic function.
φ	Gaussian probability density.
$\boldsymbol{\Psi}$	Set of functions.
Ψ	Fourier spectrum of a function ψ.
ψ	Basis function.
ω	Angular frequency.

B.3 Math notation

$|x|, |\mathbf{x}|$	Absolute value of a scalar x or the length of a vector $\mathbf{x}$.
$|\mathbb{A}|$	Cardinality (the number of elements) of a finite set $\mathbb{A}$.
$g * w$	Convolution of two functions, g and w.
$\langle g, w \rangle$	Dot product of scalar functions g and w.
$a \in \mathbb{A}$	Element a of a set $\mathbb{A}$.
$\emptyset$	Empty set.
e^t; $\exp(t)$	Exponential function with an exponent t.
$w : \mathbb{A} \rightarrow \mathbb{V}$	Function w mapping a set of values, $\mathbb{A}$, to a set of values, $\mathbb{V}$.
∇_g	Gradient of a scalar function g of two or more variables.
$l \leftarrow l + \Delta$	Incrementing an integer variable l by Δ.

$m \bmod n$	Modulo (a non-negative remainder of integer division $\frac{m}{n}$).
$\lfloor t \rceil$	Rounding a floating-point value, t, to the nearest integer.
$\mathbb{B} \subseteq \mathbb{A}$	Set $\mathbb{B}$ is a subset of or equal to a set $\mathbb{A}$.
$\mathbb{A}^2$	Set of all pairs, (a, a'), such that $a, a' \in \mathbb{A}$.
$s \in \mathbb{Q}$	The variable s is contained within the set $\mathbb{Q}$.
$\approx$	Approximately.
$\ominus$	Binary erosion, a morphological operation performed on binary images.
$\oplus$	Binary dilation, a morphological operation performed on binary images.
$\circ$	Binary opening, a morphological operation performed on binary images.
$\bullet$	Binary closing, a morphological operation performed on binary images.
∞	Infinity.
$\int$	Integral operator.

Appendix C

Abbreviations

1D	One-dimensional.
2D	Two-dimensional.
3D	Three-dimensional.
AC	Active contour.
ACM	AC model.
ASM	Active shape model.
a.k.a.	Also known as.
CH	Cumulative histogram.
CT	Computed tomography.
DCT	Discrete cosine transform.
DFT	Discrete Fourier transform.
DHT	Discrete Haar transform.
DoG	Difference of Gaussians.
DoOG	Difference of offset Gaussians.
DWT	Discrete wavelet transform.
e.g.	*exempli gratia* (Latin), or "for example".
etc.	*et cetera* (Latin), or "and so forth".
FFT	Fast Fourier transform.
FN	False negative.
FP	False positive.
FT	Fourier transform.
GAC	Geodesic AC.
GLH	Grey-level histogram.
GLCH	Grey-level co-occurrence histogram.
GLDH	Grey-level difference histogram.
HDR	High dynamic range.

HSI	Hue-saturation-intensity colour space.
HS-map	Hue saturation map.
i.e.	*id est* (Latin), or "that is".
IR	Infrared.
IRF	Independent random field.
LBP	Local binary pattern.
LDR	Low dynamic range.
LoG	Laplacian of Gaussian.
LTP	Local ternary pattern.
LUG	Local uniformity grade.
LUT	Look-up table.
MLE	Maximum likelihood estimator.
MRA	Multi-resolution analysis.
MRF	Markov random field.
MRI	Magnetic resonance imaging.
MTF	Modulation transfer function.
MWT	Moving-window transform.
NIR	Near IR.
OTF	Optical transfer function.
PCA	Principal component analysis.
p.d.	Probability distribution.
p.d.f.	Probability distribution (*or* density) function.
PDM	Point distribution model.
PhTF	Phase transfer function.
POI	Point of interest.
PSF	Point spread function.
RGB	Red, green, and blue primary colours.
RMS	Root mean square.
ROI	Region of interest.
SDF	Signed distance function.
SDR	Standard dynamic range.
SE	Structuring element.
SIFT	Scale-invariant feature transform.
SNR	Signal-to-noise ratio.
std; st.d.	Standard deviation.
SURF	Speeded up robust features.

SUSAN	Smallest univalue segment assimilating nucleus.
TIR	Thermal IR.
TN	True negative.
TP	True positive.
USAN	Univalue segment assimilating nucleus.
UV	Ultraviolet.
w.r.t.	with respect to.
WT	Wavelet transform.

Bibliography

Alahi, A., Ortiz, R., and Vandergheynst, P. (2012). FREAK: Fast Retina Key-point, in *Proceedings of the 2012 IEEE Conference on Computer Vision and Pattern Recognition (CVPR 2012), Providence, RI, USA, 16–21 June 2012* (IEEE), pp. 510–517.

Aubert, G. and Blanc-Féraud, L. (1999). An active contour model without edges, *International Journal of Computer Vision* **34**, 1, pp. 19–28.

Bay, H., Ess, A., Tuytelaars, T., and Van Gool, L. (2008). A computational approach to edge detection, *Computer Vision and Image Understanding* **110**, 3, pp. 346–359.

Berg, M. de., Cheong, O., van Kreveld, M., and Overmans, M. (2008). *Computational Geometry: Algorithms and Applications*, 3rd edn. (Springer-Verlag, Berlin, Heidelberg).

Blake, A., Kohli, P., and Rother, C. (eds.) (2011). *Markov Random Fields for Vision and Image Processing* (The MIT Press, Cambridge, MA, USA).

Bovik, A. C. (2005). *Handbook of Image and Video Processing*, 2nd edn. (Academic Press, Burlington, MA, USA).

Bovik, A. C. (2009). *The Essential Guide to Image Processing* (Academic Press, London, Boston).

Broughton, S. A. and Bryan, K. (2009). *Discrete Fourier Analysis and Wavelets: Applications to Signal and Image Processing* (John Wiley & Sons, Hoboken, NJ, USA).

Burger, W. and Burge, M. (2009). *Principles of Digital Image Processing: Core Algorithms* (Springer, London).

Burger, W. and Burge, M. (2013). *Principles of Digital Image Processing: Advanced Methods* (Springer, London, New York).

Calonder, M., Lepetit, V., Strecha, C., and Fua, P. (2010). BRIEF: Binary Robust Independent Elementary Features, in *Computer Vision – ECCV 2010. 11th European Conference on Computer Vision, Heraklion, Crete, Greece, September 5–11, 2010. Proceedings, Part IV, Lecture Notes in Computer Science*, Vol. 6314 (Springer), pp. 778–792.

Canny, J. (1986). A computational approach to edge detection, *IEEE Transactions on Pattern Analysis and Machine Intelligence* **8**, 6, pp. 679–698.

Caplier, A., Delmas, P., and Lam, D. (1999). Robust initialisation for lips edges detection, in *11th Scandinavian Conference in Image Analysis (SCIA'99)* (Springer), pp. 523–528.

Caselles, V., Kimmel, R., and Sapiro, G. (1997). Geodesic active contours, *International Journal of Computer Vision* **22**, 1, pp. 61–79.

Chan, T. F. and Vese, L. (1999). An active contour model without edges, in *Scale-Space Theories in Computer Vision*. Second International Conference (Springer), pp. 141–151.

Chan, T. F. and Shen, J. (2006). *Image Processing and Analysis: Variational, PDE, Wavelet, and Stochastic Methods* (Society for Industrial and Applied Mathematics, Philadelphia, USA).

Chen, L. M. (2014). *Digital and Discrete Geometry: Theory and Algorithms* (Springer International Publishing, Switzerland).

Cooley, J. W., Lewis, P. A. W., and Welch, P. D. (1967). Historical notes on the fast Fourier transform, *IEEE Transactions on Audio and Electroacoustics* **15**, 2, pp. 76–79.

Cooley, J. W. and Tukey, J. W. (1965). An algorithm for the machine calculation of complex Fourier series, *Mathematics of Computation* **19**, 90, pp. 297–301.

Cootes, T. F., Taylor, C. J., Cooper, D. H., and Graham, J. (1995). Active shape models-their training and application, *Computer Vision and Image Understanding* **61**, 1, pp. 38–59.

Dempster, A. P., Laird, N. M., and Rubin, D. B. (1977). Maximum likelihood from incomplete data via the EM algorithm, *Journal of the Royal Statistical Society* **39B**, 1, pp. 1–38.

Efford, N. (2000). *Digital Image Processing: A Practical Introduction Using Java^{TM}* (Pearson Education Limited, Harlow, Essex, England).

El-Baz, A., Gimel'farb, G., and Suri, J. S. (2016). *Stochastic Modelling for Medical Image Analysis* (CRC Press, Boca Raton, FL, USA).

Fisher, R. B. (2014). *Dictionary of Computer Vision and Image Processing*, 2nd edn. (John Wiley & Sons, Chichester, UK).

Förstner, W., Dickscheid, T., and Schindler, F. (2009). Detecting interpretable and accurate scale-invariant keypoints, in *Proceedings of the 12th IEEE International Conference on Computer Vision (ICCV'09). Kyoto, Japan, 29 September–2 October, 2009* (IEEE), pp. 2256–2263.

Förstner, W. and Gülch, E. (1987). A fast operator for detection and precise location of distinct points, corners, and centres of circular features, in *Proceedings of the ISPRS Intercomission Conference on Fast Processing of Photogrammetric Data, Interlaken, Switzerland, 2–4 June 1987* (ISPRS), pp. 281–305.

Gonzales, R., Woods, R., and Eddins, S. (2004). *Digital Image Processing Using MATLAB* (Prentice Hall, Englewood Cliffs, NJ, USA).

Haralick, R. M., Shanmugam, K., and Dinstein, I. (1973). Textural features for image classification, *IEEE Transactions on Systems, Man and Cybernetics* **SMC-3**, 6, pp. 610–621.

Harris, C. and Stephens, M. (1988). A combined corner and edge detector, in *Proceedings of the Fourth Alvey Vision Conference, Manchester, UK, 31 August–2 September 1988*, pp. 147–151.

Kass, M., Witkin, A., and Terzopoulos, D. (1988). Snakes: Active contour models, *International Journal of Computer Vision* 1, 3, pp. 321–331.

Leutenegger, S., Chli, M., and Siegwart, R. Y. (2011). BRISK: Binary Robust Invariant Scalable Keypoints, in *Proceedings of the 13th IEEE International Conference on Computer Vision (ICCV'11), Barcelona, Spain, 6–11 November 2011* (IEEE), pp. 2548–2555.

Li, S. Z. (2009). *Markov Random Field Modeling in Image Analysis*, 3rd edn. (Springer, London, UK).

Lowe, D. (2004). Distinctive image features from scale-invariant keypoints, *International Journal of Computer Vision* 60, 2, pp. 91–110.

Mallat, S. (1999). *A Wavelet Tour of Signal Processing*, 2nd edn. (Academic Press, San Diego, CA, USA).

Marr, D. and Hildreth, E. (1980). Theory of edge detection, *Proceedings of the Royal Society of London B: Biological Sciences* 207, 1167, pp. 187–217.

McInerney, T. and Terzopoulos, D. (1996). Deformable models in medical image analysis: a survey, *Medical Image Analysis* 1, 2, pp. 91–108.

McLachlan, G. J. and Krishnan, T. (2008). *The EM Algorithm and Extensions*, 2nd edn. (John Wiley & Sons, Hoboken, NJ, USA).

Nixon, M. S. (2008). *Feature Extraction and Image Processing*, 2nd edn. (Academic Press, Amsterdam, Boston, London).

Ojala, T., Pietikäinen, M., and Mäenpää, T. (2002). Multiresolution gray-scale and rotation invariant texture classification with local binary patterns, *IEEE Transactions on Pattern Analysis and Machine Intelligence* 24, 7, pp. 971–987.

Oppenheim, A., Schafer, R., and Stockham, T. (1968). Nonlinear filtering of multiplied and convolved signals, *Proceedings of the IEEE* 56, 8, pp. 1264 – 1291.

Osher, S. and Fedkiw, R. (2006). *Level Set Methods and Dynamic Implicit Surfaces* (Springer-Verlag, New York).

Otsu, N. (1979). A threshold selection method from gray-level histograms, *IEEE Transactions on Systems, Man, and Cybernetics* 9, 1, pp. 62–66.

Petrou, M. and Petrou, C. (2010). *Image Processing: The Fundamentals*, 2nd edn. (John Wiley & Sons, Chichester, UK).

Pietikäinen, M., Hadid, A., Zhao, G., and Ahonen, T. (2011). *Computer Vision Using Local Binary Patterns, Computational Imaging and Vision*, Vol. 40 (Springer-Verlag London Ltd).

Pratt, W. K. (2014). *Introduction to Digital Image Processing* (CRC Press, Boca Raton, FL, USA).

Richardson, I. E. G. (2004). *The MPEG-4 and H.264 Standards* (John Wiley & Sons, Ltd), ISBN 9780470869611, pp. 85–98, doi:10.1002/0470869615.ch4.

Rosenfeld, A. (1969). *Picture Processing by Computer* (Academic Press, New York, NY, USA).

Rosenfeld, A. and Kak, A. C. (1976). *Digital Picture Processing*, Vol. 1, 2nd edn. (Academic Press, Orlando, FL, USA).

Rosten, E. and Drummond, T. (2006). Machine learning for high-speed corner detection, in *Computer Vision – ECCV 2006. 9th European Conference on Computer Vision, Graz, Austria, May 7–13, 2006. Proceedings, Part I, Lecture Notes in Computer Science*, Vol. 3951 (Springer), pp. 430–443.

Rublee, E., Rabaud, V., Konolige, K., and Bradski, G. (2011). ORB: an efficient alternative to SIFT or SURF, in *Proceedings of the 13th IEEE International Conference on Computer Vision (ICCV'11), Barcelona, Spain, 6–11 November 2011* (IEEE), pp. 2564–2571.

Russ, J. C. and Neal, T. B. (2016). *The Image Processing Handbook*, 7th edn. (CRC Press, Boca Raton, FL, USA).

Schowengerdt, R. A. (2007). *Remote Sensing: Models and Methods for Image Processing*, 3rd edn. (Academic Press, Burlington, MA, USA).

Shih, F. Y. (2009). *Image Processing and Mathematical Morphology: Fundamentals and Applications*, 2nd edn. (CRC Press, Taylor & Francis Group, Boca Raton, London, New York).

Smith, S. M. and Brady, J. M. (1997). SUSAN – A new approach to low level image processing, *International Journal of Computer Vision* **23**, 1, pp. 45–78.

Soille, P. (2004). *Morphological Image Analysis: Principles and Applications*, 2nd edn. (Springer-Verlag, Berlin Heidelberg).

Sonka, M., Hlavac, V., and Boyle, R. (2015). *Image Processing, Analysis, and Machine Vision*, 4th edn. (Cengage Learning, Stanford, CT, USA).

Tikhonov, A. N. and Arsenin, V. Y. (1977). *Solution of Ill-posed Problems* (V. H. Winston & Sons, Washington, DC, USA).

Ulrich, M. L. (1969). FFT's without sorting, *IEEE Transactions on Acoustics and Electroacoustics* **17**, 2, pp. 170–172.

Van Fleet, P. J. (2008). *Discrete Wavelet Transformations: An Elementary Approach with Applications* (John Wiley & Sons, Hoboken, NJ, USA).

Winkler, G. (2012). *Image Analysis, Random Fields and Dynamic Monte Carlo Methods: A Mathematical Introduction* (Springer, Berlin, Heidelberg).

Yang, S., Li, B., and Zeng, K. (2016). SBRISK: speed-up binary robust invariant scalable keypoints, *Journal of Real-Time Image Processing* **12**, pp. 583–591.

Yuille, A. (1991). Deformable templates for face recognition, *Journal of Cognitive Neuroscience* **1**, 3, pp. 59–70.

Index

cascaded, 60
cepstral, 206
convolution, 49
fast box, 56
Gaussian, 60, 61, 202
high-pass, 202
homomorphic, 205
inverse, 203
kernel, 50
linear, 49, 50
low-pass, 55, 60, 201
mean, 55
median, 63
morphological, 99
nonlinear, 49, 62
rank, 67
separable filter, 54
unsharp masking, 203
Fourier series, 181
Fourier spectrum, 181
  amplitude spectrum, 184
  centring, 185
  DCT, 187
  DFT, 183
  FFT, 191
  phase spectrum, 184
  power spectrum, 184
  windowing, 186

greyscale morphology, 110
  closing, 114
  dilation, 113
  erosion, 112
  opening, 114
  SE, 111
  smoothing, 115
  top-hat transform, 115

harmonic, 177, 178
  angular frequency, 179
  basis, 180
  frequency, 179
  period, 179
human vision, 2
  dynamic range, 6
  resolution, 5, 10

image
  bit-depth, 6, 12
  continuous, 4
  digital, 7
  dynamic range, 6
  GLCH, 14, 20
  GLCH descriptors, 21
  GLDH, 14, 22
  GLH, 13
  gradient, 133, 138
  Hessian, 133, 138
  structure matrix, 133
imaging device, 2
  CT, 2
  MRI, 3
  pinhole camera, 3

noise
  additive, 47
  linear channel, 206
  multiplicative, 48, 205
  salt-and-pepper, 47
  SNR, 47, 63
normalisation
  $\alpha - \beta$-percentile, 36
  equalisation, 37
  min-max, 35

quantisation, 21, 73
  vector quantisation, 87

region map, 8, 13

segmentation, 73
  accuracy measures, 74
  adaptive thresholding, 77
  colour thresholding, 86
  connected components, 90
  contextual, 74
  EM, 80
  Gaussian mixture model, 79
  histogram thresholding, 77
  non-contextual, 73
  region models, 76
  unimodal thresholding, 80

www.ingramcontent.com/pod-product-compliance
Lightning Source LLC
Chambersburg PA
CBHW050556190326
41458CB00007B/2064